# MUSLIMS IN BRITAIN

*An Introduction*

SOPHIE GILLIAT-RAY

CAMBRIDGE
UNIVERSITY PRESS

CAMBRIDGE UNIVERSITY PRESS
Cambridge, New York, Melbourne, Madrid, Cape Town, Singapore,
São Paulo, Delhi, Dubai, Tokyo

Cambridge University Press
The Edinburgh Building, Cambridge CB2 8RU, UK

Published in the United States of America by Cambridge University Press, New York

www.cambridge.org
Information on this title: www.cambridge.org/9780521536882

First published 2010

Printed in the United Kingdom at the University Press, Cambridge

*A catalogue record for this publication is available from the British Library*

*Library of Congress Cataloguing in Publication data*
Gilliat-Ray, Sophie, 1969–
Muslims in Britain : an introduction / Sophie Gilliat-Ray.
p.   cm.
Includes bibliographical references and index.
ISBN 978-0-521-83006-5 – ISBN 978-0-521-53688-2 (pbk.)
1. Muslims–Great Britain.   2. Muslims–Great Britain–Social conditions.
3. Muslims–Great Britain–History.   4. Islam–Great Britain.   5. Islam–Great
Britain–History.   6. Great Britain–Religious life and customs.   I. Title.
DA125.M87G55 2010
305.6'970941–dc22
2010014634

ISBN 978-0-521-83006-5 Hardback
ISBN 978-0-521-53688-2 Paperback

*Dedicated to my cohort of British Muslim sisters:*

*Batool, Farat, Fauzia and Karima*

*'This is my jihad – to give the British people a true picture of Islam, a picture of love, respect and peace.'*

*(Shaykh Ibrahim Mogra, Imam, Leicester)*

# Contents

# Contents

# Figures

# Tables

x

# *Preface*

This book aims to provide an accessible introduction to the history, the institutions and the diversity among Muslims in Britain, drawing upon the academic scholarship of the past three decades. As the television journalist Rageh Omaar has observed, there is 'a hunger for an understanding of Islam in relation to British experience' (Omaar 2006: 11), but so far there are few sources to which students of contemporary religion might turn. This book aims therefore to meet the need for an introductory academic text, which reflects and synthesizes the wealth of interdisciplinary writing and research about British Muslims that now exists.

Writing about communities of people, including British Muslims, is in any circumstances difficult:

> It is inadequate to seek to define what Islam is and what being a Muslim implies primarily or even exclusively on the basis of observations of the actual behaviour of a group. The most accurate description of a Muslim community does not necessarily reflect what Islam can and does mean to many Muslims. In all religious traditions and communities, there are persons and events that obscure rather than reflect what many of those who live in it see as the true character of their faith. (Bijlefeld 1984: 220)
>
> The religious label accorded to Muslim citizens does now appear to have some problematic dimensions. Increasingly, Muslim identity is viewed as reified and exaggerated. A criminal is now a 'Muslim thief', the local GP is a 'Muslim doctor', and so on. The trouble with this is that Muslims cannot be seen simply as human beings: they have to be perceived mainly through the religious prism. Giving them a one-dimensional description, however important, undervalues the complexity of that person. (Hussain, D. 2008: 40)

Mindful of these warnings, I have nonetheless sought in these pages to sketch out the key debates and issues surrounding Muslims in Britain. Some degree of generalization is unavoidable, but the consequences of this can be leavened to some extent by quoting the personal stories and reflections of individual travellers, biographers and pioneers, both past and present.

The answer to the straightforward question 'who are British Muslims?' might seem obvious at first. But 'Muslim' is a description or label which may not always be important to those to whom it is applied. Likewise, the self-ascription 'Muslim' can be more or less meaningful at different times in the life of an individual:

> The stereotype of Muslims assuming an identity that is religious above all else and that is incompatible with the secularized, modern public sphere belies the highly variable ways in which Muslims practice and conceive of relationships between religion and politics and between cultural difference and membership in the public. (Nagel and Staeheli 2009: 99)

When I refer to Muslims in Britain in this book, I am aware that I am privileging a particular (religious) identity over other multiple identifications primarily to define my field of study (Kalra 2000), and with awareness of the danger of constructing essentialized notions of what 'British Muslims' are like, individually or collectively. By prioritizing religious identity over other identifications, there is a danger of artificially presenting a supposedly 'authentic community' (Eade 1996a: 63) purely on the basis of religion, which then goes on to become subject to political and academic interventions which further reinforce particular conceptions of what being a 'British Muslim' involves. So there are considerable difficulties in writing about Muslims in Britain, and indeed about 'the Muslim community', because of the supposition of homogeneity contained within the word 'community', and because of the problems of artificially prioritizing one identity (religious) over others (class, gender, ethnicity, generation, politics) (Samad 1998). In order to avoid giving the impression of a monolithic 'Muslim community', or 'Muslim world', a new lexicon is often advocated both within and outside academic discourse (Quilliam Foundation, July 2009)[1] and this new vocabulary rests upon the idea of diverse and distinctive 'Muslim communities'.

Despite the diversity within and outside Muslim communities, I believe it is still meaningful to consider Muslims in Britain as constituting a distinctive social group, on the basis of a generally shared set of core religious beliefs. These translate into religious practices that are often undertaken as part of 'belonging' (however loosely) to a distinctive faith 'community'. Clearly, the boundaries of any group are permeable, and the manner in which individual Muslims express or practise

---

[1] See the Quilliam Foundation 'Media Briefing: Welcome Change of Lexicon away from "the Muslim world"', www.quillliamfoundation.org/index.php/component/content/article/515, 4 July 2009.

their faith is highly subjective, and shaped by context and circumstance. Notwithstanding the strategic and variable deployment of individual and collective identity claims, Muslims in Britain arguably have sufficiently shared beliefs and practices to warrant their categorization as a distinctive group (see also Open Society Institute 2005: 56). Many Muslims in Britain (though by no means all) have themselves been pressing for this particular recognition for at least the past two decades.

Much contemporary discussion about Muslims in Britain is now taking place against the background of the current 'Preventing Violent Extremism' agenda. This has generated a wealth of speculative journalistic writing that has sometimes had the unfortunate consequence of framing British Muslims in definite and distorting ways, as 'Potential Violent Extremists'. This kind of framing does not contribute to an informed understanding of British Muslim lives, or an appreciation of either the history or the diversity within Muslim communities. Much contemporary writing about British Muslims presents an

apocalyptic account of the threat posed to Britain by extremist Islam. (Indeed a fair proportion of the books published about 'Islamic terrorism' adopt this tone.) (Reddie 2009: 140)

This book is intended to rebalance current discourse by focusing on issues that are perhaps much closer to the 'ordinary' daily lives of British Muslims. The scholarly literature about Muslims in Britain that has been produced over the past thirty to forty years, and which this book aims to synthesize and reflect, has sought to document the history and settlement of Muslims, the processes of institution-building, and the ways in which Muslims think about their lives in British towns and cities. This book aims to bring that valuable scholarship, much of it contained within specialist academic journals, to a new and more general audience. Arguably, it is only possible to understand currents of extremism and so-called 'radicalization' among a small minority by acquiring a better appreciation of British Muslim religious history, the contemporary socio-economic situation and major religious institutions. So, while being mindful of the political, religious and social consequences of 'crisis' events over the past three decades (such as the 'Rushdie affair',[2] and the terrorist atrocity in London on 7 July 2005), and the need to take their impact on British

---

[2] The Rushdie Affair generated much academic writing, a small selection of which includes Akhtar (1989 ); Cohn-Sherbok (1990); Modood (1989); Modood (1990a); Weller (2009).

Muslims and wider society seriously (Abbas 2005), this book deliberately shifts the focus back towards the 'everyday' lives of British Muslims.

My writing has been informed by a background of teaching and research based in the City of Cardiff. Compared with the cosmopolitanism and metropolitanism of London, and the particular dominance of South Asian Muslims in cities such as Birmingham, Bradford, or Leicester, during the past decade I have come to appreciate the distinctive spirit of internationalism and multiculturalism that is discernible in Cardiff. Perhaps this is a legacy of the City's historic importance as an international centre for commercial shipping. Muslim seafarers, students and merchants from diverse origins have been passing through and often settling in Cardiff. This history is today embodied in the intergenerational memories of those now living and working within a short radius of the University, and has helped to provide a unique setting for the writing of this book.

# *Acknowledgements*

I would like to record my thanks to numerous people for their support during the writing of this book, beginning with my colleagues in the Centre for the Study of Islam in the UK at Cardiff University. I am also grateful to the staff of the Arts and Social Studies Library: Helen Brill, Sue Austin and Tom Dawkes deserve particular mention.

Key supporters of my work in Cardiff include Akmal Hanuk, Saleem Kidwai OBE and Shaykh Dr Abdalla Yassin Mohamed OBE, all from the Muslim Council of Wales. They have been true friends, and it has been an inspiration to feel that we share so many common objectives in the promotion of a better understanding of Islam.

Thanks are also due to Kate Brett, Gillian Dadd, Laura Morris and Aline Guillermet at Cambridge University Press, for their thoroughness and helpful assistance. It is a pleasure for an author to work with a production team who have been unfailing in their prompt and considered responses to communications, and who have continued to believe in the project at all stages of its evolution.

I would like to record posthumous thanks to my mother, Janet Gilliat, who provided editorial assistance with two draft chapters in 2004–5, while undergoing chemotherapy. Her wisdom on matters of spelling, grammar and punctuation were of inestimable help, and later chapters of the book are the poorer without her input.

Two people have acted as 'critical friends' for me during the production process. The first of these is the former Head of the School of Religious and Theological Studies at Cardiff University, Professor Stephen Pattison, now at Birmingham University. I am grateful to him for offering timely advice at all stages. The second of my 'critical friends' is Yahya Birt, currently at Kube Publishing, Markfield, Leicester. Yahya's own writing has always been a fine example and inspiration to me, and I knew there could be no better supportive critic from within the world of British Muslim scholarship. I, of course, take full responsibility for the completed manuscript, and its various shortcomings.

Throughout my professional career, I have made many friends around the UK within different Muslim communities, and within various university departments. I am very appreciative of these friendships and would like to express my gratitude for the kindness that has been shown to me over the years. I would like to record particular thanks to my friends in the Muslims in Britain Research Network, the BSA Sociology of Religion Study Group, and the British Association for the Study of Religions.

My greatest debt of gratitude is to my husband, Dr Keith Ray. He has provided strategic advice during the writing process, and he has also helped editorially. I offer my thanks for all the discussions about chapter headings, paragraphs to add or take out, or the nuances of particular phrasing. As an archaeologist, Keith has also encouraged me to consider how insights from history, conservation, material culture and heritage studies might inform this book, and I have truly enjoyed the intellectual stimulation that has come from engagement with these disciplines and fields. Above all, I wish to thank him for his continual encouragement, and for being patient.

Cardiff
August 2009

# *Abbreviations*

| | |
|---|---|
| BMI | British Muslim Initiative |
| BMF | British Muslim Forum |
| CRB | Criminal Records Bureau |
| FAIR | Forum Against Islamophobia and Racism |
| HT | *Ḥizb al-Taḥrīr* |
| MAB | Muslim Association of Britain |
| MCB | Muslim Council of Britain |
| MINAB | Mosques and Imams National Advisory Board |
| NUS | National Union of Seamen; also, National Union of Students |
| PVE | Preventing Violent Extremism |
| SMC | Sufi Muslim Council |
| TJ | *Tablīghī Jamā'at* |

# PART I

# Historical and religious roots

It is a common assumption that the presence of Muslims in Britain and the influence of Islamic culture and history on British society is a recent phenomenon, confined mainly to the post-Second World War era. The period after 1945 is certainly distinctive in terms of the scale of Muslim migration to Britain, but the history of Muslim settlement here, and wider British engagement with Muslim majority countries, goes back much further. The extent to which the first two chapters of this book explore this history is a reflection of the fact that ideas, impressions and encounters from the past have a considerable impact on apprehension and understanding in the present. The first chapter offers an overview of some key aspects of the complex history of Muslims in Britain and, particularly, English perceptions of Islam, from the earliest times to the mid nineteenth century.

During the later nineteenth century and early twentieth century, there was a qualitative and quantitative shift in the nature of Muslim settlement in Britain. The character of Muslim communities began to change with the rapid expansion of the British Empire. Large numbers of unskilled Muslim labourers came to Britain as part of the colonial enterprise and by the late 1800s a distinctive Anglo-Muslim community had begun to emerge in Britain (Murad 1997). In some cases this was led by notable British converts to Islam. Discussion of this, and the subsequent arrival of Muslims to Britain after the Second World War, is the focus for the second chapter. Here it becomes possible to see also the 'routes' of more recent migration, and the socio-political circumstances which have led to the emergence of vibrant Muslim communities in Britain today.

Alongside the importance of a broad historical understanding, it is also essential to appreciate the religious 'roots' of Muslim communities, and to grasp the significance of religious ideas and interpretations that have led to the development of multiple Islamic discourses over time. The religious, social and political identities of Muslims in Britain today have been shaped by the legacy of Islamic religious movements established in predominantly Muslim countries. These influential socio-political and religious schools of thought continue to shape British Muslim experience. Two chapters explore the principal currents of religious thought that emerged in the Middle East and in South Asia respectively from the eighteenth century onwards. Considerable attention is paid to the way in which such thinking has found new expression in the lives of Muslims living in British towns and cities. Here the focus is not so much upon the movement of people over time, but more upon the transmission of religious ideas and the new interpretations to which these ideas are subject as they move from one social context to another.

Overall, then, Part I of the book is devoted to providing sufficient background to enable a social, historical and religious 'placing' of Islam and Muslims in Britain today. The dynamics of Muslim institutions and the themes that are explored later in the book can only be fully understood against this backdrop.

# CHAPTER I

# The roots of Islam in Britain

## INTRODUCTION

This chapter identifies some of the ways in which the Islamic world has been encountered, engaged with, understood and, of course, substantially misunderstood in Britain from an historical perspective.[1] The historical narrative ranges from early encounters and impressions, through to the settlement of the first traders, sailors and students. What has brought Muslims to Britain across the course of history? How has the character of Muslim communities developed over time? How have perceptions of Muslims changed? Finally, some instances of contact and engagement between Britain and majority Muslim regions, especially from the sixteenth century onwards, are brought into focus. Fascinating insights emerge about the first converts to Islam, and the establishment of embryonic Muslim communities in the seventeenth century.

It is important at the outset to consider where information about Islam and Muslims in Britain has come from over the course of history, and the limitations and biases of difference sources. Any understanding of the relationship between Islam and Britain is inevitably shaped by the available evidence, so whether we are examining Christian ecclesiastical texts, travel diaries, captivity narratives, parliamentary papers, literary fiction, or stage plays, there are inevitably inherent limitations and biases. Misunderstandings of Islam and Muslims in one genre are often reproduced in another. So, for example, in the Anglo-Saxon world, information about Islam and Muslims was understood within a framework of Christian theological ideas and assumptions that pre-dated Islam

---

[1] I use shorthand phrases such as 'Islamic world' or 'Muslim world' with full awareness that they can potentially be very homogenizing descriptors, masking the enormous linguistic, racial, cultural and religious diversity among Muslims living in different parts of the world. I use these phrases with awareness of this diversity, and also with mindfulness of the opposition that can be (unhelpfully) implied by reference to a supposedly monolithic 'Muslim world' and other non-Muslim 'worlds'.

(Scarfe Beckett 2003). Perceptions contained within travel diaries in the fifteenth and sixteenth centuries directly influenced later impressions of Islam among playwrights. In the medieval period, alongside prodigious theological and literary writing about Islam that was often negative (and rarely supported by actual personal encounter with Muslims), there was also secular engagement with Muslim states via trade and commerce. Scholars today therefore have access to numerous literary records about Islam produced by medieval ecclesiastics, but they do not have other kinds of data, such as trade records or visual representations, except in the form of material culture such as ceramics or coins (Petersen 2008). Such material simply has not survived as a source of information which might enlighten and diversify perceptions of Islam that are otherwise almost wholly shaped by literary (and mostly theological) records. Furthermore, some periods of history have been studied in more depth than others. For the study of Islam and Muslims in the West, 'there are still many dark corners and some subjects which have scarcely been touched' (Southern 1962: 2). This is especially true of 'remoter' times. Given that the relationship between Islam and Britain in history has not been systematically investigated, there is scope for considerably more exploration and study.

Bearing in mind this limitation in scholarship so far and the extent of available data, it becomes critical to think about *who* was writing about Islam and Muslims from the eighth century onwards, and with what authority, knowledge, power and evidence. What kinds of agendas and assumptions are likely to have framed their perceptions? Such writing has never emerged from a void: it has always been shaped by prior assumptions and received impressions. Furthermore, over the course of history existing information about Islam and Muslims has been subject to fresh interpretations, to serve newly emerging interests. At different times in the past, the specifically 'religious' aspect of the Muslim world has been both highlighted and, paradoxically, at the same time more or less ignored (Daniel 1979: 7–8). Consequently, across different eras of British history, there have been multiple perceptions of, and engagements with, Muslims and the Islamic world, often existing in parallel, and also often contradictory.

It is not wise, therefore, to make generalized assumptions about perceptions of Islam or Muslims across time because the nature of the relationship and the character of engagement have been diverse and constantly changing. Over the course of history the Islamic world has been resisted, traded with, studied, negotiated with, written about and plundered. The British have therefore apprehended Islam and the Muslim world in multiple and often paradoxical ways. Looking back historically:

accurate knowledge of Islam as a religion and polity and of Muslims in daily life jostled with hearsay, wishful thinking, polemic and received opinion; information was acquired, generalised, distorted, consolidated and in some cases apparently created from scratch, and yet, in other cases, the received opinion survived for a surprisingly long time despite its patent inaccuracy. (Scarfe Beckett 2003: 230)

It might be plausibly argued that this 'received opinion' is still alive and well.

## THE WRITINGS OF BEDE AND THE TRADING OF KING OFFA

The Prophet Muhammad was born in 570 and died in 632. By the time of his death, the Islamic faith was spreading rapidly. As new information about Islam and Muslims became known during the early medieval period, it was accommodated within pre-Islamic theories about the 'Saracens'. So as the English monk, scholar and writer Bede (673–735) began shaping some of the first medieval understandings about Islam in England from his monastery in Northumberland, he was indebted to the earlier writings and perceptions of St Jerome (342–420), a Christian scholar and early church father, 'widely seen as a pre-Islamic authority on the Orient' (Scarfe Beckett 2003: 22). So, right from its inception, Islam was not apprehended on its own terms, but understood within pre-existing frameworks of thought about 'the Other' derived from Christian dogma and biblical exegesis. Instead of being apprehended matter-of-factly, as a people living by their own values and social norms, Muslims were framed within an entirely Christian perspective.

Living and writing at a time when textual authority rested upon quotation from the works of scholars, it was almost inevitable that Bede would accommodate his understanding of the newly emerging Islamic faith within a set of assumptions about the Orient originally derived from Jerome. For Jerome, there was a direct connection between the desert-dwelling 'Saracens' and all that was 'dark' or within 'shadows'. He defined Arabia as 'evening', the beginning of night and sin, and he contrasted this spiritual darkness with 'the light of scriptural knowledge' (Scarfe Beckett

2003: 103).[2] Just as Jerome stigmatized the 'shadowy' ones, Bede describes the 'Saracens' (Muslims) as enemies of the Christians. These kinds of connections, associations and prejudices, established so early in Christian Anglo-Saxon views, appear to have resulted in a unique kind of opposition and antipathy towards Islam within English-speaking Christendom, a legacy of which arguably remains evident in the contemporary world today.

Hearing about the rapidly expanding borders of the Islamic world in the early eighth century, especially in southern Europe, Bede had vivid contemporary evidence to support negative and prejudicial views about Muslims. Without ever actually meeting a Muslim, Bede nevertheless writes about the 'hatred'[3] that invading Muslim armies had for Christians. In his writings he draws a sharp distinction between the Christian 'us' and the Islamic 'them', although a full antipathy between Islam and Christianity was not to emerge until the Crusades. Muslims, he says, are 'undifferentiatedly shiftless, hateful, aggressive (*uagos, incertisque sedibus; exosi et contrarii*)' (Scarfe Beckett 2003: 20). From as early as the eighth century therefore, the power and literary influence of a single English monk, regarded as the 'father of history' among the Anglo-Saxon peoples, shaped a dominant perception of the Islamic world that was wholly negative, with Muslims characterized as an obdurate and callous 'Other'. Bede was one of a number of influential European theologians who laid the foundations for anti-Islamic prejudice in the Christian world (Kalin 2004).

However, clues from contemporary material evidence indicate a striking contrast. For instance, within decades of Bede's writing, the Anglo-Saxon king, Offa of Mercia (757–96), issued a gold coin bearing an inscription featuring the Islamic declaration of faith, the *shahādah*, as well as the Latin formula 'Offa Rex' ('King Offa')[4] engraved on the coin. The coin is a copy of a gold dinar originally minted in 774 by the Abbasid Caliph Al-Mansur, and there have been lively debates about why Offa might have chosen to produce such a coin.[5] These even include the proposition that King Offa was Britain's first convert to Islam. This is highly implausible given, for instance, Offa's promotion of a new archbishopric

---

[2] See Scarfe Beckett (2003: 100ff) for an explanation of Jerome's commentary on Genesis 4:14–16.
[3] See Scarfe Beckett, p. 18, for the original Latin text.
[4] Another example of the influence of the Islamic world is the 'Ballycottin' cross from Ireland. It is a piece of jewellery in the form of a cross with a glass bead in the centre inscribed with the *Bismillah* in Kufic script (Porter and Ager 1999).
[5] A number of theories are explored by Shaykh Abdullah Quilliam, writing as Professor H. M. Leon in 1916: www.masud.co.uk/ISLAM/bmh/BMH-AQ-offa.htm. See also Allan (1914).

Figure 1. Offa's dinar, British Museum (Cat. CM1913–12–13–1). Copy of 'Abbasid dinar dated AH 157 (AD 773–4) made for King Offa of Mercia. Reproduced by kind permission of the British Museum

at Lichfield. Moreover, it has been noted that the Latin inscription on the coin was inserted upside down among the lines of Kufic script, suggesting that neither Offa nor his moneyers had any idea of the form or meaning of the Arabic (Metcalf, D. M. 1982). The coin was found in Rome, so another possibility was that it was part of a payment to the see of Rome (Scarfe Beckett 2003).

The very existence of this coin nevertheless indicates some degree of influence of the Islamic world upon Anglo-Saxon economics and politics.[6] Offa may well have wished to imitate what was an internationally recognized trade coin of the time, widely respected for its high gold content. This would accord well with Offa's reputation for projecting an image of himself as entrepreneurial, cosmopolitan and outward-looking (Wormald 1982). Ultimately, it was probably therefore commercial acumen and political aggrandizement that lay behind the decision of the Mercian court to authorize such a coin.[7]

---

[6] There is moreover evidence that Muslim cartographers and geographers were aware of the British Isles as early as 817. The mathematician, astronomer and geographer Muhammad bin Musa al-Khwarizmi in his 'Kitab ṣurat al-Ard (*The Face of the Earth*) refers to a number of places in Britain (Sherif 2002), and we can deduce that at least some of the seventy or so geographers working with him might have visited Britain during their explorations. A more definite record of Muslim visitors to England comes in the twelfth century, when al-Idrisi (1100–66), a North African scholar, travelled to the west of England as part of his geographical endeavours (Watt 1972: 21).

[7] A range of Muslim coinage has been found in Britain dating from the early medieval period. These coins arrived via Mediterranean and Scandinavian trade routes. Later, the treasury of Henry III (1207–72) contained significant quantities of Islamic gold coins (Grierson 1974).

In the history of the relationship between Britain and various Muslim nations, the determinant role of economic and material interests in shaping contact and influence is repeated continually, as we shall see. When Britain has been in a position of relative weakness, interests have tended to be negotiated with the Muslim world. But when Britain has been more powerful, economically and politically, negotiation has usually been replaced by the imposition of terms and conditions detrimental to Muslim participants both in trade and in politics. Paradoxically, therefore, throughout history negative assumptions about Islam and Muslims have coexisted alongside very different secular views about the material culture of Muslim countries. Bede himself is a good example of this irony. For example, on his deathbed in Northumberland in 735, Bede requested one of his monks to gather his fellow priests around him, so that he could distribute the goods in his 'treasure box'. Bede's treasures included pepper and incense, products of the Arab Middle East and which 'must have passed through Muslim hands' (Scarfe Beckett 2003: 61) before finding their way to Bede's box. So while he might have regarded the Muslims as the hateful 'Other', he was appreciative of the unusual products that emanated from their world. Throughout medieval England, a taste for the exotic was acquired, and there is evidence for a whole range of medicinal ingredients,[8] spices, silk and ceramics having been imported from the Muslim world during the late first millennium (Petersen 2008).[9]

Alongside the theological and symbolic 'darkness' brought about in the Anglo-Saxon mind by the advent of Islam, there was also a very real perception of threat from Muslim armies. Bede was writing at a time when Muslim forces were advancing rapidly into territories under former Christian control. Long before the Crusades, Christian Europe therefore had reason to fear the advent of a 'new world order', at least as it affected the Mediterranean and Iberia. The first Caliphate saw not only the invasion of Sicily and the Balearics, the Maghreb and Spain, but also an apparently unstoppable advance of Muslim armies northwards into France. Only the Battle of Poitiers (732) – also known as the Battle of Tours – saw the halting of a northern advance by Muslim armies led by Amir 'Abd al-Rahman. During the battle the Franks, led by Charles Martel, defeated

---

[8] Anglo-Saxon medical recipe books include references to a number of ingredients which could only have arrived from territories ruled by Muslims (Scarfe Beckett 2003).

[9] Ceramics from the central Middle East, especially Syria, Iran and Iraq, were regarded in particular as luxury items in the twelfth and thirteenth centuries. 'The pieces found in Britain are all of the blue under-glaze painted variety which would certainly have looked exotic and sophisticated within the context of British green, yellow and brown glazed earthenwares' (Petersen 2008).

the Muslims. The victory has been subsequently interpreted as one of the decisive and most important military exchanges in the world (Watt 1972). Martel was seen as the saviour of Western Christendom for generations. A no doubt apocryphal story has it that when news of the victory at Poitiers became known in France, local bakers began to bake bread in the shape of the Islamic crescent in celebration of Charles's victory. The *croissant* that remains so popular on breakfast tables across Europe today may therefore have entirely unacknowledged origins in an event that took place 1,200 years ago – a symbol of a perceived epoch-making European victory over the Muslim world.

But was the Battle of Tours really as significant for relations between Islam and Europe as historians have claimed? The famous eighteenth-century English historian Edward Gibbon clearly regarded Charles Martel as the 'saviour of Christendom' and noted that without his victory over the Muslims 'perhaps the interpretation of the Koran would now be taught in the schools of Oxford, and her pulpits might demonstrate to a circumcised people the sanctity and truth of the revelation of Mahomet'.[10] The assumption that the Battle of Tours was somehow a 'salvation of Christendom' from the Islamic world is regarded today in some quarters simply as a myth constructed by modern historians (Mastnak 2002: 99). The historical validity of such a claim has never been closely challenged, and Mastnak notes also that contemporary chroniclers of the battle did not give it the same significance as did later historians. At the time, it was pictured as 'just one of many military encounters between Christians and Saracens – moreover, as only one in a series of wars fought by Frankish princes for booty, power and territory' (Mastnak 2002: 100). It was the lure of the East and the foundation of Baghdad that diverted the dynamic emergent Islamic world away from Christian Europe:

The eastward pull of the vast mass of Persia in the Islamic empire was the salvation of Europe ... not the Frankish cavalry of Charles Martel at Tours. The division of East and West, which had been blurred throughout the Late Antique period by the confrontation of Byzantium and Persia along the Fertile Crescent [the area between Turkey and Iran], came to rest along the shores of the Mediterranean itself. The Muslim world turned its back on its poor Christian neighbours across the sea. The cultivated man drew his language from the desert, and the style of his culture from eastern Mesopotamia. In the more stable world created by this vast shift of the balance of culture, Western Europe could create an identity of its own. (Brown 1971: 203)

[10] Edward Gibbon cited in Mastnak (2002: 99).

So while the emergence of the *croissant* following the Battle of Tours could be interpreted as an indicator of the defeat of the Muslim world, it is only later that it has been reinterpreted as the 'salvation of Christendom'. The quotation above indicates what a Euro-centric perception of history this actually constitutes (Herrin 1989).

Bede certainly had cause to be fearful of the incursion of Muslims into former Christian territory, however, not only in Spain, but also in other parts of the world previously under Christian control, for example in the eastern Mediterranean and areas of Africa and Asia. The boundaries of the Christian world were being markedly reduced by the spread of Islam. However, Bede's response was not a call to political or military action, but rather the creation of a polemical 'othering' of Muslims. The Islamic world was an ideological resource in Bede's worldview. By portraying Muslims as opponents of Christianity itself rather than simply of Christian states, Bede created a rhetorical means of pushing them back into the desert whence they came. Thus the Muslims 'act as a foil for the virtue and eventual success of the Christians and, at last, confirm their righteousness … Bede's representation of the Saracens constitutes an aggrandizement, however small, of the institution of the medieval church' (Scarfe Beckett 2003: 21). Bede's treatment of Muslims and Islam can thus be regarded as a tactical device in reference to the situation of his own religious community.

### THE CRUSADES AND THEIR LEGACY

By making Jerome's views of the Saracens even more widely known and by presenting Muslims also as spiritually deviant and 'anti-Christian', Bede helped shape prevalent negative ideas about Islam within and beyond the medieval church. In this way, he provided the kind of religious sanction that fuelled the Crusades. Whereas resistance to Muslim influence upon Europe had prior to the Crusades been predominantly theological and literary in England, it now became military and material, if heavily idealized and 'penitential' (Riley-Smith 2008: 29–44). Crusading was believed to be 'directly authorised by Christ himself, the incarnate God, through his mouthpiece the pope' (Riley-Smith 1987: xxix), as for instance by Pope Urban II in his 'launch' of the First Crusade at Clermont in France on 27 November 1095 (Tyerman 2004: 27–8). The most tangible aim of the Crusades, beyond securing the safety of Christian pilgrims to Jerusalem, was to wrest back control of the holy places, and especially the Church of Jerusalem, 'from the savagery and tyranny of the Muslims' (Riley-Smith

1987: xxix). While they were undoubtedly viewed by Christians as featuring 'holy' battles against the Muslims, the ultimate goal of Jerusalem
made the Crusades also a form of pilgrimage.[11]

The earlier Crusades met with some success, and one result of the First
Crusade was that a Christian Kingdom of Jerusalem was established in
1099, with coastal ports at Tyre and Acre. Churchmen from across Britain
also participated in these early Crusades and many died in battle or
through illness. Jerusalem was recaptured by the forces of Salah al-Din
('Saladin') in 1187. The Christian response to this was to organize a further
Crusade (the 'Third Crusade', 1189–92) in which Richard I of England
(also known as 'the Lionheart') was a prominent leader. Although the
Third Crusade was in several respects the high point of the Crusading
movement (Philip I of France and Richard I of England were extremely
powerful monarchs, Richard being the ruler of the Anglo-French 'Angevin
Empire'), Richard failed in his bid to recapture Jerusalem.

Richard was by no means an untutored interloper in the Levant,
however. Adelard of Bath (*c.*1080–*c.*1160), who had tutored Richard's
father, Henry II, had travelled extensively in the Middle East, especially
in Syria and Palestine, and had translated many Arabic works in the
fields of astronomy and mathematics (Wolff 1968). He was perhaps the
first person to popularize Islamic science in the Western world, and as
a result of his endeavours the use of Hindi-Arabic numerals was introduced into Britain, and so too was the concept of 'zero'. Just as significant as Adelard's learned translations and writings was his admiration
for the methodology of scholastic learning which he observed from his
Arab masters (Burnett 1997). Fundamentally, this depended upon put-
ting reason and critical understanding above all else in the matter of
natural knowledge. Makdisi argues that the scholasticism that emerged
in twelfth-century Europe was indebted to the scholarly methods of the
Muslims, and this methodology went on to influence later scholars such
as Albertus Magnus (1208–80) and Roger Bacon (1214–94) (Makdisi
1974). Important new ideas about learning and scholarship were received
from the Islamic world, even if there was a reluctance to admit the intellectual superiority of the Muslim world at the time (Cochrane 1994;
Kalin 2004).

[11] For a short introduction to the religious dimensions of the Crusades see Riley-Smith (2002),
especially chapter 4. Recently Riley-Smith has yet more strongly emphasized the spiritual motivation of the Crusaders: 'it was the belief that Crusades were collective acts of penance, re-pay-
ments through self-punishment of the debts owed to God for sin' (Riley-Smith 2008: 33). See
also, however, *Fighting for Christendom, Holy War and the Crusades* (Tyerman 2004).

Even by the time of the Fourth Crusade the ideals of the early Crusades were becoming markedly distorted, as exemplified in the infamous sack of Constantinople, the capital city of Christian Byzantium, in 1204. In the later medieval period, the focus of attention of the Europeans shifted from the attempt to recapture the Christian holy places, towards containing the impact of a resurgent Islam upon Europe itself. This resurgence encompassed the Ottoman Muslim capture of Thessalonica (1361) and the victory of Sultan Murad I at Kosovo (1389). It culminated in the fall of Constantinople (1453) and the first of the two sieges of Vienna (1529).

The influence of Islamic culture and scholarship on medieval English society has often been underestimated and downplayed (Makdisi 1974), while the extent to which there is a distinctly 'Islamic' character to the legacy of Muslim scholarship is also contested. Burnett's account of Arabic influences on English scholarly life from the eleventh to the thirteenth centuries reveals the extent to which Western scholars were indebted to the Arab world in the fields of philosophy, mathematics, medical sciences, astrology and other sciences (Burnett 1997). But this debt to Muslim scholarship is not attributed to the nature of Islam itself in Burnett's work, whereas scholars such as George Makdisi stress that the particular nature of Islamic *fiqh* (jurisprudence) directly influenced the scholastic method of the Arab Muslim world on which Western scholars later came to depend (Makdisi 1976).

In the fourteenth century, the English author Geoffrey Chaucer pursued an interest in medieval science and philosophy and, like other intellectuals of the time, he was aware of Muslim scholarship. There are references to Islamic scholars in the *Canterbury Tales* (1386) and the influence of Arabic terminology is evident in his writings. As a result of his literary works, about twenty-four Arabic loanwords entered English vocabulary, such as 'almanac', 'nadir', 'alkali', 'tartar', 'satin' and 'checkmate' (the latter from the Arabic/Persian *shah mat* meaning 'the king is dead'). The adoption of these words by Chaucer illustrates the extent to which in a wide variety of fields of knowledge, and especially in the sciences, Muslim scholarship contributed to the culture of medieval England.

The medieval period was therefore characterized among other things by mutual influences and encounters between the Muslim world and English society. There was conflict and 'holy war', but there was also

trade across the Mediterranean, and the balance of it changed in the course of time; from the eleventh and twelfth centuries onwards the Italian ports expanded their trade, and, in the fifteenth and sixteenth centuries, ships from the ports of northern Europe began to appear in the Mediterranean and the Indian ocean.

There was an exchange of ideas, and here the traffic moved mainly from the lands of Islam to those of Christendom. (Hourani 1991: 7)

During the sixteenth century, the Ottoman Empire dominated the Mediterranean world. English travellers and traders in the Eastern Mediterranean and North African regions therefore knew they were meeting a 'powerful religious and military civilization which viewed them as an inferior people with a false religion' (Matar 1998: 3). During the sixteenth and seventeenth centuries, despite a complex background of anti-Islamic polemic, especially in theological and literary writing, there nevertheless emerged forms of contact that brought the first substantial numbers of Muslims to the British Isles while also bringing about the first known conversions to Islam.

The first Muslims so far documented as having landed on English shores were predominantly North Africans and Turks. They had been freed from galley slavery on Spanish ships by English pirates and privateers in the mid to late sixteenth century. Few became permanent residents, and most were granted permission to return to their native lands. The 'Spital Sermons' in London collected funds to send 'divers mariners' back to their countries of origin (Harrison 1931: 273). Interestingly, these freed slaves were not identified specifically as 'Muslims' at the time. Rather, they were referred to as 'Moors' or 'Turks'. It is hard to give an accurate estimate of numbers, but Nabil Matar estimates the figure in terms of hundreds by 1660, a cumulative figure derived from government (Privy Council) papers of the time (Matar 1997).

The release of these Muslim slaves from Spanish ships has to be set in a wider political context, however. The England of Protestant Queen Elizabeth I was a small trading nation without extensive overseas possessions, vulnerable to attack from the Spanish Catholic world-empire. Elizabeth wanted to cultivate good relations with the Muslim Ottomans, not only as a way of improving trading relations, but more especially as a means of resisting the Spanish, politically and militarily. The release of the galley slaves was therefore an instrument of diplomacy. Elizabeth's successful approach to Sultan Murad for assistance in 1588, for instance, helped to divide the naval force intended for the Spanish Armada. This led ultimately to its defeat, potentially saving England from coming under Spanish rule.

Elizabeth I's administration was the first to co-operate openly with a Muslim power, and to initiate diplomatic visits and exchanges (Birt, Y. 2006c). However, the engagement with Muslims as an immigrant group was less favourable. In January 1601, for instance, the Queen issued a proclamation that could be regarded as the first recorded anti-immigration tract. She was 'highly disconcerted to understand the great numbers of Negroes and Blackamoores which are carried into [the] realm [England] ... the most of them [being] infidels having no understanding of Christ or his Gospel'. Accordingly, they were to be with 'all speed avoided and discharged out of this Her Majesty's realms' (Fryer 1984; Walvin 2005: 79). It is instructive to note here that when these 'Blackamoores' began to constitute a 'problem', Elizabeth I made specific reference to the fact that they were not Christians. She highlighted what made them fundamentally 'different', and therefore problematical (Kundnani 2007a: 11).

In 1627 there were 'nearly forty Muslims living in London, working as tailors, shoemakers, button makers and even one as a solicitor' (Ansari 2003: 27), and in 1641 a 'sect of Mahometans' (Matar 1997: 46) was reported in London, but we are not told the ethnic background of these Muslims. Even if the precise origins of these early Muslims cannot be discerned, it can be said with reasonable confidence that Turkish Muslim culture was beginning to make a dramatic if localized impression on English society during the mid to late seventeenth century with the introduction and spread of the 'coffee house'. In the early 1650s, an English merchant who had been trading in the Ottoman Levant returned to London accompanied by a Turkish servant who introduced the technique for making coffee, Turkish-style. By 1652 the first coffee house had opened in London, and within a decade more than eighty establishments thrived in the city (Farazi 2004).

The coffee house became a central institution in urban life in London because it provided a forum for unregulated debate and discussion for a broad spectrum of the population. Not surprisingly, therefore, major public institutions in contemporary Britain, such as the stock market, insurance companies and political parties, had their birth in the coffee house on account of the free exchange of public opinion and information that took place within them (Ellis 2004). Despite the wide appeal of the coffee houses, they were also a cause of concern and anti-Islamic polemic. Some writers termed coffee the 'Mahometan gruel' or the drink of Satan, fearing that there was only a short step between drinking coffee and converting to Islam (Matar 1997: 111). It was claimed that coffee had been brought to the British Isles by the Ottomans as a way of 'preparing Englishmen for apostasy' (Matar 1997: 113). The fact that some coffee-house owners adopted the turban (a 'sign' of Islam) exacerbated a sense of threat, and a wider fear of the Islamization of London, if not of English society.[12]

Alongside military and trading co-operation, piracy was a common occurrence in the waters surrounding the British Isles, with individual English, Turkish and North African vessels being vulnerable to attack from one another. English passenger, trader, and fishing boats off the coasts of Devon and Cornwall were particularly susceptible, their crews being taken prisoner and held in major centres in the Ottoman Empire (Colley 2000). The scale of this human trafficking can be estimated by the degree of political pressure applied to Parliament to secure the safe release of these captives, usually by raising enough money to buy their freedom, and by sending diplomatic missions which sought to negotiate the release of the captives. In 1584 money was collected in London to 'redeem sixty English captives among the Muslims' (Matar 1998: 6), while between 1620 and 1621 the English Ambassador in Istanbul noted that over one hundred ships had been taken by the North Africans (Matar 1998: 6). These captures caused local financial and emotional hardship, but there were bigger implications for the economy as whole. The abduction and captivity of British subjects in the Ottoman Empire put a strain on trade relations by destabilizing the commercial production and manufacture of exportable goods, such as cloth, tin and lead. Trade with Islamic societies was essential for the healthy balance of exports and imports (for instance, currants, cotton, wool, spices, chemicals and silk were frequent imports from 'the East').

What is largely unknown, and has been perhaps deliberately down-played in the narration of English history, is the extent to which conversion to Islam occurred during the sixteenth and seventeenth centuries. But the first converts to Islam were not the imbibers of caffeine in London coffee houses but English traders, travellers and seafarers captured and held by raiding Ottoman and Barbary corsair ships during the sixteenth and seventeenth centuries (Colley 2000). Not surprisingly, accounts differ as to the kind of numbers involved. Bernard Lewis regards the extent of conversion as 'minimal' (Lewis 1993: 14) and dismisses the early converts as simply idiosyncratic religious 'adventurers' in search of the exotic (Lewis 1993: 25). However, Matar and others provide detailed evidence

---

[12]  See Matar 1993 for an explanation of the significance of the 'turban'.

to suggest this view is questionable (Colley 2000; Matar 1998; Murad 2003). Historical records indicate that the first well-known and recorded conversion was a certain 'John Nelson'. Nelson was a servant on board an English vessel journeying to Tripoli in the 1580s, and he was in fact the first of many hundreds of converts.[13] Linda Colley's *Captives* (Colley 2002) shows that entire armies in North Africa consisted of European renegade converts to Islam, many of whom were from the British Isles. Regardless of precise numbers (which are probably impossible to estimate with any accuracy), the extent of conversion was perceived as high: 'so much did the direct encounter with Islam and the subsequent conversion to "Mahometanism" concern Britons that the topic appears in literary and theological writings in every decade in the period under study [1558–1685]' (Matar 1998: 19). Also notable is the fact that the Spanish word *renegado* (a 'renegade' being a convert from Christianity to Islam) enters the *Oxford English Dictionary* in 1583, suggesting that conversion was sufficiently widespread to warrant a dedicated entry, reflecting an assumed social reality.

Conversion to Islam among seafarers, travellers and merchants arose for a number of reasons. Seafarers were often poor. Some may have seen conversion to Islam and subsequent residence in the Ottoman Empire as a means of improving their material circumstances (Matar 1993). Sir Thomas Shirley, ambassador to the Ottoman Empire, noted the large number of 'roagues and the skumme of people whyche are fledde to the Turke for succour and releyffe' (cited in Dalrymple 2002). There is evidence that some of the *renegados* went on to become prosperous in terms of material and social status (Colley 2000; Matar 1993; Murad 2003).

Travellers and seafarers witnessed the toleration of religious diversity in the Ottoman Empire, and observed for themselves the largely amicable relationships between Christians, Muslims and Jews. They were impressed by the general lack of racial discrimination, and the apparent equality of opportunity that existed among the Ottomans. For illiterate Christian seafarers with little understanding of religious matters, it is possible that conversion to Islam was not seen as a substantial change of religious identity. After all, a number of early Christian theologians initially regarded the advent of Islam as simply a Christian heresy, rather than a new faith derived from the Judeo-Christian tradition (Kalin 2004). The extent to

---

[13] The evidence for John Nelson's conversion derives from an account of *The Voyage made to Tripoli* (1583) by Thomas Saunders, cited in Matar (1998).

which conversion to Islam was voluntary, 'expedient', or forced, we shall never know. However, it was always regarded negatively in England, not least because the renegade was seen as an 'enemy within' (Matar 1993: 2), an individual who had renounced not only his religion, but also his culture and society:

From Italy news is come of Sir Anthony Shirley, that went out of England the last winter giving out that he would serve the Emperor against the Turk, but now it appeareth that he doth serve the Turk against the Emperor; and so is he turned from a Christian to a Turk, which is most monstrous. No doubt if it be so the Lord will punish the same. (Harrison 1931: 294)

It is unfortunate for today's scholars of religious conversion that there are so few self-authored accounts by the *renegados*.[14] This is probably because a significant number of converts were illiterate cabin boys or fishermen, and so lacked the ability to offer a written narrative of their journey to Islam. Moreover, they were rarely of high social status, so their conversion did not cause the same kind of social concern that might have arisen had a wealthy nobleman or ambassador decided to 'turn Turk', another expression for conversion to Islam (MacLean 2007). In this context, the conversion in 1606 of the English Consul in Egypt, Benjamin Bishop, is perhaps noteworthy. Tellingly, following his conversion, he 'disappeared from public records' (Dalrymple 2002). Many converts also chose to adopt a new name, and to remain within the Ottoman Empire; few returned home to tell their story. There was after all little incentive, given the hostile reception they must have known they would receive:

The renegade was an Other in the midst of English society because he reminded priests and writers, urban theatre goers and village congregations of the power and allure of the Muslim Empire ... [he] threatened the idea of England ... he was renouncing all that defined England to Englishmen. (Matar 1997: 71–2)

As a consequence, returning *renegados* could expect to be harshly interrogated. A number of converts were subject to the trials of the Inquisition Court. For instance, in 1610 no fewer than thirty-nine Britons were questioned: ten were from London, six from Plymouth, and the others from Middlesbrough, Lyme and the Channel Islands (Murad 2003). Some converts were tortured until they renounced their new faith and re-converted to Christianity. For those that refused, the punishment was

---

[14] There are between ten and fifteen documented accounts, the first being written between 1571 and 1577 by George Gascoigne (Matar 2001).

often death: 'in 1671 a Welshman was put to death by impalement after refusing to re-convert' (Murad 2003: 63).

Despite the general lack of captivity and conversion accounts, there are some notable exceptions such as the account by Thomas Pellow, written in 1740: *The Adventures of Thomas Pellow of Penryn, Mariner, Three and Twenty Years in Captivity Among the Moors* (Brown 1890). Pellow's story has become increasingly well known through its recent retelling in Giles Milton's *White Gold: The Extraordinary Story of Thomas Pellow and North Africa's One Million European Slaves* (Milton 2004).

Travel narratives and captivity diaries became crucial for the production of knowledge about Islam in the sixteenth and seventeenth centuries (Parr 1996) and they provided ample material for dramatic representations of Turks, Moors and Muslims on the stage. These fed the curiosity in England for the Muslim (and especially Moorish and Turkish) 'Other' (Vitkus 2001), but none of these written sources provided accurate information about Islam. As a genre of writing, such travelogues had many limitations:

Most travellers were too isolated to observe and understand more than the externals. Legally subject to the *millet* system, which placed them under the rule of their ambassadors, they lived around the embassies and seldom learned enough of the language or customs to penetrate their stereotypes. Their knowledge of the Turks was gleaned from books they had read, rumours they had heard from other Europeans ... and direct observation of events whose internal causes and significance they did not understand. (Jones 1978: 169)

The value of these accounts lies largely therefore in the data they provide about the interests and preoccupations of the travellers themselves, rather than about their destinations, or the people they met. Likewise, captivity accounts, such as that of Thomas Pellow, were distorted by selective recall of events, and the temptation to exaggerate their stories in the hope of selling a more exotic and dramatic tale of their experiences on their return. They are 'imperfect, idiosyncratic, and sometimes violently slanted texts' (Colley 2002: 15) and accordingly they provided bizarre and distorted impressions of Islam for later use by English novelists and playwrights.

## WRITING ABOUT ISLAM IN SIXTEENTH AND SEVENTEENTH CENTURY ENGLAND

Over the course of history, Islam, Muslims and the person of the Prophet Muhammad have each been the subject of extensive English literary, dramatic and scholarly treatment. This was especially so during the sixteenth and seventeenth centuries. Writing offered a strategy for giving some meaning to the growing power and influence of the Muslim world, especially the expansion of the Ottoman Empire and the activities of the Barbary Corsairs. Not surprisingly, the literature and dramatic works that emerged during this time reflected the xenophobia of the period, and were legitimated by other propagandist works such as Richard Knolles' *The Generall Historie of the Turkes* published in 1603. Over the past century, the work of Renaissance playwrights and theologians has been subject to analysis, evaluation and scholarly critique (Chew 1937; Sharafuddin 1994; Smith, D. 1977), and this remains an area of current academic interest. Specialist scholars of English Renaissance and Jacobean literature continue to critically examine the portrayal of Muslims, 'Moors' and Turks in the works of Shakespeare, Webster, Fletcher and other dramatists (Bak 1999; Fuchs 2000; MacLean 2007; Malieckal 1999). Clearly, the potential volume of literature on English perceptions of Islam, the Prophet Muhammad and Muslims is extensive, and this chapter can only give a broad sense of sources and studies. A good place to begin this necessarily brief examination, however, is with the question of the first translations of the *Qur'ān* into English, many of which were prefaced by a commentary.

Establishing what counts as the first translation of the *Qur'ān* into English is problematical, not least because of the inaccuracies and biases that dogged early efforts. According to some, the first translation into English was by Alexander Ross, chaplain to Charles I, in 1649. But the difficulty with his work was the fact that he was not an Arabic speaker, and was reliant upon a faulty French translation, regarded by a later translator (George Sale) as being full of omissions, additions and faults (Mohammed 2005). When the news spread that Ross was about to publish a translation of the *Qur'ān*, there was widespread concern that it would lead to a 'wave of apostasies', that is, conversions (Milton 2004: 162). The printers were arrested and Ross himself summoned before the Council of State. Yet he made some forceful arguments for the publication of his *The Alcoran of Mahomet translated out of Arabique into French, by the Sieur Du Ryer ... And newly Englished, for the satisfaction of all that desire to look into the Turkish vanities.* He was clear that knowledge of the Muslim world was essential for its overcoming: 'there have been continual wars, and will be still between us ... it concerneth every Christian who makes conscience of his ways, to examine the cause and to look into the grounds of this war' (cited in Milton 2004: 163). Furthermore, a banning of the translation would probably have been illegal, since just four months previously 'two Whitehall councils had voted for the toleration of all religions in England, 'not excepting Turkes, nor Papists, nor Jews' (cited in Milton 2004: 163). In his translation, Ross's own motivation for publication becomes clear, revealing his own deepseated prejudice: 'I thought good to bring it to their colours, that so viewing thine enemies in their full body, thou must the better prepare to encounter … his Alcoran' (cited in Kidwai 1987). Not surprisingly, his efforts became raw material for 'countless bilious sermons and diatribes against the Islamic world … his *Alcoran* was pillaged and bastardized, and whole sections of the book were cited as proof of the falsehood of Islam and the dangers of apostasy' (Milton 2004: 163).

Following Ross, other translators saw the importance of their work as part of a wider missionary effort to refute Islam, and to promote as far as possible the conversion of Muslims to Christianity. These later translators included George Sale (1697–1736) and Sir William Muir (1819–1905). Like Ross, Sale prefaced his translation with an account of Islam and the life of the Prophet Muhammad. However, he was much less worried about the possibilities of the subsequent conversion of readers to Islam because the *Qur'ān* was full of 'contradictions, blasphemies, obscene speeches, and ridiculous fables …' (Sha'ban 1991 cited in Kalin 2004: 159).

Meanwhile, English dramatists including Shakespeare, Webster, Fletcher, Marlowe and others, with no personal understanding of Islam or Muslims, used their literary licence to the full by portraying 'Turks', 'Moors' and English converts to Islam in a negative light. For example, they wrote exaggerated accounts of the circumcision that new male converts to Islam were assumed to undergo. They also inflated the stories that a very small number of returning 'renegades' told about their apparently forced conversion and/or circumcision. In this way, dramatists in particular had considerable power to define for at least part of the general public the nature of Islam and Muslims. Robert Daborne's play *A Christian Turn'd Turk* (1612), for example, elaborates and embellishes the story of the historical pirate Captain John Ward. It focuses on Ward's 'descent to what the prologue calls "the heart itself of villainy" – religious apostasy' (Fuchs 2000: 52).[15] The stage provided a context where Islam could be defeated, and in relation to renegades this was made possible through

---

[15] See also MacLean (2007), chapter 4.

depicting either their miserable end, or their re-conversion to Christianity (Matar 1993).

For English dramatists, the association of Muslims with darkness becomes prominent once again, but this time the physical darkness of Moors is explicitly a manifestation of spiritual darkness:

The blackness of Moorish characters in drama was so important as to be embedded into play texts themselves, with both Moorish and European characters calling attention to the blackness of Moors as their defining characteristic. In almost all instances, this blackness was used to identify Moors as physical and spiritual outsiders ... The association of Moors with blackness, blackness with Satan, and therefore Moors with Satan ... [was] influential in the early modern period. (Bak 1999: 206, 215)

Alongside playwrights, influential European theologians between the fifteenth and seventeenth centuries such as Martin Luther (1483–1546), John Calvin (1509–64) and George Fox (1624–91) alluded to the interaction between Islam and Christianity in their writings, and assured their readers of the divine punishment that converts would experience. For Luther, the Turk was the 'scourge of God, sent to chastise Christendom for its sins' (Jones 1978: 163). But alongside such outright rejection of Islam as a religion, there was also an appreciation of its cultural and intellectual heritage. Nowhere is this more evident than in the work of George Sandys (1578–1644) in his *Relation of a Journey begun An. Dom. 1610. Foure Books. Containing a description of the Turkish Empire, of Aegypt, of the Holy Land, of the Remote Parts of Italy, and Islands adioyning.* Alongside polemical comments about the *Qur'ān* and derogatory remarks about the Prophet Muhammad, there is praise for Muslim philosophers (Haynes 1986) and detailed observations about Turkish politics, social life and customs. It nonetheless remains the case that works which derided the Prophet Muhammad and attacked Islam remained popular throughout the seventeenth and eighteenth centuries, such as Humphrey Prideaux's *The True Nature of Imposture fully displayed in the life of Mahomet* published in 1697. For many years following its publication, this work was regarded as an authoritative account of Islamic belief and practice in England, because Prideaux himself had sought to stress his impartiality. In the Introduction, he told his readers that he was not deliberately presenting Islam 'in the foulest colours' (cited in Milton 2004: 164). Moreover, he insisted that his account was based upon years of careful scholarship, evidenced by his extensive footnoting and referencing of sources. The book was outstandingly popular, and was reprinted nine times.

During the seventeenth century possibilities for a more informed understanding of Islam and Muslims began in scholarly circles. William Bedwell, a mathematician and specialist in Semitic languages at Cambridge University, earned a reputation as the 'father of Arabic scholarship in Britain' (Jones 1978: 170). Through his mastery of Arabic he was able to encounter Muslim religious thought at first hand. Although his improved understanding of Islam was still put to use in sharpening the polemic against it (Jones 1978), his command of Arabic was the inspiration behind later influential scholars such as Edward Pococke (1604–91), the first Professor of Arabic in Oxford University, who combined his knowledge of Arabic with scholarship and travel in Muslim lands. The scholarship of Arabists such as Pococke, combined with the atmosphere of dissent that surrounded the years of the English Civil War (1642–51), meant that some of the theological and literary polemic against Islam could be constructively challenged. In this context, perhaps the first sympathetic account of Islam and the life of the Prophet Muhammad in English was written by the remarkable Henry Stubbe, a scholar of Latin, Greek and Hebrew, and a friend of Pococke. Stubbe's *An Account of the Rise and Progress of Mahometanism, and a Vindication of him and his Religion from the Calumnies of the Christians* was so admiring of Islam that he dared not publish it, and it was not until 1911, when a group of Ottoman Muslims in London found the manuscript, that it became publicly available in its entirety (Murad 1997). Until this time, it had circulated only among his friends and other 'freethinkers' (Jacob 1983).

Stubbe was an historian who regarded the beliefs and doctrines of the early Christian church as a corruption of the original Christian message. According to Stubbe, it was only the advent of the Prophet Muhammad and Islam which restored Christian doctrine to its original purity (Jacob 1983). He argued that the early Christians never saw Christ as the natural son of God, and that the doctrine of the Trinity would have been regarded by them as 'tending to blasphemy and polytheism' (Stubbe cited in Jacob 1983). Here is Stubbe on Islam:

This is the sum of the Mahometan religion, on the one hand not clogging Men's faith with the necessity of believing a number of abstruse Notions which they cannot comprehend, and which are often contrary to the dictates of Reason and common Sense; nor on the other hand loading them with the performance of many troublesome, expensive, and superstitious Ceremonies, yet enjoining a due observance of Religious Worship, as the surest Method to keep Men in the bounds of their Duty both to God and Man. (Holt 1972: 22–3 cited in Kalin 2004: 157)

It is not surprising that Stubbe's work was not published during his life-time. His understanding of the life and legacy of the Prophet Muhammad and his interpretation of the 'Five Pillars' of Islam differed dramatically from most other perceptions of Islam that were prevalent in England at the time. However, even Stubbe, like most other English commentators on Islam and Muslims from the time of Bede onwards, saw the advent of Islam against the background of Christianity. Yet where Bede wanted to draw a distinctive theological line between a Christian 'us' and an Islamic 'them' as a means of affirming the righteousness of the Christian church, Stubbe used the advent of Islam as a radical device to challenge contemporary English Christian practice and governance. 'Stubbe's *Account* is not merely descriptive and explanatory of the past; it is a prescriptive critique of contemporary religion and government' (Jacob 1983: 75). For Stubbe, *Mahometan Christianity* provided a template for English religious life, civil society and government.

At the close of the seventeenth century, the magnitude and influence of the Muslim world had not only significantly changed the lives and religious identity of significant numbers of native Britons, but had also played a major role in shaping English (and European) history and identity. 'It was always engaged and alluded to, recalled and examined – and became part of the English worldview in the same way that the Communist bloc during the Cold War partly shaped Western self-understanding' (Matar 1998: 14). During the late seventeenth century, Muslim countries became even more important, not only for the shaping of national identity, but also for the English economy. The pursuit of commercial profit on an entirely grander scale would begin a new chapter in the relationship between Islam and Muslims in England.

## THE EAST INDIA COMPANY AND EARLY MUSLIM SETTLEMENT IN BRITAIN

During the seventeenth century, Britain's trading links around the world developed and expanded into the further reaches of Muslim lands. In particular, the East India Company, established by Royal Charter in 1600, became an important conduit for the immigration of Muslims to the British Isles. The Company was initially formed to profit from the Indian spice trade, which until the 1600s was dominated by the Spanish and the Portuguese. It is an ironic twist of fate that Sultan Murad's intervention in the defeat of the Armada in 1588 gave the English an opportunity to break the monopoly held by Spain and Portugal. Eventually, the

East India Company went on to become not only a commercial enterprise but also a ruling power, acting as an agent of British imperialism
in India from the early eighteenth century until the middle of the nineteenth century.

Agents of the Company and their families in India sometimes chose to
return to Britain accompanied by their Indian servants and *ayahs* (nan-
nies), some of whom were Muslim (Robinson-Dunne 2006). They were
often favourite employees, familiar with the ways of the household. At a
time when all things Indian were considered exotic, they were also status
symbols, and they were a clear indication of good fortune and wealth
(Visram 2002). Many eventually returned to their homeland, but some
remained in British homes.

As the East India Company developed its commercial activities, it
needed increasing manpower for its trading vessels. Initially, English sailors were used for this purpose, but when the supply diminished through
illness, death, or desertion, Indian sailors were recruited, and sometimes
press-ganged to take their place. These Indian sailors were known as *lascars* (from the Urdu word *lashkar*). Many of these sailors worked in unsatisfactory employment conditions and, not surprisingly, some of them
'jumped ship' and settled in Britain, usually in London. Although the law
obliged the East India Company to take responsibility for these sailors,
many of them living in Company hostels were kept on the verge of star-
vation, and there was a high rate of mortality. There are various sources
which document the rise in the number of *lascars* arriving in Britain over
time, recently estimated as 470 in 1804; 3,000 in 1842; 10,000–12,000
in 1855 (Ansari 2004: 35). The vast proportion were Indians, with small
numbers of Arabs, Turks, Somalis and Malays. It is not surprising that
we have relatively few accounts of their life in Britain by social historians: 'many of them resided in imperial spaces such as dockyards, seaport
towns and areas inhabited by the migratory, labouring poor considered
*outside the English nation*' (Robinson-Dunne 2003, emphasis added). So
the first substantial numbers of Muslims in Britain were marginalized
and peripheral, historically as well as physically. But there is evidence that
these Muslim seafarers were quite prepared to challenge the boundaries
which might have otherwise kept them within imperial spaces. In 1805,
the *Gentleman's Magazine* reported the celebration of a 'Mahommedan
Jubilee' in the East End of London, an apparently festive street procession
made audible and visible through pantomimic dances and drumming
(Robinson-Dunne 2003; Robinson-Dunne 2006).

Meanwhile in India, the exploitative commercial activities of the East India Company caused a great deal of local resentment, bringing a stream of Muslim emissaries and petitioners to Britain in order to complain about the Company and to seek redress for the land and property they had lost. One such visitor was Mirza Itisam ul-Din, who came to Britain in 1766 on behalf of the Mughal Emperor, Shah Alam, to petition George III over disagreements on tax and revenues (Seddon 2003). He travelled extensively around Britain, and his popularity with the British public was apparently considerable. He was entertaining, exotic and refined, and as such presented a dramatically contrasting impression of Muslims compared to that produced by the poor uneducated *lascars* with whom people were more familiar. Other 'noble' Muslim visitors included Mirza Abu Taleb Khan, a Muslim scholar who travelled around Africa and Europe between 1799 and 1803. During his time in Britain he was received by the upper echelons of British society, and was eventually dubbed in the popular press the 'Persian Prince' (Seddon 2003). Following a reception with King George and Queen Charlotte, he wrote:

Both these illustrious personages received me in the most condescending manner, commanded me to come frequently to court. After this introduction, I received invitations from all the Princes; and the Nobility vied with each other in their attention to me. Hospitality is one of the most esteemed virtues of the English; and I experienced it to such a degree that I was seldom disengaged and enjoyed every luxury. (Khan 1810: 161–2)

Among the more entrepreneurial Muslims to come to Britain was Shaykh Din Muhammed (or the more usual 'anglicized' 'Sake Dean Mahomed'). Born in 1759 to a noble family, at the age of ten he joined the English East India Company Bengal Army as a trainee surgeon (Visram 2002). At the age of twenty-five, he accompanied his army captain to Ireland in order to work as the house manager and to learn English. While in Cork, he met a wealthy local lady known as Jane Daly, and eventually they eloped to London and married.

Shaykh Din Muhammad turned his hand to a number of enterprises while in London, but with relatively little success. He opened the first Indian restaurant in London in 1810 and was proprietor of the 'Hindoostanee Coffee House', just off Baker Street. Neither were to be enduring concerns, and within only a few years he was bankrupt. But Shaykh Din's real talent lay in bringing together an ingenious combination of aromatherapy and hydrotherapy healing treatments. In the 1770s and 1780s, Brighton was becoming a fashionable resort and was receptive to the establishment of 'Mahomed's Indian Medicated Vapour Baths', which he claimed gave full relief to a variety of ailments of the joints and limbs. He acquired no less than a national reputation. Hospitals referred patients to him, and the ultimate recognition came when he was appointed as 'Shampooing Surgeon' to both George IV and William IV.[16] He became so successful that another branch of his enterprise was opened in London. Eventually known as 'Dr Brighton', he died aged 102 in 1851 and was buried in St Nicholas's Churchyard in the town that had made him famous.

During the eighteenth century, Britain became a major economic and military power. Having usurped the established powers in India, Britain went on to dominate the Persian Gulf region and many other majority Muslim states over the following century. This included Egypt and other regions of the Middle East, Zanzibar and Somaliland. Eventually Britain also acquired the port of Aden in the Arabian Peninsula to serve as a staging post for commercial shipping. The expansion of the British Empire into the Islamic world meant that whenever there was a need for cheap labour, Muslims formed a large proportion of the workforce.

By the mid nineteenth century Britain's influence on global politics and trade had made it an attractive destination for entrepreneurs, scholars and travellers from all over the world. A new demand emerged in Britain for teachers of Eastern languages and culture, and so Muslims increasingly came to Britain to both impart and gain education. *Munchis* (teachers) were found in regular employment for the teaching of Arabic and Persian, and well-known teachers included Munchi Ismail, who came to Britain in 1772 (Seddon 2003).[17] However, proportionately more Muslims came to Britain to gain knowledge than to impart it. Many educated and elite members of Muslim societies felt that their own advancement under imperial rule was conditional upon learning about European ideas and systems of thought, hence the growing traffic of Muslim students to Britain. From the 1840s there was a steady stream of Indian students to

---

[16] At this time, shampooing referred not to washing hair, but to massaging the body in vapour baths.

[17] Perhaps the best known of these Muslim teachers was Munchi Abdul Karim who became Queen Victoria's teacher in the social norms, languages and religions of India soon after her Golden Jubilee in 1887. He was named 'Indian Secretary' in 1894 and was awarded the Companion of the Order of the Indian Empire (CIE), such was the degree to which Queen Victoria was impressed by him. But following Queen Victoria's death, Abdul Karim became the victim of ongoing racist prejudice and was eventually deported back to India.

British (and especially Scottish) universities. From only four in 1845, the number had grown to 700 by 1910 (Ansari 2004), including Muhammad Ali Jinnah, the 'founding father' of Pakistan. Inevitably, some of these Muslim students never returned to their homelands and settled in Britain permanently.

## CONCLUSION

This chapter has covered a long historical period, over a thousand years from the eighth century to the mid nineteenth century. It has summarized some of the main trends in the relations between Muslims and the British Isles. Inevitably, it has provided only a generalized and selective outline of a subject that has deservedly been examined in more depth by others, and will no doubt be re-examined afresh from time to time in the future. Looking back on this long history of engagement between Islam and British society, there has no doubt been an under-appreciation of the impact and presence of Islam and Muslims in Britain, perhaps especially in 'remoter' times. It is a history that is largely unknown, at least outside of fairly narrow academic circles.

In this regard, important scholarly work remains to be done, to reverse the common assumption that the Muslim presence in Britain is only a relatively recent phenomenon, and that Islamic scholarship in the medieval period made little impact on English society. There is a vast range of sources at our disposal to further this exploration, from government papers, to diaries, to travelogues, to theological texts. So far, much of this data has been examined almost exclusively by historians and those working in literary studies, but it could provide fertile material for a much wider, interdisciplinary, critical scholarship.

# CHAPTER 2

# The development of Muslim communities

## INTRODUCTION

For the mid nineteenth century onwards, there are more diverse resources available for understanding the place of Islam in British society, and evolving perceptions of Muslims in Britain and abroad. Travel narratives, parliamentary papers, newspapers, novels, poetry and scholarly studies are supplemented by detailed trading documents, missionary reports, oral histories and photographs. These sources have limitations and biases, but the scope for comparative analysis opens up possibilities for a greater range of interpretations. Some of these sources, especially literary works, have recently been subject to critical evaluation (Khattak 2008).

Moreover, from this time Muslims in Britain were actively producing and publishing their own newsletters and journals. Given that this is a history that, through new research, continues to reveal itself even in the present day,[1] this chapter can only be introductory, time-bound and selective. Similarly, it remains necessary to be mindful of who exactly has recorded and documented the history of Muslims in Britain, the sources they have relied upon, and the perspectives that might be shaping their analysis.

During the late Victorian period, greater numbers of Muslims were coming to Britain as traders, teachers and university students. At the same time, a number of high-profile British public figures converted to Islam. These developments are examined in general outline here, but most of the focus is upon the 'Muslim history' of three maritime ports that provide case studies of Muslim activity and settlement in Britain in the late nineteenth and early twentieth centuries: South Shields, Cardiff and

---

[1] A good example of more publicly available resources is the recent acquisition in late 2005 of the 'Quilliam Collection' by the Islamic Foundation in Leicester. This collection comprises both hard-copy and CD-ROM data reflecting the publications and activities of the Liverpool Muslim community in the late nineteenth and early twentieth centuries.

Liverpool. The choice of these places as case studies rests upon the overall importance of major ports during this phase in British Muslim history, as well as the significance of particular charismatic personalities associated with them. Of particular importance were two individuals: Abdullah Ali al-Hakimi in South Shields and Cardiff, and Abdullah 'Henry' Quilliam in Liverpool. Readers with an interest in other important locations for Muslim settlement and activity, such as Woking, London or Glasgow, or in other significant British Muslim personalities, such as Khwaja Kamal-ud-Din, Syed Ameer Ali or Marmaduke Picthall, are directed to further sources.[2]

In the second half of the chapter, the main features of Muslim migration and settlement in Britain from 1945 are further documented. This most recent history could be presented in great detail, such is the extent of scholarly research and the availability of primary sources. There have been in-depth studies of Muslims arriving and settling in particular towns and cities, such as Bradford, Manchester and Oxford. There has also been research that has focused upon the settlement of particular ethnic groups, such as Pakistanis and Bangladeshis. Space does not permit a detailed discussion, but again there is reference to further sources.

1860–1945: THE BACKGROUND TO MUSLIM SETTLEMENT

In the mid nineteenth century, a major technical transformation that took place in the world's merchant shipping industry had almost immediately a most profound effect on Muslim settlement in Britain: most freight ships were no longer powered by sails, but by steam from coal-fired engines. At this time, the Durham and South Wales coalfields were among the most productive in Britain, and their proximity to major ports such as Cardiff and South Shields gave these places a particular strategic advantage in the world of commercial shipping. But the transition from sail to steam vessels created work that was hot, dirty and tiring, and this form of labour was increasingly rejected by white European workers. New recruits on these trading ships were therefore drawn from colonial territories with strong merchant shipping traditions, such as coastal India, Yemen and

---

[2] For more information on Woking and the personality of Khwaja Kamal ud-Din see Ansari (2002); Ansari (2004); Brown (2004); 'Khwaja Kamal-ud-Din – the torch-bearer of Islam' (1922); Siddiq (1934); and the website of the Woking Muslim Mission, www.wokingmuslim.org.uk. To learn more about the history of Muslims in London see Ansari (2004); Bugby (1938); and www.masud.co.uk/ISLAM/bmh/BMH-IRO-historical_overview.htm. For a history of Muslims in Scotland see Dunlop (1990); Maan (2008). To learn more about Marmaduke Picthall see his biography (Clark 1986).

Somalia. They were employed primarily as firemen and stokers on vessels moving between Britain and the Far East (Aithie 2005; El-Solh 1993; Lawless 1995).

Given the extent and diversity of the British Empire, the seafarers were not all Muslim of course. There was a certain amount of religious stratification on board ship, with Muslims tending to work together in the engine rooms, Hindus on the decks and Christians in the saloon (Lawless 1997). There was also considerable diversity among the Muslim seafarers themselves. Pathans, Punjabis and Mirpuris were recruited in Bombay, while Bengalis, especially from the Sylhet region, were recruited in Calcutta. The availability of workers for the ships varied according to the vibrancy of the agricultural industry at the time, since most recruits were peasant farmers. The opening of the Suez Canal in 1869 added a further impetus to Muslim migration to Britain as the volume of trading between Britain and Asian countries increased.

The Muslim seafarers were prepared to undertake arduous work in the engine room for considerably less financial reward than their British counterparts, their wages being between one-third and one-quarter those of a British seaman (Lawless 1997). Because of their poor wages and inferior living and working conditions, some Muslim seafarers 'jumped ship' and sought a new life for themselves in Britain. Many chose to remain in the maritime ports that had brought them to Britain originally. Life for these former seafarers was often harsh. There was considerable unemployment, and during the winter months *lascars* were sometimes found dead on the streets of London, having succumbed to cold and hunger (Salter 1873).

The plight of destitute seafarers led the Church Missionary Society to open a Strangers' Home for Asiatics, Africans and South Sea Islanders in London in 1857 (Beckerlegge 1997). As part of this initiative, a missionary named Joseph Salter from the London City Mission was appointed to offer pastoral support to members of other faiths in Britain, and especially *lascars*. His forty years of missionary work around Britain became the subject of two volumes (Salter 1873; Salter 1895). Although they are 'highly polemical' (Beckerlegge 1997: 225) in relation to Islam and Muslims, Salter's books provide valuable insights into inter-religious relations in Britain in the mid nineteenth century, and the beliefs and practices of members of various religious traditions.[3] For example, he notes

---

[3] In terms of polemic, a good example is the way in which Salter consistently refers to the *lascars* as 'heathens' with 'dark minds' (Salter 1873: 21).

the strict observance of Ramadan in one of the households in London occupied by *lascars*, and records their perplexity at and suspicion of the missionary efforts being made towards them (Salter 1873).

The way in which Muslim seafarers in British towns and cities were perceived in wider society during the mid to late nineteenth century had as much to do with class tensions and conflicts as with religious difference. They were outsiders, not only because of their origins and visible racial difference, but also because they were regarded as being part of a migratory labouring underclass. They were 'beyond the pale of the true English nation' because their 'circumstances and lifestyles resembled those of other English people who seemed to threaten the social order' (Robinson-Dunne 2003: 2), such as pedlars, criminals and vagrants. Their relationships with English women did nothing to improve such perceptions. They married women who were often from poor dockland areas of the cities, and were usually regarded as part of the uncivilized lower strata of society. At a time when a woman's social position was often determined by the status of her father or husband, 'women could be "Orientalized" by lascars [but] lascars could not be Anglicized by their new companions' (Robinson-Dunne 2003: 2). Women nonetheless played a vital role in community-building. They were expected to cater for predominantly male-only gatherings, and to keep open house for needy seafarers and travellers. In reference to Cardiff, Marika Sherwood has noted: 'if there was a unified "community" in The Bay, it was cemented together by the women' (Sherwood 1988: 67).

Perceptions of Muslims were also shaped by international and diplomatic forces. Britain's relations with Muslims in colonial India and with the Ottoman Turks in the closing decades of the nineteenth century were politically very important. British rule in North India and the frontier with Afghanistan was sustained by maintaining close relations with Indian Muslim 'elites', while the Turks were the allies of the British until the growth of German influence in the period from 1900. However, despite the importance of Britain's links in numerous parts of the Muslim world, stereotyped images of Islam and the Prophet Muhammad that had originated in the medieval period were still in evidence. For example, the *British Quarterly Review* in 1872 commented on the spread of Islam beyond Arabia being 'the greatest of curses to mankind' (Beckerlegge 1997: 244, citing Almond 1989: 82). These views had consequences for Muslims living in Britain, in terms of discrimination and prejudice.

There were considerable differences of language, ethnicity and interpretation of Islam among the Muslim seafarers, and their distinctive identities and differences became more – not less – apparent through their proximity in Britain. At the same time, however, their collective experiences of exclusion and their common religious identity as Muslims created the basis for new bonds of association. These often revolved around religious figures and places of worship, as will be noted below. The largely transient population of Muslims living in Britain included not only poor working seafarers, however, but also students from wealthy elite Indian families. They were isolated from the hardships of working life, in the confines of British universities which were training grounds for future political leaders in the Indian subcontinent, such as Muhammad Ali Jinnah (1876–1948), the founder of Pakistan, who came to Britain to study law. So education and socio-economic differences also had a determining influence on where Muslims were located on the precarious and porous boundary of inclusion and exclusion in British society.

The number of Muslims in Britain at the end of the nineteenth century is estimated to be in the region of 10,000 (Ansari 2004). But what do historical records tell us about the early Muslim communities in Britain? To what extent did they practise their faith, and how did these embryonic communities change over time? To answer some of these questions, we can look at Muslim communities in particular British cities, beginning with Tyneside and South Shields in the north-east of England, just a stone's throw from the site of Bede's monastery at Jarrow (see chapter 1).

TYNESIDE AND SOUTH SHIELDS (SHAYKH ABDULLAH ALI AL-HAKIMI)

Although Indian seafarers constituted the greater proportion of seamen employed on British merchant ships in the mid to late nineteenth century, more Arab (especially Yemeni) and Somali seafarers than Indian counterparts became domiciled in Britain. There is therefore more documentary evidence about their lives in Britain, and this evidence has been used as the basis for a number of studies of Arabs in Tyneside (Carr 1992; Collins 1957; Lawless 1995). However, these studies are limited by a heavy reliance upon documents which reflect the immediate interaction between Arab seafarers and wider society, such as newspaper reports. Perhaps not surprisingly, when Muslims figured in the local press it was due either to their exoticism, or to their involvement in an incident regarded as newsworthy, such as a civil disturbance. Furthermore, wider social and political factors had a bearing upon the nature of reporting; when seafaring fell into decline after the First World War, resulting in considerable unemployment, Arab Muslims were the target of substantial local hostility that was reflected in local newspapers. Compared with such newspaper evidence, much less material is available to illuminate the internal dynamics of the community. However, Lawless has provided important insights through the interviews he conducted in South Shields.

It is evident that Arab Muslims were beginning to settle in South Shields by the early 1900s. While the number of permanent residents was quite small (Lawless gives a figure of twenty to thirty in 1913), there was a constant stream of seafarers living in the town on a temporary basis. By the First World War, the Immigration Office in Newcastle reported the existence of eight Arab boarding houses accommodating between 300 and 600 seafarers:

For Arab seamen arriving in a strange land with little knowledge of its language and customs, the Arab boarding house was virtually essential for their survival … it provided not only accommodation and food that was lawful according to their religion, but essential assistance in securing another ship, and credit if their resources ran out before they signed on for the next voyage. (Lawless 1997: 23)

Lawless has provided detailed accounts of the lives of these seafarers in the north-east of England. He describes how they struggled, economically, politically and socially, and their efforts to create mosques, religious associations and burial facilities. He also documents their day-to-day religious observances of prayers, fasting and rites of passage. Most of the Yemeni Muslims belonged to the *Shāfiʿī* legal school of Sunni Islam, and they clearly made every effort to adhere faithfully to Islamic practice, a point confirmed by other scholars (Serjeant 1944). Most of the boarding houses allocated a room for communal prayers, with the role of imam carried out in turn by different seamen. Festivals of *Eid* were celebrated (and sometimes reported in the local newspapers), and by 1928 boarding-house owners had established permission from the South Shields Corporation for the halal (lawful) slaughter of animals on their own backyard premises. Islamic funerals rites, sometimes described at length in the press, were taking place from 1916. Moreover, some of the Yeminis living in South Shields undertook the pilgrimage to Makkah during the early twentieth century (Lawless 1995). But it was the arrival in Britain of Shaykh Abdullah Ali al-Hakimi in 1936 that transformed and projected the largely private practice of Islam in the boarding houses into the streets and public consciousness of South Shields.

Religion and politics (both international and local) were closely intertwined in the three Muslim organizations that were active in Tyneside from around the turn of the century onwards. They played a pivotal role as mediators between Arab seafarers and local authorities, and their concerns encompassed both religious and secular matters. The first of these, the Islamic Society, emerged out of another British Muslim organization, the Pan-Islamic Movement (headed by Abdullah Suhrawardy in London), and it was most active between 1915 and 1919. Some of the members of the Islamic Society were also involved with the Woking Muslim Mission in Surrey[4] and the British Muslim Society. The stated objectives of the Islamic Society were 'to promote the religious, moral, social and intellectual advancement of the Muslim world', with patrons including senior British government officials such as Lloyd George (Lawless 1995: 215). This organization played an important advocacy role for Muslims in South Shields following the First World War, when employment and racial tensions saw members of the Yemeni community suffering abuse and prejudice which, at its worst, culminated in street riots in 1919. One of the most active members of the Islamic Society was an Indian barrister, Shaykh Dr Abdul Hamid. After these urban disturbances, he played an important intermediary role between the seafarers and local government officials.

In 1930 a new British Muslim organization was formed in London called the Western Islamic Association, headed by Dr Khalid Sheldrake, a convert who was also associated with the Woking Muslim Mission. A branch of this new organization was established in South Shields (and another in Cardiff), and Sheldrake acted as an advocate for the Arab seamen in relation to the National Union of Seamen (NUS). By the late 1920s and early 1930s, with the shipping industry in sharp decline, there were even fewer employment opportunities. Tensions between Arab and white seafarers (additionally fuelled by jealousy and moral outrage at the relationships between Arabs and local white women) led the NUS actively to campaign for the deportation of Arabs. There was also controversy over the introduction of a new 'rota system' that ensured that seamen who had been ashore the longest were given first refusal for new voyages. Sheldrake campaigned on behalf of the Arabs, on the strength of being 'a Britisher and also as a Mohammedan' (*Shields Daily Gazette*, 11 September 1930, p. 6, cited in Lawless 1995: 39).

Unlike the Islamic Society and the Western Islamic Association, both of which were London based and led by educated professionals, the Zaouia Islamia Allawoulia Religious Society of the United Kingdom was pioneered by a Sufi *shaykh* of the *'Alawī ṭarīqah* (Sufi order), from Yemen.

---

[4] www.wokingmuslim.org

During the mid 1930s, Shaykh Abdullah Ali al-Hakimi established religious centres (*zāwiyah*) in South Shields, Cardiff, Hull and Liverpool, but most of his energy was devoted to religious activity in South Shields, and then in Cardiff. al-Hakimi had a transformative effect on religious life in both cities, resulting in the 're-Islamization of the Arab seafaring communities' (Lawless 1995: 42). Religious festivals were celebrated less in private and more in public. Following the arrival of al-Hakimi, photographs from local newspapers depict lively street processions, with participants dressed in typical Yemeni clothing:

> Green banners inscribed with the words *la ilaha illa 'llah* (there is no God but God) together with a white crescent and stars, were always carried aloft at the head of the procession and those taking part chanted 'Alawi *nashids*' or praises to God. These processions attracted hundreds of curious onlookers ... and were reported in some details, though with numerous inaccuracies, in the local press which was obviously intrigued by the 'picturesque pagentry' of these occasions. (Lawless 1995: 221)

al-Hakimi negotiated his way through local politics with apparent skill and ease. He was regarded by civic leaders in both South Shields and Cardiff as having a 'representative' role, despite the fact that he confined his work almost exclusively to the Yemeni Muslims. He actively cultivated civic figures such as leading councillors, the Mayor and the Chief Constable. They in turn appeared to regard his efforts as socially useful, especially where he channelled the energies of otherwise unemployed Arab seafarers into constructive religious activity. In relation to Cardiff, Evans is clear about why al-Hakimi's work would have won local support: he did not challenge the local status quo, and his organization, which encouraged self-discipline, was probably 'encouraged by the authorities ... as a supplement to social control' (Evans 1985: 102). With this level of support and recognition, it was perhaps not surprising that al-Hakimi began to regard himself as the 'Head of the Muslim Community of the UK' (Lawless 1994).

al-Hakimi had interests beyond Britain. He travelled periodically in Europe, in North Africa and in the Middle East. During his absences, he would deputize to another *shaykh* from his Sufi order, Shaykh Hassan Ismail. Over the course of the mid twentieth century, trans-global Yemeni politics began to cause a rift between al-Hakimi and his deputy. One supported the existing regime of Imam Yahya (Hassan Ismail), while the other campaigned for the 'Free Yemeni Movement' (al-Hakimi). International politics were played out on the streets of Tyneside and Cardiff, and led to rivalries and factionalism in both communities. The height of these came after the Second World War, but the seeds were sown in the interwar period.

## CARDIFF: SHAYKH ABDULLAH ALI AL-HAKIMI AND SHAYKH HASSAN ISMAIL

The Muslim community that formed in Cardiff during the late 1800s was larger and much more significant than that in South Shields, but it has not received so much scholarly attention. Lawless attributes the lack of research on Muslim settlement in South Wales to the lack of local documentary sources, but recently substantial new evidence has emerged. Since Lawless published his book in 1995, the Butetown History and Arts Centre has been established in Cardiff.[5] This project has sought to enable different generations of Muslims (and others) to record and celebrate their history in the City, resulting in the donation of photographs and other documentary sources, as well as the active collection of oral histories. These resources, combined with further interviews, are part of an ongoing project to document the history of Muslims in Cardiff.[6] Meanwhile, snippets of data recorded during the interwar period by sociologists and social historians provide other important insights; matters of religion are second in priority to issues of employment, race, and politics, though on occasion they intertwine.

In the late 1800s, the patterns of Muslim settlement evident in South Shields were also evident in Cardiff. By 1881, there were enough transitory seafarers to warrant the establishment of a so-called 'Home for Coloured Seamen'.[7] Boarding houses owned and managed by Yemenis (mostly from the *Shamiri* tribe) provided a physical, social, religious and economic base for Muslim seafarers. The social historian Neil Evans has collected together a wide range of documentary sources about the lives of Arab seafarers in Cardiff during the interwar period, especially reports in the *Western Mail* and City Council papers. He provides a sense of local life in 1920s and 1930s Butetown (also known as 'Tiger Bay') which was the base for many Muslim seafarers. He reports that they were effectively isolated from the rest of the city in a cosmopolitan international

---

[5] For an indication of the resources held at BHAC see their website: www.bhac.org/collections.html

[6] This project is being undertaken by Dr Jody Mellor in the Islam-UK Centre at Cardiff University: www.cardiff.ac.uk/relig

[7] Over the past ten years, some scholars and historians have claimed that the first mosque in the UK was established in Cardiff in 1860. This is in fact not the case. See Gilliat-Ray (2010).

ghetto comprising seafarers from over thirty different countries (Evans 1985). Running from one end of Butetown to the other, Bute Street linked the docks to the heart of the capital and acted as the 'the jugular vein of the Welsh economy' (Evans 1985: 69). Welsh Office records suggest a population of 5,000 Arab seamen in Cardiff around the turn of the century (Aithie 2005: 22); by 1930 the number of recorded 'Alien Coloured Seamen' included 1,241 Arabs (mostly Yemenis), 227 Somalis, 148 Indians, 121 Malays and 49 Egyptians (Evans 1985: 71). Nearly all these seamen were of course Muslims.

The outbreak of the First World War produced a rapid expansion in demand for maritime manual labour, and the number of Muslims increased in all Britain's seaports. Cardiff was no exception. Wages rose sharply, and seafaring became an attractive proposition. But prejudice against Muslims was clearly discernible. This took the form of anti-Arab and anti-'coloured' sentiment, rather than what we might today call 'Islamophobia'. The *South Wales Daily News* on 2 September 1916, for example, noted with some concern that 'there are more Arabs ... entering Cardiff than ever before'. However, after the First World War ended, the coal trade declined and young Welsh soldiers returned to Cardiff. Muslims then began to experience particular prejudice, and some suggested that they should 'go home'.[8] The tensions led to violent race riots and attacks on boarding houses inhabited by Muslim seafarers in 1919, resulting in a warning that 'Moslems all over the world will require an explanation of why their brothers in Cardiff ... should have been treated in the scandalous manner they have by an unruly mob' (Evans 1980: 20). Anti-Arab feeling led to the repatriation of 500 men (originally from Aden) in 1921, and between the two wars there was mass unemployment for Muslims. 'Out of the 690 unemployed seamen on the Cardiff Dock Register, on 1st June 1936, 599 were "coloured"' (Ansari 2004: 44).

However, employment issues were not the sole cause of ill-feeling towards Muslims in Cardiff in the interwar years. Relationships between Arab/Muslim men and local white Welsh women were also a catalyst for prejudice. The *Western Mail* (13 June 1919), found 'such consorting ... ill-assorting; it exhibits either a depravity or a squalid infatuation; it is repugnant to our finer instincts in which pride of race occupies a just and inevitable place'. The Chief Constable of Cardiff sought to make sexual relations between 'coloured' seamen and white women illegal (Ansari 2004), and there was an almost complete segregation of the Muslims in

---

[8] For more information about race relations in Cardiff see Sherwood (1988).

Figure 2. Shaykh Said, Imam of the South Wales Islamic Centre, Cardiff.
Reproduced by kind permission of the Institute of Welsh Affairs

Tiger Bay from the rest of Cardiff society. Words such as 'undesirable', 'unsavoury' and 'disreputable' were the kind of terms used to refer to the homes and cafés of Muslims. Ansari notes that they were 'forced to live in deprived areas and then [were] blamed for creating the miserable conditions' (Ansari 2004: 107).

al-Hakimi left South Shields for Cardiff in May 1938, though he had been moving between the two cities frequently for the previous two years. He established premises for the Zaouia Islamia Allawoulia on Bute Street but this was insufficient for the number of Muslims in the City. Although by 1936 there were six mosques in Cardiff associated with boarding houses, the community raised funds for the purchase of some terraced houses in Peel Street in 1938. Funding came from a variety of sources, and assistance was sought from the British authorities who readily agreed, initially, to back the project for its 'propaganda value' (Lawless 1994: 43) at a time when a second world war was looking increasingly likely. In the end, no money was forthcoming from the British government, but the community nevertheless managed to acquire the premises and convert them into what became known as the Nur al-Islam Mosque.

al-Hakimi returned to Cardiff following the Second World War, using it as his base for opposition to the political regime in Yemen. As part of his efforts, he published one of Britain's first Arabic newspapers, *Al-Salam*, from the Nur al-Islam Mosque. Tension between him and his deputy continued into the 1950s, but when he left Britain in 1952 his Deputy, Shaykh Hassan Ismail, took his place as the spiritual leader of the Yemenis in Britain. He was himself then succeeded by Shaykh Said, his adoptive son, who continues to be an important figurehead for Muslims in South Wales, despite his advancing years (Figure 2; Gilliat-Ray 2005c).

## LIVERPOOL (ABDULLAH QUILLIAM)

During the mid 1800s, the size of the docks in Liverpool and the scale of cargo that they could handle meant that Liverpool was regarded by some as England's 'first port of Empire' (Neal 1988: 1). There were particularly strong connections with India and Egypt, and visiting Egyptian dignitaries were often well received by civic officials. Liverpool grew rapidly during the nineteenth century. It was a city characterized by 'constant motion ... of people, products, and ideas' (Robinson-Dunne 2003). This cosmopolitan entrepreneurial atmosphere attracted migrants from other parts of the British Isles as well as from overseas. As a consequence, Liverpool was perhaps more accommodating of difference and diversity than other places in Britain, especially where this was perceived to relate directly to increased prosperity.

This vibrant, outward-looking maritime city provided an ideal location for the emergence of a new British Muslim community, the history of which is directly linked to the figure of William Henry Quilliam[9] (Robinson-Dunne 2006). Quilliam was born in Liverpool in 1856.[10] By 1878 he had qualified as a solicitor, having worked as a journalist to support his legal training. He became a prominent member of civic associations in the north-west of England, but on grounds of ill health he was advised to travel to warmer climes in 1882. With this advice, he set out for Morocco. During and after his extensive travels in North Africa he began

[9] Beckerlegge (1997) offers a number of references for biographical information about Quilliam's life, including local Liverpool newspapers and the periodical *Islamic World* (p. 246). For more information about Quilliam see also Pool (1892), especially his chapter 'Islam in England' where he recounts his visit to Liverpool as Quilliam's guest in 1891.

[10] For a biography of Quilliam see Geaves (2010).

to learn Arabic. When in 1887 he publicly announced his conversion from Christianity to Islam he became known as Abdullah Quilliam, and almost immediately he began to propagate the message of Islam, through both public speaking and the publication of pamphlets. His wearing of 'Islamic dress' (typically a Moroccan fez) made his new-found faith publicly conspicuous.[11] Within six years of his conversion he was recognized as an *ʿālim* (Islamic scholar) *ʿulamāʾ* by the Islamic University in Fez, and in the following year the title 'Sheikh-ul-Islam of the British Isles' was conferred upon him by the Sultan of Turkey and the *Amīr* of Afghanistan.[12] This made him the 'universally-acclaimed leader of British Islam during the period' (Murad 2005: introduction).

Quilliam used his extensive connections with particular Muslim countries to further his cause in Liverpool. He secured funding for the establishment of the Liverpool Mosque and Muslim Institute and various other concerns, such as the Medina Home for Children opened in 1896.[13] At its most active, the Liverpool Muslim Institute included a mosque, a library, a lecture hall, a school and a printing press producing the weekly publication *Crescent* (1893–1908) and the monthly *Islamic World* (1893–1908). But the vibrancy of the Institute was heavily dependent upon the figure of Quilliam himself, the 'life and soul' of the movement (Pool 1892: 395). When he left England in 1908, the cohesion and energy that he had brought to Muslims in Liverpool started to dwindle.

Reflecting on his legacy, he clearly made Islam personally relevant to significant numbers of native Britons. The Annual General Meeting of the Institute in 1896, subsequently reported in *Islamic World* (August 1896: 99), refers to 150 new members. Beckerlegge surmises that about two-thirds of the Institute's members were probably converts (Beckerlegge 1997). It is not for nothing that Quilliam has been described as the 'the founder of the Anglo-Muslim movement' (Murad 1997), perhaps on account of the number of British people attracted to Islam through his influence. Some of his poetry has been set to indigenous folk tunes, and in 2005 the Quilliam Press published a collection called *Muslim Songs of the British Isles* (Murad 2005).[14]

---

[11] See Robinson-Dunne (2003) for an excellent interpretation of the social meaning of 'Oriental' dress in Britain.

[12] See 'An Enquiry into the status of the Sheikh-ul-Islam of the British Isles' by Yahya Birt: www.yahyabirt.com:80/?p=138 for more discussion of this designation, and its significance.

[13] See www.bbc.co.uk/legacies/heritage/england/liverpool/article_1.shtml for more information about the Institute. The Abdullah Quilliam Society was founded in 1998 to celebrate Quilliam's work.

[14] To listen to some of these songs go to the website www.britishmuslimsong.co.uk/

The Muslims of Liverpool would not have escaped the complexities underpinning public perceptions of Islam and Muslims during the late nineteenth century. However, there were particular reasons why the Liverpool Institute and more especially the person of Quilliam himself were regarded with additional suspicion in some quarters. In parallel with the flourishing of the Institute, the question of Britain's relationship with the Ottoman Empire loomed large; diplomatic relations were delicate. Quilliam's close personal relationship with the Ottoman Sultan was regarded as an indication of divided loyalties: 'a Muslim living according to the imperatives of Islamic law was seen to be answerable to authorities beyond and other than the British monarch and the British state' (Beckerlegge 1997: 261). So just as the sixteenth- and seventeenth-century 'renegades' were seen as the 'enemy within' (Matar 1993: 2), so too some Muslims in Britain in the nineteenth century were confronted with questions about their identity and loyalty. But these challenges were not just about religious identity and spiritual deviance. They were actually bound up with assumptions about political sympathies that were regarded as conflicting with British interests, at the time. Thus the kind of religious liberty assumed to be implicit within Victorian Anglican Protestantism had definite boundaries, the borders of which fluctuated according to wider socio-political circumstances. But the end result was often the same, with Muslims placed on the margins of society.

## THE DIVERSITY OF MUSLIM EXPERIENCE AND SETTLEMENT

Surveying the Muslim presence in Britain from 1860 to 1945, it can be seen that port cities like Cardiff, Liverpool, Hull and Glasgow were crucial places of settlement. It was specifically the imperial ports, those engaged in international trading around the British Empire, that had the most significance. If Liverpool was the first 'port of Empire' (Neal 1988: 1), Glasgow was regarded by some as the 'Second City of Empire' (Ansari 2004: 36) in the late nineteenth century. It was a major centre for the import and export of jute (from Bengal), and the institutions associated with shipping (such as the Glasgow Sailors' Home) provide evidence for the presence of Muslim *lascars* in the City. Joseph Salter's accounts of his missionary work in Britain also mention the presence of *lascars* in a number of other Scottish towns and cities such as Aberdeen and Dumbarton (Salter 1873).

Of similar importance to the maritime ports were metropolitan manufacturing cities, such as Manchester, Birmingham and Bradford. For
example, Manchester became pivotal in the global manufacture and
export of textiles, and it attracted Moroccan and Arab traders from at
least as early as 1830. By the end of the nineteenth century there were over
a dozen Moroccan families in the city, and up to 150 Middle Eastern merchant houses, the occupants of which preserved their languages, religious
identity and cultural norms (Halliday 1992b). The history of Muslims in
London could be an entire study in its own right; it has always been a significant location for Muslim settlement. Being both a maritime port city
and an international centre for manufacture, trade, diplomacy and politics, it is not surprising that an established Muslim presence in the city
goes back over a number of centuries.

Besides Quilliam, the late nineteenth century and early twentieth century saw other high-profile and aristocratic British public figures convert to Islam, such as Lord 'Abdullah' Headley.[15] Whereas the mainly
poor uneducated British converts to Islam in the sixteenth and seventeenth centuries often remained living in the Muslim world, these new
British converts often practised their faith in Britain. And unlike their
sixteenth- and seventeenth-century predecessors, they were usually seen
less as 'the enemy within' (Matar 1993: 2), and rather as 'eccentrics of the
Raj'.[16] Although they attracted suspicion, they were nevertheless generally tolerated in diplomatic and military circles owing to their potential
ambassadorial role.

There is a lack of in-depth research on Muslims in Britain during the
interwar years, and relatively little evidence as to how they were bound
up with, and affected by, the major events and trends of the times, such
as the Great Depression, the rise of fascism in the 1930s, communism
and changing social mores. However, a number of important projects
are attempting to develop scholarly understanding,[17] and there is scope

---

[15] Another example is Sir Archibald Hamilton, former master of foxhounds and President of the
Selsey (Sussex) Conservative Association (*Islamic Review*, March 1924, p. 117). Although the
appeal of Islam to British people from a variety of backgrounds was noted in British Muslim
publications of the early 1900s, upper-class/aristocratic converts were often named in reports, as
if they added particular legitimacy and significance to the Muslim community in Britain. See
also the biography of the first British Muslim woman to go on pilgrimage to Makkah in 1933,
Lady Evelyn Cobbold (Cobbold 2008).

[16] www.masud.co.uk/ISLAM/bmh/BMH-IRO ('Muslims of London: a brief historical overview').

[17] For example, 'Making Britain: South Asian Visions of Home and Abroad 1870–1950' (Open
University, Oxford University, King's College London) will contribute to knowledge of (South
Asian) Muslims in Britain between the two world wars: www.open.ac.uk/Arts/south-asians-
making-britain/

for more research on this era of British Muslim history. These studies are likely to show how the widespread recession after the First World War forced Muslims in Britain towards other entrepreneurial activity. Alongside the economic gloom of the post-First World War period, there were growing prospects in newer industries such as chemicals, electrical goods and car manufacturing, and there was a new demand for unskilled and semi-skilled workers. Between the two world wars, therefore, the geographical distribution of Muslims to Britain altered as cities in the Midlands, such as Birmingham, and large textile mills in the north of England began to attract former seafarers and dock labourers. These workers were at the 'starting end of migratory chains' (Ansari 2004: 49) in cities which, after the Second World War, would attract substantial numbers of Muslims. But these cities were also vital during the Second World War years as many of them had armaments factories providing abundant work for ex-seafarers. For example, the first Muslims to settle in Bradford in 1941 were former sailors, and most worked in factories that supported the war effort. Likewise, about thirty Muslim ex-seafarers were directed by the Ministry of Labour from Cardiff to Birmingham in 1940 (Dahya 1974).

Muslim contributions were as vital to Britain in the Second World War as they had been in the First World War. When Britain declared war against Germany in 1939, it did so

on behalf of India, Burma and the Colonies ... for approximately 48 million people in Britain, 63 million in the colonies in Africa and the Caribbean, 370 million in the Indian sub-continent and 15 million Burmese. People of all these countries fought *with* the British forces against Germany, Italy and Japan. (Visram 2002: 341, emphasis original)

Because of India's manpower potential, its location and its material resources, its contribution to the war effort was critical. Visram outlines at some length the extent of Indian contributions in terms of foodstuffs, jute, cotton, timber and leather, not to mention financial aid (Visram 2002). The Indian army, which included large numbers of Muslim soldiers, constituted the largest volunteer army on the battlefield and their bravery was recognized by the number of military awards that followed subsequently (Visram 2002). But for the 6,600 Indian seamen who lost their lives in the war, many of whom were Muslim, there is virtually no record of their names, and no monument to their losses. Many 'perished, unnamed, as is if they never were' (Visram 2002: 347).

### MUSLIMS IN BRITAIN FROM 1945

Muslims who had contributed to the war effort were demobilized in Britain. Some returned to their countries of origin, but others became domiciled in the UK. The post-war period, especially from 1950 onwards, also saw the new arrival of large numbers of Muslim immigrants to Britain, especially from the Indian subcontinent. There is more familiarity with this phase of Muslim immigration, not only because it is relatively recent, but also because it has been studied more systematically (Adams 1987; Ansari 2004; Anwar 1979; Dahya 1974; Jeffery 1976; Kalra 2000; Lewis 1994; Saifullah-Khan 1975; Shaw 1988; Werbner 1990). Because of the availability of a wide range of literature and resources about the history of Muslims in Britain in the post-Second World War period, this is not examined in great detail now. However, a general account of the reasons for migration to Britain and an overview of settlement patterns provides important contextual background for later chapters. Given that the majority of Muslims coming to Britain post-1945 were from the Indian subcontinent, much of the following discussion describes the settlement of Pakistani, Bangladeshi and Indian Muslims. Towards the end, the arrival of Muslims with different origins, especially Arabs, Iranians and Turks, is considered.

There are three distinctive themes within theoretical discussion surrounding migration (Kalra 2000). 'World systems theory' examines the movement of people on the basis of worldwide dynamics of supply and demand in the labour market (Castles and Kosack 1973). 'Push and pull' theories consider the structural drivers of migration – away from poverty, flood or political unrest – towards parts of the world where there is demand for labour. Much of the literature surrounding Muslim immigration to Britain has been understood in terms of 'push and pull' factors. However, the limitation of this perspective is that it undermines the agency of migrants themselves, and fails to recognize the social relationships that enable human movement from one part of the world to another. So 'network theory' has developed to consider the human support systems that facilitate the emotional, spiritual, and economic transition involved in migration (Kalra 2000). Relatively few studies of Muslim migration to Britain, especially of South Asians, have given sufficient attention to the history that precedes a migratory move. A notable exception is Kalra's study of (Azad) Kashmiri settlement in Oldham. He considers the full political, historic and economic context which already made areas such as Mirpur 'environments of migration' (Kalra 2000: 63), and in his analysis the outcomes of both 'push and pull' and 'network' theories are made evident.

In relation to the history of Muslim settlement in Britain after 1945, what were the 'push and pull' factors? Firstly, the economic boom and development of manufacturing industry in Britain during the post-Second World War period meant that there was an abundance of work for unskilled and semi-skilled workers. Towns and cities such as Oldham and Bradford were at the centre of the wool textiles industry, as well as other expanding trades such as building and electrical engineering. Fieldwork conducted in Bradford in the mid 1960s found that there were approximately 1,500 Bangladeshis, mostly from Sylhet, while the 12,000 Pakistanis in the city were from rural villages in Mirpur (Azad Kashmir), Campbellpur district (the Chhachh), and to a lesser extent Jhelum, Lyallpur and Rawalpindi (Dahya 1974: 80). There was a tendency to view Pakistanis settling in Britain as being one homogenous community of people, but Pakistanis defined themselves in a much more nuanced way, placing emphasis on the precise region in Pakistan from which they had migrated. Among the Pakistanis in Britain, those from Mirpur and Campbellpur dominated (Saifullah-Khan 1976). Most of these Pakistani settlers were small rural landholders who came to Britain as temporary economic migrants. There were clear expectations from their extended families back in the Indian subcontinent that remittances would substantially improve the long-term material and social circumstances of the whole family, for example through the building of a better house or the acquisition of more land. A Select Committee on Race Relations report during the late 1960s found that Pakistani Muslims in Britain were annually sending between £50 million and £60 million pounds 'back home' (Dahya 1973). In other words, more than half of what most men were earning in Britain was sent back to the Indian subcontinent.

Muslims coming to Britain in the 1960s were usually male, often single, and they suffered hardship in living and working conditions on the assumption that they were only transient settlers.[18] Migration was driven almost entirely by economic motives; religion was usually irrelevant, although it provided an important personal and collective resource once in Britain:

For many Muslims of the older generation, the observance of Islam was less about piety and more to do with participation in communal life. Whether sincerely

---

[18] For an in-depth anthropological description and discussion of Pakistani migration and settlement in Britain see Shaw (1988); Werbner (1990).

undertaken or not, the performance of rituals, the attendance at mosques and the undertaking of fasting during Ramadan were aspects of a social life which established a semblance of community for the older generation of South Asian migrants, and the dense network of relationships that such activities helped to sustain would provide them the stability and support they needed in an unfamiliar environment ... it seems that this *collective* observance is what motivated the older generations in their adherence to Islam rather than any particular sense of personal religiosity. (Mondal 2008: 4–5)

Migration to Britain was also spurred on by a number of significant 'push' factors. For example, the creation of Pakistan as an independent Islamic state in 1947 created a large number of refugees. 'Approximately seven million refugees from India put a severe strain on Pakistan's economy and social order ... [unsurprisingly] Indian Muslims [already] living in Britain became anxious about relatives and fellow villagers [and] these pioneer settlers from India began to send for their kinsfolk' (Ally 1979: 3). A further impetus behind immigration was the Pakistani government's decision to build a dam at Mangla in 1960, in order to produce more water and electricity for large areas of the Punjab. The Mirpur region lost some 250 of its villages, forcing entire communities to migrate. Once the migration process began, others were encouraged to follow. The compensation received as a result of the dam-building project was used by some to buy a one-way ticket to Britain.

Another group of Muslims to arrive in Britain during the 1950s were Turkish Cypriots. Civil unrest was one 'push' factor, but it was compounded by the 'inability of the Cypriot labour market to keep pace with the rising aspirations of a fast growing and youthful population' (Ally 1979: 3). By 1995, there were 65,000 Turkish Muslims in Britain (Kucukcan 1999: 59). Many settled in or close to London, relying on kinship networks to facilitate their settlement. Educational ambitions also drew Muslim students from the West Indies, from Trinidad, Tobago and Guyana, and some of them chose to remain in Britain once their education was completed.

Just as the 'boarding house' had provided a vital socio-economic base for Muslim seafarers earlier in the century, so too lodging houses in major industrial cities such as Bradford, Manchester and Birmingham provided a similar foundation for South Asians arriving and working in Britain.[19] They were centres of 'chain migration' whereby one settler would sponsor

---

[19] For information about the settlement of Muslims in Northern Ireland, and the process of constructing an Islamic environment, see Marranci (2004).

Table 1. *Numbers of Britons of Pakistani and Bangladeshi descent, and percentage born in Britain, 1951–2001*[20]

|      | Total     | % born in Britain |
|------|-----------|-------------------|
| 1951 | 5,000     | –                 |
| 1961 | 24,000    | 1.2               |
| 1971 | 170,000   | 23.5              |
| 1981 | 360,000   | 37.5              |
| 1991 | 640,000   | 47.0              |
| 2001 | 1,029,811 | 46.0              |

(*Source:* Lewis 1994, Census 2001)

another male relative or friend to join him, often working in the same factory or enterprise, and often sharing the same all-male dormitory-style accommodation. As a result, the settlement of Muslims in Britain has been 'selective in terms of specific areas and specific families of origin' (Dahya 1974: 86). In other words, distinct kinship networks were re-formed in specific cities in Britain, and sometimes within discrete areas of particular cities.

This process was accelerated by the arrival in the later 1960s and 1970s of women and children, especially from South Asia. The rising numbers of immigrants during the 1960s began to give the government cause for concern, and legislative measures were taken to limit the influx. Unrestricted immigration ended on 30 June 1962 with the Commonwealth Immigrants Act, which set down conditions for entry into Britain. By 1971 even tougher entry conditions effectively brought immigration to a halt. But in order to 'beat the ban' of the increasingly restrictive immigration laws, large numbers of Muslim women and children came to join their husbands or fathers working in Britain. Because they could anticipate a time when family reunion (if they so chose) would become nearly impossible, women and children who might have otherwise remained in the Indian subcontinent decided to join their menfolk in Britain. Some women were also prompted to migrate on hearing rumours that their husbands might take new wives in Britain.

Permanent family settlement began to replace temporary male residence and, as a consequence, more efforts were made to establish facilities and services for the long-term future of communities. In 1964 women and children represented 66 per cent of all incoming migrants from Pakistan.

[20] See p. 119 for statistics on the number of Muslims in Britain in recent decades.

By 1966 this had risen to 93 per cent (Hill 1969: 38). Proportionally less income was sent 'back home', and Muslims began investing more money in their communities in Britain. Over time, returning to Pakistan became an increasingly unattractive proposition, especially as the number of children in a family rose. It would have been expensive to leave, and the benefits and standard of living in Britain were generally much higher than those, for example, in Pakistan. Gradually, all-male boarding houses gave way to nuclear family homes, with relatives from the same kinship network often living as close neighbours. This change in residence patterns also allowed a certain amount of internal differentiation to take place, in terms of language or dialect and village or town of origin. Particular areas of cities such as Bradford and Birmingham began to be associated with Muslims with distinctive ethnic, linguistic or South Asian regional origins. The availability of easy access to transport networks, factories and mills, and the availability of cheap housing for purchase, reinforced this process. These districts have tended to be just outside the inner city area, or in what Dayha termed 'zones of transition' (Dahya 1974: 90). They quickly became identifiable as places of Muslim settlement because of the growth in the number of businesses and facilities that emerged to serve the needs of the community, such as places of worship, grocers and butchers, travel agencies, bookshops, import and export firms, estate agents and so on. The identification of these facilities by means of signage in community languages such as Urdu or Bengali, or the display of posters depicting Islamic holy sites, helped to reinforce religious and ethnic identification. But seen from another perspective, while they cushioned the process of arrival and settlement for later migrants, they also 'hindered the acquisition of the skills needed for participation and full access to the advantages of the majority society' (Saifullah-Khan 1976: 222). Though this probably did not concern those living with the assumption of returning 'home' one day, it did have consequences for the acquisition of social capital for later generations born in Britain.

Business networks played an important role as 'clearing houses' (Dahya 1974: 92) for information-sharing, especially in relation to employment. The geographic scope of these businesses went beyond the confines of a particular town or city. Most early post-war Pakistani Muslim settlers relied upon them as a means of remaining in contact with relatives and friends living in other parts of Britain. An individual was thus part of a much larger interconnected system of relationships that rested upon shared interests, trust, honour and expectations of mutual self-help, all of which contributed to sustaining ties of loyalty and kinship, and reinforced informal mechanisms of social control. But these networks and relation-ships were also international. During his fieldwork among Pakistani Muslims in Bradford and Birmingham in the late 1960s, Dahya treated 'the migrant community in Britain and the society of origin as parts of a single system of socio-economic relationships' (Dahya 1973: 247). Early Pakistani migrants in Britain had little regard for their status or approval in British society, because the 'significant others' from whom they sought recognition were their fellow migrants and their relatives 'back home'. Consequently, experiences of racial or religious discrimination in Britain were generally suffered rather than challenged, because there was per-ceived to be no long-term benefit to be derived from the distracting pro-cess of seeking redress.[21]

With the settlement of women and children and the growth of reli-gious facilities, attitudes towards Britain and the future began to change. The early emphasis on austere living, remittances and hardship gradually gave way to a new set of aspirations. This gradual change in attitude took place over several decades, and was driven by a concern to maintain reli-gious and ethnic identification among children who had been born in Britain. Less and less money was invested in enterprises 'back home', and more was spent on the establishment of mosques, schools and other facil-ities in Britain which might help to transmit religious and cultural trad-itions to the next generation.

But alongside an evident commitment to a qualitatively better life in urban Britain, many Pakistani Muslims, especially the initial post-war migrants, still expressed the intention to return home eventually, although many never did. So pronounced was this unrealized intention to return home that it has been termed by one Pakistani Muslim soci-ologist the 'myth of return' (Anwar 1979). Early migrants justified their continued 'sacrificial' residence in Britain, to themselves and to others, as a necessity for the sake of the uninterrupted education of their children. But by making such choices, an important change in psychological orien-tation took place. Identity that once rested heavily upon the approval and expectations of kin abroad was gradually replaced by a more individualis-tic outlook on life shaped by the needs of a new British-born generation. This change in attitude was probably also reinforced by the experience of making short return visits 'back home' (Akram 1975). Many Pakistani

---

[21] Similarly, there was limited involvement in trade unions, resting upon the assumption that 'this is not our country, we are here to work and then return home and do not have time to get involved in such organisations' (Dahya 1973).

Muslim migrants found that things had moved on in their absence and the nostalgic memories they once held about their villages and relatives were revised: migrants 'begin to assess the adequacy of [their] beliefs about [their] past and the present, and revise [their] images and beliefs about the future' (Dahya 1973: 263). For instance, although some of the social norms of non-Muslim Britain were criticized, such as the perceived lack of respect for elders, some of the actual benefits of life in the UK, such as state-funded education and healthcare, began to figure in future thoughts and planning.

Whereas the first substantial wave of South Asian Muslim settlement in Britain after 1945 was almost entirely driven by economic motives, the later migration of Muslims from other parts of the world, such as Turkey, Iran and the Middle East, rests upon a greater range of factors. Some have come to Britain as refugees, as international traders or as highly skilled professionals. But as with their South Asian counterparts, wider global political and economic forces have often underpinned their decision to come to Britain.

The more mobile, interconnected world of the 1970s, combined with the rise in oil prices, facilitated the settlement of wealthy Arabs in Britain (from Saudi Arabia, the Gulf states, Syria, Lebanon, Egypt, Palestine and Jordan). Some felt that their investments would be more secure in Britain than in their own politically unstable countries (Ansari 2004). Research in 1997 estimated that about half of all Arabs living in Britain were based in London, and Egyptians constituted the largest subgroup (Karmi 1997).[22] Skilled professionals from Muslim countries such as Iran, Afghanistan and Iraq also chose to migrate in the 1970s and 1980s, sometimes 'pushed' by civil war or repressive regimes in their own society, and 'pulled' by the attractions of working in more liberal economic and intellectual surroundings in Britain. Some were already familiar with British society, perhaps having studied in a British university, or having been to Britain on business. At least some of these factors were behind the migration of some 20,000 Iranians to Britain in the late 1970s following the Iranian revolution (Ansari 2004: 161). The educational background of Middle Eastern Muslim migrants to Britain in the later decades of the twentieth century was extremely diverse, but often predominantly middle class and professional. It is not surprising, then, that the worldview of these Middle Eastern Muslims was often quite different from that of

---

[22] Census data from 1991 put the number of Egyptians in Britain at 22,582, but Karmi (1997) regards this as an underestimate.

their co-religionists from South Asia. Though sharing a common religious identity, albeit characterized by a great deal of internal diversity, their backgrounds in terms of language, history, ethnicity and education were often very different.

Some Muslims coming to Britain after the Second World War were involuntary migrants, escaping human rights abuses and civil war in their own societies. For example, the early 1960s saw the arrival of many Asians from East Africa. They had initially gone to Africa to service the British colonial administration, and to assist with building the communications infrastructure, principally railways. Uganda became a 'British Protectorate' in 1896 and achieved its independence in 1962. But following a coup led by Idi Amin in 1971, there was a strong nationalist political ideology and the minority Asian communities were treated with suspicion and hostility. Amin regarded the Asians as 'colonial consequences' and expelled them. Britain agreed to resettle 28,600 of the 80,000 Ugandan Asians expelled by Amin in the autumn of 1972 (Gelsthorpe and Herlitz 2003: 16). Though many of these Ugandan Asians were Hindu, there were also Muslims among the refugees.

Asians from East Africa were not small rural landholders, like the majority of Pakistanis in Britain, and nor were they single males. Complete families migrated at the same time. They were predominantly middle-class Gujarati merchants and 'far more cosmopolitan in outlook than the Muslims of the South Asian subcontinent, and already had a knowledge of English' (Ally 1979: 3). They had a strong sense of commerce, and worked hard to try to establish a new life for themselves in Britain. About 6,000 of these Ugandan Asians were re-settled in Leicester, and they have contributed substantially to the developing prosperity of the city.

Asylum-seekers from Algeria, Bosnia, Somalia and Kurdistan came to Britain during the later decades of the twentieth century. For Somalis, Britain was a natural destination owing to the existence of already-established communities in cities such as Cardiff and London (Berns McGowan 1999; El-Solh 1993). From the mid 1980s and throughout the 1990s, some 15,000 Somalis arrived in Britain (Ansari 2004: 162). The 2001 Census counted 43,515 Somalis in the UK while more recent estimates suggest 75,000 in 2005 (Sporton *et al.* 2005), to over 100,00 in 2009 (Change Institute/Communities and Local Government, 'The Somali Muslim Community in England: Understanding Muslim Ethnic Communities', 2009b). These new Muslim migrant communities have tended to be somewhat 'invisible' in the literature on Islam in Britain, which is why an annotated bibliography devoted exclusively to the literature on new Muslim migrants has become a valuable research resource (Hussain 2005), as has the effort to record oral histories via the web, such as www.moroccanmemories.org.uk. In 2008, Communities and Local Government commissioned the Change Institute to undertake a survey of thirteen of the most significant Muslim ethnic diaspora communities in England. Although valuable surveys, the omission of Wales and Scotland is unfortunate, especially given that cities such as Cardiff, for example, have very well-established Somali communities.[23]

CONCLUSION

In understanding the growth of the Muslim population in Britain over the past century or so, the 'circumstances for leaving a country (labour, political strife, and conflict); the places and experiences [Muslims] encountered before reaching Britain; the changing legal, socio-economic and political frameworks and barriers they face in Britain; and the transformations of the "home" country are all conditions which need to be explored' (Spellman 2004: 6). The general overview in this chapter has provided a brief glimpse of some of these issues, and has indicated the diversity of experiences, backgrounds and circumstances that have led to a Muslim population in Britain that today numbers about 2.4 million.

What becomes clear through this survey is that there has been a shift in the character and significance of different places of Muslim settlement around the UK, and that this has reflected socio-economic change in wider British society. So with the decline of commercial shipping, maritime ports such as Liverpool and Cardiff are now somewhat less prominent in the overall social geography of Islam in Britain. Meanwhile, the growth of manufacturing industries and the subsequent development of the service sector in the Midlands and in Yorkshire has led to particularly sizeable Muslim communities in cities such as Birmingham and Bradford. These cities have become synonymous with 'Muslims in Britain' in the popular imagination. However, cities such as Liverpool or Cardiff remain important, not so much for the size or diversity of their Muslim populations, but more because of the historicity of the communities in these places, and the cultural legacy they can provide for new generations. In both Cardiff and Liverpool, various projects now exist to document and celebrate the history of their Muslim communities, thereby providing an

---

[23] www.communities.gov.uk/communities/racecohesionfaith/research/understanding-muslimcommunities

opportunity for Muslims to connect with, and take pride in, their historical roots and achievements in Britain.[24] Contrary to media stereotypes, the very existence of these projects provides compelling evidence that many Muslims in Britain are keen to feel a sense of belonging to their historical past in this country, which itself is revealing of generational shifts and important future trends.

This book has so far been concerned primarily with historical perspectives. The importance of history as a lens through which to view the present has become increasingly evident, particularly where it helps to explain the social, ethnic, linguistic and economic diversity within Muslim communities in Britain today. However, parallel to an historical appreciation of British Muslim 'roots', similar discussion is necessary regarding the religious origins of Muslim communities. The following two chapters aim to illuminate the way in which Islamic discourses originating from the Middle East and South Asia now shape the character of contemporary Islam in Britain.

[24] See the section on heritage in chapter 10.

# CHAPTER 3

# Middle Eastern religious reform movements

## INTRODUCTION

Intense competition exists among Muslims in Britain today about what counts as the most authentic and authoritative interpretation and practice of Islam. Religious reform movements that have their origins in nine-teenth- and twentieth-century Arabia and South Asia, each of which claims to reflect an authentic and correct expression of Islam in the con-temporary world, now influence some young British Muslims. Many of the historic debates about religious authority and authenticity that have taken place in Muslim majority countries are now taking place in Britain. The questions are simple, but profound: 'Who speaks for Islam *here?*' 'What is the most authentic way of being a Muslim in Britain *today?*'

Religious movements with origins in the Middle East have made par-ticularly strong claims to be interpreting and practising Islam in a way that reflects most closely the supposed purity and authenticity of Islamic belief and practice in the Prophetic era. These Middle Eastern move-ments, and the implications of their efforts to return to the roots of Islam within the context of contemporary Britain, are the focus of this chap-ter. Movements which trace their origins to South Asia are considered in the next chapter. But what both Middle Eastern and South Asian reform movements have shared in common throughout their history is a spirit of revival, and an effort to restore and reinvigorate a self-assertive form of Islam. But before considering these movements in detail and the way in which they have found new expression among British Muslims, we need to consider some of the theoretical and linguistic challenges arising from an examination of religious diversity in Islam.

## DESCRIBING DIVERSITY IN ISLAMIC THOUGHT

Because there is a core of belief and practice that broadly unites Muslims across time and space, many Muslims reject the divisiveness that is conveyed by the term 'sectarian', and prefer instead to talk about different 'schools' or 'trends' of thought (*maslak*). These phrases more adequately reflect the assumption that while there are differences of interpretation or practice, there is nevertheless a fundamental body of belief and practice that unites Muslims throughout the world and across history. When non-Muslims enquire about the internal differences in Muslim communities, any diversity in practice or interpretation is often downplayed in favour of an emphasis upon a common allegiance to Islam, in 'a community which would rather regard itself as unified' (King 1997: 133) . This is a possible reflection of the emphasis in Islam upon God's indivisible 'oneness' (*tawḥīd*). The terminology used by many Muslims themselves has guided the choice of vocabulary made in this volume, and thus the various ideological movements within British Muslim communities are referred to as 'schools of thought'.

While there are distinctive schools of thought among British Muslims, there are often significant differences of interpretation or practice within these trends. The boundaries of membership or identification are often overlapping and fluid, and as a consequence they are often the sites for contested disputes and vigorous competition for members, resources or influence. As Geaves notes in relation to many faith groups:

in every religious community there are those who have a vested interest in claiming orthodoxy and marginalizing others within tradition. One way of achieving this is to assert ownership of a supposed core of essentials that are divinely provided. (Geaves 2005: 86)

What kind of analytical framework can be used to try to understand how the various schools of Islamic thought are distinct from one another? One option is to examine how the movements concerned have developed identifiably different attitudes towards society, law and politics across time, both here in Britain and in their countries of origin. For example, some movements reactively and defiantly orientate themselves against everything in society that they consider to be 'anti-Islamic'. They moreover call for a new religious political order to bring about change, often inspired by, or modelled upon, historic methods of Islamic governance, real, imagined or idealized (Afshar 1998). Other movements can be characterized as more isolationist, seeking to protect and preserve religious identity from the corrupting influences of society using piety, knowledge and contemplation. Another trend in thought and action seeks to engage fully with the wider society, working through existing political structures but using distinctively Islamic perspectives to try to bring about deliberate social change and the modelling of society upon Islamic values. In this chapter, and the next, examples of all these options are cited. Most were triggered by the impact of colonialism and post-colonialism in the Muslim world during the nineteenth and twentieth centuries, which also drew upon antecedents from the sixteenth century.

## THE NATURE OF AUTHORITY IN ISLAM

Throughout the history of Islam, there has been recognition that along-side the religious authority that derives first from divine revelation, and secondly from Prophetic example, scholarly individuals are also import-ant as mediators and interpreters of these sources. The concern here, and in chapter 4, is therefore not so much with authority as with authorities. By this is meant individuals who are able to claim, or to exercise, author-ity within a particular context: in this case Britain. However, the prolif-eration of religious teaching mediated via mass communications means that debates surrounding religious authorities and religious knowledge also take place beyond the boundaries of particular ideological or geo-graphic communities.

Some of the individuals most strongly associated with the emergence of different schools of thought are descendants of the Prophet Muhammad. Others are able to trace their spiritual roots back to some of the major historical religious figures in early Islam through the bonds that link one teacher to another. Some Islamic movements, especially those with con-nections to Sufi orders, therefore regard authority as resting upon spirit-ual and scholarly genealogies that are believed to bestow some degree of divinely sanctioned religious legitimacy. 'Here we have a manifestation of the idea, ubiquitous in Islamic thought, that the closer an individual is to the source of an event, the more authoritative is their interpretation of that event' (Brown 1996: 49). As we shall see in the following chapter, in many religious movements deriving from South Asia, and in various Sufi orders, the ability to trace spiritual or scholarly links back to the ori-gins of Islam, or to an established religious scholar, can constitute a key dimension of an individual's claim to authority, or to authentic religious practice.

In most Islamic religious movements, religious authority rests on the relationship between individuals or institutions that are regarded as carrying authority, and those that follow them. There are a number of important criteria that determine whether an individual can be regarded as authoritative. Firstly, authoritative individuals must be trusted, and they should embody and exemplify religious truths. They can then be perceived as 'authority figures'. Secondly, authority must be achieved within a particular social context, and this often means the development of religious associations that compete for legitimacy and primacy against rival interpretations. These institutions might be formal religious movements, Sufi teachers or religious scholars, depending upon the context, but they each contend for influence in an atmosphere of competition which centres upon the right to interpret and promote particular religious truths and symbolic capital. Thirdly, the authority of particular individuals is heightened by virtue of the role they play for their followers. By articulating and drawing boundaries around what counts as authentic religious practice and the associated criteria for membership or belonging, they confirm their authority and thus earn the right to act as mediators of a particular tradition or school of thought.

During the history of Islam in Britain, various authority figures have emerged who illustrate some of these criteria. For example, the late Shaykh Dr Zaki Badawi (1922–2006) was an important figurehead for Muslims in Britain during the 1980s and 1990s. As a graduate of Al-Azhar University in Cairo, he was part of a well-established, historic, authoritative scholarly tradition, and yet he also derived credibility from his familiarity with Western academic systems of thought. His various religious leadership roles, as imam at the Regent's Park Mosque in London, as Principal of the Muslim College in Ealing and as founder and chairman of the Imams and Mosques Council of the UK (1984), offered him platforms from which he could exercise authority. But his leadership role was also achieved through his ability to exercise influence at moments of crisis. During the 1980s and early 1990s there was a vacuum in authority and leadership within British Muslim communities, and this provided an opportunity for an articulate and knowledgeable individual to become prominent. This was further stimulated by the media and by the political 'establishment'; Dr Badawi was a figure to whom they could relate. While he resisted both the title and the implication of being dubbed the 'Grand Mufti of Islam in Britain' in media circles (O'Sullivan 2003), such a characterization nevertheless bestowed an authority on him undoubtedly perceived more beyond Muslim communities than within them. Although he was isolated in many ways from the predominantly South Asian Muslims in Britain and therefore rarely regarded by them as 'representative', many nevertheless recognized Dr Badawi's scholarly credentials and the energy he invested in helping British Muslims, individually and corporately. His relative isolation from South Asian communities could even be regarded as an advantage to his achievement of authority. This is because he stood outside many of their internal tensions and disputes. The emergence of authority figures, and the prevalence of particular Islamic 'schools of thought' in Britain today, therefore needs to be understood as a distinctly social process strongly conditioned by context and opportunity.

Many authority figures associated with Islamic religious movements appeal to the Islamic *past*, in order to justify the actions they regard as necessary in the *present* to bring about the social or religious changes they are striving to achieve in the *future*. 'Tradition acts, in effect, both to legitimize criticism of the status quo and to facilitate revolutionary as well as incremental changes' (Eickelman and Piscatori 2004: 35). Yet at the same time, what counts as authentic Islamic tradition can be equally subject to re-evaluation, reinvention and manipulation in changing circumstances. Assertions about the purity or timelessness of particular beliefs, texts or traditions obscures the fact that the meaning of ideas and practices can change as human societies develop over time: 'Divine texts may be unalterable, but the ingenuities of human interpretation are endless' (Asad 1993: 236). However, just as tradition can be manipulated to enhance the authority of particular individuals or ideologies, so too can rhetoric. Religious authority figures routinely make dramatic and rhetorical appeals to the *Qur'ān* and *Sunnah* in speeches and sermons. A visit to virtually any British mosque on a Friday lunchtime will underline this point. By demonstrating their ability to memorize particular texts, and through appropriate use of the principles of citation, authority figures directly promote their own image as religious leaders and authority figures among their congregation, some of whom are unable to discern the accuracy of the messages they are hearing. Some young British Muslims, although perhaps more knowledgeable about their faith than their parents or grandparents, will not necessarily have sufficient knowledge of Arabic or original Islamic sources to follow religious arguments in detail. They nonetheless recognize the outward forms and conventions of authority, as exemplified in particular individuals.

The utility of religious vocabulary and symbolism is particularly evident at times of social upheaval. In these situations, authority figures have the capacity to 'modify and rework the symbols in specific circumstances and for particular purposes' (Eickelman and Piscatori 2004: 13), often in competition with other religious authorities or institutions. In this way, Islamic movements or groups headed by charismatic religious authority figures can offer Muslims in Britain a sense of religious identity and agency. They can provide a framework for Muslims to understand themselves and their world in a context often shaped by their relative disadvantage, discrimination and exclusion.

## 'Authenticity' in Islam

The different Islamic movements present in Britain today share some common characteristics, irrespective of their geographic or historical origins. For example, they nearly all regard the time of the Prophet Muhammad and his Companions as providing a template for Islamic practice and belief. They are seeking to relive that assumed pristine time in the modern world (Metcalf, B. 1982). The variation arises from differing understandings about *how and in what ways* Muslims should *actually* go back to the social mores of the Prophetic era. Fundamentally, the various schools of thought differ in their *methodology* for trying to *interpret* and *achieve* this religious reality, and the place of Prophetic tradition within this process:

There is fierce competition to control the process by which the content of tradition is defined, and for modern Muslims, sunna has become the bitterest point of conflict. Thus, the modern problem of sunna arises out of conflict among Muslims over the definition and content of the authentic tradition, and over the method by which that tradition is to be defined … sunna is the fulcrum on which the central debates over religious authority turn. (Brown 1996: 3)

The relationship between the *Qur'ān*, the *Sunnah* and the *Ḥadīth* and the precedence that one source should have over the other in matters of religious thought and practice provides the fulcrum of debate in Britain today (and further afield) about the most 'correct' and 'authentic' way to be a Muslim. Because Muslims believe that Muhammad had God-given insight, and was the best person to interpret and exemplify the *Qur'ān*, his words and actions have subsequently been regarded as an authentic interpretation of Qur'ānic text. As a consequence, the ability to ascertain and recall the actual words of the Prophet with absolute accuracy has been an ongoing quest for Muslims throughout the ages, and has rested on the ability to trace Prophetic utterances via an unbroken chain of reliable and pious scholars and transmitters (*isnād*). The contemporary quest for authenticity is therefore part of an historical debate about what constitutes correct, genuine Islamic practice and interpretation, and who constitutes a reliable, credible and authoritative guide. Throughout Islamic history, and certainly for members of most revivalist reform movements, the *Sunnah* is a key dimension of Islamic authority. Debates about its interpretation have inevitably been vigorous and competitive, since it provides such an important means by which scholars and reform-ers can claim authenticity, while also asserting independence and flexibil-ity to interpret Prophetic traditions in a way that is consonant with new concerns and problems. The scope to reject, reinterpret or make selective use of the *Sunnah* provides a means for Muslim scholars to deal with new social realities. Sometimes, the debate becomes essentially an 'argument about how to argue' (Roff 1983: 336), particularly in new circumstances and contexts.

## SPLITTING A DIFFERENCE: SUNNI AND SHĪʿA

The distinction between Sunni and Shīʿa traditions in Islam is often regarded as the most significant historical and ideological division among Muslims, and this therefore serves as a very useful point of departure for reviewing concrete expressions of difference, authority and authen-ticity within Islam. Very simply, following the death of the Prophet Muhammad in 632 there were different views about who should succeed him. Some assumed that it should be determined according to lineage and descent, while others suggested that it should instead be a matter of personal knowledge of the life and example of the Prophet. The view pre-vailed that Muhammad's closest male companion and one of the earliest converts to Islam, Abu Bakr, should assume the role of leader or Caliph (meaning 'representative' or 'delegate' of God and his Prophet), and the proponents of this view were termed 'Sunnis' – or those that followed the example of the Prophet (the *Sunnah*). The alternative viewpoint was argued by those who advocated that the Prophet's cousin and son-in-law, ʿAli, should be his legitimate successor on the basis of descent, and this grouping became known as the Shīʿa (party of ʿAli). Arising out of this difference of opinion about succession is a division rooted especially in politics, and later compounded by theology. For this reason, the religious differences between Sunni and Shīʿa should not be exaggerated. However, the contested leadership of the Muslim community after the death of the Prophet did reflect a fundamental difference about the principles that should take precedence in the ordering of the Islamic community in its wider sense. Should authority rest on 'descent via kinship' or 'descent through practice'? Should it be visceral or intellectual? Although in theo-logical terms many Muslims suggest that the difference is marginal, or is one of inflection, it nonetheless represents a tension that exists within both Sunni and Shīʿa traditions, sometimes leading to mutual accusations of being 'unbelievers' (*kāfir*).

## THE SHĪ'A IN BRITAIN

Muslims from the Shī'a tradition account for up to 15 per cent of the worldwide Muslim population. They are significant for this book because there are now major centres for Shī'a worship and activity in most large British cities, frequented by Pakistanis, Iranians, Iraqis, Bahrainis, Lebanese, Afghanis, East African Indians and Yemenis in particular. Shī'as in Britain are so far under-researched, and as yet there has been no systematic study of this diverse community, though they formed part of a study of religious diversity among Muslims in Britain conducted in 2007–8 (Baksh *et al.* 2008), and there has been a study of one particular branch of Shī'as (the Nizari *Ismā'īlīs*) (Mukadam and Mawani 2009). The Iranian community in Britain, with particular reference to religious activity, has also been studied, but of course this does not capture the extent of Shī'a activity overall (Spellman 2004). Clearly this is going to be an important area for future research, especially with growing British media coverage of Shī'a concerns and traditions following the war in Iraq (such as the destruction of the Askariya shrine in Samarra, north of Baghdad, in February 2006 ... an event which clearly had personal religious repercussions for many Shī'a in Britain). As with other Muslim groups, transnational ties remain important for Shī'a self-identity, and events 'back home' resonate in Britain.

A rough estimate of the number of Shī'as in Britain is about 320,000.[1] The largest ethnic group is probably Pakistani, and their migration pattern is similar to that described in chapter 2 for Pakistani Muslims in the post-Second World War period. The next largest ethnic group is Iraqi, present since the 1940s, mainly in London. They were typically professionals, some of whom had little interest in their faith. However, most Iraqis have arrived in Britain more recently, as a result of war and sanctions in Iraq. The current population is estimated to be 70,000–80,000 (in England) of which a significant number are likely to be Shī'a (Change Institute/ Communities and Local Government, 'The Iraqi Muslim Community in England' 2009a).

It is beyond the scope of this volume to engage in detailed discussion of the different schools of thought within the Shī'a tradition but in brief they each accord significance to a line of imams following the death of the Prophet Muhammad's son-in-law, 'Ali. There are three main branches, differing according to the significance they place upon imams, and the

---

[1] I am grateful to Iqbal Asaria, Ahab Bdaiwi and Mustafa Field for providing estimates.

degree to which they view the imam as a supernaturally endowed person representing God on earth. The *Zaydīs* are closest to Sunni Muslims, in that they accept the legitimate rule of Abu Bakr and 'Umar (and partially 'Uthman), but do not view the imam as supernaturally representing God on earth.[2] There are only a very small number of *Zaydīs* in Britain. The *Ismāʿīlīs* ('Severners'), are named after Isma'il, the eldest son of Imam Ja'far al-Sadiq (d.765 CE), the sixth imam. The distinctive school of law developed by Ja'far al-Sadiq has since 1959 been recognized as a 'fifth' legal school of thought by Al-Azhar in Cairo alongside the four schools of Sunni religious law (Sivan 1989). The *Ismāʿīlīs* have divided into a number of major branches over the course of history. The *Nizari* branch, for example, recognize the Aga Khan as their imam, and there are an estimated 10,000 members of this branch in Britain today (Mukadam and Mawani 2009). A branch of the *Ismāʿīlīs* known as the *Dāʾūdī Bohrās* is active in Britain, and they are distinctive for recognizing seven (rather than five) pillars of Islam.

The *Ithnā ʿAshariyyah* ('Twelvers' or '*Imamis*'), are the largest grouping within the Shīʿa world and this is reflected in their number and influence in Britain. They believe in a succession of twelve imams following the death of the Prophet Muhammad, the first being the Prophet's son-in-law 'Ali, and the last being Muhammad al-Mahdi who is believed to be in occultation (a state of religious concealment) ready to return at the 'end of time' as the messianic imam who will restore justice and equality on earth (Esposito 2003: 292). They too follow the *Jaʿfarī* school of law. An important group within the *Ithnā ʿAshariyyah* in Britain are the *Khojas*, who originate from Gujarat in India. There are estimated to be approximately 10,000 Khojas in Britain today, who arrived in Britain following the expulsion of South Asians from Uganda by Idi Amin in 1972. The headquarters of the worldwide movement is now based in London, reflecting the energy and organizational capacity of the late Alhaj Mulla Asghar Ali Jaffer (Al-Khoei 2000).

Some of the diversity within the Shīʿa tradition is reflected in the range of active centres and institutions in Britain. These include mosques, educational institutions, increasingly well-organized student groups, women's organizations and charities.[3] Many of the larger

---

[2] However, a sub-group of the *Zaydīs*, the Jarudiyya, are quite distinct from Sunni Islam and are considered to be closer to the 'Twelver' Shīʿas.

[3] These include the Majlis Ulama-e-Shia Europe (an organization of South Asian Shīʿa with approximately thirty centres in the UK, the largest one being in Birmingham); the Dar al-Islam

organizations are based in London. There are estimated to be approximately seventy Shī'a mosques in Britain, mostly supported by members of a particular ethnic group. Some of the main Shī'a organizations, and well over half the Shī'a mosques, are now members of MINAB (see chapter 7), the constitution of which includes scope for 20 per cent Shī'a representation.

One of the older Shī'a organizations in Britain is the Al-Khoei Foundation in London, opened in 1989. Over the past two decades, staff have been engaged in lobbying on Shī'a interests, ensuring that Shī'a perspectives shape British Muslim affairs and government policy. As well as being a religious centre, the Al-Khoei Foundation administers two schools in Britain which provide education in accordance with the National Curriculum at primary and secondary level. Four other prominent Shī'a educational initiatives include the Institute for Ismaili Studies in London founded by the Aga Khan, the al-Mahdi Institute in Birmingham established in 1993, the educational wing of the World Federation of Khoja Shī'a *Ithnā 'Ashariyyah* (Dar al-Tabligh) and the Hawza Illmiya, a college in Willesden, London, which was opened in 2003. The Hawza Illmiya has close collaborative ties with the Islamic College for Advanced Studies (ICAS), a thriving college offering A levels, and undergraduate degrees in Islamic studies (Gilliat-Ray 2006). The first graduates of the Hawza are now completing their studies, meaning that a new generation of British-born Shī'a religious leadership is likely to play an increasingly active role in shaping future directions, and consolidating an emergent and distinctive Shī'a identity in Britain.

## SUNNI SCHOOLS OF THOUGHT

In Sunni Islam, the practices and sayings of the Prophet provide the template for an Islamic 'way of life'. Some Sunni Muslims define their practice by following one of four major schools of Islamic law (known singularly as *madhhab* or in the plural as *madhāhib*), while others look to

Foundation; the Abrar Foundation in London www.abraronline.net; the Council of European Jamaats www.coej.org/; the Rasool A'tham Mosque www.imam-hussein.org; the Idara-e Jaferia www.idara-e-jaferia.org; the Mohammadi Trust www.mtrust.org.uk; the World Ahlul Bayt Islamic League www.wabil.com; Sakina Trust www.sakinatrust.org; Islamic Universal Association www.arafeh.co.uk; Mahfel Ali www.sicm.org.uk; the Islamic Centre of England, Maida Vale www.ic-el.com; the Ahl-ul-Bayt Islamic Mission, www.markaz.org.uk; the al-Khoei Foundation www.alkhoei.org; the World Federation of Khoja Shī'a Ithna-Asheri Muslim Communities www.world-federation.org and their associated educational programme (Dar al-Tabligh); the Imam Ali Foundation www.najaf.org.uk.

the time of the Prophet and his Companions for their religious guidance.[4] The four schools of law in Sunni Islam formed around the scholarship of individual teachers, namely Abu Ḥanifa (d.767 CE) (*Ḥanafī*); Malik ibn Anas (d.795 CE) (*Mālikī*); Ahmad Ibn Hanbal (d.855) (*Ḥanbalī*); and Muhammad ibn Idris ash-Shafiʿi (d.822 CE) (*Shāfiʿī*). Different schools of law tend to predominate in particular Muslim countries, and the two most prevalent legal traditions, the *Shāfiʿī* and *Ḥanafī* schools, are particularly influential among Arabs in the Middle East and among Muslims in South and central Asia respectively.

During the early years of Islam, the development of Islamic law was highly flexible, to accommodate the changing needs and circumstances of a rapidly expanding religious community. But by the tenth century, there was general consensus that the parameters and principles of Islamic law had been broadly established, and that no further interpretative effort (*ijtihād*) should be invested in the textual sources of Islam (Sonn 2004). Thereafter, it was broadly assumed that the consensus (*ijmāʿ*) of scholars and the imitation of past precedents (*taqlīd*) was all that was necessary to derive new legal rulings. However, over the passage of time, the apparent inflexibility of Islamic law inherent in the method of *taqlīd* was highlighted by some Islamic scholars (for example, by Ibn Taymiyah in the fourteenth century). This was a realization that later accelerated in the face of challenges from European colonialism.

Some of the religious revival movements present in Britain today are divided about the degree to which new interpretation of Islamic law has once again become a religious obligation for Muslims, and essential for the vitality of Muslim life and thought. Others are wary of what they regard as the virtual abandonment of generations of scholarly tradition. Given that this is largely an internal debate, it has tended to remain unintelligible outside various closed spheres of discourse. However, the new proximity of representatives of various schools of thought as a consequence of migration, travel and media communications has extended the boundaries of this debate and it has become a matter of public and political discussion in wider society.

Besides the different legal schools of thought, brief mention should be made of theological schools of thought which reflect different views on philosophical and mystical truths, such as the relationship between

---

[4] The translation of the Arabic word '*madhhab*' into the English word 'law' does not fully reflect the entirety of meaning. 'Law' in the Islamic sense refers not only to 'details of conduct in the narrow legal sense, but also minute matters of behaviour, what might even be termed "manners", as well as issues related to worship and ritual' (Rippin 2005: 88).

reason and revelation, free will and determinism, punishment and reward. There are four major theological traditions, some of which are associated with particular thinkers. These schools are known as the 'Ashari', after Abu-al-Hasan Ali ibn Ismail al-Ashari (d.935), the 'Maturidiyyah', after Abu al-Mansur al-Maturidi (d.944), the Murji'a and the Mu'tazila.[5]

## SUFISM

Sufism has always been integral to Islam. The word *sufi* describes those Muslims who seek direct personal experience of God, hence the linkage often made between Sufism and parallel mystical traditions in other religions. As Muslim societies expanded in the eighth and ninth centuries, gradually acquiring greater material wealth and political power, mystical and sometimes ascetic religious practices and traditions developed to counter the potentially distracting world influences. Those who chose the mystical path could be identified by the coarse woollen garment (*ṣūf*) that they often wore as a marker of their ascetic practices. The word *ṣūf* is probably the etymological root for the Arabic word for Sufism, *taṣawwuf*. The word 'Sufism' has also been claimed to have an etymological connection with the Arabic word *ṣafā* meaning 'purity'. While the origins of Sufism are not clear, across the centuries many different styles and traditions emerged, usually organized in the form of a spiritual order or path (*ṭarīqah*) at the heart of which is the relationship between a spiritual teacher and his devotee (*murīd*). The *shaykh* is regarded as having been endowed with God's blessing (*barakah*) and is considered to be sufficiently adept spiritually to be a guide for his followers. Before his death, the *shaykh* will normally nominate a spiritual successor, so that there is an unbroken chain of spiritual blessing and succession (*silsilah*). Despite the importance of mystical religious practices in Sufi devotions, most Sufis also stress the centrality of proper observance of Islam and adherence to the *sharī'ah*.

Sufism manifests in Britain in a number of ways. Geaves has developed a four-fold typology to capture the diversity of Sufi expression (Geaves 2000). Firstly, he argues, there are Muslims who may have a very loose association with Sufism, neither formally belonging to an order nor actively identifying themselves as Sufis, yet practising a form of Islam that is shaped by Sufism. Secondly, there are Muslims who belong to a Sufi

---

[5] For further information about these theological schools of thought see the *Encyclopaedia of Islam* (Bearman *et al.* 2007).

order, but one that is confined to a particular ethnic group. Membership of the order is likely to be fairly homogeneous in terms of ethnicity, and therefore is confined principally to Pakistanis, or Bangladeshis, or Turks, and so on. An example of this category is the *Tijāniyah* order, which has a strong Nigerian following in London. Thirdly, some Sufi orders have transcended ethnic boundaries, and have large transnational followings, usually revolving around the charisma of a particular *shaykh*. An example might be the *Haqqani Naqshbandī* order of Shaykh Nazim who has a community of followers from different ethnic and linguistic backgrounds all around the world. Fourthly, some expressions of Sufism have lost their moorings in Islam altogether. Various Sufi movements have transcended not only ethnicity, but also their connection to the Islamic *ummah*. Associated with this 'universal' Sufism were thinkers such as Idries Shah (1924–96) and Hazrat Inayat Khan (1882–1927), and organized networks associated with these thinkers are active in Britain.

Having outlined some of the broad contours of diversity within Islam, attention now turns to the emergence of various major religious reform movements that originated in the Middle East, and that find expression in Britain today. Clearly, it has not been possible to survey all of them, so there is a particular focus upon those movements that have become especially influential among British Muslims.

## THE DEVELOPMENT OF SUNNI ISLAMIC REFORM MOVEMENTS IN THE MIDDLE EAST

At the turn of the twentieth century, many regions in the Middle East were under the rule of European colonial powers. The presence of foreign colonial rulers exposed the limitations of traditional institutions, and religious leaders were often seen as ineffective in their responses to the overbearing imperial ideologies of the colonizers. To make matters worse, Orientalist scholars such as William Muir and Alois Sprenger raised critical questions about the authenticity of many traditional Islamic sources. Eventually, a number of Islamic movements emerged to counter the intellectual, religious, economic, social and political impact of colonialism and post-colonialism (Hashem 2006: 32; Vertigans 2007).

European empire-building was sometimes bolstered by reference to a romanticized Crusading past. The consequences of this are evident in the contemporary world, according to the historian Jonathan Riley-Smith (Riley-Smith 2008). He notes that some Islamic ideologues were taken in by such nineteenth-century Crusading rhetoric, and that their reaction to it resurrected a largely forgotten Muslim memory of the actual Crusades. Some Muslim political activists in the nineteenth and twentieth centuries thereby came to believe that 'the West, having lost the first round in the Crusades, had embarked on another' (Riley-Smith 2008: 61), and they went on to shape their anti-colonial ideologies around such ideas. For example, Sayyid Qutb (see below) noted that crusaderism underpinned colonialism, and that the West was reviving its hatred of Islam once again (Haim 1982). In the contemporary world this re-imagining of the actual Crusades in a manner divorced from the lived medieval reality has provided both fuel and inspiration to the anti-Western jihadists. Much of the discourse of Osama bin Muhammad bin Laden, for instance, is suffused with the language of anti-crusaderism (Riley-Smith 2008: 75).

In the early post-colonial period, Islamic movements also derived further impetus from what many regarded as failed secular modernization projects in the Middle East. The rapid socio-economic transformations that took place in these societies created a highly unequal distribution of resources. This led to the rise of a wealthy westernized elite minority, while a large proportion of the population suffered poverty, social exclusion, housing shortages and unemployment. In a post-colonial world, the activities of Middle Eastern religious movements reflected a struggle for stability within traditional societies that had been disrupted by 'haphazard modernization projects and failed nationalisms' (Hashem 2006: 24). These movements provided an ideological response and an alternative to the perceived corruption and ineffectiveness of dominant social, political and economic elites (Wiktorowicz 2005: 12). Underpinning many of the movements that emerged in this context was reference to the *salaf* (literally, 'to precede'), meaning the first three generations of Muslims and the immediate Companions of the Prophet Muhammad (*'al-salaf al-ṣāliḥ*) (Shahin 1995). Derivatives of this Arabic term, particularly the words *salafiyah* and *salafi*, have become part of the routine discourse around Muslims in Britain.

### Salafis and the Salafiyah movement

A *salafi* is an individual who draws primarily upon the *Qur'ān* and the *Sunnah* for religious guidance. The early Muslims and Companions of the Prophet are regarded as having a particularly pure understanding and practice of Islam by virtue of their proximity to the Prophetic era, hence the reference to their time and religious practice. Today, the term *salafiyah* is also used to refer to a modern religious reform movement established in the Middle East at the turn of the twentieth century.

The term *salafiyah* cannot be confined to a narrow current of thought or a certain period of history. Rather it is best understood as a system of thought that has found expression in different times and places where reform and revival of Islam have been regarded as necessary in the face of upheaval or threat. *Salafiyah* thought is therefore not represented in a formal institution. Where the original *salafi* thinkers placed the emphasis on doctrinal purity and a return to the example and teachings of the Companions of the Prophet, later exponents have used the original sources of Islam as a means for reviving Islamic thought in the struggle against colonialism. *Salafiyah* therefore refers to, and characterizes, a very fragmented and diverse range of movements which may not have much in common with one another except for a shared concern to return to a supposedly pure Islam, free from what they regard as un-Islamic cultural accretions.

Amid their concern with 'purity' and the discernment of what is or is not permissible in terms of both belief and practice, *salafiyah* movements have tended to be intolerant of difference. This has often resulted in the denouncement of other expressions of Islam, and accusations that followers of different schools of thought are unbelievers (*kafirūn,* sing. *kāfir*) who have deviated from 'true' Islam. When such a belief becomes allied to political ambitions, and the idea that Muslims should be governed entirely according to the principles of the *Sharī'ah* within an Islamic state, the ideological conditions are created for the rise of more militant groups, some of which reject violence, others of which advocate violence and terror as the only means to achieve their ends. So while *salafis* share a broadly similar ideological orientation, they differ markedly in terms of their methodological strategies.

In the social and religious climate of the eighth century, characterized by diversity, conflict and debate among various schools of Islamic theology (*kalām*), Ibn Hanbal (780–855), founder of the fourth major school of Sunni law, advocated a return to the purity of the *Qur'ān,* the *Sunnah* and the *Ḥadīth.* For him, revealed text and Prophetic example took precedent over other means for establishing religious truths, such as independent interpretation (*ijtihād*), and he outlined strict rules for the practice of reasoning by analogy (*qiyās*). Later scholars developed his approach, especially Taqi al-Din Ibn Taymiyah (1263–1328), a Hanbali theologian and jurist, who was critical of what he regarded as un-Islamic innovations (*bid'ah*) in religious belief and practice, especially those associated with Sufism (Nafi

2004). He re-emphasized the importance of God's oneness, rejected the idea of adherence to, or imitation of, past precedents and developed techniques and rules for analogical reasoning.

As Muslim communities have had to respond to new social, political, cultural and religious realities and upheavals over the course of history, there has often been a corresponding emphasis on a return to 'pure' Islamic teachings and practices, a rejection of innovations or accretions, and a call to unity among Muslims (Shahin 1995). Thus the terms *iṣlāḥ* (reform) and *tajdīd* (renewal) are central concepts, providing the impetus for enabling Muslims, both past and present, to deal with new realities (Voll 1983). It has often been at times of crisis or major social change facing Muslim communities that *salafiyah* influences have become prevalent as its approaches offer basic principles for responding to new circumstances. At the heart of both *iṣlāḥ* and *tajdīd* is the idea of 'moral righteousness' (Voll 1983: 33), from which a new social order can be established.

The modern *Salafiyah* movement was established by Jamal al-Din al-Afghani (b.Iran, 1839–97)[6] and Muhammad 'Abduh (b.Egypt, 1849–1905)[7] at the beginning of the twentieth century (Shahin 1995), as a reaction to the apparent scholastic, legalistic, and non-interpretive mode of thinking prevalent among the scholars in the late nineteenth and early twentieth centuries. Islamic law was seen as overly legalistic and unable to address contemporary religious, social and political problems and realities. Al-Afghani and 'Abduh argued that Islam and modern Western science and civilization could be harmonized, and that by abandoning the idea of imitation of past scholarly precedents and using once again the tools of *ijtihād* it would be possible to discern what was essential to Islam, and what was not. Once the 'essentials' had been established, Muslims could then undertake the kind of educational, legal and administrative reforms necessary to compete with European powers. Through lectures delivered in many Muslim majority countries, and via publications written in Europe while in exile, they sought to raise political and intellectual standards in order to combat Western colonialism.

Following their deaths, the work of al-Afghani and 'Abduh was taken up by Muhammad Rashid Rida (1865–1935). He was especially committed to the pan-Islamic ideal of al-Afghani. *Salafiyah* ideology subsequently went on to inspire a later generation of Muslim activists, including Hasan al-Banna (1906–49), founder of the Muslim Brotherhood in Egypt

---

[6] For more information on his life and work see Goldziher (2007).
[7] For more information on his life and work see Schacht (2007).

(see below), and the *Jamā'at-i Islāmī* founded by Abu al-A'la Mawdudi (1903–79) in India. However, these movements departed somewhat from the original *salafiyah* vision of reform by virtue of their often dominant political orientation.

### THE WAHHĀBI MOVEMENT

One of the most significant strands of *salafiyah* thought is the *Wahhābīyah*, which emerged in Saudi Arabia in the eighteenth century under the influence of its founder, Muhammad Ibn 'Abd Al-Wahhab (1703–92). His followers called themselves *al-Muwahhidun* ('those who profess the unity of God') and this designation is indicative of a central tenet of the movement, namely the restoration of the pristine monotheism of Islam (Peskes and Ende 2007). In 1745, 'Abd al-'Aziz ibn Sa'ud, chief of a small tribal area in north central Arabia, aligned himself with this new *Wahhābī* ideology, and it became the unifying principle for tribal solidarity in the area (Lapidus 2002). Ibn Sa'ud and his successors declared themselves 'imams of the Wahhabi movement' (Lapidus 2002: 572) and the resulting combination of spiritual and temporal power paved the way for the establishment of the current (third) *Wahhābī*-Saudi state. The maintenance of religious and political power has been consolidated through ties of marriage with neighbouring tribal groups, and particularly with the descendents of Ibn 'Abd al-Wahhab who have gone on to become the religious scholars or *'ulamā*.[8] Orthodox *Wahhābī* influences predominate in contemporary Saudi Arabian society, and there are numerous ways in which this ideology permeates the structures of society.[9] However, there is of course some degree of contradiction between the Kingdom's *Wahhābī* ideology, and the fact that it is also a close ally of the West, meaning that its legitimacy as the 'defender of the faith' of Muslims around the world has been called into question. There are principal scholars associated with the global spread of Wahhabism: Nasr al-Din al-Albani (d.1999), the former Grand Mufti of Saudi Arabia, 'Abd al-'Aziz ibn Baz (d.1999) and Shaykh Muhammad ibn al-'-Uthaymin (d.2000) (Birt 2005c). However,

---

[8] For more information on the *'ulamā'* in Saudi Arabia see Kechichian (1986).
[9] These include the issuing of religious rulings, the control of the curriculum in particular universities (e.g. the Islamic University in Medina), and an influential role in the activities of the pan-Islamic 'Muslim World League' (*Rābiṭat al-'Ālam al-Islāmī*), a non-governmental Islamic organization founded in Makkah in 1962. Religious scholars control the Ministries of Higher Education, Information, Justice, Interior, Propaganda, and Guidance and Public Morality (Lapidus 2002: 574), meaning that most aspects of public life are shaped by *Wahhābī* ideology.

it is important to note that the term *Wahhābī* is generally considered derogatory by its adherents. To them, 'Wahhabism is not a school of thought within Islam, but *is* Islam' (El-Fadl 2001).

'Wahhabism' is therefore a strand of *salafiyah* thought that has become influential and powerful through the ambitions of a state seeking local and regional legitimacy. Financial resources deriving from Saudi Arabian oil wealth in the past four decades have fuelled the ambitions of its rulers to assume religious leadership of the Muslim majority states, and this has enabled the spread of *Wahhābī* ideas beyond the Kingdom (Birt 2005c). Indeed, from the 1970s onwards Saudi Arabian-backed projects presented in terms of 'mission' (*da'wah*), such as the building of mosques and Islamic centres and the large-scale publication of books propagating *Wahhābī* thought, deliberately targeted Muslim minorities living in the West, including Britain.

## THE VARIETIES OF *SALAFĪYAH* EXPRESSION IN BRITAIN

Just as the quest for an 'authentic' Islam was particularly evident in Muslim countries during the nineteenth and twentieth centuries, the context of contemporary Britain has provided an important catalyst for a similar effort among British Muslims today. Brown's observations regarding the rise of *salafiyah* thought in nineteenth-century Egypt have some parallels with contemporary Britain. He writes:

By the mid-nineteenth century the rejection of *taqlid* [and the] promotion of *ijtihad* ... had taken hold among reform-minded men of religion in various parts of the Middle East. Historical circumstances, particularly the spread of secular education and secular legal systems and the resulting disenfranchisement of many *'ulamā'*, gave these ideas new force. Social and economic dislocation seems to have given certain segments of the religious elite reason to reject the religious status quo and the rejection of *taqlid* proved a popular tool both to oppose more conservative *'ulamā'* entrenched in their positions and to appeal to young men of secular education who sought to understand the reasons for the apparent weaknesses of Islam in the face of Western power. Thus the urgently felt need to catch up with the West was combined with the latent power of the traditionist thesis – the assurance that all could be set right by returning to the unadulterated sunna of the Prophet – to create a powerful reform movement. (Brown 1996: 30)

Within this quotation we can discern some of the reasons why some Islamic reform movements, especially those reflecting *salafiyah* thought, have also become influential for some British Muslims. Although the circumstances and context are clearly different, the upheavals created by the mass migration of Muslims to Britain in the post-Second World War period, especially from predominantly rural, uneducated backgrounds, have created the conditions where the same quest for 'authenticity' has once again become significant for some. Muslims born and brought up in Britain have sought answers to the dilemmas and tensions that arise when confronted with a powerful and often contradictory combination of social influences. For example, there is rarely meaningful overlap between secular education in mainstream schools, and religious education in *makātib*, sometimes delivered by ineffective religious leaders from the South Asian villages and towns of their parents and grandparents. This dissonance can cause some degree of educational confusion. Similarly, the conservative cultural traditions of parents and grandparents are no defence against the direct or perceived experience of Islamophobia.

In these circumstances, *salafiyah* thought, articulated by charismatic religious authority figures (in the medium of English), becomes a powerful evidence-based tool to counter the 'traditionalism' of the parental and grandparental generations. These leaders have been effective in promoting a form of Islam that is seen as especially authentic, relevant, pure and powerful. This current of thought has proven popular with converts and second-generation South Asian British Muslims, aged roughly eighteen to thirty, living in proximity to some key *salafi* centres in Britain.[10] The Green Lane Mosque and the Salafi Institute, both in Birmingham, the Masjid Ibn Taymiyyah in Brixton and the Islamic Centre of Luton are prominent in this regard (Hamid 2008a; Hamid 2008b).

These communities of meaning provided an intellectual as well as physical refuge from readings and practices of Islam that were judged to be inauthentic, inferior, and deviant. In comparison to other Muslim groups, the Salafi trend seemed to offer a cohesive identity option that young people could purchase which might explain its relatively greater attraction for converts seeking 'a rationalized Islam', one already stripped of the niceties and ambiguities of juristic reasoning, the complexities of theology, and the subtleties of Sufism. (Hamid 2008b: 11)

But the appeal of *salafiyah* approaches and ideology is not new, nor by any means confined to converts: 'In times of uncertainty and flux, it is natural for Muslims to look for guidance to the one era of certainty and stability,

---

[10] Sadek Hamid estimates that there are approximately thirteen to twenty openly *salafi* mosques in the UK, but notes that their influence is disproportionate on account of their effective web presence and literature distribution (Hamid 2008a). This is probably a conservative estimate; there may be as many as thirty *salafi* mosques in the UK, as of mid 2009.

the time of the Prophet' (Brown 1996: 138). Such an appeal effectively disregards the classical Islamic scholarship contained with the Sunni schools of law and the work of the *'ulamā'* who have perpetuated them, in favour of a presumed direct return to the sources of Islam. In this ideological frame, individual Muslims can become their own interpreters of religious issues, without having to grapple with the historicity or complexities of centuries of scholarship: 'By rejecting juristic precedents and undervaluing tradition, Salafism adopted a form of egalitarianism that deconstructed any notions of established authority within Islam … effectively anyone was considered qualified to return to the original sources and speak for the divine will' (El-Fadl 2001). There is therefore something that could be understood as distinctly democratic and empowering in *salafiyah* methods, and this has a powerful appeal for some Muslims today, especially perhaps for those who feel themselves to be powerless, marginalized or excluded in wider society.

It was during the early 1990s that a range of *salafi* groups became prominent in Britain, often because of a small minority of highly visible and vocal activists. These individuals acquired notoriety owing to their outspoken and often 'radical' preaching. Sociologically speaking, there are parallels between some *salafiyah* movements and evangelical Protestantism (Hashem 2006: 23) in terms of their often fierce assertions of independence from one another, literalist reading of religious texts, shifting alliances based on particular issues or self-interest and decentralized leadership provided by charismatic preachers who co-ordinate their activities from a particular mosque or group of mosques. The recognition of a particular individual as a teacher or authoritative spiritual guide is derived from subjective perceptions and social consensus, with the title *shaykh* being conferred informally as the individual develops a reputation for their scholarship, piety, religious rulings or sermons (Mandaville 2005a). Minor differences in the interpretation of a particular text are sometimes the only distinguishing feature between one movement and another. In this way, 'argumentation is a favorite hobby for this type of activist since their tendency is to perceive the world as an arena of clashing religious texts' (Hashem 2006: 36).

Amid the diverse expressions of *salafiyah* thought in Britain, there are some basic analytical distinctions that can be drawn. On the one hand there are non-violent pro-Saudi Arabian/*Wahhābī* groups, while on the other hand there are anti-Saudi Arabian *salafis*, a minority of whom advocate violence as a means of achieving their ends. Included in this minority grouping are supporters of Osama bin Laden and the al-Qaeda network.

The middle ground is occupied by non-violent Islamists, reformers who work through existing social and political structures to try to achieve their ends. The remainder of this chapter briefly examines three different reformist, broadly *salafiyah*-orientated movements that reflect this diversity, namely the Muslim Brotherhood, *Ḥizb al-Taḥrīr*, and 'JIMAS'. None of them advocate the use of violence, relying instead on methods such as preaching, publication and religious instruction. Each of them shares a broad *salafiyah* orientation that advocates a direct return to, and fresh interpretation of, the original sources of Islam. However, they differ from one another significantly in relation to aims, objectives and methodology.

### THE MUSLIM BROTHERHOOD — *IKHWĀN AL-MUSLIMŪN*

The Muslim Brotherhood (MB) has been described as 'the world's oldest, largest, and most influential Islamist organisation ... [but] also the most controversial, condemned by both conventional opinion in the West and radical opinion in the Middle East' (Leiken and Brooke 2007: 107). So-called 'jihadist' groups have often been critical of the Brothers' engagement with democracy and with their apparent rejection of global *jihād*, while non-Muslim Western commentators are equally suspicious of the Brotherhood, owing to its outspoken attacks on United States foreign policy and its apparently half-hearted commitment to the principles of democracy. If this represents a relatively recent analysis of the movement, to what extent does this reflect its founding origins and history?

The Muslim Brotherhood was established in Egypt in 1928 by a young schoolteacher, Hasan al-Banna (1906–49) (Mitchell 1969). In its early years, it was intended to be an apolitical religious reform and mutual aid society (Munson 2001). It only took on a more political character in the late 1930s, prompted by the Arab general strike in Palestine. By 1941 it was promoting candidates for the parliamentary elections, with a central theme of its campaign being the immediate withdrawal of British troops from Egypt and widespread social reform.[11] 'The need to rid Egypt of immoral and imperialistic Western domination through the adoption of an Islamic path formed the basic mantra of the Muslim Brotherhood' (Munson 2001: 490).[12]

---

[11] The British first occupied Egypt in 1882, and remained there until 1954. Control of the Suez Canal was vital to British economic well-being, hence the colonization of Egypt.

[12] For an analysis of Muslim Brotherhood ideology and activity 1928–53 see Simms (2002), and also Cantwell Smith (1961); Mitchell (1969).

In general, the Brotherhood advocated slow Islamization, beginning with individuals, then families, then society itself. They argued that their ultimate objectives could only be achieved gradually and incrementally. Those who were impatient with these goals, or who felt that more violent means were necessary, often left the movement for 'jihadi' groups, some of which derived inspiration from ideologues such as Sayyid Qutb.[13] These jihadi activists were very critical of the Brotherhood's engagement with democracy, arguing that 'any government not ruling solely by sharia is apostate; democracy is not just a mistaken tactic but also an unforgivable sin, because it gives humans sovereignty over Allah' (Leiken and Brooke 2007).[14]

The diversity within the movement today means that the Muslim Brotherhood is best seen as an umbrella organization for a range of national groups with differing outlooks (Leiken and Brooke 2007). Critical examination of each group, on its own terms, also helps to avoid the tendency for outsiders to see Islamist movements (of which the Brotherhood is an example) as monolithic. Branches of the movement now exist across the world, and chapters exist in most capital cities, including London (Marechal 2008).

### THE MUSLIM BROTHERHOOD IN BRITAIN

The Muslim Brotherhood does not officially exist in Britain, but there are a number of organizations which derive their general inspiration from it (Marechal 2008). Perhaps the most prominent among them is the Muslim Association of Britain (MAB), founded in 1997 by Kamal el-Helbawy who has had connections with the Muslim Brotherhood in Egypt. The link with the wider *salafiyah* movement is evident in MAB's aim to 'project and convey the message of Islam in its pure and unblemished

---

[13] Sayyid Qutb was a member of the Brotherhood, and was imprisoned in Egypt from 1960 until his execution in 1966. His publication *Milestones of the Road*, written during his incarceration, was influential in providing the ideological foundations for violent jihadi groups. He argued that armed struggle against political and military regimes that were 'un-Islamic', and therefore deemed to resemble the paganism and ignorance of pre-Islamic Arabia, was a religious duty incumbent on all Muslims.

[14] In Britain, this ideology was given vocal expression by Abu Hamza al-Masri, one-time leader of the Finsbury Park mosque. He argued that democracy is 'the call of self-divinity loud and clear, in which the rights of one group of people, who have put their idea to vote, have put their ideas and their decisions over the decisions of Allah' (Al-Masri, cited in Leiken and Brooke 2007). By giving pre-eminence to human ideology, he argued that Muslims are committing a grave sin against the idea of God's oneness and supremacy.

form'.[15] There are currently about eleven MAB branches around the UK, and most senior leaders are Arabs. MAB works in close association with the Muslim Council of Britain, and links to other Brotherhood-inspired groups in Europe through the Federation of Islamic Organizations in Europe.[16]

MAB became prominent in Britain in 2002 by engaging with the Stop the War Coalition. Based on interviews with existing and former MAB activists, Richard Phillips documents the various perceptions about working relationships between those in the coalition (Phillips 2008). Through his research, it becomes clear that MAB was 'elevated from a relatively obscure group to one with a national profile … MAB helped mobilize thousands of Muslims [achieving] unprecedented significance for British Muslims' (Phillips 2008: 105). Not surprisingly, membership grew from about 400 to 1,000 during this period.

MAB has fragmented since its formation, largely because of divergent opinions about the degree to which the organization should engage in high-profile political activity. After several years of involvement in the Stop the War Coalition, many senior members of MAB wanted to return to low-profile educational/community development programmes, fearing that the organization's new political activism and profile was pitting it 'too publicly and forcefully against the British establishment' (Phillips 2008: 107). The events of July 2005 brought these divergent opinions to a head, and by December of that year the most prominent activists, Anas Altikriti and Azzam Tamimi, lost control of the movement at a meeting which saw a new executive board elected. By February 2006, those who had taken MAB into the Stop the War Coalition and who were keen to maintain an emphasis on high-profile political activism went on to form the British Muslim Initiative (BMI) in 2006.[17] Another initiative that sprang from MAB origins was the Cordoba Foundation,[18] formally launched on 7 July 2006, the first anniversary of the London bombings. The 'Islamispeace.org.uk' campaign, initiated in 2007 to improve perceptions of Islam among the general public, overlaps with MAB and some of its offshoots through a number of shared personnel.[19]

Most of those associated with MAB and its offshoots are influenced by the religious thought and activism of international Islamic thinkers. These include Rashid al-Ghannushi, founder of the Islamic opposition

[15] www.mabonline.net    [16] www.euro-muslim.net
[17] www.bminitiative.net    [18] www.thecordobafoundation.com
[19] www.islamispeace.org.uk

'Renaissance Party' (Hizb al-Nahdah) in Tunisia in the 1980s (but now living in exile in London) and Yusuf Al-Qaradawi, spiritual and scholarly leader of the worldwide Muslim Brotherhood.[20] A theme that unites many of these individuals and reformist groups is an opposition to political and military occupation and oppression, whether in Palestine or in other predominantly Muslim countries.

In recent years, MAB has worked with the British government to try to counter more radical Islamist groups. In 2005, MAB was given control of the notorious Finsbury Park Mosque, formerly led by Abu Hamza al-Masri, in a deal to rid the mosque of extremists.[21] This pragmatism by MAB reflects a willingness to adapt the underlying resources and objectives of the Islamic movement to the concrete socio-political environment of contemporary Britain.[22]

## *Ḥizb al-Taḥrīr al-Islāmī – The Islamic Liberation Party*

Members of *Ḥizb al-Taḥrīr* (HT) would probably not regard themselves as *salafīs* in either methodology or theory/theology, and indeed, there is some merit in such a claim. However, where members of the movement do not tend to follow a single school of Islamic law, and reject the principle of *taqlīd*, there is scope to regard HT members as *salafī*, where this term is understood in its broadest sense.

HT was established in Jerusalem in 1952 by Taqi al-Din al-Nabhani (1909–77).[23] The underlying imperative of the HT was, both then and now, the effort to establish a universal Islamic state (*Khilāfah*), and al-Nabhani's writings documented the means whereby such a reality might be achieved.[24] He wrote at length on the social and economic

---

[20] See Brown (1996: 119–121, 125) for a summary of Qaradawi's contribution to Islamic reformist thought and Skovgaard-Petersen and Graf (2009).

[21] 'New Start for Extremist Mosque', BBC News 24, 11 February 2005: http://news.bbc.co.uk/1/hi/uk/4258891.stm, accessed 12/11/07. See also O'Neill and McGrory (2006), who particularly draw attention to the links between terror and organized crime.

[22] Other British Muslim organizations established by individuals inspired by the Brotherhood are the 'Muslim Welfare House', initially a hostel for students arriving from the Middle East in the 1960s, and the European Institute of Human Sciences in Lampeter, Wales, opened in 1999 (Marechal 2008).

[23] See Taji-Farouki (1996) for one of the few definitive studies of the origins and ideology of HT and, importantly, an account that members of HT largely see as being a fair reflection of their history and aims (Mayer 2004). For a shorter summary of Al-Nabhani's ideas, see Commins (1991).

[24] 'Khilafat' is the name for the Islamic state or empire that existed from the time of the Prophet Muhammad in 622 to 1924 . The term relates to the word Caliph, which can be roughly translated as lieutenant or viceroy.

models that would underpin such a state, and called upon Muslims to overthrow existing regimes in order to realize the vision of a truly Islamic society based upon *Sharī'ah* law. Because he was aiming for the establishment of a single Islamic state, initially governing all Muslim countries and eventually the entire world, al-Nabhani rejected the idea of 'nation states'. For him, nationalist ideology was introduced into the Muslim world by European powers to weaken the Ottoman Empire, to divide Muslims from one another and to pave the way for greater European influence in the Middle East region (Commins 1991). Allied to this, al-Nabhani rejected the principles of democracy and the idea that Islamic movements might work through these mechanisms. He argued that God is the only legitimate legislator, and that political systems which allowed human beings to determine laws and policy were un-Islamic. As part of the effort to re-establish the caliphate, HT activists, rather like members of other Islamic reform movements, want to re-awaken the religious identity of Muslims themselves, thereby saving Muslims from the supposedly corrupting influences of the West. Bottom-up intellectual revolution among ordinary Muslims will bring about the ultimate and eventual political revolution (Taji-Farouki 2000).

HT has been active throughout the Middle East, Central Asia, Africa and Asia, and like other Islamic movements has survived periods of repression and proscription. Surveying both the open and underground HT groups around the world, Mayer notes the remarkable degree of uniformity and ideological cohesion between them, certainly in comparison to some other Islamic movements (Mayer 2004).

### Ḥizb al-Taḥrīr in Britain

HT first found expression in Britain by accident, rather than by design. Some of its Middle Eastern activists became exiles in Britain, thereby enabling the movement to find new life in the West. Its initial aims were modest, in that it sought to influence and recruit foreign students studying in Britain, who would ultimately return to their countries of origin and bring about change in these societies. However, it quickly developed a significant following among British-born Muslims, owing to the particular charisma of Omar Bakri Mohammad.

Omar Bakri Mohammad arrived in London in January 1986 on a multi-entry business visa, having been deported from Saudi Arabia. Although he was officially suspended from HT because of his controversial activism in the Saudi Kingdom, he nevertheless set about the formal organization

of the movement in Britain, initiating study circles for students and professionals from Arab states. As membership grew and new HT groups
formed, however, the movement began to reflect the predominance of
South Asian Muslims in Britain. By the early 1990s, HT was particularly
prominent on university campuses,[25] and it acquired notoriety owing to
its controversial leafleteering and organization of large public demonstra-
tions.[26] Student unions became increasingly concerned about the distribution of anti-Zionist, homophobic and anti-Hindu leaflets on campuses
(Mandaville 2005b), while the media began to give airtime to Omar's
outlandish and provocative statements. Typical among them was his call
for the Queen to convert to Islam (Wiktorowicz 2005). This kind of mis-
placed activism drew the attention of the worldwide HT leadership, who
withdrew support for his continued control of the British branch, ultimately leading to his resignation from HT in January 1996. He subsequently
went on to form a British cell of *al-Muhājirūn* ('the emigrants'), reviving
a largely defunct organization that had provided a 'front' for his activism
in the Middle East during the early 1980s.[27] Inevitably, some members of
HT followed him into *al-Muhājirūn*, while others remained loyal to HT
itself.[28]

Omar Bakri Mohammed's departure from HT in 1996 ushered in a
new phase in the history of the movement lasting from 1996 to 2002.
Its profile during this time was much reduced as members focused on
'strategic reappraisal' (Hamid 2007: 148). With the spotlight turned on
*al-Muhājirūn* rather than on HT, the movement had an opportunity to
reconfigure its membership and consider future priorities. From 2002
onwards, the movement has been concerned to promote a more refined
image and better public relations (Mondal 2008). Although committed
to its founding ideology, HT has also been actively campaigning on
issues of common concern to Muslims in Britain, such as opposition
to the war in Iraq. It has moreover made strategic interventions into

---

[25] Wiktorowicz (2005: 9) suggests that there were 400 members of HT by 1990.

[26] For a British Muslim 'retrospective' view of Omar Bakri Mohammed, see Aziz (2006).

[27] A detailed case study of this organization was undertaken in late 1990s and early 2000 by
Quintan Wiktorowicz (Wiktorowicz 2005). Founded in 1996, it was disbanded in 2004, but is
widely regarded as still operational under different 'platforms'. It has broadly the same ideology
as HT, but differs in that HT only aims to establish Islamic states in countries where success is
likely. *al-Muhājirūn* felt that geography was not a relevant issue, and under Omar Bakri's leadership Muslims in the UK were encouraged to establish an Islamic state in Britain (Mandaville
2005b). See also Connor (2005) for an overview of the movement in Britain, and in particular its
view of issues in Palestine.

[28] Omar Bakri Mohammed was the subject of a Channel 4 documentary *The Tottenham Ayatollah*,
screened in 1997. Hamid describes his portrayal therein as an 'affable fool' (Hamid 2007: 148).

policy debates on issues such as multiculturalism and citizenship and has started to adopt a 'gradualism' that resembles some other Islamic movements (Mandaville 2005b). The message of the movement is widely disseminated through its website (Sinclair 2008),[29] magazines, leaflets and events, and although officially banned by the National Union of Students, HT continues to have an active presence on university campuses through organizations that disguise its true identity.[30] Current estimates for active membership vary between 500 to 1,000 members (Sinclair 2008) and 5,000 to 8,000 members (Lewis 2007), although the latter figure is likely to reflect occasional conference attendance rather than signed-up regular members.

For young Muslims who have become impatient with other Islamic movements, HT has always been appealing (Gilliat 1997). However, retaining members has proven to be more difficult. Ex-members have reported that their departure was caused by a sense of frustration that all issues and concerns are ultimately reduced to the singular issue of establishing the Islamic state. They are also critical of the fact that this ideology is sometimes promoted through the use of tactics that some ex-members now regard as alienating, arrogant and divisive, so reducing the likelihood of ultimate success.

Hamid regards government apprehension about HT's supposed 'radicalism' as unfounded, suggesting that 'nomadic jihadi groups' that have clustered around figures such as Abu Hamza al-Masri,[31] Abu Qatada[32] and Abdullah al-Faisal[33] pose a more dangerous threat (Hamid 2007: 155). Ultimately, he concludes that HT

offers little that is constructive beyond vague general prescriptions about the superiority of Islamic systems, and does not have much to say about the pressing social problems and issues affecting Muslim communities at the grassroots hence limiting its mass appeal … In Britain, it continues to fill a void in the Islamic landscape with a consistent, professionally marketed message. Young people who complete their education and settle down into adult life, and those who can think for themselves, usually leave. HT's long-term appeal will most

---

[29] www.hizb.org.uk

[30] These 'fronts' have included names such as the 1924 Society, the Pakistan Society, the Millennium Society, and the Muslim Media Forum. HT has been at pains to distance itself from the 'off-shoots' of *al-Muhājirūn*, variously known as the 'Saviour Sect', 'Al Ghuraba', and a recent incarnation as 'Ahle Sunnah' (Hamid 2007).

[31] For a brief profile see http://news.bbc.co.uk/1/hi/uk/3752517.stm, accessed 9/11/07. See also Mandaville (2005b: 312–15).

[32] For a brief profile see http://news.bbc.co.uk/1/hi/uk/4141594.stm, accessed 9/11/07.

[33] For a brief profile see http://news.bbc.co.uk/1/hi/uk/6692243.stm, accessed 9/11/07.

likely be determined not by the radicalism of its ideas but by the absence of alternatives. (Hamid 2007: 157–8)

This assessment accords with Winter's observation of 'Salafi burnout' (Winter 2004: 286), by which he means that the enthusiasm of initial engagement with Islamic movements can decline with greater life experience, and a realization that it is often impossible to bridge the gap between aspiration and reality.

### *Jam'iyat Ihya' Minhaj al-Sunnah (JIMAS) – 'Association to Revive the Way of the Messenger'*

Frustrated with an apparent lack of dynamism in the South Asian *Ahl-e-Hadith* movement in Britain (see chapter 4) and a refusal to prefer English over Urdu, a group of four young Muslims, all studying at the University of Kingston in Surrey, established their own breakaway religious movement (JIMAS) in 1984. The biography of conference speakers over the past few years reveals their ideological links, which indicate connections both to the global *salafiyah* movement, and to Islamist groups. Speakers such as Shabbir Ally, Yusuf al-Qaradawi and others from the Muslim Brotherhood are prominent, as are activists emerging from the Islamic University of Medina and the Imam Muhammad Ibn Saud Islamic University in Saudi Arabia. Today this group is probably the largest *salafi* group in Britain.

Following 9/11, JIMAS moved away from a politicized expression of *salafiyah* ideology towards grassroots engagement with 'ordinary' British Muslims and the issues that preoccupy them (Birt, Y. 2006a). JIMAS has fractured over the past two decades, principally along pro- and anti-Saudi Arabian lines. Those who remained loyal to the Saudi Arabian government formed OASIS (Organization of Ahl al Sunnah Islamic Societies) led by Abu Khadeejah (also known as Abdul Wahid), which in turn led to the creation of the Salafi Institute in Birmingham. This group, sometimes given the derogatory label 'Super Salafis' by its critics, is known for its 'ruthless witch-hunt tactics' (Hamid 2008b: 11). Also involved in this organization is Dawud Burbank, a British Muslim revert/convert, and alumnus of the Islamic University of Medina (Birt 2005c). This breakaway faction remained committed to the idea that correcting religious belief and practice among British Muslims was more important than political reform, and Burbank has translated many Arabic texts which reinforce this aim. Over time, Birmingham and Luton have become important centres for this group, and it has a disproportionate appeal to young Somalis and Afro-Caribbean converts (Birt 2005c). Why this should be the case has yet to be fully understood.[34]

CONCLUSION

Despite a common reformist outlook, there is substantial diversity within Islamic religious movements in terms of their methodology. At one end of the spectrum there are non-violent but highly organized and visible groups that work through formal, structured, hierarchical institutions, while at the other there are very informal social networks, such as religious instruction circles and social associations that depend upon interlinked individuals. Not surprisingly, those *salafi* groups that advocate violent action tend to be characterized by informal associations between individuals, making them difficult to study and hard for government to monitor. This situation is made more complicated by the fact that informal *salafi* groups sometimes have a parasitical relationship with more formally organized reformist groups, using them for their networking purposes. For example, the non-violent, quietist South Asian *Tablighi Jamā'at* movement has acquired undeserved notoriety simply because several of the suicide bombers in July 2005 had been associated with it at different times in their lives (Norfolk 2007). The unfortunate result is that *all* movements then tend to be designated as 'radical' merely by association. They then become grouped together as 'Islamist' or extremist, with little understanding of their real character or differences.

Radical jihadi groups that advocate the use of violence are on the margins of Islam across the globe. Although they constitute a tiny minority, their activism nevertheless cannot be ignored. The 'skillful use of rhetoric and symbols that resonate with Muslims worldwide affords them a constituency that, while not always supportive of their militant tactics, identifies with many of the issues that constitute their discourse of resistance' (Mandaville 2005b: 306).[35] In other words, in the post-9/11 world, the continued oppression of Muslims in particular places and the continued support of Western governments for corrupt and repressive regimes continues to create the space for sometimes radical dissent. In Britain, meanwhile, many Muslims across the generations have felt the effects of

---

[34] However, for a popular discussion of the growing number of Black Muslims in Britain, see Reddie (2009).
[35] See also Tibi (2007) for an analysis of contemporary jihad groups.

racism and religious discrimination. As a consequence, religious reform movements provide an important avenue for religious interpretation of these dilemmas. Such movements are powerful and appealing because of their promise 'to bring Islam back to life' (Brown 1996: 141). In so doing, they offer Muslims a vision of a self-confident Islam at ease with the contemporary world. Other faith communities are arguably engaged in their own parallel quests.

The city of London has been especially important as a location for the new expression of reformist ideologies that originated in the Middle East. The concentration of a relatively wealthy and often very mobile Arab community in London has meant that groups such as the Muslim Brotherhood or *Ḥizb al-Taḥrīr* have often been especially active here. This is to some extent in contrast with the situation in other British cities, where South Asian religious reform movements have predominated.

# CHAPTER 4

# South Asian religious reform movements

## INTRODUCTION

A range of major religious reform movements that emerged in South Asia in the nineteenth century influence many Muslims in contemporary Britain. These movements in part evolved as responses to colonialism, and have been characterized as 'the reformist *Deobandīs*, the quietist and revivalist *Tablīghī Jamā'at*, the conservative and populist *Barelwīs*, the Islamist *Jamā'at-i Islāmī* and the modernists' (Lewis 1994: 36). These broad schools of thought still shape the character of Islam in the Indian subcontinent, and consequently they remain prevalent among British Muslims also. Not surprisingly, this diversity has significant consequences when it comes to the representation of Muslim interests in the public sphere, and towards the end of this chapter some of the issues and tensions surrounding 'representative' organizations, at both the local and the national level, are considered.

The political and military domination of the British in nineteenth-century South Asia was the outcome of economic activity and trade links that had begun a century earlier, under the auspices of the East India Company. Secular European powers were successfully capturing Muslim territory owing to their superior technological, military and economic capacity. This provoked a profound sense of crisis and self-reflection as Muslims questioned why divine guidance was no longer protecting the Islamic *ummah* (Cantwell Smith 1961). There was broad agreement about the need to reform and reinvigorate Muslim civilization, but also much disagreement about how this should be accomplished. A defining moment was the Indian uprising of 1857, which saw civilians and Indian army soldiers challenging British domination. The 'mutiny' 'threw patterns of social relations into high relief' (Metcalf, B. 1982: 81) and the relative lack of power and influence of the '*ulamā*' became especially evident. As in the Middle East, these circumstances provided fertile ground for the emergence of revivalist religious movements.

The 'mutiny' brought the ruling power of the East India Company to an end, and transferred power directly to the British government (British Raj). The failure to resist the British by military means led to a retreat from armed activism, and a turn towards religious reform and revival. The '*ulamā*' largely disengaged from matters of politics. Focusing their energies on the preservation of religious heritage and the dissemination of religious instruction, 'they sought to be, and to create in others, personalities that embodied Islam' (Metcalf, B. 1982: 11). Above all, they had to learn how to live as Muslims under British rule. While united in an effort to reform and revive Islam at a time of turbulent political and social change, they had different stances towards colonial power. Initially, the different movements tended to have a localized appeal, and often attracted particular social groups. Over time, however, 'each attracted a more geographically dispersed and more sociologically heterogeneous following' (Metcalf, B. 1982: 264). Likewise relationships between the movements evolved, becoming more or less antagonistic according to changing political and social circumstances.

## THE *DEOBANDĪ* MOVEMENT

Deoband is small town 100 miles north of Delhi in India. It was here that an Islamic seminary (*dāru'l-'ulūm*) was founded in 1867 by Muhammad Qasim Nanautawi (1833–77) and Rashid Ahmad Gangohi (1829–1905), both classically trained Islamic scholars and Sufi *shuyūkh*, and both coming from families with connections to the '*ulamā*'.[1] They melded intellectual learning with spiritual experience by stressing the importance of Sufi practice alongside observance of Islamic law.

Intellectual work was highly regarded in the Deoband seminary, but teachers were not simply imparting knowledge ('*ilm*) to their students. They were also engaged in the shaping of individuals and the purifying of character (*tarbiyat*), and so a regimen for personal life was integral to the student experience. Relationships between students and staff were

---

[1] For more details about their early lives, see Metcalf 1982, pp. 76ff, who has written perhaps *the* definitive history of the foundation of the *dāru'l-'ulūm* at Deoband in English. Another important work is Faruqi (1963): *The Deoband School and the Demand for Pakistan* (Bombay).

strong and enduring, and teachers often acted as *shaykh* for their pupils, instructing them not only on the specifics of *Ḥanafī* law, but also guiding them in the spiritual practice of *dhikr* (remembrance of God). The stress upon Urdu as the common language of religious instruction and publishing served to unify Muslims from across the Indian subcontinent, and became symbolic of a distinctive Muslim identity.

The *Deobandīs* followed the *Ḥanafī madhhab* and saw legal commentaries as the basis for making future legal rulings on religious matters. They followed a 'jurisprudential position of *taqlid* or conformity' (Metcalf, B. 1982: 141). It is partly due to this that they can be distinguished from other Islamic movements today (especially those of the *salafiyah* school of thought which stresses *non-conformity* to scholarly and legal traditions). The *Deobandī* emphasis on *Ḥanafī* law and limited practice of legal interpretation (*ijtihād*) resulted in a common approach among students. This generated criticism from their opponents, for placing too great an emphasis upon the authority of the *'ulamā'* and their scholarly traditions.

*Deobandīs* were vigorously anti-colonial, and regarded themselves as morally superior to the British. To indicate their distinctiveness, the founders stressed that students at the Deoband *dāru'l-'ulūm* should not dress like Englishmen, and should wear traditional Islamic attire. This attitude of superiority and difference helped to foster self-confidence among members of the movement.

The seminary at Deoband eventually expanded beyond the limits of a single institution, and another *dāru'l-'ulūm* was founded in Saharanpur, just twenty miles away. By 1967, when the centenary of the movement was celebrated, they claimed to have established 8,943 *Deobandī* centres of learning in the Indian subcontinent (Geaves 1996b: 149), mainly in urban areas. Many of the alumni established new institutions of their own, so that the movement became self-perpetuating. Over the course of time different currents of thought have emerged, based on the teachings and political views of a number of the movement's early scholars, such as Ashraf Ali Thanawi (Zaman 2007) and Husain Ahmad Madani (Metcalf 2008).

## Deobandīs *in Britain*

The migration of South Asians to Britain in the 1960s and 1970s was the conduit for the introduction of '*Deobandī*' thought in this country. Core support for the movement appears to be among Indian Muslims, especially Gujaratis,[2] and the key centres of *Deobandī* influence are the mill towns of the north-west, Bolton, Preston and Blackburn, Leicester and West Yorkshire (Birt 2005b; King 1997).[3]

*Deobandīs* were influential in the early days of Muslim settlement in Britain after 1945 for a number of reasons. For example, the early 'house-mosques' in towns and cities such as Bradford and Birmingham were often established by well-educated Muslim migrants, often from urban areas (see chapter 8). Given the *Deobandī* emphasis upon scholarly learning, the pioneers of mosque building in Britain in the 1960s and 1970s were naturally well disposed to the orthodox traditions of the *Deobandīs* and looked to this tradition for religious leadership. The original *Deobandī* ethos of 'protecting and preserving' religion that had come to the fore in nineteenth-century colonial India came into its own once again for similarly 'protecting and preserving' the religious identity of Muslims in twentieth-century Britain.

Although the *Deobandīs* successfully created a network of mosques in many British towns and cities, their most significant enterprise has been the establishment of *dāru'l-'ulūm* or Islamic 'seminaries', particularly one at Bury in the north of England. There was a realization of the need to train a new generation of British-born *'ulamā'*, and so they have created in Britain replicas of the institution that enabled their survival and pre-eminence in colonial India. The vice-chancellor of the Deoband *dāru'l-'ulūm* visited Britain in 1971, and following his trip, he noted:

Such preachers and ulema are urgently required there who, having full command over the English language, may explain the basic principles of Islamic sciences with insight and discrimination to the people of those places and may also live for some time amongst them with financial independence. (Cited in Geaves 1996b: 159)

In the overall landscape of Islamic religious training in Britain, the *Deobandīs* dominate; approximately seventeen *dāru'l-'ulūm* in Britain are

---

[2] A number of researchers of Islam in Britain, such as King (1997: 137); and Sikand (1998: 182), note the strong Gujarati influence among *Deobandīs* in Britain, and speculate why this might be the case. One possible explanation might lie in the fact that Gujaratis in Britain (unlike Muslims from other areas in South Asia) migrated from areas where they were a religious minority. Having such a background, they would have been well disposed to the idea that Islamic education was important to resist 'un-Islamic' influences. Furthermore, the entrepreneurial skills of the Gujaratis – built upon travelling and commerce – have resulted in the accumulation of social and material capital that helps to support *Deobandī* activity.

[3] By contrast, cities such as Birmingham with a very high percentage of Pakistanis (Mirpuris and Punjabis) are described by Birt as 'Deobandi outposts' (Birt 2005b).

*Deobandī*, out of a total of twenty-six similar institutions for advanced religious training (Birt 2005b).[4]

An influential young Bury graduate in Britain today is Mufti Muhammad ibn Adam al-Kawthari, in Leicester. Having completed his studies, he went on to specialize in the issuing of *fatāwā*, thus continuing a well-established *Deobandī* tradition. Mufti Muhammad now performs his role in modern-day Leicester, rather than nineteenth-century India, but he can trace his 'lineage' back to Deoband itself. Through his Darul Iftar (office of legal judgements) website (www.daruliftaa.com) he advises British Muslims about a wide range of religious matters. By placing the questions and his responses on the worldwide web, he is simply using modern technological methods to undertake the traditional *Deobandī* practice of documenting their *fatāwā*, as a resource for future scholars. The questions posed to him tell us something about the concerns of pious Muslims in Britain today:

A member of my father's family, by marriage, works as an insurance broker. From my understanding, since most forms of insurance are considered by the majority of ulema to be haram, his income is haram. Does this mean it is impermissible to consume food at their home, e.g. if my family is invited there for dinner? If it is haram, what is the best manner in which to deal with invitations to their home?

Could you tell me if it's haram or halal to enter in prize draws? And if it makes any difference whether you have to pay for a ticket or it's a free entry?

An academic analysis of questions such as these is currently being undertaken by an Islamic legal scholar in Bradford, as part of doctoral research. The outcomes of Shaykh Amjad Mohammad's work are likely to demonstrate that Islamic law is not rigid, but 'profoundly contextual' (Eickelman and Piscatori 2004: 16; Metcalf 2002: 5).

In cities such as Leicester, where the *Deobandīs* have been particularly energetic (they influence over half the twenty mosques, and the three *dāru'l-'ulūm* are all *Deobandī*), more radical expressions of Islam are less discernible (Birt 2005b). Birt suggests that this is because Muslims are brought into the *madrasah* system while young. The well-organized system of *Deobandī* education for young Muslims, relying upon a carefully constructed curriculum, appears to provide a bulwark against the influences of more 'radical' groups.

---

[4] The 'Muslim Faith Leader's Review' undertaken from 2008 to 2009 estimated a total of thirty-nine seminaries. The discrepancy between Birt's figure in 2005 and this recent estimate is probably indicative not of recent growth but of different criteria at work for evaluating 'what counts' as a *dāru'l-'ulūm*.

## TABLĪGHĪ JAMĀ'AT (THE 'PREACHING PARTY')

The *Tablīghī Jamā'at* (TJ) movement is an offshoot of the *Deobandī* tradition. Maulana Muhammad Ilyas Kandhlawi (1885–1944) was a graduate of the Deoband *dāru'l-'ulūm* and a charismatic *'ālim* (teacher) at its sister institution in Saharanpur in India. Against the background of the political, religious and social tumult of late colonial India, he saw the need for an entirely new style of Islamization, and the need to fashion programmes of Islamic education that could bring nominal (or spiritually misguided) Muslims back into the fold of 'authentic' Islam:

Tablighi Jamaat took its impetus from a desire to move the dissemination of Islamic teachings away from the madrasah, the heart of *Deobandī* activity, to inviting 'lay' Muslims, high and low ranking, learned and illiterate, to share the obligation of enjoining others to faithful practice. (Metcalf 2002: 8)

The organization that he founded in the 1920s, the *Tablīghī Jamā'at*, is firmly within the *Deobandī* tradition, but its methods have been quite different. The movement has become distinctive for door-to-door preaching, and a strict Sufi-inspired ethos of self-discipline and service among its members. This is encapsulated in a six-point programme comprising profession of the faith (*shahādah*), prayer (*ṣalāt*), remembrance of God (*dhikr*), respect for all Muslims, sincere intentions and the giving of time, especially in missionary activity. Soon after the movement's foundation, 'a pattern emerged of calling participants to spend one night a week, one weekend a month, 40 continuous days a year, and ultimately 120 days at least once in their lives to engage in *tablighi* missions' (Metcalf, B. 1982: xviii).[5]

During the course of its history the TJ has developed influence on a global scale. It has a presence in about a hundred countries of the world (King 1997), and preaching tours are made possible through transnational networks and personal connections linking members around the globe. The movement can be characterized as egalitarian and anti-intellectual, and can be credited with having successfully brought the message of Islam

---

[5] Missionary tours comprise about ten men and sometimes women who go to another town or region (or country) to preach their faith, dressed very simply, carrying few belongings and sleeping in mosques *en route*. Being a 'quietist', internal grassroots missionary movement – only operating within the Muslim community – the *Tablīghī Jamā'at* is largely invisible to outsiders. The focus is upon (nominal) Muslims, and not the wider non-Muslim society. 'The goals and satisfactions that come from participation … have little to do with opposition or resistance to non-Muslims or "the West"; their own debates focus on other Muslims, an internal, not an external "Other"' (Metcalf 2002: 16).

to rural, less educated Muslims.[6] By focusing its activities upon Muslims themselves, it 'implicitly fosters the privatization of religion associated with the modern liberal state' (Metcalf 2002: 17). Being highly individualistic, and so concerned with personal salvation, it has been regarded as a 'very modern movement' (Metcalf 1993: 606).

However, the movement has been subject to sharp critique in some quarters. It is accused of 'depoliticizing Muslims by preaching other-worldliness and disdain for power' (Sikand 2006: 186). By withdrawing from active engagement in politics and social affairs, the movement has come to be regarded by some as implicitly supporting the separation of religion and politics – a *de facto* secularism – which many would regard as contrary to the all-embracing nature of Islam as a complete 'way of life'.

When Maulana Muhammad Ilyas Kandhlawi died in 1944, his immediate successor was his son, Maulana Muhammad Yusuf (d.1965). In his hands, the movement rapidly expanded its reach beyond the Indian subcontinent (Masud 2000), and London was seen as an important new centre for the movement's activities on account of the growing Muslim population in Britain.

### *Tablīghī Jamāʿat in Britain*

The first recorded TJ preaching tour in Britain was organized on 20 January 1945 in an Indian quarter of London (Sikand 1998). The response of the Muslims in London was said to be enthusiastic.[7] Although missionary tours came to Britain in the later years of the 1950s, it was not until the 1960s that the movement made concerted efforts to reach British Muslims. In 1962–3, preachers were dispatched to Britain from the TJ headquarters in Delhi, and as a result of their activities a number of mosques and *madrasahs* were established. This was a time of rapid institution-building among British Muslims, and the movement was actively involved in the process. The focus of its activities was straightforward teaching about the basics of Islam. There was a concern that as Muslims in Britain became wealthier, they might be drawn away from Islamic

---

[6] Its annual religious meeting, held in Raiwind near Lahore in Pakistan, attracts between 1 million and 2 million participants each year, the second largest gathering of Muslims after the annual *ḥajj*. Some have suggested that it is perhaps the largest Muslim movement in the world today (Sikand 1999).

[7] This is according to Sani Hasni, the principal biographer of Maulana Yusuf: *Sawaneh-i-Hazrat Maulana Yusuf Kandhlawi Rahmatullah Aleih*, Lucknow, Department of Publications and Dissemination, Nadwat-ul-Ulama, 1989), cited by Sikand (1998).

practice (Geaves 1996b). Children were perceived to be particularly vulnerable to the potentially corrupting influences of British society. Because the movement focused particularly upon basic teachings, it was able to work effectively among Muslims from many different backgrounds. The networks and mosques established by the movement were steeped in South Asian culture, thereby providing a social and spiritual refuge for Muslims trying to overcome the dislocation of migration.

Having developed a presence in a number of major British towns and cities during the 1960s, there was a growing need for the movement to establish a British headquarters from which to co-ordinate activities. The driving force behind the establishment of the UK headquarters was Hafiz Muhammad Ishaq Patel, a migrant factory worker of Gujarati origin living in Coventry. Patel was well known for his knowledge of Islam (although he was not a classically trained scholar), and eventually he was invited by a small Muslim community living in Dewsbury, Yorkshire, to teach them the fundamentals of Islam. A residential property became the focus for *Tablīghī* activities, but soon outgrew its premises. This led to the construction of a new purpose-built centre opened in 1982 (also in Dewsbury, in the Saville Town area) with an adjacent mosque and *dāru'l-'ulūm* known as the Jamiat Talimul Islam, the 'Institute of Islamic Education' (Gilliat-Ray 2006).[8]

The TJ centre in Dewsbury serves as the European headquarters of the movement. Some 8,000 to 15,000 activists attend the annual winter gathering. Its anti-intellectual ethos, combined with its emphasis on equality and piety (as against wealth or educational attainment), 'would seem to hold a particularly strong appeal for educationally and economically less privileged individuals' (Sikand 1998: 183). While this might be true among rank-and-file activists, influential leaders of the movement often come from more educated, middle-class backgrounds. Their social and educational capital often provides an important resource for the movement (Sikand 1998: 183).

Speculating about the future of the TJ in Britain, Sikand is not optimistic. Youth do not appear drawn to the distinctive preaching methods of the movement, and their political concerns about issues of racism in society and global injustice are apparently not being addressed: 'by turning a blind eye to the real-world concerns of British Muslims, movements like the Tablighi Jamaat are bound to lose their appeal in the years to come' (Sikand 1998: 188). However, there is a new feeling of optimism and

[8] See Faust (2000), Gilliat-Ray (2006) and Lewis (1994) for a description of the curriculum.

entrepreneurialism in the TJ movement. It is currently in the process of preparing a planning application for a new centre (*markaz*) in West Ham in London, adjacent to the new Olympic stadium. The ambitious plans are controversial, not least because of the scale of the project. Regardless of how and whether this project is actually realized, the ambition behind it indicates a degree of commitment and energy that might enable the *Tablīghī Jamā'at* to find a new place within British Muslim society, especially among the youth.

### THE 'BARELWĪ' MOVEMENT (AHL AL-SUNNAT WA-AL-JAMĀ'AT – THE PEOPLE OF THE SUNNAH)

If the *Deobandīs* have been ideologically and institutionally dominant among South Asian Muslims in Britain, Muslims with *Barelwī* sympathies have been more significant numerically. An understanding of the character of the *Barelwī* movement is important for an appreciation of Islam in Britain today, because the ideas and practices of this school of thought reflect the religious worldview of many South Asian Muslims in Britain.

The *Ahl al-Sunnat wa-al-Jamā'at* movement evolved through the life and work of Maulana Ahmed Riza Khan (1856–1921), from Bareilly, in northern central India. Members of the movement do not think of Ahmad Riza as a 'founder' of a movement as such, but more of a 'reviver' of the Prophetic *Sunnah* (Sanyal 1996). He can be credited with having established a 'unified identity for a strand of Islam which is by nature disparate and lacking central organization' (Geaves 1996b: 96). Because Ahmad Riza was born in a society where a person's family name often reflected his or her place of birth, occupation, or family lineage, the movement became known as 'Bareilly' simply because of the town in which Ahmad Riza was born. Members of the movement usually reject the name and identity *Barelwī*, preferring to be known as members of the *Ahl al-Sunnat wa-al-Jamā'at*, or *Ahl-i Sunnat*' in short. This translates as 'people of the *Sunnah*' or 'people of the Prophetic path'. This identification is a direct and political claim to be members of the majority Muslim community (Sanyal 1996:166).

The *Barelwī* worldview is shaped by distinctive ideas about the qualities and characteristics of the Prophet Muhammad, who is widely believed to be blessed with superhuman qualities and characteristics. He is regarded as an emanation of God's light, with unique knowledge of the unseen world, and with limitless virtues and abilities (Sanyal

1996: 153). It is believed that Allah created the Prophet before anything else existed, and, while physically dead, He nevertheless remains spiritually alive in His tomb (as do other Prophets and saints after Him). For *Barelwī*s, there is a necessary and hierarchical path to reach God that depends upon the intercession of the Prophet Muhammad and also, crucially, of one's *pīr*, a Sufi teacher who is regarded as having saintly and supernatural spiritual qualities. A true *pīr* has to be a pious and exemplary scholar with an unbroken chain of lineage back to the Prophet Himself. Thus, the *pīr* intercedes with the Prophet Muhammad on behalf of the believer, and the Prophet in turn intercedes with God. For Ahmad Riza just as *'ulamā'* were necessary for knowledge of the *Qur'ān* and *Sharī'ah*, so *pīr*s were necessary for full understanding of spiritual matters.

The *Barelwī* also believe that deceased saints have intercessory powers between God and humankind by virtue of their capacity to converse directly with and through the Prophet Muhammad. Upon death, their tombs and relics become shrines, and pilgrimage to these sites is undertaken with the objective of bringing about cures for illness, or some other good fortune:[9]

> [The] spirit [of the *pīr*] is so powerful and so dominant over the body that the body itself does not die or decay but is merely hidden from the living. The *baraka* [blessing] of the saint is not dissipated at the saint's death. It is both transmitted to his successors, and remains at his tomb, which becomes a place of pilgrimage for later followers. The *pīr* does not actually die in the ordinary sense of the term. He is 'hidden', and over time continues to develop spiritually, so that his *baraka* increases, as does the importance of his shrine. (Ewing 1980: 29, cited in Sanyal, p. 106)

On the anniversaries of their births (*mīlād*) and deaths (*'urs*) the spirits of deceased saints are believed to be particularly alert to the needs of their followers. *Barelwī* devotion towards the Prophet Muhammad means that His annual birthday celebrations are especially joyful occasions, characterized by recitations of devotional poetry (*na'ts*), readings of the entire *Qur'ān* in one night, and joyful singing in praise of the Prophet (*qawwālī*). *Barakah* is inherent in the relics and shrines of deceased saints, and thus the guardianship of these sites becomes a privileged responsibility. Before his death, a *pīr* will appoint a successor, who will not only become the caretaker of the shrine, but will also inherit something of the

---

[9] In addition, sometimes amulets containing verses from the *Qur'ān* are written on small pieces of paper, and worn on the body in the hope of bringing about the cure of illness.

*pīr*'s spiritual blessing. 'Inheritance' is usually biological as well as spiritual, with a son often succeeding his father.

Ahmad Riza differed from other nineteenth-century South Asian religious reformers on account of his political views. Riza was sometimes accused of being pro-British, because he did not align himself with distinctly anti-British organizations, such as the *Jam'iyatul 'Ulamā'-i Hind*. However, Usha Sanyal, the author of one of the few major studies of Ahmad Riza, regarded him as rather 'uninterested' in political self-determination in India, so long as Muslims were free to observe Islam without interference (Sanyal 1996: 297). So he did not actively oppose the British, as some other religious movements did, but rather 'distanced himself from it, carving out an identity removed from its concerns' (Sanyal 1996: 298).

The strongly localized character of *Barelwī* Islam in South Asia, revolving as it does around *pīrs* and shrines, makes it deeply embedded in specific ethnic and regional identities. For those British Muslims who identify with the *Ahl-i Sunnah*, this has presented a particular challenge in terms of transmitting their traditions to young people.

## Ahl al-Sunnat wa-al-Jamā'at *in Britain*

Many British Muslims do not consciously identify with the *Ahl al-Sunnat wa-al-Jamā'at* movement, but nevertheless practise a form of Islam that Ahmad Riza and his successors actively defended (Geaves 1996b: 101). This form of Islam overlaps with membership of various Sufi orders, the most prevalent of which in Britain is the *Naqshbandī* order (and its sub-branches) (Ansari 2004: 358). Various scholars of Islam in Britain have estimated that about 50 per cent of all British Muslims and British Muslim organizations reflect a general *Barelwī* worldview (Geaves 1996b; Raza 1991).[10] This has been sustained by the arrival in Britain of religious professionals (*pīrs*, *shuyūkh* and *'ulamā'*) who are able to maintain the linkages between shrines, living and deceased saints, and their followers. The religious leadership of *Barelwī* mosques in Britain can take numerous forms (Geaves 1996b). Mosques might be led by a well-trained *Barelwī* scholar (*'ālim*) without connection to any particular saint (*pīr*) or Sufi order. Others might be under the leadership of a 'living *pīr*' (*zindapir*), while some reflect a traditional Sufi structure. Far from being a

---

[10] As yet, no definitive research has been undertaken which accurately measures the prevalence of different 'schools of thought' in Britain. At present, the best guide remains the number or proportion of mosques in a particular city, and the extent of membership/attendance.

monolithic group, *Barelwīs* in Britain are divided not only on the grounds of ethnicity/region, but also according to their membership of different Sufi orders: *Qādirī, Chishtī, Naqshbandī*, and so on, each with their own subdivisions.[11] There is some degree of interaction between Sufi orders and their members, but they each also retain a degree of independence. The variations among them tend to revolve around issues of lifestyle or forms of spiritual practice.

There have been some in-depth scholarly accounts of the life of a number of influential *pīrs* in Britain, especially Pir Marouf Hussain Shah in Bradford (Lewis 1994: 81ff), Sufi Abdullah Khan in Birmingham (Geaves 1996a; Werbner 1996b; Werbner 2002b),[12] and Pir Abdul Wahab Siddiqi in Coventry (Asif 2006; Geaves 2000).[13] It is worth considering the life and legacy of Pir Abdul Wahab Siddiqi in some depth, given his pioneering influence in the establishment of the first *Barelwī dāru'l-'ulūm* in Britain.

Pir Abdul Wahab Siddiqi from Coventry (1942–94) was a *Naqshbandī* Sufi (of the *Hijazi* branch), who originated from Sheikhpura in Pakistan. He came to Britain in 1972, in the hope of promoting the education of his children, rather than for the more typical migrant intention of improving material prosperity. He established an Islamic Study Centre in Coventry to train Islamic scholars (*'ulamā'*) in 1982, and was instrumental in founding Hijaz College in nearby Nuneaton, one of the first formal *dāru'l-'ulūm* in Britain for the training of *Barelwī 'ulamā'*. His educational philosophy (and that of the College today) is that traditional Islamic learning must be pursued alongside other 'secular' disciplines, such as law, medicine and so on. For him, the combination of two educational forms, one divinely inspired (the *Qur'ān* and *Ḥadīth*), the other of human origin, would equip Muslims with the knowledge needed to engage with contemporary issues.

[11]  A full discussion of the diverse expressions of Sufism in Britain is beyond the scope of this chapter, though detailed scholarly accounts can be found in Draper (1985); Geaves (2000); Werbner (1990); Werbner (1996b); Werbner (2006). Membership of a Sufi order is usually achieved by taking an oath of allegiance to a particular *shaykh*.

[12]  The saintly authority of a 'living *pīr*' is confirmed when he successfully inscribes his charisma onto a new place (Werbner 1996b). Sufi Abdullah achieved this by organizing marches through the streets of Birmingham on significant religious occasions, such as the birthday of the Prophet Muhammad. Processions led by living *pīrs* 'sacralize' the space and locality, because of the sanctity that they embody (Werbner 1996b), and so certain streets, parks and procession routes in some British cities are becoming sacred for *Barelwīs* in Britain. Marches can be interpreted as acts of 'spatial appropriation', 'reverse colonization' and a 'decentering of Western dominance' (Werbner 1996b: 334).

[13]  Many Sufi teachers or *pīrs* are also giving the honorific title '*Ḥaẓrat*', which is a title of courtesy and respect, and means 'master', and is applied to a revered individual.

Figure 3. The shrine of the late Pir Abdul Wahab Siddiqi, Hijaz College, Nuneaton.
Reproduced by kind permission of Ron Geaves

When he died in 1994, responsibility for developing his vision fell to his four sons, all university graduates but also schooled in Islamic sciences. His son Faiz ul-Aqtab Siddiqi now serves as the College Principal, and is himself a living *pīr*, guiding his students and followers as his father before him.[14]

The shrine of the late Pir Abdul Wahab Siddiqi is within the Hijaz College grounds, and it has inevitably become a place of pilgrimage and devotion. It is considered the first and only Sufi shrine in Western Europe (Asif 2006).

Another important current of diversity within the *Ahl al-Sunnat wa-al-Jamā'at* stems from the activity and popularity of Shaykh Nazim 'Adil Al-Haqqani an Naqshbandī, a Sufi Shaykh of the *Haqqani Naqshbandī* order. He first came to Britain in 1973, and because of his Turkish-Cypriot origins found a ready audience among Turks living in London. However, his charisma has enabled a broadening of support, which now includes British-born Pakistanis and converts to Islam, with significant centres

---

[14] A postgraduate dissertation has been written about Hijaz College (Asif 2006).

in Birmingham, London, Sheffield and, more recently, Glastonbury in Somerset (Draper 2004; Geaves 2000).

British Muslims who are influenced by the *Ahl al-Sunnat wa-al-Jamāʿat* have a particular devotion towards the Prophet Muhammad, and as a consequence they were among the most vocal in condemning the insults of the Prophet in Salman Rushdie's novel, *The Satanic Verses*. However, while they were numerically the most active campaigners, they were usually unable to take up positions of leadership in the organization of major protests. This was because of the fragmentation and diversity of the *Ahl al-Sunnat wa-al-Jamāʿat* in Britain, combined with a general lack of conscious identification with a distinctive 'movement'. The *Barelwīs* lacked the organizational structures of their *Deobandī* counterparts, and in the late 1980s did not really have a leadership that could present a unified and articulate defence of their position, in the medium of English. However, as a result of the Rushdie Affair, British Muslims who identified with the ethos of the *Ahl al-Sunnat wa-al-Jamāʿat* recognized the power that could be derived from unity, and the novel was (among other things) a catalyst for efforts to address organizational issues.

As in the Indian subcontinent, so in Britain; rivalry with other South Asian reform groups has helped to cement a common *Barelwī* identity in recent years, and this has found expression in the formation of two organizations to represent *Ahl-i Sunnah* interests in the public sphere. In March 2005, the 'British Muslim Forum' (BMF) was established to provide a national body for mosques and 'grassroots' organizations reflecting 'traditional' Islam, and their website (archived by the British Library on 25 July 2005)[15] claimed some 250 members (listed by name on the website). In reality, the BMF was formed to give a national voice to *Barelwī* Muslims in Britain, who felt 'unrepresented' in the Muslim Council of Britain. The BMF had a presence at the launch at Westminster of a second organization, the Sufi Muslim Council (SMC) on 19 July 2006. The SMC claims to provide a voice for the 'eighty per cent of UK Muslims who are Sufis' (King 2006). This is a dubious claim to make in view of the academic evidence that many British Muslims do not actively identify with the *Ahl al-Sunnat wa-al-Jamāʿat*, or with a particular Sufi order (Geaves 2000). Press releases about the new movement provide no evidence to suggest how and to what extent they really do reflect the worldview and aspirations of the vast majority of British Muslims. The launch of the new organization attracted a great deal of media publicity, no doubt reinforced by the

---

[15] www.webarchive.org.uk/tep/12353.html; www.bmf.eu.com

Westminster setting and the involvement of senior New Labour politicians, representatives from the Board of Deputies of British Jews, and senior church leaders. The circumstances, patronage and timing behind the emergence of this organization has raised numerous questions and speculation, most evident on websites and blogs.[16] The long-term future for the SMC remains uncertain, as does its relationship with the BMF with whom it is likely to overlap (and possibly compete) significantly.

### JAMĀ'AT-I ISLĀMĪ ('THE ISLAMIC SOCIETY')

The schools of Islamic thought discussed so far emerged in nineteenth-century India, and they emphasized the preservation and protection of Islam from non-Muslim rulers. But the conservatism that often sprang from their isolationist stance left Muslims ill-equipped to deal with the changes that would occur in the twentieth century as new Muslim nations were seeking (and winning) their independence from colonial rule. In a post-colonial world, it was the ideological legacy of colonialism that provided the challenge, rather than direct colonial rule itself. Against this background, the *'ulamā'* were regarded by some as out of touch with major changes in international politics and developments, and unable to represent the interests of Muslims in real-world debates and decision-making. In these new socio-political circumstances, there was an ideological space to be filled between post-colonial secular nationalism on the one hand and individually orientated personal piety on the other. The founder of the *Jamā'at-i Islāmī*, Maulana Mawdudi (1903–79 CE), stepped into this space, simultaneously criticizing so-called 'Western' values (especially nationalism and secularism)[17] while also asserting the primacy of Islam. During the 1920s he became interested in politics and journalism, but by the closing years of the decade he had begun to forge his own political path, and devoted his time to writing and research. In 1941, he founded the *Jamā'at-i Islāmī* (The Islamic Society/Islamic Party), and acted as its *amīr* (leader) until 1972. Mawdudi has been described as a 'trailblazer of contemporary Islamic revivalism' (Esposito 1992: 120).

Mawdudi shared many of the same reformist assumptions about the need to revive 'pure' Islam as did his predecessors. However, he placed an emphasis upon the need to transform *all* social, economic and political

---

[16] Perhaps the most critical scholarly reflection about the new organization has been written by Shehla Khan from Manchester University (Khan, S. 2006).
[17] To read Mawdudi's views on nationalism, see Donohue and Esposito (2007: 74–7)

structures according to the teachings of Islam. Mawdudi suggested that it was only in an Islamic theocratic state where *Sharī'ah* law was in place that the oppressive political and ideological forces of colonialism could be defeated. He was critical of scholars who obscured 'Islam's dynamism with medieval commentary and fossilized law: he argued for the need to move beyond conformity to the teachings of Islamic law, and for the exercise of *ijtihād*, or interpretative effort' (Lewis 1994: 41) in order that the spirit of Islamic teaching could be applied to real-world issues. This amounted to a direct critique of the *Deobandī* and *Barelwī* 'schools'. While acknowledging the contribution that earlier reform movements had made to the cause of Islam, he was critical of their Sufi tendencies and the scholar–pupil relationship in particular.

The revivalist spirit that inspired Mawdudi and his followers has often been called 'Islamist', but what does this term actually mean, and how does it relate to the related word 'Islamism'? The French word *Islamisme* was first coined in the eighteenth century to refer to the religion of Islam. It was derived from the Arabic *Islamiyyun* (*The Search for Common Ground: Muslims, non-Muslims and the UK Media. A report commissioned by the Mayor of London* 2007: 84). These terms became widely used in Algeria in the 1970s, to describe people who were seeking to use the beliefs, narratives, symbols and language of Islam to inspire and mobilize political activity:

The term 'Islamists' (*al-islamiyyun*) is used by Muslim activists, to refer to adherents of the 'Islamic movement', for whom it contextually implies ideologically motivated Muslims. Islamist authority to remake the world derives from a self-confident appropriation of what they believe to be 'tradition'. (Eickelman and Piscatori 2004: 45)

*Islamisme* referred to a general approach to politics and the organization of civil society, and was used to describe a wide range of very different social movements. These ranged from formally organized religious-political parties that operated within legal structures, to religious groups that were merely concerned to defend Islamic beliefs and practices and to spread the Islamic 'way of life' in society. The term was also used to describe those engaged in armed struggle. Some movements combined these different approaches.

The French word *Islamisme* translated into the English 'Islamism' in the mid 1980s, and from the mid 1990s quickly acquired negative connotations as a result of the way that journalists and commentators used the word to refer pejoratively to aspects of Islam that they found distasteful.

It was no longer being used to refer to a general approach to society and politics. Not surprisingly, the terms 'Islamist' and 'Islamism' became offensive to many Muslims. Those who were sympathetic to the original and broad meaning of 'Islamism' began to refer to themselves as members of the 'Islamic Movement' instead. This was generally understood as the effort of individuals and organizations inspired by Islam, to work towards the establishment of an Islamic state. However, in situations where Muslims are in a minority, such as in India or Britain, the 'Islamic Movement', of which the *Jamā'at-i Islāmī* is one expression, places less emphasis upon the creation of a theocracy and more upon the spreading of Islamic virtues, teachings and values in public life (Geaves 1995).[18]

Unlike many other Islamic reform movements in South Asia, the *Jamā'at-i Islāmī* built its power base not upon the teachings and activities of the *'ulamā'*, but upon the development of a well-trained elite of core committed leaders, mostly drawn from the educated middle and lower middle classes. Typical *Jamā'at-i Islāmī* activists were engineers, doctors, lawyers and academics, all of whom had received 'Western' education (Esposito and Voll 2001). Mawdudi was concerned with quality, not quantity, in his activists. As a result, the movement has not made a significant impact upon the 'popular' religious culture of the uneducated rural masses, and is unsympathetic to their traditions of worship at shrines. The current activities of the movement focus upon research institutes, social services, publications, student outreach, preaching and youth work. From its headquarters near Lahore, it houses a hospital, offices, visitor accommodation, research facilities, a mosque and a library.[19] The Pakistan Islamic Front, established in 1993, is the political wing of the movement, but it has so far failed to attract sufficient voter support. It remains merely a voice of political opposition.

## Jamā'at-i Islāmī *in Britain*

At a formal organizational level, the *Jamā'at-i Islāmī* does not exist in Britain (Geaves 1995). However, through the effort of individuals who worked closely with Mawdudi and who were inspired by him, there are

---

[18] For a useful overview of the history and politics of terms such as 'fundamentalism' and 'Islamism', see Kramer (2003).

[19] During visits to Pakistan in 1993 and 1994, I spent one month on each occasion staying in the homes of several very senior *Jamā'at-i Islāmī* members. During my time in Lahore, I was shown around the headquarters of the movement, known as 'Mansoorah', and interviewed both male and female activists, as well as representatives from the student wing of the movement.

now a number of prominent Islamic organizations in Britain which reflect the broad *Jamā'at-i Islāmī* vision to spread Islamic values. They have consistently been less concerned with political activity, and more preoccupied with spreading Islamic teaching through education and social welfare. In other words, the directly political aspects of Maududi's original vision have become dissociated from their activities, and the emphasis has been upon mission and *da'wah*. It is unfortunate that many journalists and media commentators have failed to recognize this evolution in thought and activity. Individuals inspired by Mawdudi's writings share a common reformist vision which emphasises 'the importance of family networks; a strong framework for morals; [and] social responsibility' (Masood 2006b: 20). A survey of three key organizations provides insight into the expression of the *Jamā'at-i Islāmī* in Britain.

The *UK Islamic Mission* (UKIM)[20] was established in August 1962, from the initiative of a small group of Muslims who felt the need for a British-based organization that would convey the 'true spirit' of Islam to the Western world. With headquarters in London, it now has over forty 'branches' around Britain. Most of these administer a mosque, usually staffed by imams recruited from overseas. The Mission principally works in the fields of education and welfare, and an analysis of its website and Annual Reports provides evidence of its vibrancy. Its educational work includes seminars, exhibitions (for instance in libraries/schools), and courses about Islam for young people and community groups. The movement is engaged in active fundraising for causes in Britain and overseas, and works with interfaith organizations both locally and nationally.

As the Mission has developed confidence and resources over time, it has sought to influence opinion formers in wider society, including politicians, academics, senior religious leaders and influential bodies in civil society.[21] 'Influence' essentially means promoting awareness and understanding of Islam and Muslims, and the contribution that Islamic perspectives can make to contemporary debates, in wider society.

The *Islamic Foundation*[22] was established in 1973 by senior members of the *Jamā'at-i Islāmī* from Pakistan, several of whom had undertaken postgraduate studies in British universities. Having lived and studied in Britain, they were deemed especially well qualified to realize the

---

[20] www.ukim.org
[21] Prior to its 2004 conference, letters of support for the Mission were written by the Prime Minister, the Mayor of London and the Home Secretary conveying support and appreciation for its work. They had clearly been invited to attend the event in person.
[22] www.islamic-foundation.org.uk

educational aims of the movement. Initially the Foundation was located in the city of Leicester, but in the 1990s it moved to larger premises eight miles from the city, in a village called Markfield. From this base, the Foundation is able to organize and host residential and non-residential conferences and training courses.[23]

The Foundation can be regarded as the main educational, training and publication 'wing' of the Islamic Movement. Most of its energies are focused on research, writing, and contributing to scholarly and policy debate. An assessment of the Islamic Foundation dating from the mid 1990s suggested that it perceived itself as the 'think-tank of the Islamic Movement in Britain ... [creating] an Islam which is suited to the environment of the West without losing the fundamentals of the faith' (Geaves 1995: 202). More recent evaluations capture important developments in the past decade which reflect generational changes in the staffing of the institution (Mandeville 2001; McLoughlin 2005c; Peter 2003). For example, McLoughlin notes that there is a gradual transition towards a 'reformist Islamism' through the work of some of the Foundation's young Islamic intellectuals, who are 'increasingly evolving innovative, cosmopolitan and self-critical reformulations of their tradition' (McLoughlin 2005c: 64). With the appointment of each successive new Director General, the significance and influence of the *Jamā'at-i Islāmī* in Pakistan has gradually begun to recede.

The Islamic Foundation works largely through the medium of English, and staff originate from a variety of backgrounds. The Foundation regards itself as non-sectarian and international in outlook, and this self-perception has made its ideology and approach attractive to educated and relatively affluent urbanized Muslims in Britain who are sympathetic to the wider 'Islamic Movement'. However, in many less educated and more conservative Muslim communities in Britain, the Foundation is regarded as simply 'too liberal'.

The educational imperative of the original *Jamā'at-i Islāmī* vision found expression in 2000, with the launch of 'Markfield Institute of Higher Education' (MIHE),[24] a postgraduate college occupying the same site at

---

[23] In the past two decades, considerable energy has been expended in supporting 'new' Muslims (converts to Islam) through a New Muslims Project which provides practical, educational and spiritual assistance for those new to the faith. The Foundation also provides 'cultural awareness' training programmes, which aim to offer public sector workers (such as police officers and social workers) some exposure to an 'Islamic' environment and basic training about the fundamentals of Islam.

[24] www.mihe.org.uk

Markfield. Over the course of time, degrees have been validated by a range of British universities (Portsmouth, Loughborough, Gloucestershire) and the college provides an Islamic environment for courses in Islamic economics, chaplaincy, counselling and Islamic studies. The former Director of MIHE, Dr Ataullah Siddiqui, is a well-established international academic authority on Christian–Muslim relations, and is actively involved in global interfaith initiatives. A recent essay by one of the staff of the Islamic Foundation and MIHE reviews some current projects which all reflect the outward-looking spirit of engagement that is becoming a hallmark of these institutions (Hussain 2007).

The *Islamic Society of Britain*[25] was founded in 1990, to 'provide a vehicle for committed British Muslims to combine their knowledge, skills and efforts for the benefit of one another and British society as a whole, through the promotion of Islam and Islamic values' (ISB website, accessed 21/6/06). The collective experience of activists was brought together to form a new organization, to work across all the different 'schools of thought' in Britain. However, the *Jamā'at-i Islāmī* background is unmistakable if one traces the background of key activists, most of whom have direct connections to other institutions or organizations that were originally inspired by Maulana Mawdudi. Over time, the ISB has successfully developed a number of innovative projects to try to engage both Muslim and non-Muslim audiences. These include an 'Islamic Scouts of Britain' project and 'Islam Awareness Week', a campaign that was initiated in 1994 'to raise awareness and remove misconceptions surrounding Britain's second largest faith group'.

The various expressions of the *Jamā'at-i Islāmī* in Britain surveyed above have been remarkably resourceful and innovative in their work with and for Muslims in Britain, adapting their activities in keeping with broader developments. There are other organizations that might have also been discussed, such as the East London Mosque[26] and the Islamic Forum of Europe,[27] but as yet there has been virtually no academic research on these institutions. Indeed, scholarly evaluations of the impact of the many organizations inspired by the *Jamā'at-i Islāmī* in Britain are few and far between, and are increasingly dated. This signals the opportunities for new research in the future.

[25] www.isb.org.uk   [26] www.eastlondonmosque.org.uk
[27] www.islamicforumeurope.com

### AHL-I-ḤADĪTH ('PEOPLE OF THE ḤADĪTH')

The ideological roots of this movement can be traced back to Arabian scholarly influences, in particular Ibn 'Abd Al-Wahhab (d.1791 CE) and Ibn Taymiyah (d.1328 CE). Meanwhile the South Asian roots lie with Syed Ahmad Sirhindi (1564–1624 CE) and Shah Wali Alla (1702–63 CE) and their successors. The organizational development of the *Ahl-i-Ḥadīth* movement proper began, however, with Nazir Husain of Delhi (1805–1902) and Siddiq Hasan Khan Bhopali (1832–90) in the 1850s. Like the founders of some of the other religious reform movements in South Asia, they regarded the Muslims in India as religiously misguided, and living in a society that had lost its link to 'authentic' Islamic beliefs and practices. They felt that Muslims had drifted away from the centrality of God's indivisible 'oneness' (*tawhīd*). The religious movement that evolved around their ideas was established to purify Islamic teaching, but also (and in contrast to the other reform movements) 'to remove the rigidity and irrational approach' (Azami 2000) of the lawmakers.

From the outset, the movement had a profoundly different view of religious law compared to most other South Asian groups examined so far. Rather than looking to one of the four legal traditions of Islam for guidance on religious matters, they advocated direct use of the sources of Islam, the *Qur'ān* and the *Ḥadīth*, which they interpreted 'literally and narrowly' (Metcalf, B. 1982: 265). For this reason, the movement has also been dubbed the 'Wahhabi movement of India' (Ahmad 1966; Azami 2000), given its broadly similar approach in terms of belief and principles.

In taking this stance towards the law, the *Ahl-i-Ḥadīth* movement aimed to popularize jurisprudential practice among 'ordinary' Muslims, effectively bypassing the *'ulamā'* and placing responsibility for legal and religious interpretation in the hands of individual believers. This worked well in the scholarly and elite circles in which *Ahl-i-Ḥadīth* ideas were popular, and where a reasonably high degree of education and literacy made such independent scholarship possible. It was of course another matter entirely among the many ordinary Muslims who were illiterate and uneducated.

The expansion and cohesion of the movement can be attributed in part to the material and social capital at its disposal. The *Ahl-i-Ḥadīth* worked among the elite, the educated and the wealthy, but ultimately its 'intensity and extremism' (Metcalf, B. 1982: 268) and assumptions about scholarship meant that it was not able to have the same influence as some of the other schools of thought. Despite the position of opposition that the *Ahl-i-Ḥadīth* movement adopted in relation to other reform movements, this didn't stop it from trying to establish a common standard of Islamic thought and practice that could be accepted by all Muslims in India.

### Ahl-i-Ḥadīth *in Britain*

Except for a short booklet published as the outcome of a postgraduate project in the 1990s (Azami 2000), the *Ahl-i-Ḥadīth* movement has not been the subject of research, and there are no substantial academic papers about its activities in Britain so far. Sources of information are therefore extremely limited, and this fact is reflected in the discussion and analysis below.[28]

The first signs of *Ahl-i-Ḥadīth* activity in Britain emerge in 1962, when Moulana Fazal Karim Asim came to Britain as a factory worker. With degrees in religious sciences and long experience of working in educational administration in Pakistan, he became the first leader (*amīr*) of the movement when it was formally constituted in 1975. Initially, he worked within the *Jamā'at-i Islāmī* inspired 'UK Islamic Mission', but by 1974 he could see that a range of reform movements in Britain were beginning to formally organize and distinguish themselves from one another. He felt that members of the *Ahl-i-Ḥadīth* were being marginalized and excluded amid this organizing process, and he therefore decided to form a separate body, the *Jamiat Ahl-e-Hadith*, with assistance from two students from the Islamic University of Medina.

The scale of the movement in Britain is proportionate to its size and influence in South Asia. Azami estimated the number of followers who held formal membership of the *Jamiat Ahl-e-Hadith* in Britain UK at 5,000 but thought that its overall following was likely to be about 9,000. The movement's website claims that there are forty-two branches in the UK, centred in London/theSouth, the Midlands and Northern England, with two in Scotland, but some branches do not necessarily have their own premises or mosque. The headquarters of the movement is in Small Heath (Green Lane Mosque) and Alum Rock in Birmingham.

### LOCAL AND NATIONAL REPRESENTATION OF MUSLIMS IN BRITAIN

The quest for local and national representation for Muslims in public life and vis-à-vis the state was not an urgent concern in the years immediately after the Second World War. Most Muslims who arrived in Britain

---

[28] www.ahlehadith.co.uk/

for unskilled and semi-skilled work in the post-war years did not envisage either the eventual migration of their families, or their permanent long-term settlement in Britain. Those formal or semi-formal associations that were formed by Muslims in Britain in the 1960s and 1970s tended to revolve around the interests of particular ethnic groups, and were often internally directed initiatives which aimed to provide practical help and support in terms of housing, employment, immigration or welfare. They were often highly localized projects. 'Community leaders' arose out of these projects, and such individuals often went on to acquire a role as representatives of Muslims, especially locally (Burlet and Reid 1998).[29] They were rarely religious specialists, but rather educated Muslim professionals, such as doctors, businessmen, and lawyers, with a strong command of English (Dahya 1973: 259). Many had connections to the Islamic Movement, and especially with the various expressions of the *Jamā'at-i Islāmī* in Britain.

Pnina Werbner's study of Pakistanis in Manchester describes the process whereby 'community leadership' emerged in the 1970s and 1980s (Werbner 1990: chapter 10), and it is clear that, then as now, much depended upon establishing trust and esteem within 'the community', but also the ability to make generous and often extravagant donations to local causes. These donations constitute

highly potent symbolic acts ... and serve to increase individual power and influence. Through such public generosity, members of an elite establish their credentials as men of high status, and attempt to legitimize their claims to positions of leadership. The basic attitude [is one of] benevolent paternalism – it is the duty of the rich to represent the community and themselves to carry the cost in time, money and effort. In return they expect a measure of prestige and personal kudos. (Werbner 1990: 306)

Through giving, they are indicating some degree of willingness to take responsibility, thus establishing their credentials for the assumption of power and leadership (Gouldner 1973, cited in Werbner 1990: 311). These individuals were (and many still are) willing to give their time and personal resources to community development and welfare.

However, being largely self-appointed, they have not always achieved a mandate for their eventual 'representative' role, so the degree to which they can be regarded as legitimately reflecting the real needs and interests

---

[29] The role of local community leaders has sometimes extended beyond their immediate geographic area, and they have gone on to acquire a role as 'representative' of Muslim interests for an entire county, region or nation.

of local Muslim communities is problematic (Burlet and Reid 1996; Burlet and Reid 1998; Dahya 1973):

The fact that Asian [Muslim] immigrant brokers ['community leaders'] are often 'middle class', educated, wealthy or anglicized is generally regarded as a key aspect of their non-representative status. The implicit critique of this apparent 'leadership from the periphery' tends, however, to miss the essentially dualistic orientation of immigrant groups, their tendency to stress, in certain contexts, the values they *share* with the wider society. [Community leaders] have mastered some aspects of the wider culture and are concerned to bridge the gap between the community and the society as a whole. They do so by attempting to increase their influence among local politicians and other representatives of the state. In their negotiations with them the emphasis is placed upon shared symbols and values. (Werbner 1990: 321–2)

Werbner thus argues that the 'non-representative' status of community leaders should not be seen as entirely problematic. By hosting formal dinners for the benefit of local MPs and other non-Muslim civic leaders, organizers are manifestly articulating a discourse which demonstrates that Muslim communities are becoming embedded in wider society. The personalities are less important than the discourse itself, she argues, especially in a context where Muslim communities are still in a position of relative political weakness.

Many of the organizations founded by 'community leaders' have been enduring, and have helped to establish better understanding about Islam and Muslims in civil society. The organization of public events, formal charity dinners and educational events to which local dignitaries and politicians can be invited are effective means for helping to build bridges of local understanding (Werbner 1990). As an outcome of their efforts, community leaders have often acquired a certain amount of semi-official recognition and status as 'representatives' of Muslim communities in the locality vis-à-vis the state (Saifullah-Khan 1976), as evidenced by their role as spokesmen (and they are nearly all men) (McKerl 2007) in the local media and in local political forums, but in reality they may be able to exert influence rather than actual power (Dahya 1973).

However, the role and influence of British Muslim 'community leaders' is being somewhat superseded (or at least supplemented) by the emergence in the past two decades of a new group of professional specialists engaged in anti-racist and other equality work. Furthermore 'traditional male leaderships are being challenged by the political participation of well-educated professional women in public spaces' (McLoughlin 2005a: 545), as well as by the emergence of vibrant youth organizations. Despite these signs of change, Kundnani remains highly critical of the influence wielded by some local 'community leaders' and their respective organizations:

these organizations have little interest in mobilizing at the grassroots in struggles for social justice or civil rights; it is rather the state that they aim to mobilize to intervene in the community on their behalf – for example by funding educational and cultural activities that endorse their ideology. The result is, often, the closing down of spaces, particularly for the young and for women, where communities can come together to tackle the injustices they face. (Kundnani 2007a: 183)

There are obvious local exceptions to this somewhat generalized view,[30] but Kundnani's observation nevertheless encourages a critical view of how the state, both locally and nationally, engages with minority groups, including Muslims. As far as he is concerned, it is simply an 'updated version of colonial-style strategies' whereby the state selectively supports those individuals 'who are chosen on the basis of their effectiveness in containing dissent and serving strategic interests, often as much linked to foreign policy as domestic affairs' (Kundnani 2007a: 181).

If there is truth in this observation, it is much easier to discern at the national level, than at the local level. By looking at the emergence and long-term fortunes of bodies that have aimed to represent Muslims nationally, the essentially problematic and politicized nature of 'representation' becomes clear.

The first attempt to establish a national platform for the representation of British Muslims after the Second World War came in 1970, with the foundation of the Union of Muslim Organizations (UMO) established by Syed Aziz Pasha. This organization is still active today, but has never really achieved the representative status it was established to provide. There are a number of reasons for this. Firstly, its creation was premature relative to the development of Muslim communities in Britain more generally. During the 1970s, many of the religious movements discussed above and in the previous chapter were primarily concerned with their own interests and immediate development needs, and thus UMO was essentially ahead of its time (Nielsen 2004: 49). Secondly, during the 1980s the Foreign Office was actively backing Saudi-linked organizations to provide national representation for Muslims. This included, for example, the

---

[30] For example, the Muslim Council of Wales has been particularly energetic in funding activities for young people (e.g. supporting the events held by the student Islamic Society).

Council of Mosques in the UK and Eire, established in 1984 through the London office of the Makkah-based Muslim World League.

As a direct response to this, a rival Council of Imams and Mosques was initiated in the same year by the late Dr Zaki Badawi, former director of the Islamic Cultural Centre in London, and later Principal of The Muslim College, in West London. This new body successfully linked mosques of *Barelwī* sympathy, although Dr Badawi was himself Egyptian and an influential graduate of Al-Azhar in Cairo. However, both these Councils were later eclipsed by the emergence of the UK Action Committee on Islamic Affairs (UKACIA) established in 1988 to co-ordinate a response to the publication of the *The Satanic Verses* by Salman Rushdie. UKACIA was an important milestone in the attempt to develop national representation for Muslims since the individuals and organizations associated with it were encouraged by the former Conservative government in 1994, and subsequently by the New Labour government, to establish a Muslim Council of Britain (MCB) (Radcliffe 2004).[31] Modelled along the same lines as the Board of Deputies of British Jews, this body was eventually formed in November 1997, and brought together a range of Sunni Muslim groups reflecting diverse schools of thought. Both then and now, activists reflecting *Jamā'at-i Islāmī* and *Deobandī* sympathies predominate, and there are some notable omissions in make-up, with Shī'a and *Barelwī* Muslims having only a limited presence (Pedziwiatr 2007).

The extent to which British Muslims perceive the MCB to be representative has fluctuated over the first decade of its existence. While some 400 British Muslim organizations, such as mosques and religious centres, are affiliated to the MCB, it has been accused of being out of touch, remote and elitist, and presenting a monolithic view of Muslim opinion to government, media and policy-makers (Radcliffe 2004: 371). Not surprisingly, much of this criticism has come from *Barelwī* perspectives. However, the degree to which government has regarded the MCB as the representative body for Islamic affairs in Britain has also fluctuated over time. In the period immediately following the invasion of Afghanistan in 2001, the government expected the MCB to manage British Muslim anger at the 'war on terror' (Kundnani 2007b: 182), but under increasing pressure from the grassroots the MCB eventually spoke out critically about

---

[31] The evolution of the MCB was encouraged by New Labour's consultative style of government. It was essentially looking for a 'one-stop shop' for partnership projects and consultation: www.mcb.org.uk

British foreign policy, thus winning some new credibility from a new constituency of British Muslims (Birt 2005a; 'MCB comeback?' 2007).[32]

In the years following the London bombings of July 2005, the government has 'fundamentally rebalanced' its relationship with British Muslim organizations (Ware 2006) on the grounds that the MCB has been regarded as not having tried hard enough to combat terrorism and extremism. The result has been active government support for the new British Muslim Forum and Sufi Muslim Council, not because they are necessarily considered to be any more 'representative' than the MCB, but simply because they are regarded as less openly critical of government foreign policy (Kundnani 2007b; Pedziwiatr 2007). Kundnani is not optimistic about the consequences, and nor is he alone in his criticism of this direction (Bodi 2006):

This double state strategy of seeking suitably compliant community leaders who can act as surrogate voices for their community, while, at the same time, demonizing that community and systematically violating its civil rights, is the worst possible combination for creating a genuinely cohesive society. Its effect is to generate a permanent state of fear, anger and resentment among the 'suspect community', whilst suppressing any kind of constructive public expression of those feelings. (Kundnani 2007b: 182)

CONCLUSION

The Islamic religious movements established in colonial India were trying to define correct and authentic religious practice in an atmosphere of religious competition, and under the rule of a foreign colonial power. The positions these movements adopted in relation to one another, to other faith communities and to their rulers have to some extent been reproduced in Britain. Past precedents have provided templates for how Muslims might live as a minority group in multi-faith Britain. Many of the same questions about authenticity, authority, correct practice and, in particular, relations with the State at both local and national level are being contested once again. Centripetal and centrifugal forces are being exerted simultaneously upon British Muslims. On the one hand there is

[32] For an insightful discussion of the issues bound up with 'representation' and 'leadership' of Muslims in Britain, and especially the MCB's role, see the analysis and deconstruction of the BBC *Panorama* programme ('A Question of Leadership') broadcast on 21 August 2005, in *'The Search for Common Ground: Muslims, non-Muslims and the UK Media. A report commissioned by the Mayor of London'*, 2007. London: Greater London Authority, pp. 75–98, www.london.gov.uk/mayor/equalities/docs/commonground_report.pdf

a clear need for a united voice on issues of common concern,[33] but on the other, the divisions that have historically and theologically divided Muslim communities constitute obstacles to unity.

However, as this chapter has also demonstrated, not all British Muslims actively identify with a particular school of thought, and the question of which organizations or individuals should 'represent' them in the public sphere can seem very remote from daily lived experience. Their own 'self-representation' and personal development within family life, within educational and employment settings, or within local religious institutions is, for many, a much more immediately pressing consideration. Just how this is playing out in the rapidly moving context of early twenty-first-century Britain is not always easy to establish. It forms, however, much of the narrative and the subject matter of the second part of the book.

[33] Most recently, twenty-one major British Muslim organizations wrote a joint letter to the Prime Minister, published in *The Guardian* newspaper, expressing their concerns regarding the atrocities in Gaza in December 2008 (*The Guardian,* 31 December 2008). The BMF, BMI, MCB, ISB, the UKIM and the Stop the War Coalition were among them (see list of abbreviations for full names of these organizations).

PART II

# Contemporary dynamics

The focus of this book now turns to the organizations and activities that sustain British Muslims, individually and corporately, in their religious identity and practice. Prefaced by a chapter that provides a socio-demographic profile of Muslim communities, the later chapters explore the ways in which religious identity and individual development are shaped by family life, by education, by religious leaders and institutions, and then by gender. The progress and success of British Muslim media, artistic, sporting, political, cultural and trading initiatives are sketched in the final chapter, and this indicates the many ways in which Muslims have become embedded within, and contribute to, wider British society.

Through this thematic exploration, the dynamics and dynamism of British Muslims are emphasized. These chapters portray the myriad ways in which Islamic traditions have found new expression in Britain through the entrepreneurialism and creativeness of individuals and organizations. Particular attention is drawn to the different ways in which British Muslim youth negotiate not only their cultural inheritance but also their religious identity. At the same time, it becomes evident that many young Muslims are actively participating in the world that is most relevant to them, namely modern (and largely secular) Britain and Europe, without succumbing to either passive assimilation or unquestioning acceptance of exploitative materialism.

Within this dynamism there are nonetheless tensions. Many Muslims, both in Britain and further afield, are engaged in an effort to determine what is Islamically 'non-negotiable', while also establishing what may be legitimately subject to change in the light of new circumstances. So, for example, some British Muslim religious leaders draw upon the example of the Prophet Muhammad in order to find a 'role model' for their relatively new involvement in publicly funded chaplaincy in prisons and hospitals. Within the domestic sphere, ways of contracting marriages are both 'traditional', in that conventions of modesty and parental involvement are usually maintained, and yet at the same time 'modern', where dedicated internet sites and chat rooms provide an opportunity for 'meeting' a potential spouse on-line. Through the discussion that follows, it becomes clear that intergenerational conflict is often the fulcrum where the struggle to reconcile forces of tradition and change is taking place.

At the heart of this struggle for reconciliation is a particular tension between individual and communal aspirations. To what extent can individuality and personal agency, so valued in Western societies, be negotiated within the structures and expectations of communities and family traditions, and also within the basic principles of Islam? Members of other faith traditions are no doubt engaged in similar debates and struggles. Unlike other faith communities, however, British Muslims are subject to heightened political and media visibility that makes their particular efforts especially public, and increasingly subject to (often uninformed) scrutiny, comment and intervention.

The following chapters attempt to describe and analyse some of these inner dynamics and social interrelations of British Muslim communities. They identify some of the new institutions and initiatives that have ensured a vibrant and increasingly self-confident social nexus for future generations.

# CHAPTER 5

# Profiling British Muslim communities

## INTRODUCTION

This chapter examines Muslim communities in Britain today from a demographic and sociological perspective. British Muslims are profiled here in terms of age, gender, ethnicity, household composition, residential patterns, geographic distribution, employment, health and socio-economic status. These are of course major topics in their own right, and some of them have been systematically studied in depth. For the purposes of this book, a survey of some of the most significant patterns and trends is provided to contextualize later discussion, and reference to more in-depth research is provided accordingly.

Unless otherwise stated, much of the statistical data in this chapter is derived from the findings of the 2001 Census, and especially from a series of reports, Focus on Religion.[1] Understanding of the demography and socio-economic structure of Muslim communities in Britain has also been substantially improved owing to quantitative analysis of 2001 Census data conducted by Serena Hussain, as part of doctoral research (Hussain, S. 2004; Hussain, S. 2008). It is worth noting, therefore, the time-bound nature of the evidence in this chapter, but the level of detail arising from the 2001 Census is such that it is likely to inform debate and policy-making until the next Census in 2011. During the intervening period there will inevitably have been significant changes in the Muslim demographic profile, particularly in terms of population growth.

Mutual self-interest on the part of British Muslims and national government has been a significant driver for gaining better information and statistical evidence in recent years. Muslims have pressed for greater recognition and more equitable service provision on the basis of their religious identity, and in so doing they have argued for the production of accurate

---

[1] 'Focus on Religion' – National Statistics Online: www.statistics.gov.uk/cci/nugget.asp?id=964. Also see Peach (2006) for an overview of Muslims in the 2001 Census.

evidence to support their claims. The collection of more detailed information enables better internal Muslim community planning and prioritization, as well as more effective lobbying of government and other service providers.[2] From a government perspective, the social capital bound up in 'faith communities' is being increasingly harnessed and co-opted as part of government regeneration initiatives and community cohesion projects. In this way, data about the size and character of faith groups has become a valuable government resource in shaping and meeting strategic equality and diversity targets (Weller 2004). The main outcome of these social and political processes was the inclusion of a voluntary question about religion in the 2001 Census in England and Wales, for the first time since 1851.[3]

Against the background of relatively little quantitative research about Muslims in Britain, there were, during the early and mid 1990s, increasing calls for a question on religion to be included within the 2001 Census.[4] British Muslims were supported in their campaign by the Commission for Racial Equality, the Inner Cities Religious Council, the Board of Deputies of British Jews, the Runnymede Trust, the British Sikh Federation and the Home Secretary's Race Relations Forum, to name but a few organizations (Aspinall 2000). Prominent academics (especially sociologists and policy advisers) supported the move. However, the campaign orchestrated within the Muslim community was reinforced also by a number of the theological premises existing within Islam itself. It has been suggested, for instance, that 'Muslims have a strong dislike for "ethnic" labels' (Sardar 1996), owing to the racially inclusive ethos of Islam. For many Muslims, their religious identity is the only one that really 'counts'. Therefore, the inclusion of a question on religion in the 2001 Census meant that Muslims could define themselves on their own terms, rather than upon the basis of classifications imposed by others. Moreover, one might argue that it is more useful for the government to be aware of how significant sections of the population truly understand themselves.

---

[2] For a full account of the efforts by sections of the Muslim community for a question on religion in the Census see www.mcb.org.uk/downloads/census2001.pdf. For an overview of the wider social and political processes leading to the inclusion of the religion question(s) see Southworth (2005).

[3] For technical information on the religion question in the 2001 Census see www.statistics.gov.uk/cci/nugget.asp?id=984

[4] The 2001 Census was the first to ask a question about religion (in England and Wales) since 1851. The question was voluntary, but was answered by 92 per cent of the population. The Scottish Census asked additional questions about religion (a) to determine the denominational differences within the category 'Christian', and (b) to measure conversion/religious change (a question about religion of *upbringing*).

THE SIZE OF THE BRITISH MUSLIM POPULATION

Establishing with some degree of accuracy how many Muslims there are in Britain has been a matter of concern for decades, both within and outside Muslim communities. From the mid 1970s, articles began to appear in British Muslim publications, debating the total number of Muslims in Britain then estimated at about 500,000 (Huq 1975). With the gradual realization of the 'myth of return', planning for the future became a priority, and this could not be done without some sense of scale and demographics. Furthermore, Muslims realized that their claims for recognition and economic support as a distinctive religious minority group would be more successful if their overall numerical strength was measured, using the best available sources of data. For several decades, this meant extrapolating from the Census. Using figures for the size of different ethnic groups, and then estimating the percentage of Muslims within each ethnic group, a rough figure for the composition and size of the British Muslim population could be established. For example, in 1991 it was safe to assume that the vast majority of the 476,000 Pakistanis in Britain were Muslim; likewise the 162,835 Bangladeshis. The outcome of this rather haphazard process of guesswork was widely varying estimates of the number of Muslims in Britain. For several decades, the range was anything between 550,000 and 3 million (Anwar 1993b; Aspinall 2000), with the most common estimate being about 1 million to 1.5 million.

According to the 2001 Census, the Muslim population of England and Wales in 2001 was 1.54 million, with about 40,000 Muslims in Scotland (Census 2001; General Register Office, Scotland). The estimated total British Muslim population was therefore around 1.6 million.[5] Muslims constituted about 3 per cent of the British population in 2001, but this percentage has increased in recent years. New figures from the Labour Force Survey (Office of National Statistics) published early in 2009 estimated a figure of 2.4 million Muslims in Britain (and constituting 4 per cent of the population) (Kerbaj 2009). This significant increase in the intervening years may be attributed to recent immigration, the growing birth rate (Penn and Lambert 2002), some conversion to Islam, and perhaps also an increased willingness to self-identify as 'Muslim' on account of the 'war on terror'.

---

[5] The Muslim population in Britain is rapidly increasing on account of the high birth rate. 'The Muslim population has the youngest marrying age for women so ... Muslims also have the highest actual and potential fertility rate' (Beckford *et al.* 2006: 17).

The 2001 Census provided data for Muslim religious identification. It is more difficult to assess the significance of this affiliation, in terms of how it relates to actual belief and practice. Census data is therefore best understood as reflecting the broad religious background of a section of the population. One newspaper report in 2002 estimated the size of the active, practising Muslim population at 760,000.[6] However, a study in the mid 1990s found that 74 per cent of Muslims reported their religion as being 'very important' to them (Modood *et al.* 1997: 301). This latter figure suggests a much larger practising and actively engaged religious community.

The 2001 Census provided for the first time some insight into the approximate number of converts to Islam in Britain. This is because the Census questionnaire in Scotland included a question not only on religious affiliation, but also on religion of birth. The findings from these questions exploded the myth that Islam is Britain's fastest-growing religion on account of new converts. Any rapid growth in the size of the Muslim population in Britain derives from higher birth rates and new immigration, not conversion. The evidence from Scotland suggested that Islam is the religion people are 'least likely to leave, or convert to' (Birt 2003: 20). The Scottish data revealed that only 3 per cent of Muslims were converts (59 per cent converting from Christian denominations; 27 per cent converting from a non-religious background; the rest converting from other faiths).

If the Scottish data is used as a model for speculation on conversion to Islam in the rest of Britain, at the time of the 2001 Census the global figure is 14,200 converts, of which about 61 per cent were white, 31 per cent were Black Caribbean, with the remainder from South Asian ethnic backgrounds (Birt 2003: 20). Assuming that converts still constitute approximately 0.9 per cent of the Muslim population, as they did in 2001, there are likely to be approximately 20,000 to 21,000 converts in Britain today.

The phenomenon of conversion has been the subject of several academic studies (Kose 1996; Zebiri 2008). These consistently point to the fact that converts often choose the path of Islam in the face of disillusionment with 'Western' morals and attitudes, and after a long period of careful study of Islamic texts and doctrines. Zebiri regards converts as

---

[6] The Guardian Research Department, 'Special Report: Muslim Britain, The Statistics' – 17 June 2002. Cited in Open Society Institute, *Muslims in the UK: Policies for Engaged Citizens* 2005, p. 111.

Table 2. *Local authority areas in Britain with the highest*
*Muslim populations based on 2001 Census*

Tower Hamlets – 71,000 (36%)
Newham – 59,000 (24%)
Blackburn – 27,000 (19%)
Bradford – 75,000 (16%)
Waltham Forest – 33,000 (15%)
Luton – 27,000 (15%)
Birmingham – 140,000 (14%)
Hackney – 28,000 (14%)
Pendle – 12,000 (13%)
Slough – 16,000 (13%)
Brent – 32,000 (12%)
Redbridge – 29,000 (12%)
Westminster – 21,000 (12%)
Camden – 23,000 (12%)
Haringey – 24,000 (11%)

'making a disproportionate contribution to the indigenization of Islamic practice, thought and discourse in the West' (Zebiri 2008: 1). In reality, it may simply be that converts are disproportionately more active in their newly adopted religion, and more vocal.

## GEOGRAPHICAL DISTRIBUTION

Throughout history, Muslims have settled in those British towns and cities that have offered the best prospects for employment and entrepreneurialism. The opportunities for work (especially in the post-Second World War period) and the sustenance of South Asian kinship networks and 'chain migration' mean that Britain's Muslims are unevenly distributed around the country: 'Muslims are disproportionately represented in the most deprived urban communities – 75 per cent live in 24 cities or authorities … and within these cities Muslims are highly concentrated spatially' (Open Society Institute 2005: 13).

Many local authority areas have a significant Muslim population. For instance, 36 per cent of the population of Tower Hamlets in East London is Muslim. In contrast, some areas record few, if any, Muslims living within them. An example is the Isles of Scilly, which at the time of the Census had none. Furthermore, in those local authority areas with high numbers of Muslims, particular ethnic groups sometimes dominate. So, for example, the Muslim population of Tower Hamlets overwhelmingly comprises Bangladeshis, as opposed to Pakistanis or Arabs. In fact, Bangladeshi Muslims are much less evenly distributed compared, for example, to Pakistani Muslims. On the whole, Bangladeshis are concentrated in large numbers in fewer areas (Anwar and Bakhsh 2003: 10).

South Asian Muslims predominate in northern England and the West Midlands, but the Muslim population of London represents the largest overall concentration and is much more diverse. About 1 million Muslims live in London, where they constitute 8 per cent of the overall population and represent around 38 per cent of all the Muslims in Britain. About 14 per cent of Muslims live in the West Midlands area, and there are other significant communities in the north-east (Middlesbrough and Newcastle-upon-Tyne), the north-west, the south-west (Bristol and Gloucester), and the Yorkshire and Humber regions.

### THE ETHNICITY OF BRITISH MUSLIMS

The term 'ethnicity' refers to a social group bound together by a more or less shared sense of historical (and sometimes geographical) origins which may be based upon language, culture, religion and so on. It is therefore to be distinguished from 'race', 'kinship' or 'nation', mainly because there is some degree of flexibility in ethnic identification according to context or circumstances. Around three-quarters of Britain's Muslim population is from an Asian ethnic background, particularly Pakistani (43 per cent), Bangladeshi (17 per cent), Indian (9 per cent) and Other Asian (6 per cent). A further 6 per cent of Muslims are of Black African origin (especially Somalia, Nigeria and other North and West African countries). Some 4 per cent of Muslims described themselves as of white British origin, and a further 7 per cent from another white background (including Arabs, Turks, Cypriots and East Europeans – especially refugees from Bosnia, Albania and Kosovo) (Peach 2006).

Bangladeshis are the most homogeneous ethnic group within the Muslim community, with nearly all originating from the Sylhet district of Bangladesh. In contrast, Britain's Pakistani community traces its origins back to the Punjab, Mirpur in Azad Kashmir, and Afghan border districts (Pathans), each region having its own distinctive language, culture and so on. So while most Muslims in Britain share a common religious identity, the expression of their faith is likely to be shaped by their ethnic or national origins. For example, when it comes to dress, there are many

Table 3. *Muslims in Britain by age, 2008*

| | |
|---|---|
| 0–9 | 537,000 |
| 10–19 | 405,000 |
| 20–29 | 502,000 |
| 30–39 | 440,000 |
| 40–49 | 257,000 |
| 50–59 | 156,000 |
| 60–69 | 68,000 |
| 70+ | 56,000 |

(*Source:* Labour Force Survey, UK Government
Office of National Statistics, January 2009)

different stylistic interpretations of how to conform to Islamic expect-ations of modesty. Even among distinctive ethnic groups, such as Pathans or Sylhetis, the fluid and changeable nature of ethnicity is evident in the cultural fusions and transformations taking place among young British-born Muslims.

### AGE AND GENDER

The Muslim population in Britain is demographically 'young'. Around 50 per cent are under the age of twenty-five. In contrast, only about 5 per cent of Muslims in Britain are over the age of sixty, compared to the aver-age (in England) of 20 per cent. The average age of Muslims in Britain is twenty-eight, thirteen years below the national average (Open Society Institute 2005). Given the age profile of Muslims in Britain, 'government policies aimed at children and young people will have a disproportionate impact on Muslim communities' (Open Society Institute 2005: 13) and should thus be drafted and implemented with sensitivity to the needs of Muslims.

On account of the recent immigration history of Muslims to Britain, men slightly outnumber women by a ratio of 52 per cent to 48 per cent, but among younger Muslims there is a more equal proportion of males and females.

### COUNTRY OF BIRTH AND LANGUAGE USE

Nearly half of the Muslims living in Britain were born in this country (46 per cent), the remainder having been born in Pakistan (18 per cent),

Bangladesh (9 per cent) and other Muslim majority states. This is already having implications for the self-description and identity of younger Muslims, who increasingly think of themselves as 'British Muslims' as opposed to Asians or Pakistanis (Afshar *et al.* 2005; Hussain and Bagguley 2005; Jacobson 1998). Regardless of country of origin, the large majority of Muslims in Britain hold British citizenship, on account of the fact that the British Nationality Act of 1948 gave citizens of the Commonwealth the right to enter, work and settle with their families in the UK as permanent residents (Open Society Institute, 'Monitoring Minority Protection in the EU: the situation of Muslims in the UK' 2002: 135). Later legislation in 1981 (British Nationality Act) confirmed their right to citizenship, for themselves and their children.

Country of birth bears some relation to language use. The predominant languages spoken by Muslims in Britain are thus English, followed by Urdu and Punjabi (and related dialects, such as Mirpuri), Pushto, Bengali (especially the Sylheti dialect), Arabic, Turkish, Somali and Gujarati. The now somewhat dated Fourth National Survey of Ethnic Minorities (1997) estimated that among South Asians in Britain, about three-quarters of men spoke English fluently or fairly well, but among Pakistani and Bangladeshi women only 54 per cent and 40 per cent respectively were competent speakers of English (Modood *et al.* 1997: 60). These figures are likely to have changed in the years since the Fourth Survey was conducted, but the key variables for language use are still likely to be significant, such as gender, length of residence in Britain, age and the proportion of people of the same ethnic background in the neighbourhood. Older Muslim women of South Asian origin (particularly those who came to Britain later in life), living in communities where more than 10 per cent of residents are of a similar background, are therefore still probably the least likely to be able to speak English fluently (Modood *et al.* 1997: 62).

## HOUSEHOLDS AND RESIDENTIAL PATTERNS

On the whole, British Muslims live in inner-city, formerly run-down, areas with an inherited high general level of housing deprivation (Anwar and Bakhsh 2003: 30). Among the key issues are overcrowding and poor housing quality. It is also clear that there are too few affordable properties that can accommodate Muslim families which are, on average, larger than the national average. The average household size for Muslims (in England) in 2001 was 3.8 (compared to the national average of 2.4), and one third of Muslim households (34 per cent) contained five or more people. Compared to other faith groups, households headed by a Muslim are more likely to contain children; 63 per cent of Muslim households had at least one dependent child, and 25 per cent had three or more dependent children. These findings reflect the younger age structure of the Muslim population, and the socio-cultural norms and expectations within many Muslim communities.

Above-average family size, and the concentration of Muslim households in flats or terraced homes, means that Muslims in Britain experience a higher than average degree of overcrowding. This is an indicator of low income and possibly unhealthy physical and mental living conditions (Beckford *et al.* 2006: 19). One-third of Muslim households (32 per cent) lived in overcrowded accommodation (just 6 per cent of Christian households experienced overcrowding). Other indicators of housing deprivation (such as lack of central heating or sole access to a bathroom) also reveal the vulnerable position of Muslims. Only 52 per cent of Muslims are homeowners, and Muslim households are the most likely to be living in social rented accommodation compared to all other faith groups; 28 per cent of Muslims were in this kind of accommodation in 2001.

Residential patterns are strongly determined by historic employment and housing opportunities. In the post-Second World War period, Pakistani and Bangladeshi migrants lived in cheap private housing located close to textile mills, and often took up unpopular night-time factory shifts (Simpson 2004). Their concentration in particular streets and neighbourhoods has been reinforced over time by the desire to live, or to remain living, close to extended family members, or associated community facilites (such as mosques). Owing to population growth and new migration, the Muslim population of some neighbourhoods has increased markedly.

The perceptions arising from this growth, particularly following the urban disturbances in Bradford, Oldham and Burnley in 2001, have led to unfounded charges of Muslim self-imposed isolationism and segregation. In the reports following these events, it was claimed that white and minority ethnic communities were living 'parallel lives' and that the disturbances reflected divisions in patterns of settlement, education, and cultural practices (Cantle 2002). Some of the assumptions behind this isolationist discourse have recently been challenged (see for example Phillips 2006; Simpson 2004), on the grounds that they fail to take sufficient account of 'the power of structural constraints (economic and institutional racism) and popular racism to shape minority ethnic housing and neighbourhood choices' (Phillips 2006: 29). In other words, it is likely that choices and decisions made by the majority white community exert a greater impact on Muslim residential patterning than the self-determining but 'bounded choices' and decisions of Muslims themselves. There are therefore both positive and negative reasons for the residential clustering of Muslims, but among the more significant negative ones are fear of racism and harassment in areas that are perceived to be 'white'. Among the positive reasons for living in close-knit communities is the availability of social, cultural and religious support that is not provided by indigenous religious and social networks (Simpson 2004). However, alongside inner-city clustering, the research conducted by Phillips and Simpson indicates that there is also a parallel process of slow outward movement to other more affluent parts of Bradford. For Simpson, who has undertaken a detailed analysis of residential patterns in Bradford in relation to overall population growth and migration, the idea of pro-active Muslim self-segregation is simply 'a myth' (Simpson 2004: 677).

## EMPLOYMENT AND THE LABOUR MARKET

'The position of Muslims in the labour market is a fundamental aspect of their position in British society' (Anwar 1993a: 38). Because of the predominance of South Asian Muslims in Britain, our understanding of British Muslims and employment is overwhelmingly shaped by the experiences of South Asians. Recognition of how this skews the data helps avoid stereotypical assumptions about the working lives of all Muslims in Britain. After all, Muslims are employed in virtually all sectors of the economy and in all levels of politics, education, business, medicine, law, media, the arts, engineering and so on.

Many South Asian Muslim men came to Britain to work in unskilled and semi-skilled occupations in manufacturing (especially textiles) and they, like everyone else in British society, were vulnerable to changes in the economy. Industrial decline in the later decades of the twentieth century meant that many Muslims had to turn to alternative means of economic activity. This often meant developing self-employment and service sector opportunities, such as taxi-driving, market-trading and catering. Despite this entrepreneurialism, Muslims in Britain are today less economically active compared to other faith groups, but 80 per cent of this economic inactivity is accounted for by the low rate of female participation in the workforce (Brown 2000; see below for further discussion).

The national average rate of economic participation for those aged over twenty-five is 67 per cent, but for Muslims the figure drops to 50 per cent. Nearly 18 per cent of Muslims aged sixteen to twenty-four are unemployed and nearly 14 per cent of those aged over twenty-five are economically inactive. In 2001–2, Bangladeshi Muslims had the highest rate of unemployment in Britain at 20 per cent, four times the rate for white British men (Cabinet Office, 'Ethnic Minorities and the Labour Market', 2003). This situation is even worse among young Bangladeshi men under the age of twenty-five, where over 40 per cent are unemployed (Cabinet Office, 'Ethnic Minorities and the Labour Market', 2003). Given these statistics, Muslims in Britain are, not surprisingly, over-represented within the lowest income bands (Brown 2000).

Economic activity or inactivity is shaped by a number of determining factors, especially gender and age: 'The odds of an individual being unemployed are found to be higher if the individual is young (16–24); male; never-married; without qualifications; lacks fluency in spoken English; lives in a ward where unemployment is relatively high … [but] the odds of being unemployed also vary significantly by religion' (Brown 2000: 1047). For example, Indian Muslims are twice as likely to be unemployed as Indian Hindus (Cabinet Office report, *Ethnic Minorities in the Labour Market*, 2003). But the relationship between religion and economic inactivity is not clear-cut, and while it is possible to demonstrate differences between (and within) religious groups in economic activity, establishing why this is the case is more difficult. For example, there are apparent differences in rates of employment *within* Muslim communities. Using data derived from the 1994 National Survey of Ethnic Minorities, Mark Brown found that more Indian Muslims than Pakistani Muslims are likely to be in full-time employment (Brown 2000), making it difficult to discern a clear 'religious effect'. In a Cabinet Office report, it was noted that 'religion may be a proxy for other factors determining employment, such as education and fluency in English … judging whether religion is a factor that affects employment chances of a given individual is complex' (Cabinet Office, *Ethnic Minorities and the Labour Market*, 2003: 33). So it is possible to speculate that those Muslims who migrated to Britain from different countries and regions brought with them different kinds of social and human capital, and that it is these differences, rather than religion, that accounts for their relative position in the economy of Britain today. This is clearly an area that warrants greater research.

For those Muslims who are in employment, their place in the labour market is vulnerable. Some 33.7 per cent of Muslim men work in semi-skilled and unskilled occupations, and they are least likely to work in senior professional roles. Only 42 per cent of Muslim men work in the main white-collar groups of the Standard Occupational Classification 2000 (managers, senior officials, professionals, associate profession-als, technical occupations, and administrative and secretarial occupa-tions) compared to the national average of 50 per cent (Beckford *et al.* 2006: 19). Compared to men from other faith groups, Muslim men are more likely to be employed (often on a self-employed basis) in spheres with little career progression, such as taxi-driving and restaurant work. In fact, according to the 2004 Labour Force Survey one Muslim man in ten was working as a taxi driver in 2004. Also in 2004, 37 per cent of Muslim men in employment were working in the distribution, hotel and restaur-ant industry compared with 17 per cent of Christian men and no more than 27 per cent of men in any other group.

One of the determining factors of British Muslim economic marginal-ity is the relatively low level of participation of women in the workforce, as noted above. According to the Census, less than 30 per cent of Muslim women in Britain over the age of twenty-five are economically active (compared to 60 per cent for all women of that age). This partly reflects the decision that many Muslim women make, especially as mothers of young children, that their primary role and responsibility is mother-hood. Islam accords a high degree of respect to the status of motherhood, and numerous Qur'ānic verses and sayings of the Prophet Muhammad allude to the important role that mothers have as those who nurture and educate future generations. This does not mean, however, that Muslim women who are mothers are confined to this role alone. Muslim commu-nities in Britain still need female teachers, for example, and those who fulfil such roles are often doing so alongside their domestic responsibil-ities. However, the way that data is collected about employment and eco-nomic activity is such that a good deal of work done by Muslim women is probably invisible to statisticians. As part of a report on 'Women and Society' conducted by the BBC (28 May 2002), Heidi Safia Mirza noted that current figures 'don't record home-working, time spent on family-run businesses, and unpaid work, so the idea that they do not participate is not very helpful' (Mirza 2002). Given the widespread transition into the service sector, it is likely that the (unpaid) labour of women is a key resource that helps to give Muslim-owned enterprises competitive advan-tage (Kalra 2000: 162), but also potentially at the expense of women's health and well-being (Afshar 1989). However, just as there are differen-tial rates of economic activity among Bangladeshi, Pakistani and Indian

Muslim men, so too there are differential rates among women from these groups. Compared to the national average, there is still a relatively low rate of Indian Muslim female employment, but it is still higher than for Pakistani and Bangladeshi Muslim women (Brown 2000).

The marginal position of Muslims in Britain in terms of economic activity and earnings is likely to have some relationship to racial or religious discrimination, actual or imagined (Bowlby and Lloyd Evans 2009). Research carried out in 2003 found that almost half of the respondents in the study perceived Muslims as being disadvantaged in the field of employment (Anwar and Bakhsh 2003). If this is the case in reality (as opposed to perception), it is serious, because Muslims are then 'disadvantaged both economically and socially, in a society which defines status largely by reference to employment' (Anwar and Bakhsh 2003: 25). Among other things, the study called for better provision for the religious needs of Muslims by employers (such as time to say prayers, or flexibility regarding religious holidays), and better protection from racism and discrimination in the workplace. In relation to the latter, new legislative measures now offer much greater protection from religious discrimination in employment, with the passing of the Employment Equality (Religion or Belief) Regulations in 2003. However, as this section has noted, the employment situation of Muslims is made complex by a wide range of issues that have little or no direct bearing on religion itself, but more upon other indicators of limited social capital and deprivation, one of which is health.

HEALTH AND WELL-BEING

Compared to other faith groups in Britain, Muslims report the highest rates of ill-health. Given the evidence presented above in relation to housing deprivation and overcrowding, employment prospects and the poverty associated with both, poor health outcomes are not surprising. In 2001, 13 per cent of Muslim men and 16 per cent of Muslim women described their health status as 'not good' compared to a national average of 8 per cent. After taking account of the different age structures of faith groups in Britain, Muslims had the highest rates of disability. Almost a quarter of Muslim females (24 per cent) had a disability, as did 21 per cent of Muslim males. Permanent sickness was reported among 8.2 per cent and 7.3 per cent of Muslim men and women respectively (Peach 2006). However, Muslims appear to be vulnerable to particular kinds of illness, such as diabetes, metabolic, heart, and respiratory diseases, frequently attributed to smoking and relatively high levels of saturated fats (oil) presumably associated with South Asian cooking.[7] A considerable amount of research has been conducted on the relative vulnerability of ethnic minorities (which includes Muslims) to particular kinds of illness (Nazroo 1997), but issues of religion have rarely been at the heart of these. However, in recent years a number of publications have emerged which consider the particular health needs and worldviews of Muslims with suggestions for how to improve their access to public health services in Britain (Gatrad 1994a; Rozario 2009; Rozario and Gilliat-Ray 2007; Sheikh and Gatrad 2000).

Alongside the use of conventional medicine, some Muslims in Britain rely upon alternative therapies and 'Islamic medicine', known as *unani tibb*. The 'medicine of the Prophet' aims to restore health and vitality from a holistic perspective, and in accordance with the sources of Islam. The degree to which Muslims resort to *tibb* practitioners, or indeed to other kinds of religious or spiritual help, varies according to the nature of the health problem, and is also likely to be conditional upon cultural background, educational levels, and understanding and practice of Islam itself. Some disorders might be perceived as being related to bad spirits (*jinn*), and imams might be consulted for help in dealing with such matters. Meanwhile, health difficulties associated with genetic disorders, for example, might be more usually regarded as biomedical in character, at least initially, and more appropriately treated with conventional therapies. Regardless of perceptions about the source of illness, however, there is evidence for a wide range of religious strategies for coping with it (Rozario 2009; Rozario and Gilliat-Ray 2007).

CONCLUSION

The 2001 Census provided evidence for the relative disadvantage of Muslims in Britain compared to other religious groups, especially in terms of housing, employment, education and health. There are a number of reasons for this generally poor socio-economic situation. Many of Britain's Muslims trace their origins back to uneducated, rural backgrounds in the Indian subcontinent. A majority of South Asian migrants arrived in Britain with little 'social capital', often limited capacity in English, worked in areas of long-term industrial decline, and resided

---

[7] A report in the BMA (25 May 2002) noted that 44 per cent of Bangladeshi men smoke (compared to 29 per cent in the general male population).

in communities characterized by multiple deprivation. The types of work available to them then (and to some extent now) not only determined income, but also settlement and residence patterns, educational opportunities, access to services and participation in civic life (Anwar 1993b). The opportunities for Muslims in Britain to improve their socio-economic prospects have therefore often been constrained by 'bounded choices' (Phillips 2006). In other words, their scope for decision-making and change is usually shaped by numerous external constraints that often serve to limit choices and possibilities. The consequences of post-Second World War housing and employment decisions continue to affect Muslims in Britain today, with nearly one-third of Muslims now living in some of the most deprived neighbourhoods in Britain, especially in London (Beckford *et al.* 2006).

In recent decades, the range and depth of qualitative and quantitative information about British Muslim communities has increased significantly. This data clearly indicates that British Muslims continue to suffer numerous structural and social disadvantages, particularly in relation to housing, education and employment. The effects of one kind of disadvantage are often compounded by others. In the past decade it has become easy for policy-makers, politicians and the media to inaccurately and unhelpfully associate this poverty and disadvantage with deliberate self-segregation. This has too often led to negative perceptions of British Muslims as a potential 'enemy within'. A more nuanced understanding of population and migration statistics, alongside an appreciation of the organizational vibrancy characteristic of British Muslims, indicates instead both entrepreneurialism and achievement, usually against the odds.

# CHAPTER 6

# Religious nurture and education

## INTRODUCTION

There are numerous Qur'ānic verses and sayings of the Prophet Muhammad regarding the formation, protection and continuity of the family. Approximately one-third of the legal injunctions in the *Qur'ān* deal with family matters (Waddy 1990). The centrality of the family in Islam is also reflected in the complexity of jurisprudence relating to marriage and the family in Islamic law, and the extent to which the *'ulamā'* direct their scholarly endeavours towards interpretation and application of legal principles in this area. Between 1992 and 1997, over 500 questions were posed to the late Dr Syed ad-Darsh, in his 'Ask the Imam' column in the British Muslim newspaper *Q-News*: most were related to family matters (Bunt 1998: 107).

According to Islamic teaching, everyone is born a Muslim, and Islam is the 'natural' religion of humankind (*dīn al-fitra*) (Murata and Chittick 2000). Whether this Muslim religious identity flourishes depends upon family upbringing, wider social environment and education. This chapter examines the two main institutions involved in the religious nurture and socialization of British Muslims: the family, and the education system (and especially that offered by Islamic institutions). British Muslims recognize the critical importance of a strong family life and effective education for the future transmission of Islam. This explains the degree to which they have sought to preserve, protect and strengthen these two central social institutions and their associated Islamic values against what is often regarded as the spiritually corrupting influence of secularism in wider British society (Bunt 1998: 103).

The centrality of the family to the preservation of Islam among future generations means that it has often also been at the centre of political debate, and at no time has this been more evident than in the past decade. For example, in 2002 the then Home Secretary, David Blunkett, called for 'British Asians' to speak English at home rather than their own community languages, such as Urdu or Punjabi, as a means of facilitating intergenerational communication within families. Not surprisingly, his comments sparked extensive debate and controversy, and for many Muslims his views were an unwelcome interference and intervention in private family life (Hinsliff 2002). In 2006 John Reid (another former British Home Secretary) made a remarkably ill-judged attempt to influence power relations between parents, children and the State. He called upon Muslim parents to keep a watchful eye upon their children, in order to prevent them from being 'groomed' by religious extremists intent upon recruitment to terrorist activity (Johnston 2006). Not surprisingly, many British Muslim commentators rejected the suggestion that parents should 'spy' on their children, and argued that his words created an unhelpful climate of fear and suspicion. The suggestion made in February 2008 by the Archbishop of Canterbury, Dr Rowan Williams, that some aspects of Islamic legal procedure (especially in relation to family law) might be accommodated alongside English civil law has also been controversial in some quarters (Williams 2008). This is because he raised a fundamental issue about whether British Muslim *Shari'ah* Councils should remain semi-autonomous, private and mainly informal, or become more formally recognized by the mainstream legal system.[1]

Islamic education and schools have been equally contested arenas of State intervention in recent history since both parents and society at large have an interest in the kind of values and norms transmitted to the next generation of citizens. So from the 1970s onwards, British Muslim parents have actively campaigned for mainstream schools to take account of the religious needs and identities of their children in relation to issues such as uniforms, school meals and the curriculum (Anwar 1983; Iqbal 1977; Joly 1995; Parker-Jenkins 1995). Meanwhile, they have also sought to establish their own voluntary aided faith schools (Halstead 1986; Hewer 2001; Nielsen 1989; Parker-Jenkins 2002; Tinker 2006). The activities of some Islamic groups operating within higher education institutions have created media headlines over the years (Gilliat-Ray 2000), as have the teachers and teaching methods used in some mosque-based *madāris* and *makātib* (Raza 1991). From 2007 onwards, the government has been looking critically at the teaching of 'Islamic studies' at universities in England

---

[1] See Bano (1999; 2007) for more details regarding the complexity of this issue.

(Siddiqui 2007).[2] These moves have been highlighted avidly by the media, with the result that Islamic education and schooling have become politicized in a way that the educational choices of other faith communities in Britain have not.

Although these controversies cannot be ignored, this chapter aims to focus instead upon the less public and often more subtle role of family life and Islamic community-based education in the religious nurture of British Muslims. By understanding some of the ways in which families aim to build and sustain religious identity, and the role of both formal and informal educational systems as part of this process, we can gain insight into dimensions of British Muslim life that are often inaccessible and hidden to outsiders.

## ISLAMIC APPROACHES TO THE FAMILY: A BRIEF OVERVIEW

The family is a central social institution for Muslims, providing the framework for emotional, social and financial stability. Islamic law reflects the mutual obligations that rest within family relationships that are intended to ensure the security, well-being and moral nurturing of the next generation, care and respect for the elderly, and protection of the weak and vulnerable. These networks of obligation extend, however, beyond the immediate nuclear family. The Arabic word for 'family', *ahl* is a comprehensive term, the meaning of which extends beyond immediate family relationships, to include grandparents, aunts, uncles, and cousins (Fernea 1995). As a consequence, Muslims often regard their family as including all their extended kin. British Muslims originating from South Asia often use the word *birādarī* (which literally means 'brotherhood') to refer to this wider kinship network, and there is an extensive vocabulary to describe different extended family relationships, and the mutual obligations that pertain to these various relations.

The primary textual sources of Islam, the *Qur'ān* and *Hadīth*, are especially concerned with establishing the principles for the regulation of conduct between spouses, and between parents and their children. Islamic law enables the practical application of these principles in individual circumstances, in matters such as inheritance, divorce and the custody of

---

[2] The scope of this chapter does not allow for detailed consideration of British Muslims in higher education, but for recent research on this subject see Ahmad, F. (2007); Appleton (2005a); Modood (2005a; 2006).

children. Values such as respect, decency, honour, mercy, kindness, self-sacrifice, generosity and love are encouraged, particularly in relation to parents and especially towards mothers (*Sūrah* 17: 23–4: *Sūrah* 29: 8: *Sūrah* 31:14; *Sūrah* 46: 15–18).

The Prophet Muhammad provides an example to Muslims (especially men) for considerate conduct within the household. His wife, Aisha, reported that he was fully involved in family life, and regularly engaged in household chores, from preparing food and sewing his own clothes, to repairing his shoes (Ramadan 2007: 168). Although the Prophetic example suggests that the practical business of running the home is ideally a shared activity and joint responsibility within the marital relationship, Islam nevertheless confers leadership and authority upon the husband as the head of the household, and the person primarily responsible for its material and financial well-being. However, the example of the Prophet once again suggests that this leadership role should be undertaken in a spirit of negotiation and consensus-seeking: 'Muhammad had accustomed his wives to attention and dialogue … he listened to their advice' (Ramadan 2007: 168).

If the breadwinner role is the primary responsibility of men, women are first and foremost responsible for (and ideally respected for) the part they play as mothers in the transmission of values, and the religious education of the next generation. Numerous verses of the *Qur'ān* allude to the importance of the motherly role, and the duties incumbent upon men to support their wives in their childcare duties, even to the extent that a Muslim woman can require payment from her husband for breastfeeding a baby. In a study of how male Muslim community leaders in East London represent women's roles and the family, they were emphatic in their affirmation of women's responsibilities:[3]

> There is a big responsibility, as far as Quran and Hadiths are concerned … the mother is the first nursery for a child. If she provides good moral values to a child, he will be a successful person … (Howe 2007: 11)

Given this role as the guardians of future collective identity, women's bodies and sexuality have been subject to particular expectations of modesty. The parental family will normally be responsible for ensuring the (hetero)sexual purity of women prior to their marriage as a way of

---

[3] This emphasis upon the role of women ignores the obvious importance of fathers in child-rearing. This is an issue that has been raised in the British Muslim press in recent years (Khan 2004a), and by organizations such as Fathers Direct and the An-Nisa Society (Khan 2007).

ensuring the future 'production' of community, both biologically and
culturally.

Although marriage is a social and religious contract in Islam rather
than a sacrament, it nevertheless has profoundly spiritual dimensions.
The joining together of husband and wife in order to raise children as
God-fearing and devout Muslims, marriage and procreation, are widely
regarded by observant Muslims as a form of worship (*'ibādah*) which can
bring spiritual rewards in this life and the next. Unlike those world religions that regard celibacy as a means of religious discipline, Islam dis-
courages this lifestyle and promotes marriage and family life as a means
of salvation. Children are viewed as a blessing within Islam, not least
because they provide parents and others with the opportunity to emulate
the care and kindness that the Prophet Muhammad himself extended to
children (Mogra 2005).

Ideas of modesty and the importance of marriage and family (and
especially the role that women play) have been remarkably persistent
throughout Islamic history and within a variety of Islamic societies.
When Muslims find themselves living as a minority group, assumptions
about the importance of family life and the religious nurture of children
can often take on particular significance. In a society that does not reflect
Islamic values, traditions and practices, family relations and domestic
homes play an even more critical role in religious nurture and education.

## MUSLIM HOUSEHOLDS IN BRITAIN

The structure and make-up of Muslim households in Britain have changed
considerably over the course of the past four decades. The 1970s and 1980s
saw the arrival of many Muslim women, mainly from South Asia, to join
their menfolk in Britain. The change in household structure, from temporary male residence to permanent family settlement, led to a reinvigoration of Muslim family life. The arrival of women and children and
a new generation of British-born Muslims provided the impetus for the
revival of religious nurture and education, centred on the family. It also
gave rise to a new genre of academic literature, especially ethnographic
monographs, which reflected a predominant concern with issues such as
migration and kinship systems, household arrangements, gender relations
and family honour. According to Ahmad, with notable exceptions (such
as Brah 1996), generalizing assumptions about the insular, repressive and
constraining structure of most Muslim/South Asian families were both
implicit and explicit in much of the research and writing about British

Muslim families in the 1980s and 1990s, contributing to their pathologization in the popular imagination (Ahmad 2006: 274).

At the time of the 2001 Census, there were 400,000 Muslim households in Britain. The composition and socio-economic situation of these households has been systematically investigated by Serena Hussain (Hussain, S. 2008), and her analysis shows that many of the Islamic ideals regarding marriage, children and the family are reflected in Census data. For example, caring responsibilities, which are deeply embedded within Islam, are reflected in the Census. Eighteen per cent of Muslims in Britain (both genders) are likely to be looking after home or family (compared with 7 per cent nationally). Muslim men and women (3 per cent and 34 per cent) are three times more likely than all men and all women in Britain to be exclusively caring for the home and family (1 per cent and 12 per cent nationally). Given the age demographics of the British Muslim population, Muslims have the lowest proportion of pensioner households and they are least likely to be residing in care homes for the elderly, although there are now a number of retirement homes in Britain that cater for 'Asian' and Muslim residents.

British Muslim households are of above average size. Two-thirds (63 per cent) have at least one dependent child, while one-quarter of Muslim homes in Britain have three or more dependent children. Muslims are the least likely to have two-person households – only 15 per cent, compared to the national average of 33 per cent. There are low rates of cohabitation among British Muslims (3 per cent) (Peach 2006: 639), although more surprisingly Muslims have the highest proportion of lone parent households (11.9 per cent, with the national average 11.6 per cent) compared to other faith groups.[4] Marital breakdown is probably the single most likely explanation, although within this statistic there is likely to be a small proportion of women who are married to husbands in polygamous marriages, who, for the purposes of the Census, only indicated their residence at one of their marital homes.[5]

The nature of Muslim households, and especially their above-average size, has particular implications for policy-makers, especially in terms

---

[4] This is also confirmed via other sources: 'Single parent households make up a greater proportion of Muslim households than is the case for the general population (12 per cent compared to 10 per cent)' ('Muslims in the UK: Policies for Engaged Citizens', 2005, Open Society Institute: 14).

[5] Hussain offers other possible explanations, such as geographical separation (e.g. spouses living or working abroad, or awaiting residence in the UK), or deliberately falsifying information about household composition and family relationships in order to increase benefits (Hussain, S. 2008: 112).

of housing, education, youth and family services. Any policies in these areas will have a disproportionate impact upon Muslim households, compared to other faith groups (Open Society Institute, 'Muslims in the UK: Policies for Engaged Citizens' 2005), especially in those parts of the country where Muslims form a significant percentage of the population.[6]

It is in such communities that Muslims have shaped their domestic homes and local areas to create 'moral spaces' (Werbner 1996b: 310) where religious identity and nurture can flourish. This often depends upon extended family relationships and networking, especially among South Asians. It is important to note, however, that the significance and implications of institutions such as *birādarī* are likely to vary in different localities, and among families who might have very different attitudes towards their extended family. Likewise, the idea of locality could have various meanings for different families such that 'Somalis in Cardiff or Turin may be consulted regularly on decisions affecting their families or households in Mogadishu' (Eickelman and Piscatori 2004: 136–7). With these caveats in mind, consideration of the ways in which Islam can influence the organization of space and social relations illustrates some of the dynamics of religious nurture within British Muslim homes.

SPACE, HOME AND RITUAL

A short extract from Rageh Omaar's biography, in which he describes a visit to Muslim friends in West London, illustrates some of the ways in which 'Islam structures time, space, action and thought with shapes that are coherent, deliberate, prescribed and defined' (Reeber 1990:6), especially in relation to domestic spaces:

A young woman in her twenties opened the door to us. She was dressed in a long Islamic gown, her head covered in a shawl to hide her hair. We greeted her in the traditional way by touching our chests rather than reaching out to shake her hand, and she showed us through the hall to the neat sitting room. Islamic posters were hung on the walls. The largest picture was a bird's eye view of the Grand Mosque in Mecca at night, the magnificent pillars lit up by hundreds of carefully directed lights. On the far wall attached by thumbtacks were two black and white scrolls inscribed with verses from the Quran, asking God to bless the

[6] This is especially the case given that Muslim families in Britain experience particularly high levels of socio-economic deprivation, and are particularly likely to be receiving state benefits and support. Muslim children experience high levels of risk associated with poverty – with 42 per cent living in overcrowded accommodation (compared to 12 per cent for the British population as a whole) (Halstead 2005: 112).

house and the family who lived in it. A woman's voice called out to the girl who had led us in. 'Have you offered them some tea?', she asked. (Omaar 2006: 87)

Contained within this apparently uneventful description of arrival, some of the ways in which Islam shapes domestic homes and social interactions are revealed. Forms of greeting, the nature of internal decorations, respect for guests and the importance of hospitality are clearly evident. These are significant in most Muslim homes across the world.

Among Muslims living in Britain, homes are the site for imparting cultural knowledge, religious teaching, language, history and a sense of identity to children (Lloyd Evans and Bowlby 2000). Women are often central to this process, and for this reason

feminine space is the space of the home. It includes spaces for women and for their close male relatives, and is a domain into which the entry of other men is restricted. Spaces outside the home are largely masculine. (Mohammad 1999: 30)

To protect the modesty of the womenfolk within the home, curtains tend to be drawn as a barrier to the external gaze. A front door inscribed with Arabic calligraphy (usually an adhesive sticker bearing the Islamic declaration of faith, the *shahādah*) indicates not only the identity of the household occupants, but also that 'the hostile environment of racism, discrimination, and religious intolerance [is] locked out' (Eickelman and Piscatori 2004: 137; Marranci 2004). The removal of outdoor shoes at the threshold is important for keeping floors (and therefore areas that may be used for prayer) clean. Internal decorations, such as pictures and wall hangings inspired by Islamic art, text and architecture, reinforce self-conscious Muslim identity and a sense of God-consciousness (*taqwā*). The Islamization of space through sound may be achieved by the playing of religious CDs, such as *nasheeds* (devotional songs), and recitation of the *Qur'ān*, perhaps by a well-known international reciter. The evolution of a new generation of British-born Muslim calligraphers, photographers, artists and interior designers means that homes can increasingly reveal a fusion of British, Middle Eastern and South Asian styles which affirm multiple identities.[7]

British Muslim homes tend to be simultaneously private spaces and also the sites of extensive (family-orientated) social life. The broad contours of sociability as described by Pnina Werbner in the 1970s and 1980s have changed relatively little. Homes are still important sites for mutual

---

[7] See chapter 10 for examples of British Muslim artists and designers.

exchange of news and gossip, joking and political debate, the co-operative care of children and the elderly, and the sharing of refreshments (Werbner 1990). This is made all the more possible when families are clustered together in neighbouring houses, streets or neighbourhoods. It is within the unsegregated, private space of homes that the power (and mutual empowerment) of women is often most evident, since here they share information and act with autonomy and confidence in relation to most family matters. The relationships of trust that are built up through the exchange of information, gifts, hospitality and mutual support are indicative of the active centrality of women in family life. The establishment of close-knit social networks is not, however, undertaken solely for utilitarian purposes, but in order to create 'a moral community and [to] transform the space, the house, the neighbourhood, and the city in which they live, into a moral space' informed by Islamic values (Werbner 1990: 150). Recent research has shown how effectively many Muslim women are also able to create 'home spaces' outside their own family homes (for example, in the homes of female friends and their immediate relatives). The idea of 'home as a single physical entity' therefore needs to be re-examined, especially where women are able to define 'home' not only as their own place of residence, but also places where they 'feel at home' (Phillips 2009: 32).

For many British Muslims, homes are sites for the performance of religious rituals, and most especially the five daily prayers, at dawn, just after midday, late afternoon, sunset and nightfall. Some homes have '*adhān* clocks' which signal the arrival of prayer time. This means that daily life is punctuated by an awareness of the passage of time, and the religious obligations associated with the different phases of the sun and the moon. Family members will usually try to offer prayers in congregation, rather than individually, and this usually means that worshippers will stand in a row behind the most senior male of the household. As the teachings of Islam are narrated, remembered and practised in this way, children both consciously and unconsciously learn traditions and observances, thereby developing a Muslim 'moral habitus' (Winchester 2008). The central role of women in family life gives them a pivotal role in the religious nurture and education of future generations; it is they who usually help young children learn how to undertake ritual washing before prayer, and how to perform the prayers themselves.[8]

---

[8] Religious nurture within British Muslim homes has received relatively little scholarly attention, especially in relation to children of primary school age and below. A project based at Cardiff University between 2008 and 2010 is seeking to understand how families instil religious identity in young children, especially in relation to other ethnic/racial identities (www.cardiff.ac.uk/

The undertaking of numerous daily activities, such as beginning a meal, retiring for sleep or leaving for a journey, usually begin with short religious invocations or prayers, transforming them into occasions for remembrance of God. Homes therefore become permeated by religious observance, but they are also of course the setting for more mundane activities, commonplace in most homes across the world. For example, the young British Muslim men interviewed as part of Peter Hopkins's research in 2006 constructed home as a place of relaxation and consumption – 'a place to have dinner, play the computer and watch TV' (Hopkins 2006: 340)[9] – and there was a noticeable lack of reference to the performance of household tasks, compared to the young British Muslim girls interviewed by Dwyer in the late 1990s (Dwyer 1999a; Dwyer 2000). Most young men assumed that the family home was the domain of mothers and sisters (Hopkins 2006). Most British Muslim girls (though not all) are socialized into their future roles as wives and mothers from an early age, mainly through an expectation that they will engage in housework (Dwyer 1999b: 139). The performance of domestic chores is seen as an expression of appropriate femininity. Large households often depend on the labour of young women in order to facilitate, for example, extended family gatherings involving refreshments, and care of younger siblings.

For both men and women, freedom from parental authority is often (but not always) a consequence of marriage, not coming of age (Basit 1997b). Marriage indicates the 'transfer of love, nurture and authority ... just as the bride moves from dependence on paternal authority to the authority of her husband, so too the groom moves from dependence on his mother for nurture to dependence on his wife' (Werbner 1990: 259, 275).

## MARRIAGE AND DIVORCE

Muslims often regard marriage as the joining together of two families. A good match can enhance the honour and reputation of both families, while a poor or failed marriage can bring social disgrace.[10] It is therefore a potentially risky process, and families will do all they can to mitigate the

---

socsi/research/researchprojects/religiousnurture/). This research is being conducted as part of an AHRC/ESRC-funded 'Religion and Society' programme: www.religionandsociety.org.uk/

[9] The availability of a range of satellite channels has increased the range of choice in television entertainment. Al-jazeerah, the 'Islam Channel', and a range of channels from South Asia and the Middle East dominate viewing preferences.

[10] See Ahmad (2006: 283) for a critical evaluation of the term '*izzat*'.

risk, especially when transnational marriage is involved (Charsley 2007). As a consequence, the choice of spouse is a matter of family concern, and most British Muslim parents regard it as part of their religious duty to find a suitable life partner for their son or daughter (Basit 1996: 7). In practical terms, contracting a marriage is usually a negotiated, joint undertaking between parents and children from two families, and mutual trust and knowledge are vital to the proceedings (Charsley 2007). Marriages that are 'arranged' in this way must in principle be consensual. All parties must have the freedom to agree or disagree to the proposed union, which is negotiated through a series of meetings prior to the wedding. In contrast, a 'forced' marriage, where either spouse has not given their free consent, is not valid according to Islamic law (McDermott and Ahsan 1980: 84). 'Arranged' marriages might involve on the one hand parental choice of prospective spouse, with the subsequent agreement of the young people concerned, or, on the other, parental 'approval' for a marriage sought by the young people themselves, but negotiated with full parental involvement.[11] Sometimes, there is a fine line between an 'arranged', an 'approved' or a 'forced' marriage, indicating the complexity and variety of meaning and social practice underlying these terms. Furthermore, the choice of spouse is not the only variable. The decision about *when* to marry is also becoming significant, especially as many young British Muslim women are keen to delay marriage in order to pursue further education and careers.

Most marriages among South Asian British Muslims are within the same ethnic group (Charsley 2007). Analysis of *Labour Force Quarterly Survey* data between 1997 and 2001 found that 98 per cent of Bangladeshi women were married to Bangladeshi men, and that 94 per cent of Pakistani women were married to Pakistani men (Peach 2006: 639). Ceri Peach concluded that marriage is overwhelmingly 'within religion, within caste' (Peach 2006: 639). While there is a noticeable rise in the age at which Muslim marriages occur, especially among women (Ahmad 2006), this is also evident in the population at large. Rates of consanguineous marriage are high within South Asian Muslim communities in Britain, especially among Pakistanis (Shaw 2001). Well over half of Pakistani married people in Britain are married either to a first cousin, or to another kind of relative (Peach 2006; Shaw 2001). There is no conclusive research so far documenting the extent of consanguinity among other South Asian

---

[11]  See Stopes-Roe and Cochrane (1990) for more details regarding variations of 'arranged' marriage, cited in Ahmad (2006: 275).

Muslim groups, though a small-scale study of British Bangladeshis found that 60 per cent of the married couples in the sample were blood relations (Rozario and Gilliat-Ray 2007). From an Islamic faith perspective, there is no preference or encouragement for cousin marriage; it is simply permitted.

The fact that many British Muslims of South Asian origin often choose to marry a blood relation therefore reflects cultural practices and traditions. Such marriages are widely regarded as being potentially more secure, not only because the credentials and reputation of the prospective husband and wife are usually well-known and verifiable, but also because the young people involved are seen as potentially more compatible as a result of their shared origins (Basit 1996; Charsley 2007). There is also an assumption of respectful and honourable treatment of women, since to desert the marriage, or mistreat a wife, risks the break-up and possible loss of support from the wider extended family. However, the young British Muslim girls in Basit's research conducted in the mid 1990s were more cautious about the prospect of a happy marriage as a result of marrying a spouse from the Indian subcontinent, regardless of whether or not they were related. As 'Seema' said:

I would like to marry someone in Britain because he'd be more like you and would understand you better. But someone in Pakistan – since they have grown up in a totally different society – maybe you'll find it difficult to get along with them. (Basit 1996: 13)

On the other hand, a husband and wife who are both British-born are sometimes seen as potentially 'too strong-willed' (Charsley 2007: 1124), and less likely to be willing to make the kind of compromises necessary for a happy marriage. 'Residence in Britain can thus be viewed as eroding gendered difference, damaging the complementarity between husband and wife, and leading to potential conflict' (Charsley 2007: 1124). The continued popularity of bringing prospective spouses from the Indian subcontinent (Ahmad 2006; Charsley 2007), often to marry a cousin living in Britain, reflects this concern, as well as other social preferences and considerations. For example, cousin marriages might be a means of sustaining transnational kinship ties, or fulfilling family obligations to enable (especially male) migration to Britain. Spouses from abroad are also seen as potentially more devout, enhancing the religious education and subsequent spiritual well-being of any children born within the marriage.

Contrary to popular media stereotypes, research conducted over the past three decades consistently indicates that the vast majority of young

British Muslims have 'arranged' or 'approved' marriages, rather than 'forced' marriages (Brah 1996: 77). However, as noted above, it might be difficult to distinguish clearly in every case between these categories. Samia Bano notes that of the twenty-five women in her study, thirteen had 'arranged' marriages, eight had a parentally 'approved' marriage, and four were 'forced' (Bano 2007: 49). Sonia Nurin Shah-Kazemi found that of 308 marriages studied as part an empirical project on matrimonial dispute and divorce cases brought to the Muslim Law Shariah Council, London, twenty-eight were 'forced' (Shah-Kazemi 2001). Research shows that many young British Muslims welcome parental involvement in their choice of spouse, and the following quotation from Basit's research with young British Muslim teenage girls in the mid 1990s illustrates the point:

I'd prefer an arranged marriage. If you choose someone yourself and you have problems, then you have nowhere to go. But if your parents choose the person, they know what they are doing and you have their support even if there are problems … (interview quote in Basit 1996: 8)

The rapid growth in recent years of websites offering matrimonial services, complementing matrimonial pages in the Muslim/Asian press, indicates that rates of 'approved' marriage are likely to grow as British Muslims purposefully use the internet to seek their own partners, alongside, or in preference to, conventional parentally initiated 'arranged' marriages (Ahmad 2006: 286). The web provides an apparently 'halal' space for single Muslims to become acquainted with potential marriage partners. There are no fewer than fourteen such sites registered in Britain (as of May 2008), some with up to 100,000 registered members. The site www. singlemuslim.com boasts 'four success stories a day'. Sites such as The Muslim Matrimonial (www.themuslimmatrimonial.co.uk) and Muslim Marriages (www.muslim-marriages.co.uk) are a clear indication that the business of finding a spouse is changing and being renegotiated, potentially allowing more space for individual agency. One reason why some Muslims are using these services is because they are not entering into a first-time marriage. The sites provide access to potential marriage partners for those who are perhaps divorced, widowed or single parents, or for those who simply do not have parents who are able to undertake marriage negotiations on their behalf, such as converts to Islam.

If families have a pivotal role in the contracting of marriage, they likewise usually have an important part to play when a marriage has broken down. Census data indicate high levels of family breakdown among British Muslims and the percentage of lone parents (12 per cent) is higher than would be anticipated given the efforts to secure lasting marriages described above (Peach 2006: 640).[12] However, this figure is likely to reflect a range of other contributory factors, such as extended visits to the homeland by one or other parent, or families that are divided while undergoing formal asylum-seeker status. Among those British Muslims who are divorcing, the main grounds are escaping from a 'forced' marriage, avoiding family interference, adultery, a 'clash of upbringing', or leaving a situation of emotional, sexual or physical abuse (Bano 2007: 55). British Muslims therefore clearly divorce for many of the same reasons as members of the wider population.

A certain degree of legal pluralism surrounds British Muslim marriage and divorce, because the demands of both British and Islamic legal systems have to be met.[13] Fulfilment of Islamic requirements remains central, but the extent to which marriages are registered and/or dissolved via mainstream legal procedures is unclear. British Muslims are subject to the same inconveniences as many other ethnic minorities who must 'marry twice, divorce twice and do many other things several times in order to satisfy the demands of concurrent legal systems' (Pearl and Menski 1998: 75, cited in Bano 2007: 45). Many British Muslims will therefore seek the advice of a *Shari'ah* Council in the effort to secure a divorce, and the work of these Councils, especially the capacity of women to instigate and negotiate divorce proceedings, has been studied extensively in recent years (Bano 2007; Shah-Kazemi 2001). *Shari'ah* Councils emerged in Britain in the 1980s, often as an extension to the services provided by mosques. These Councils serve three principal functions: they seek to reconcile matrimonial (or other family) disputes; they issue religious divorce certificates; and they produce reports and expert opinion for civil courts. Bano found that 'women's experiences of marriage, divorce, and family and community relationships were messy, fragmented and complex' (Bano 2007: 65), not least because of the workings of *Shari'ah* Councils, which tended to rely upon very traditional assumptions about women's roles in Islam. The statistics indicate that British Muslim marriages are under pressure, but that family life more generally is subject to other tensions and difficulties which have an effect upon religious nurture, and some of these are discussed in the next section.

[12] In the report 'Marriage and the Dissolution of Marriage in Shari'ah' following a symposium organized by the Muslim Women's Helpline in May 2003, it was noted that calls to the Helpline concerning marital difficulties rose from 21 per cent in 1991 to over 50 per cent in 2002.
[13] For a fuller discussion of the complex legal position surrounding marriage and divorce, see Carroll (1997) and Warraich and Balchin (2006).

## INTER-GENERATIONAL RELATIONS AND THE 'DECLINE' OF THE FAMILY

Social scientists who specialize in the sociology of the family note the growing pressure on family life in general (Allan and Crow 2001; Cheal 2002; Scott *et al.* 2007). There is much debate about the extent to which this can be attributed to the growth of 'individualism' (Scott 1997). The British Muslim religious and community leaders interviewed as part of Howe's research in 2000 were sure that Muslim youth were the agents of family breakdown, and they identified 'British culture, and its emphasis on individualism, as the ultimate source' (Howe 2007). However, they were also concerned about other economic and structural factors which undermined British Muslim family life. For example, the limited availability of large affordable housing meant that extended family living arrangements became less feasible, with the likely consequence that grandparents and other family elders might no longer pass on attitudes such as respect and responsibility at close quarters. Meanwhile, the availability of various state benefits potentially reduced financial dependence upon the wider kinship network and facilitated the break-up of families. They noted that the economic advantages of migration to Britain had been gained at a very high price.

If there is concern regarding the breakdown of inter-generational family relationships in Britain, there are also worries about the decline in transnational links 'back home':

I go every year to see my family, my distant relatives ... my son won't go visit. Family ties are coming to an end, you know? ... After us, after we go, there won't be any family tie from here to Bangladesh ... That's why I am worried ... I told them, 'without your ancestors, more or less you are nothing' ... You don't know where you are from. You should *know*. (Imam from Bangladesh, interviewed by Howe 2007: 18, emphasis original)

Religious and cultural identity is perceived as under threat, especially by the elder generation, as a result of the perceived 'decline' of the family. Differences of opinion between generations are of course inevitable in most communities, but among Muslim families, young people who see their future in Britain are sometimes extremely critical of the aspirations and loyalties of their parents and grandparents. So, for example, the relevance of caste, clan, tribal or regional ties, often important in the worldview of elders, is regarded as increasingly outdated by many young British-born Muslims who feel disconnected from their origins 'back home' (Ansari 2004: 217). By the 1990s, inter-generational tension was a distinctive theme in much writing and research about young Muslims in Britain. The older generation continues to feel that they are not respected by their children and grandchildren, as Gardner found in her research with Bengali elders (Gardner 1998b). This was also the perception among younger British Muslim fathers (Khan 2007). However, more recent research contradicts the dominant discourse that young Muslim men are in inevitable conflict with their parents' generation (Hopkins 2006; Khan 2007). Hopkins found, for example, that young men in his sample extended respect towards their parents, based on recognition of their sacrifices and hard work in the later decades of the twentieth century.

## DEATH AND BEREAVEMENT

With a growing British Muslim elderly population, there is now a need for new research to explore the changing meanings and rituals that surround death, dying and bereavement. As an inevitable consequence of the migration history and demographics of the Muslim population in Britain, relatively little research has been done on death and dying, although there are notable exceptions (Gardner 1998a; Gatrad 1994b). There are a number of customs surrounding death that are universal among Muslims, such as the requirement to be buried and not cremated, for the body to be ritually washed and draped before the burial, and for the face of the deceased to be turned towards Makkah. British Muslim institutions have gradually developed to enable these religious needs to be met, while local authorities and hospitals have become more familiar with the rites and rituals that surround Muslim death and dying. As in families of many other faiths, there is a strong preference among Muslims in Britain for death to occur at home, and for the dying person to be supported by the prayers of loved ones as the time of death approaches. Palliative care often involves giving holy *Zam-zam* water from Makkah to the dying patient.

It used to be commonplace for the bodies of many deceased South Asian migrants to be returned 'home' for burial in their villages or towns in the Indian subcontinent. This was a direct reflection of their sense of place and 'homeland'. However, this practice has been increasingly discouraged by Islamic scholars in Britain, because embalming the body in alcohol to enable its preservation during transit is *haram* (forbidden). More British Muslims are now buried in Britain for a combination of religious, social and practical reasons.[14] Their preferences arguably reflect a new sense that Britain is their 'home':

> Death is not solely a matter of individual experience and emotion but is also inherently social … the meanings and practices which surround death are, then, the products of particular social, cultural and historical circumstances. Since these rituals are central to the identities and meanings which groups construct for themselves, they can be viewed as windows, which open out to the ways societies view themselves and the world around them, and the changes and conflicts which they may be undergoing. (Gardner 1998a: 507)

The overall management of death and dying is slowly passing away from Muslim families in Britain, and into the hands of professional Islamic funeral services. This process was vividly captured in a compelling Channel 4 documentary, *God's Waiting Room* (26 November 2007), which profiled the work of a Muslim funeral director, Mr Ghulam Taslim, of East London's 'Taslim Funerals'.[15] While there is an inevitable sadness about death, of course, Islamic beliefs about death and dying offer hope and reassurance for devout families. Muslims believe that life on earth is merely a temporary phase in the journey towards the hereafter: 'The firm Muslim belief in the immortality of the soul and the existence of an afterlife perhaps lends a lesser finality to death and greater acceptance of the end of life as a natural transition' (Balchin 2007). Children are encouraged to mourn with adults, and to consider that both their origination and their passing are subject to the will of God: 'As He originated you, so you will return' (*Sūrah* 7: 29). The rites of passage associated with birth and death are therefore equally occasions for religious nurture and education in many British Muslim homes.

### RELIGIOUS EDUCATION AND NURTURE BEYOND THE FAMILY

Islam has a rich tradition of education that goes back well over a millennium (Nielsen 1989). Islamic scholarship led the world for hundreds of years in virtually every known academic discipline, and universities in the Islamic world pre-dated Western universities by several centuries (Halstead 2004). Part of the reason why Muslim scholars were so

---

[14] A Bengali undertaker in Tower Hamlets interviewed for Gardner's research estimated that about 60 to 70 per cent of corpses are sent back to Bangladesh for burial (Gardner 1998a). This percentage is likely to have reduced in the years since fieldwork was conducted.

[15] At the time of writing, it was possible to view this documentary on-line at: http://video.google.com/videoplay?docid=-8312558074382407564

pioneering was the importance that is attached to knowledge in the *Qurʾān*. The *Qurʾān* is full of exhortations to pursue knowledge (*Sūrah* 20: 114), and it proclaims the superiority of those who have knowledge over those who do not (*Sūrah* 58: 11). The *Qurʾān* makes it clear that knowledge is a characteristic of God himself and that all knowledge comes from Him. This applies whether the knowledge is revealed or humanly constructed, and it means that knowledge must be approached reverently and in humility.

The *Qurʾān* accordingly makes the pursuit of knowledge a religious obligation upon all believers (Parker-Jenkins 1995). It is not a monopoly of a few individuals, or a certain class, group or gender. To acquire knowledge is a key responsibility for each person throughout their lifetime. Furthermore, it is not limited to a particular field of enquiry, but covers all aspects of human life and awareness, and the entire spectrum of natural phenomena. The *Qurʾān* particularly emphasizes the importance of knowledge in relation to the achievement of justice in society. One is an instrument for achieving the other. Only when knowledge is widely and easily available to everyone can justice be established. Ultimately, education is necessary in order to 'attain success in this life and the next' (Association of Muslim Social Scientists/FAIR, *Muslims on Education: A position paper*, 2004: 2).

Islam places a particular responsibility upon parents to educate their children in the faith. A group of British Muslim fathers from diverse ethnic backgrounds who took part in a focus group discussion about parenting between 2004 and 2006 emphasized the importance of imparting religious knowledge to their children (Khan 2007). They recognized the connection between such education and the achievement of a secure religious and personal identity for their offspring. Educational institutions that build upon religious nurture in the home are therefore of paramount importance to Muslims throughout the world, and some of the first major national organizations established by Muslims in Britain were concerned with teaching and learning about Islam.

The comprehensive nature of education in Islam is reflected in the expectation that a teacher should 'exemplify in her/his life the content of that which is taught' (Hewer 2001: 521). In other words, teachers should not simply transmit knowledge and information but should also act as guides and exemplars in all aspects of personal conduct. The education and religious nurture that children receive at home is therefore ideally matched by teachers who reinforce and exemplify the values and teachings of Islam at school, thereby enabling children to understand the holistic and all-encompassing way of life that is intrinsic to Islam and a secure Muslim identity (Nielsen 1981).

The remainder of this chapter explores the development of educational institutions within Muslim communities in Britain, especially mosque-based *makātib* and independent and state-funded Muslim schools, established over the past three decades. However, initiatives have often occurred in parallel with, or in response to, the efforts of parents and Islamic organizations to support the education and religious identity of Muslim children in mainstream state schools where, of course, the vast majority of children are still educated. The extent of research into these different kinds of educational provision is variable. There are, for instance, few academic studies focusing on Muslim supplementary schools compared to the relatively extensive literature around debates such as state funding of Muslim faith schools.[16]

A key theme to emerge from the debate concerning the schooling of Muslim children is, paradoxically, parental ambivalence. On the one hand, Muslim parents who are keen for their children to be academically successful often see mainstream schools as the most likely place where these ambitions can be fulfilled (Joly 1995). On the other hand, these same schools are seen as potentially undermining Islamic values that have been cultivated within the home (Nielsen 1989; Osler and Hussain 2005). The emergence of academically successful independent and state-funded Muslim schools over the past twenty years has in many ways enabled a reconciliation of what were once mutually exclusive choices. These institutions are nonetheless still only able to educate a relatively small minority of Muslim children in Britain. This means that the education of Muslim children beyond the home is likely to remain an ongoing subject for research and media headlines well into the future.

To set the following sections in context, the age demographics of the British Muslim population today means that Muslim children currently make up between 5 and 6 per cent of the total school population (Beckford *et al.* 2006). In some regions and cities of the country, such as

---

[16] By now there have been a number of studies that consider different aspects of British Muslims and schooling, for example in relation to gender (Abbas 2003; Afshar 1993; Archer 2003; Basit 1995; Haw 1998; Mustafa 1999), parental perceptions and aspirations (Afshar 1993; Joly 1984; Osler and Hussain 2005), teacher perceptions (Abbas 2002a; Abbas 2002b), the debate around state funding of Muslim schools (Hashmi 2003; Hewer 2001; Kelly 1999; McLoughlin 1998b; Meer 2007; Parker-Jenkins 2002; Tinker 2006), to cite a number of examples. There have also been studies which examine educational issues in particular cities, such as Birmingham and Bradford (Abbas 2002b; Hewer 2001; McLoughlin 1998b), or particular schools, such as the Islamia School in Brent (Dwyer and Meyer 1995).

Bradford, Muslim children will represent up to 33 per cent of the school population (Halstead 2005). In particular schools therefore, the vast majority of pupils are from Muslim homes.

## BRITISH MUSLIM CHILDREN IN STATE SCHOOLS

As Muslim children gradually began to form a significant proportion of the school population in the 1960s, parents and Muslim organizations began to campaign for greater recognition of their particular needs and preferences. Calls for the provision of halal school meals,[17] adaptation of school uniform rules and procedures to accommodate Muslim expectations of modesty (for boys and girls), adjustments to the curriculum and timetable to allow for exemptions for *Eid* holidays and Friday prayers, and provision of single-sex education were the kind of issues that brought British Muslims into public view for the first time. Their concerns challenged the assimilationist assumptions of the Establishment. These had often presumed that the distinctive identity of Muslim children (often viewed through the predominant lenses of race and ethnicity) could and should be absorbed into 'British' culture, and that diversity was fundamentally disruptive to the educational process (Ansari 2004: 300).[18] The reaction of local education authorities to these calls from Muslim parents were regionally variable, confused and often ad hoc (Nielsen 1989: 225).[19] Meanwhile, the relative lack of effective lobbying from organizations within Muslim communities added to a sense of mutual frustration.

By the end of the 1970s, successive educational policies introduced more multicultural and anti-racist approaches to education, and by the 1980s some schools had largely resolved the issue of uniforms and provision of halal school meals. However, these measures did not address some of the specifically religious concerns of Muslim parents, particularly in relation to the religious education (RE) curriculum. The idea that religions should be studied from a secular, often phenomenological viewpoint, and the fact that Islam was often taught by ill-qualified

[17] Given the levels of socio-economic deprivation in Muslim homes, many children were (and still are) entitled to free school meals, and thus the provision of Islamically permitted halal meals was (and still is) an important issue.
[18] This stance found particular expression again in the mid 1980s in Bradford, at the height of the Thatcher years, when headteacher Ray Honeyford caused controversy for his views about Pakistan and the education of children from Pakistani homes in Britain.
[19] See Joly (1995), chapter 7, on Muslims and education in Birmingham.

teachers using outdated 'Orientalist' textbooks, continued to cause parental concern at a time when parents were beginning to be more familiar with their children's schools and with educational policy more generally. Their worries and growing criticisms of schools (Joly 1984) were amplified by emerging evidence of poor academic performance among Muslim children during the 1980s, extrapolated from data about the educational attainment of, for example, children of Pakistani and Bangladeshi descent.[20] Statistics produced by the Inner London Education Authority in 1986, for instance, found that only 16.1 per cent of Pakistani children and only 3.6 per cent of Bangladeshi children were leaving school with five or more O level passes (Ansari 2004). The evidence of a significant gap in educational performance between pupils from different ethnic groups continues, and it has become less feasible to attribute this to recent arrival in Britain. Attention has begun to turn to other, 'cumulatively disadvantaging processes' (Ansari 2004: 307) that might be contributing to the generally lower educational attainment levels of many Muslim children.[21]

Although many schools have become more accommodating regarding, for example, school meals or uniforms, such adjustments do not address more fundamental pedagogical and practical issues which can amount to discriminatory practice. For example, a Euro-centric curriculum, poor home–school communications, racist/Islamophobic bullying of pupils, and stereotypical views held by some non-Muslim teachers (especially in relation to girls) now provide evidence for low self-expectations on the part of some Muslim pupils. This produces the conditions for a vicious circle of continuing under achievement. Many of these matters remain key policy issues today (Association of Muslim Social Scientists/FAIR, *Muslims on Education: A position paper*, 2004; Halstead 2005). British Muslim organizations are actively lobbying to promote greater parental involvement in schooling issues, such as by encouraging Muslim parents to become school governors,[22] or promoting Muslim teachers as role

---

[20] It is commonplace to talk of Muslim 'underachievement' at school, but this term is not without difficulties. See Haque (2000). A number of explanations have been put forward to account for poor educational performance, such as socio-economic deprivation, parental expectations and educational experiences, pupils' experiences at school and teachers' expectations. Haque notes the difficulty of establishing the cause owing to the complexity and interlinking character of the issues, and she calls for further qualitative and quantitative research. See also Modood (2005a).

[21] Statistics indicate that, in 2000, 35 per cent of children from Pakistani backgrounds and 37 per cent of children from Bangladeshi backgrounds achieved five or more GCSEs at grade A*–C ... compared with 47 per cent of students overall (Osler and Hussain 2005: 141).

[22] See *The Muslim Governors: Making a Difference* video produced by the Association of Muslim Governors, which can be viewed on-line: www.youtube.com/watch?v=RjpbXK_E71Y&fmt=18

models (Halstead 2005).[23] As Muslim parents have become more familiar with a range of educational and social issues, the question of separate
Muslim schools has become more significant, particularly where parents
have sought schooling which they regard as more consonant with religious nurture provided at home (Osler and Hussain 2005).

## INDEPENDENT AND STATE-FUNDED MUSLIM SCHOOLS

There are currently 115 fee-paying full-time Muslim schools in Britain,
and seven state-funded schools (Odone 2008a).[24] The popularity and
demand for places in these schools is demonstrated by their long waiting
lists, and their overall growth in numbers over the past twenty years from
just twenty in 1990, to forty-six in 1996, to eighty in 2002 (Association
of Muslim Social Scientists, *Muslims on Education: A position paper*,
2004: 20).

Approximately 3 per cent of Muslim children in Britain are currently
educated in fee-paying, independent Muslim schools. Lacking state support, these schools have often been financially vulnerable, with obvious
consequences for the employment and retention of qualified staff, and
limitations upon physical and material resources. Less than 0.5 per cent of
Muslim children are currently educated in state-funded Muslim schools,
but these institutions are seen to be of symbolic significance as a demon-
stration that British Muslims have the legal right to a distinctive form of
education alongside other faith communities in Britain (Halstead 2005).
The arguments for and against state-funded Muslim schools have been
well documented in recent years (Halstead 1986; Hashmi 2003; Meer
2007; Tinker 2006), and the issue provides an interesting lens through
which major philosophical and political questions concerning religion in
public life come into view (Meer 2007). The academic quality of Muslim
schools as measured by levels of achievement in standard national tests
(SATS) is variable, but well-resourced Muslim schools often out-perform
other local authority, community-based schools (Halstead 2005). Recent
evidence suggests that these Muslim schools, which are often single sex,
can also be very significant for the future higher education of girls: 'the
proportion of girls in Muslim faith schools who go on to higher education

---

[23] A BEd degree was established in Birmingham in 1991, specifically to encourage Muslims into
teacher training (Hewer 2001).
[24] The activities of many of these schools are co-ordinated by the Association of Muslim Schools,
established in 1992.

is more than twice as high as in secular state schools' (Odone 2008a; Odone 2008b).

Among the motivating factors underpinning parental preference for a distinctively Islamic school is the fact that teaching and learning about Islam from a committed perspective is embedded into the curriculum, as are other subjects which support religious learning, such as Arabic language classes. As a consequence, some of the responsibility that Islam places upon parents in terms of religious education and nurture becomes shared between school and home environments. Children attending a Muslim school make less use of after-school Muslim supplementary schooling which currently serves as the main avenue for religious socialization and nurture for many British Muslim children beyond the home.

SUPPLEMENTARY SCHOOLS

Apart from a study of a Bengali mosque in Bradford in the 1980s, which included a chapter about the education of children (Barton 1986), and two postgraduate dissertations from the University of Birmingham (Amer 1997; North 1986), relatively little research has been conducted

Figure 4. A class for Muslim boys at a mosque in Redbridge, London, 2004.
The teacher is sitting with his back to the wall, listening and checking boys' correct
recitation of the *Qur'ān*. Reproduced by kind permission of Bill Gent

concerning Muslim supplementary schools in Britain (Halstead 2005). However, given their importance for the religious education of young British Muslims, and the recent availability of a new insightful study (Gent 2006), it is worth considering these institutions in more depth.

Supplementary schools, often based in mosques but sometimes based in private homes, provide a range of educational activities for Muslim children, such as mother-tongue classes (for example in Urdu or Bengali), and homework support. However, their main role has been in teaching children the basics of Islam, and the linguistic skills necessary for correct recitation of the *Qur'ān*. For this reason, they are sometimes also known as 'complementary' schools, or 'mosque schools' (as with the term 'Sunday School', often used to describe Christian religious education provided by churches) (Martin *et al.* 2004). Many Muslim children in Britain between the ages of five and fourteen years spend up to two hours each day at their local mosque, usually after school, receiving instruction about Islam. It is usual for boys and girls to learn in separate spaces, and to be taught by a teacher of their own gender. These institutions are usually known as *makātib* (sing. *maktab*), or *madāris* (sing. *madrasah*), the latter suggesting a more formal or advanced place of learning. It is difficult to know exactly how many young Muslim children are receiving supplementary/complementary religious education, but one recent estimate of 90 per cent attendance (Mogra 2004, citing Parker-Jenkins 1995: 30) could well be inflated (Halstead 2005: 133). Whatever the exact figure, these institutions play a pivotal role in religious education for the vast majority of young British Muslims.

Research among Muslim families of Kashmiri origin in Birmingham in the 1980s revealed that supplementary schools for religious instruction were already well-established across the city (Joly 1995). In 2001 in Bradford, there were sixty-three supplementary schools (Ouseley 2001). Meanwhile in the Kirklees area (around Huddersfield, Dewsbury and Batley in Yorkshire) approximately fifty *makātib* provide education for some 10,000 children (Hafez 2003). This is indicative of the priority that Muslim parents give to the more formal religious education and nurture of their children, and the energetic establishment of these institutions within one generation of post-Second World War migration to Britain.

Barton's description of the Bengali *maktab* in Bradford in the 1980s indicates the various ways in which the religious identity of children and their sense of belonging to the Muslim community is inculcated (Barton 1986). A key route is through the memorization and recitation of a 'catechism' or statement of basic principles of Islamic belief. This 'catechism' begins with the question 'who are you?', to which children are instructed to respond 'I am a Muslim'. Barton comments that 'the beginning of the Muslim child's knowledge of himself and of his faith lies not in his individual identity, nor in his relationship to his family, but in his membership of the household of Islam' (Barton 1986: 162).

In recent years, a number of concerns have been expressed by Muslim educationalists about mosque-based religious education (Halstead 2005; Mogra 2004). For example, it has been suggested that the requirement to spend several hours each day at the *maktab* following a day of learning at school may place undue pressure upon the time and energies of children. Furthermore, the dissonance between the style and methods of education they receive at community-based state schools, which normally rely upon critical questioning of knowledge and of teachers themselves, is in sharp contrast to the teaching and learning methods used in mosques. Most *makātib* operate on the basis of the unquestionable authority of the teacher, strict discipline and rote learning. The qualifications of teachers and imams who deliver this teaching has sometimes been questionable, as has their ability to contextualize the learning in order to make it relevant to young British Muslims.

There are, however, signs of change, particularly due to more innovative teaching and learning methods and greater investment in resources and personnel (Hafez 2003; Mogra 2004). Such change has come about in part because of the sharing of good practice among Muslim educationalists. However, research can itself provide contributions to a better understanding of *makātib* and their potential. An example is the study carried out by a local education authority adviser in the London borough of Redbridge (Gent 2005; Gent 2006).[25] Gent's important work illuminated the profound and positive impact of traditional learning methods, especially memorization of the *Qur'ān*, upon the wider educational and personal development of the pupils in the class he studied. Far from being critical of 'rote learning', he uncovered evidence that the boys' ability to memorize the *Qur'ān* 'by heart', and thereby to acquire the prestigious title *ḥāfiz*, brought them (and their families) religious and social capital that had deep significance in many aspects of their lives. The ability to memorize and visualize written text, and to then recite aloud in public, also provided them with transferable skills which were put to good use in

---

[25] See also Gent and Redbridge SACRE (2003), available to download from: www.redbridgerenet. co.uk/publications.html.

their work at school, not to mention the development of character traits such as determination and self-discipline:

Qur'ānic memorization … is an educational process whereby the *Qur'ān* becomes embodied within the person of the memorizer, usually a child. Memorization, in this case, is a process that seamlessly unites the physical and the mental in the formation and enactment of religious and cultural practice. Seen in this light, memorization is more than the following of tradition, more than sustained discipline or indoctrination, and even more than the passing on of religious rituals. The embodied *Qur'ān* serves as a source of ongoing knowledge and protection to the child as he/she journeys through life. (Boyle 2004: 84)

A key outcome of Gent's work was a realization of the significant mutual benefits that could accrue from co-operation between supplementary schools and mainstream community-based state schools.

## CONCLUSION

'Metaphorically, a child is often represented as a seed,' wrote Imran Mogra, a Muslim educationalist at Birmingham City University (Mogra 2005). He went on to say that 'with prayer, attention, dedication, needs assessment and appropriate provisions, self-evaluations and strategies, children can grow to become stronger than oaks' (p. 63). So it is within British Muslim family homes that the process of religious nurture and education ideally begins. It is then ideally supplemented by more formal religious learning beyond the home. By now, a body of literature has emerged that illuminates our understanding of educational experiences for British Muslim children within a range of educational settings, and some of that literature has been discussed in this chapter. So far, however, there has been much less research into the contexts in which children (especially younger children) have been given the opportunity to reflect upon their own growth, from 'seeds' to 'oaks'. This process of religious nurture, of 'becoming' Muslim in Britain today, is therefore now the central point of focus for a new research project at Cardiff University (2008–2011).[26]

The concept of 'intersectionality' (Brah and Phoenix 2004) is likely to become a valuable theoretical device for enabling an understanding of the project's findings about childhood and religious nurture among contemporary British Muslim families. Intersectionality is

the complex, irreducible, varied, and variable effects which ensue when multiple axes of differentiation – economic, political, cultural, psychic, objective and

---

[26] See note 8 above.

experiential – intersect in historically specific contexts. The concept emphasises that different dimensions of social life cannot be separated out into discrete and pure strands. (Brah and Phoenix 2004: 76)

This means that understanding the education of young Muslim children in Britain today will involve making visible their multiple positionings in everyday life, rather than reducing them to the single category 'Muslim'. It will also entail an examination of their capacity to contest and engage with the social and power relations that structure their daily lives, at home, at school, in mosques and in other contexts where their identities are shaped (Phoenix and Pattynama 2006). Research methods that place children's subjectivity and experience at the centre, and that focus upon the accounts that children give of their everday practices, are likely to illuminate the interpersonal and community politics that surround them.

# CHAPTER 7

# Religious leadership

## INTRODUCTION

It is often said that there is 'no clergy' in Islam (Haneef 1979: 94; Murata and Chittick 2000; Ruthven 1997). Up to a point this is true, mainly because Islam's religious specialists exercise no sacramental or priestly functions (Tayob 1999). Within Sunni Islam there is no formal, structured hierarchy of religious professionals, such as may be found in some Christian churches, or in some Buddhist monastic orders, for example. In the belief that there should be no form of human intercession between God and humanity, Islam encourages all believers to know and understand their faith and to exercise their own interpretive judgement. However, Muslims are also exhorted to learn from scholars with specialist knowledge of the *Qur'ān* and other Islamic sources, and to emulate the moral conduct of pious individuals.

It would be difficult to put an exact figure upon the number of Muslim religious professionals in Britain today. There are a number of reasons for this. Firstly, there are a variety of both formal and informal centres for Islamic religious training (*dāru'l-'ulūm*). These offer programmes of learning at different levels, with emphasis upon the acquisition of particular skills or knowledge such as memorization of the *Qur'ān*, or study of the sources of Islamic law (Gilliat-Ray 2006). Not all graduates of these programmes will go on to become salaried religious professionals, not least because there is a shortage of employment opportunities for them (Birt 2005b: 687). They may nonetheless periodically perform religious duties informally, while pursuing more secular occupations. Secondly, the decentralized character of Islam in Britain means that there is no formal comprehensive national directory of religious professionals, compared for example to *Crockford's Clerical Dictionary*, or the Year Books produced by other religious communities in Britain. There is quite simply no systematic process for recording the existence of individual Muslim religious professionals in Britain. However, among British Muslim communities, an informal process of collective recognition of the knowledge and piety of particular religious scholars is well established, and is made evident through public speaking and mosque networks.

With these caveats in mind, and in the knowledge that there are approximately 1,200 to 1,500 mosques in Britain (some of which employ more than one religious specialist) we can assume that there are approximately 2,000 to 3,000 Islamic religious scholars in Britain today who derive their sole or primary living from the performance of a variety of religious functions. Most of them originate from overseas, but there are now also a growing number of British-born, British-trained imams, as we shall see.

This chapter surveys some of the debates and developments that have taken place concerning professional Muslim religious leadership in Britain over the past three decades. It soon becomes clear that there are new demands and expectations about the role and function of imams in Britain. These are being articulated not only by British Muslims but also by government and public institutions, especially since the London bombings in July 2005. Religious leadership and training is accordingly becoming highly politicized, and is one of the most vigorous areas of debate between British Muslims and the government.

Relative to other topics of study, remarkably little academic research has been conducted on Muslim religious leadership and training in Britain and there is a paucity of scholarly literature (Gilliat-Ray 2006).[1] Given the currency of the issues, however, it is likely that there will soon be a burgeoning relevant literature. The most important contributions will probably come from those British Muslim scholars who can combine an understanding and appreciation of traditional Islamic religious training and roles with critical insights derived from the academy, and/or from professional skills in public service, such as chaplaincy (Gilliat-Ray 2008). This is because such individuals have the potential capacity to bridge the worlds of public life and local Muslim communities and the respective institutions of both.

THE SCOPE OF ISLAMIC RELIGIOUS LEADERSHIP

A necessary prerequisite for a discussion of Muslim religious leadership in Britain is some explanation of terminology, and some consideration of

[1] This point is also confirmed in the Muslim Council of Britain report, *Voices from the Minaret: MCB Study of UK Imams and Mosques* (Rahman *et al.* 2006).

the range of different leadership roles. In Britain, some Islamic religious titles have become especially familiar, such as *mullah*, *muftī*, imam and *maulvī*. There is often little appreciation, however, of the fact that all of these titles have very distinct nuances and meanings and usually convey different degrees of knowledge and authority.

Religious specialists in Islam fall into four broad yet frequently overlapping categories: ritual, textual, scholarly/legal and spiritual. Because the majority of Muslims in Britain originate from South Asia, especially Pakistan, the vocabulary associated with religious specialists from this part of the world has become particularly familiar. Muslims from South East Asia, Turkey or various African countries use different terms to refer to their religious specialists. However, because the range of religious roles is broadly the same in most Muslim majority countries, and because the Arabic language is the universal means of religious and textual communication, there is usually sufficient sharing of a common religious terminology to enable religious titles to be universally understood.

The meaning of particular titles is nonetheless sometimes circumstantially and contextually dependent. For example, the term 'imam' within South Asian village contexts tends to denote a man with little secular or religious learning: 'the village community regards him as a low-ranking functionary equal to the barber, washerman, cobbler, or carpenter' (Syed 1984: 219–20). There is little social prestige to be derived from being a village imam in India, Bangladesh or Pakistan. However, in another context, the title 'imam' can convey immense respect, and signify religious, scholarly and spiritual authority. Ascertaining the degree of respect or authority in relation to a particular title usually means evaluating who is using it, when, where and for what purpose.

The word 'imam' derives from the *Qurʾān*, and more specifically from the Arabic verb *amma*, 'to precede' or 'to lead', but it connotes also a person who guides and exemplifies. In essence, an imam is a ritual specialist, responsible for leading congregational worship. While we usually speak of the imam in the masculine as 'he', and indeed most imams in history have been men, there is no reason why women cannot act as leaders of prayer for groups of female Muslims. In fact, there is no religious professional role formally barred to women. They can exercise their right to preach, teach and issue legal verdicts on an equal footing with men (at least where socio-cultural circumstances are in their favour), in accordance with their religious knowledge.

Although the leading of prayer is at the core of the imam's role, other functions are usually associated with it. These include presiding over rites

of passage, such as whispering the *adhān* (call to prayer) in the ears of
a newborn baby, officiating at a *nikāḥ* (signing of a wedding contract)
and leading the funeral prayer (*ṣalāt al-janāzah*). Other functions include
delivering the Friday sermon (*khuṭbah*), daily teaching of Arabic to children in order that they can recite the *Qur'ān*, and offering general advice
on religious matters. Imams often also have an important role as local
community mediators, offering arbitration in the case of interpersonal
disputes. The degree of authority and knowledge and the range of functions that imams perform will, as already noted, often depend upon the
context in which they work.

The term 'imam' can also be used to denote the leader of a particular
community or group. So for example, the founders of the major schools of
Islamic law are referred to by the title 'imam'. The word can also convey
an honorific title, as in the case of Imam al-Ghazali, the eleventh-century
Persian philosopher, theologian and mystic. Finally, the term 'imam' also
has a particular meaning among the Shī'a where it signifies an individual with supernatural knowledge and authority. This places such a person
almost on a par with the Prophet Muhammad himself, and for Twelver
Shī'as (also called '*imamis*'), the imam is regarded almost literally as an
intermediary between God and humanity.

Alongside the imam with his core role as the leader of ritual prayers,
there are other religious leadership roles in Islam. Their titles convey different levels of social or religious prestige. For example, a *mullah* is usually
in charge of a local mosque, and the education of children in the *maktab*
or *madrasah*. The title, literally meaning 'master', 'patron' or 'protector'
(Lewis 1994), is not especially prestigious (Ahmed 1993). Indeed, one
British Pakistani anthropologist noted that 'mullahs are often derided in
private' (Saifullah-Khan 1976: 227). A more respectful way of referring
to a person who broadly carries out the same function is *maulānā* (or
*maulvī*), meaning 'our learned master'. A *khaṭīb* is someone with religious
knowledge but also outstanding oratory skills who is delegated to give the
Friday sermon (*khuṭbah*).

Another category of religious specialism relates specifically to the
*Qur'ān*. For example, *ḥāfiz* denotes an individual who has memorized the
entire *Qur'ān* by heart, while a *qāri'* has learnt the techniques for the correct recitation of the *Qur'ān* (a skill known as *qirā'āt*). This is an accom-
plishment that is much in demand during the month of Ramadan, during
which the entire *Qur'ān* is recited. Many mosques in Britain will employ
a *qāri'* and/or a *khaṭīb* to complement the imam, on either a temporary or
a permanent basis.

The *'ulamā'* (singular, *'ālim*; feminine, *'ālima* – to refer to female scholars) are 'the learned', those recognized as scholars and authorities in religious matters. The *'ulamā'*

present themselves as custodians of an authoritative dogma, reproducers of an authoritative legacy, and interpreters of an authoritative law. In public they have always acted as a distinctive category of dignitaries or as Allah's elite among His people, [men] wearing distinctive costumes and a distinctive type of beard. (Ghozzi 2002: 317).

The *'ulamā'* are often employed to work in mosques, or as teachers of Islamic studies in seminaries (*dāru'l-'ulūm*). They are recognized as having the knowledge and competence to make decisions on everyday religious matters. A scholar with particular expertise in legal matters is known as a *muftī*, and such an individual has the authority to issue legal opinions (*fatāwā*). A *qādī* (or *qazi/kadi*) is a 'judge' who exercises this authority specifically within a court of law. In many Muslim societies, the *'ulamā'* have often fulfilled an important but usually indirect role as watchdogs of the conduct and behaviour of elites, especially those in political power.

The term *shaykh* (also spelt *sheikh*) means literally 'elder' or 'old man', but conveys the meaning of one who has spiritual authority, or who is especially revered as a guide on the religious path. It is a respectful, prestigious term, and is also often used to refer to Sufi teachers. In the Indian subcontinent, the term *pīr* is widely used, yet it has a slightly different meaning to the word *shaykh*. It is a Persian word, 'denoting a holy man who is a spiritual master and guide, endowed with Divine power and blessing which he can also confer upon others, both in his lifetime and after death' (Barton 1986: 32).[2] Because many British Muslims originate from the Indian subcontinent, it is common to hear them refer to their *pīr* in the villages and towns from which they originally migrated, and there are also some well-known *pīrs* in Britain itself (see chapter 4).

Another religious title which entered mainstream vocabulary in Britain in the 1970s and 1980s was the word *Ayatollah* (from the Arabic *Āyat Allāh*, meaning 'sign of God'). This term is distinctive to the Shī'a, and refers to a senior-ranking religious official. After the Iranian Revolution in 1979, and the *fatwā* passed by Ayatollah Khomeini in Iran against the novelist Salman Rushdie in 1989, the word *Ayatollah* gained prominence in the British media, but usually with little understanding of its true meaning or its particular association with the Shī'a.

[2] See Shaw (2000) for an explanation of the role of *pīrs* among Pakistanis in Oxford.

Although Sunni Islam has religious leaders of differing status, Shīʿa Islam has a much more formal clerical hierarchy. Scholarship remains, however, the necessary prerequisite to rise from *talabeh* (student), to *hojja-toleslam* (advanced seminary student), to *mujtahid* (those who have completed 'seminary' studies), to *Ayatollah* and finally to *Ayatollah al-Uzma* ('Grand Ayatollah'), a title conferred upon only four or five living scholars at any one time.[3]

IMAMS IN BRITAIN FROM 1970: CRITICAL PERSPECTIVES

From the 1960s and 1970s, as Muslim communities in Britain began to establish mosques and other religious centres, the demand arose for specialist religious personnel to lead prayers, to officiate at rites of passage, and to teach children the basic skill of Qurʾānic recitation. The Muslim religious professionals recruited to undertake these roles mostly came from the Indian subcontinent, reflecting the predominantly South Asian origins of British Muslims. They usually had their origins in the same rural communities from which their sponsoring community in Britain also traced its roots. With strong post-migration kinship ties, it was not difficult to find imams in the Indian subcontinent who were willing to come to Britain. These imams often had no advanced religious knowledge, and usually spoke little or no English. However, there was often a comfortable familiarity between the worldviews of these imams and their sponsoring communities, at least initially.

Imams from the Middle East were also recruited to work in British mosques, especially in large, high-profile, well-established centres such as the London Central Mosque at Regent's Park. Their salaries were usually provided by the Saudi Arabian government, and many still are. There were (and continue to be) important local variations on these arrangements however. For example, the 'South Wales Islamic Centre' in Cardiff has a long tradition of employing new Al-Azhar graduates from Egypt to serve the predominantly Arabic-speaking Yemeni congregation. These graduates arrive and leave on a rotating basis and work under supervision of the permanent British imam.

During the 1960s and 1970s the role of the imam was largely confined to leading prayers, presiding over rites of passage, perhaps giving the Friday sermon, and teaching Qurʾānic recitation to children. As such, his

[3] This was confirmed during the author's interview with Grand Ayatollah Nasir Makarem Shirazi in Qom, Iran, 1 June 2004.

role was mosque-centred. He had little external profile or authority in wider society, and his lack of English often severely restricted his capacity to engage in civil society (Barton 1986). Muslims themselves made few demands upon the imam besides these traditional functions, and the emphasis of the role was usually on the preservation and protection of religious identity.

In the 1980s and 1990s, however, criticisms were raised concerning the quality, qualifications and role of many of Britain's imams. Issues of religious leadership were the subject of debate in the British Muslim press, and mostly reflected a concern with language and communication difficulties, pastoral ability (particularly in relation to British-born Muslim youth) and accusations of 'sectarianism'. An Indian *Barelwī* imam, writing some fifteen years after his arrival in Britain, was critical of his fellow religious leaders, especially those of South Asian origin:

the leaders do not know anything about the context in which they are resident. They can neither speak the English language nor are acquainted with the sociopolitical context of the dominating British culture. (Raza 1991: 33)

Some of these 'insider' criticisms are still current, reflecting a spirit of self-awareness and openness. For example, a recent Muslim Council of Britain study, *Voices from the Minaret* (Rahman *et al.* 2006), noted some of the following issues about imams:

[they are] mainly 'imported' with a conservative understanding of their role ... unable to adequately meet the needs of the growing demands with respect to a range of skills and knowledge of British society. (Rahman *et al.* 2006: 3.8.1 (f–g))

The Islamic religious leaders who came to Britain from the 1970s spoke little or no English. Their first language was Urdu, Punjabi, Gujarati, or perhaps Sylheti or Arabic, and their teaching, especially of children, was also therefore largely delivered in the medium of their mother tongue. Some imams promoted community languages (especially Urdu) using a religious justification, as if these languages were inherently religious and divinely inspired. In reality, they were trying to legitimate their own continued use of the only language in which they were fluent. Some also laboured under the misapprehension that the preservation of mother-tongue languages would somehow automatically protect the religious identity of the young. There was a further disincentive to learn English, reflecting the contractual and financial insecurity of 'ministers of religion' from overseas. Many were (and some still are) on short-term visas, and could be deported back to their countries of origin with little right of appeal. Under these conditions, many understandably saw no necessity to learn English or engage with wider British society.

Those suffering the consequences of poor religious leadership were often the least empowered and the most in need within the community: young people and women. Both within and outside Muslim communities there was (and continues to be) concern for the welfare of children in some mosques. Not only were some imams from overseas unaware of legislation forbidding corporal punishment in Britain, but they also did not appreciate the effects that such disciplinary methods were likely to have on children. A Bradford doctor, active for some years in Young Muslims UK, noted in 1989 that the reason why so many Muslim youth were adopting an alternative youth culture of *bhangra*, rather than furthering their knowledge of Islam, was because 'at the first opportunity [the boys] rebelled against a religion, which has sometimes been literally beaten into them' (Dr Munir Ahmed, *The Muslim News*, 15/12/89, cited in Lewis 1994: 141). At present, there is no legal obligation on Britain's mosques to run Criminal Record Bureau (CRB) checks on their employees, and the diversity and decentralized character of Muslim communities in Britain makes it difficult to impose any kind of central authority on matters of professional standards. Any efforts in this direction are largely local, and stimulated by the concern to promote 'good practice', such as the report by Shakeel Hafez in Kirklees, *Safe Children, Sound Learning* (Kirklees Metropolitan Council) (Hafez 2003).

Many young British-born Muslims are negotiating lifestyle choices and decisions that are authentically Islamic but also consistent with their lives in Britain. The complex legal, social and economic realities of their lives are not always being addressed by imams: 'Most "imported" imams are frankly not able to understand or reach out to young Muslims' (Birt 2000: 21). Some of these criticisms are still voiced today, particularly in relation to youth. The over-representation of young Muslim men in the prison population, while obviously alarming, has also been a catalyst for dynamic new initiatives on the part of some imams (Miah 2005).

Muslim women in Britain have often also suffered the consequences of poor or inaccessible religious leadership. Too many imams are still remote and unapproachable to half the community where predominantly mosque-based roles confine them to premises that women are often not permitted to enter. When women are able to access religious leadership, it is frequently unsatisfactory, as Samia Bano's research on *Sharī'ah* Councils demonstrated (Bano 2007). Muslim women seek the counsel of imams on issues concerning marriage, children, education, divorce and so on, yet few imams have been trained in counselling skills, or have the ability to relate Islamic law to the realities of contemporary Britain. Ill-qualified imams sometimes offer incorrect information or guidance, interpreting Islamic law without sufficient knowledge or competence. The advice that women receive is often inconsistent or impractical: 'It seems some of them just need a good turban and a long beard, and people will go to them ... they are not properly trained but they give out *fatawas* which are not suitable for this country' (Badawi 2004).[4]

Although there is an increasing number of British-trained imams, religious professionals still arrive in Britain from various Muslim countries. This reflects the fact that most of Britain's mosque committees continue to be predominantly constituted by post-Second World War migrants. Transnational kinship ties among this generation are still strong, and they remain keen to nurture meaningful links with their villages and towns of origin. The recruitment of imams is a way of affirming and maintaining ongoing kinship ties, these loyalties sometimes assuming more importance than the knowledge or qualifications of the imam himself. However, there are perhaps other less charitable reasons for the continued recruitment of imams from abroad. For instance, many of them are willing to work for considerably less remuneration than British-trained imams would be. Being largely unfamiliar with the notion of 'employment rights', they are dependent upon the continued support and goodwill of the committee employing them. This dependence makes them altogether more malleable and, if necessary, removable, should there be a breakdown in relationships.[5] In 1989, Lewis notes that an imam paid more than £80 a week was exceptional (Lewis 1994). Research in 2003/4 found that 'average' pay was about £150 per week, usually with some accommodation as part of the package.[6] A British-born and trained scholar (*ālim*) will know that this is considerably below the national minimum wage, and hardly a fitting reward for the length of training that many of them have undertaken.

There is now something of a crisis of religious leadership within British Muslim communities, particularly manifest among the younger

---

[4] Cited on the website for the Channel 4 series *Shariah TV*, 2004, www.channel4.com/culture/microsites/S/shariahtv/rules.html
[5] For an example of how relationships can break down, and the impact this can have on the employment of an imam, see Shaw (2000: 279).
[6] This research was conducted by Sophie Gilliat-Ray at Cardiff University, with Fiaz Ahmed. The project was entitled 'The Training and Development of Muslim Religious Professionals', and was funded by the Leverhulme Trust, 2003–4.

generations. One of the consequences of this has been the growing use of the internet for religious advice. 'Fishing for a *fatwā*', where advice is sought from several scholars before selecting the interpretation that suits one's preferences, has come about because many imams working in British mosques cannot satisfactorily address the questions being posed to them: 'they may understand the *text*, but not the *context* of the questioner'.[7] Their religious advice is often framed against the background of the culture from which they have come, which is usually the Indian subcontinent, and not British society. Accordingly, the internet provides young people with the opportunity for finding answers from further afield, suggesting that the very nature of religious authority itself – who has it, how it is constructed, and how it is displayed – is now being questioned.

Alongside the '*ulamā*', other religious intellectuals are becoming influential, such as Shaykh Hamza Yusuf (USA), Shaykh Abdul Hakim Murad (UK) and Professor Tariq Ramadan (UK). These individuals have the ability to draw a large and often well-educated following. They are also distinctive for their capacity to draw audiences which often transcend the internal diversity of Muslim communities. The emergence of these charismatic figures, along with the accessibility of religious information on the internet, is democratizing knowledge. Young British Muslims now have the option of bypassing local imams, along with their perceived sectarian differences, language difficulties and lack of wider socio-political awareness.

### IMAMS IN BRITAIN TODAY: A SOCIOLOGICAL PROFILE

So far, there is only one study which offers insight into the basic sociological profile of imams in Britain today. In 2007, Professor Ron Geaves undertook a small-scale quantitative study to investigate the place of birth, age, mother tongue, language for sermons, length of residence, place of education and qualifications of 300 British imams (Geaves 2008).[8] The results reveal that 83.7 per cent of imams were of South Asian

---

[7] Website for the Channel 4 series *Shariah TV*, 'Fatwa shopping', www.channel4.com/culture/microsites/S/shariahtv/

[8] This was undertaken via telephone interviews conducted by postgraduate students able to speak relevant community languages. The contact details for mosques were gathered from a number of sources, including the *Green Directory*, the *Muslim Directory*, and *Religions in the UK* (University of Derby/Inter Faith Network for the UK). However, it is important to be aware of the particular character of the sample, since 'one assumes that those [mosques] organised enough to place themselves in various directories, may be the ones with the best educated imams (small back street mosques that are not recorded in directories would presumably have less resources for highly

origin, while 8.5 per cent were from other overseas countries. Only 8.1 per cent were born and educated in Britain, confirming the well-established impression that most British imams are foreign. Geaves interprets this finding as confirmation that mosques remain in the control of first-generation, post-Second World War migrants who continue to prefer the services of 'imported' rather than 'home-grown' imams. Despite this, however, Geaves's work reveals that nearly half of British imams (41.5 per cent) are below forty years of age, so mosque committees are not employing 'ageing' imams. Furthermore, his findings show a gradually increasing stability within the imamate: nearly a quarter of the sample (23.1 per cent) had been in Britain for over ten years, while a further 31.3 per cent had been in Britain for between six and ten years. The largest group (39.1 per cent) nonetheless had arrived in the past five years. Taken together, his findings overall

reveal a deeply conservative body of individuals maintaining traditional languages, certain types of qualifications and still largely recruited from the place of origin. Although there are social, religious and political reasons that drive a need to transform the imamate in to a twenty-first-century British context, there is as yet little sign of the mosque imams or their employers being ready to professionalise. (Geaves 2008: 105)

## THE CHANGING ROLE OF IMAMS

Against this background of conservatism, British Muslims nevertheless have new and growing expectations about their religious leaders. Fundamentally, Muslims in Britain want imams who can provide not only ritual, textual, scholarly/legal and spiritual leadership, but also some degree of pastoral competence (Birt 2005b). Imams are now increasingly expected to engage with a broader range of constituencies, and in particular to address the needs of youth. There is a growing sense that imams should be active community leaders, engaging with and addressing the social, educational and political realities facing Muslims in contemporary Britain. The capacity to provide relevant, credible, intellectual leadership, in the medium of English, has become pressing. This expectation has, to some extent, emerged in parallel with the evolution of what might be called a distinctive 'British Muslim' identity, especially among the young (Jacobson 1998). One of the characteristics of this 'British Muslim' identity

qualified imams and even more unlikely to employ British-trained imams or use English language for example)' (Ron Geaves, personal communication, January 2009).

is the sense of connection to the *ummah* and an identity which reaches beyond the local to the global, beyond the particular to the universal. As young people, especially those with origins in the Indian subcontinent, are increasingly looking for identities which lie beyond South Asian language or culture, or 'traditional' (often parental) interpretations of Islam, so too do they appear to be expecting imams to move beyond their traditional mosque-based roles and to encompass a broader responsibility.

At the same time, however, it would seem that British Muslims, even the youth, still want imams to be carriers of historic Muslim traditions, traditions that are part of their heritage which they do not want to lose, but for which they do not want to take personal responsibility. Some youth still favour the 'importing' of imams from overseas since it gives them a sense of connection to the Muslim world, especially the Arabic/Urdu-speaking world, even when they themselves do not understand Urdu or Arabic. One interviewee in 2003/4 noted the paradox:

the role of the imam is curious in that the Muslim community *per se* is modernising, acculturating, indigenising. So they expect their imam to facilitate all their new experiences, but at the same time carry all those traditional themes that they themselves feel they should have ... but because of the new context they find themselves in ... can't really have.[9]

If this is the case, Britain's imams are perhaps beginning to undertake a role that is not dissimilar to one recently assumed by the priests and clergy of the Christian churches, as carriers of vicarious memory (Davie 2000) and bearers of culture (Schoenherr 1987).

As part of this expanding function, imams are increasingly expected to act as interlocutors between Muslim communities and the wider society. While international events weigh heavily upon them, Muslims in Britain are also concerned that imams should publicly address issues of local need and inequality. They want imams who can speak out about local Islamophobic prejudice, the problems of substance abuse, issues of global injustice and so on. Many young Muslims have suffered a whole range of disadvantages, educationally, socially and materially. Imams are potentially the only people who can provide 'bridging social capital' to help young people to benefit from the opportunities of society at large (Lewis 2006a: 273; Lewis 2006b). There are already examples of good practice. Speaking from East London, one young British Muslim noted that in his mosque

---

[9] See note 6 above for details of this research.

the imam runs support classes, does access work with people on drugs and with people coming out of prison. It's all voluntary ... he is very involved with the local interfaith community, including the synagogue next to the mosque. His good grasp of other cultures and religions is something that I aspire to. There is a huge scope for imams in playing a role in promoting community cohesion. (Miah 2005: 19)

The Muslim Council of Britain report, to which reference has already been made, also notes the multiple roles that imams are now expected to play, as

community leaders, teachers, advisors, counsellors, social workers, mediators. [Beyond this] they have to deal with the social consequences of the economic conditions of their communities. (Rahman *et al.* 2006: 3.8.1 (b))

These new expectations about the role that an imam might play are just one aspect of a move towards the apparent 'professionalizing' of British Muslim religious leadership. To some extent this is being driven by Muslim communities and organizations themselves, as well as by recent government agendas. However, it is also part of a wider trend affecting religious professionals from all faith communities.[10] It remains to be seen how far the various efforts towards change and professionalization coming from both within and outside Muslim communities are pulling in either co-operative or conflicting directions (Birt, J. 2006). The following section maps the various elements of this apparent process of professionalization, beginning with the issue of employment rights and professional standards.

## PROFESSIONALIZING INFLUENCES: EMPLOYMENT RIGHTS AND STANDARDS.

In 1984, a national conference of imams and mosque leaders was held in Wembley, London. The late Dr Zaki Badawi, former chief imam at London Central Mosque, was appointed chairman of a new body, the 'Imams and Mosques Council of the UK'. The Council's premises were based at the Muslim College on Creffield Road in Ealing, and the aim of the Council was to facilitate communication between mosques, solve

---

[10] For example, there are now new postgraduate courses relating to chaplaincy in Britain, emerging out of institutional expectations that chaplains should have recognized qualifications and certified 'competence'. Chaplains also have a self-imposed desire for recognition of their professional abilities, surrounded as they often are by other professionals. Imams are being employed in a climate of new expectations about religious professionalism more generally.

internal disputes through conciliation, and encourage co-operation and tolerance between mosques of various factions. The issue of employment rights for imams was high on the Council's agenda for some years.

At the 1999 Council meeting, the role, payment and training of imams was discussed at length. In a conference report, a number of key issues were noted. These included the accessibility and approachability of imams (especially for women seeking religious guidance), and the need to establish a 'register' of imams (employed with professional contracts of employment). The inclusion of community care, marriage counselling, mosque management and 'crowd psychology' as part of the curriculum of religious training was also realized as an issue, together with a call for proper remuneration for the work of imams (Shirwani 1999).

The late Dr Badawi took up the issue of employment rights for imams once again in 2002, this time in co-operation with FAIR (Forum Against Islamophobia and Racism) and the Al-Khoei Foundation. The report produced by this alliance of concerned individuals and organizations pointed out that imams were vulnerable to poor pay and conditions, and unfair, ad hoc disciplinary procedures. They noted that where imams pay tax and national insurance on their earnings 'it is anomalous that they have all the responsibilities of paid employees to fulfil ... but without the corresponding protection of their basic employment rights' (FAIR 2002). Another argument put forward by FAIR was that the extension of employment rights to imams would not only have practical value in eliminating poor employment practices, but would also be 'enormously symbolic' (FAIR 2002: 7) by bringing them into the mainstream with other public servants. It would amount to recognition of their role, and the growing complexity of that role in contemporary Britain. Dr Badawi was not only concerned with employment rights, however. He also promoted the creation of better Muslim religious professionals in Britain, noting:

I want the Government to help me in training better imams ... Governments plead poverty. That is their mantra. But my argument is that it is cheaper than having to combat the effect of bad imams. (Dr Zaki Badawi, interviewed by O'Sullivan 2003)

The next and most recent development in relation to employment rights and professional standards for imams took place on 27 June 2006, when the Mosques and Imams National Advisory Board (MINAB) was formally launched as an outcome of the consultations following the London bombings of July 2005. Again based on Creffield Road in Ealing, London, Maulana Mohammad Shahid Raza is the current Acting Chair of this new body. MINAB describes itself as a non-sectarian advisory body, characterized by transparency and confidentiality. It has the backing of a number of major British Muslim organizations, namely, the Al-Khoei Foundation, the British Muslim Forum, the Muslim Association of Britain and the Muslim Council of Britain. During the first two years of MINAB's existence, it undertook consultation on a formal constitution and standards for membership, the outcomes of which can be viewed on its website.[11]

What is clear from these efforts is that an attempt is being made to address many of the issues that have been at the centre of debates about imams over recent decades. Questions surrounding the involvement of women and youth in mosques are prominent, as is the expectation that mosque personnel will 'promote civic responsibility of Muslims in wider society ... actively combat all forms of violent extremism ... and encourage participation in the events of other communities' (MINAB website, accessed 2/5/2009). Likewise, mosques that register with MINAB are expected to ensure that mosque personnel are CRB checked, and will undertake suitable continuing professional development. MINAB's claim of 'transparency' is manifest within the organization's website, and there is extensive and publicly accessible documentation and feedback arising out of its consultation work in recent years. This feedback indicates that some issues surrounding the remit of MINAB and especially its powers and management procedures are still being resolved. Time will tell whether MINAB is able to evolve into an effective and sustainable organization in the future, and whether its agenda will be able to work with and through the diverse and decentralized nature of Islam in Britain.

## PROFESSIONALIZING CAPACITY: CHAPLAINCY

In recent decades, Muslim religious professionals have increasingly been employed as 'visiting ministers' and chaplains in public institutions, especially prisons and hospitals (Beckford and Gilliat 1998; Gilliat-Ray 2008; Spalek and Wilson 2001).[12] The growing role of Muslims in chaplaincy has been a significant driving force behind professionalization of Muslim religious leadership, particularly through the acquisition of management, interfaith and pastoral skills (Birt 2005b). Prisons and hospitals need

[11] www.minab.org.uk
[12] From 2008 to 2010, Dr Sophie Gilliat-Ray and Professor Stephen Pattison are undertaking research on Muslim chaplaincy in Britain generously funded by the AHRC/ESRC 'Religion and Society' programme, and in partnership with Markfield Institute of Higher Education.

Figure 5. Imam Asim Hafiz, Muslim Chaplain to HM Armed Forces,
appointed in 2005 © Crown Copyright/MOD. Reproduced with the permission
of the Controller of Her Majesty's Stationery Office

religious professionals who understand the protocols of the context in
which they are working, such as security, confidentiality, and health and
safety. Muslim chaplains have to be able to write reports, navigate their
way through bureaucratic structures, and work as part of a multi-faith
team. Their role can also extend to delivering training about the beliefs
and practices of Muslims to other staff. Public institutions now expect
professional accreditation, and so imams working in publicly funded
chaplaincy are being influenced by the standards and ethos of professionalism that is affecting 'sector ministry' as a whole.[13]

In 2009 there were 203 Muslim chaplains employed by the Prison
Service, of whom forty-one were full-time, and thirty-six were part-
time. The remainder were 'sessional' which means that that their time
was bought in for specific periods.[14] In addition, there was one part-
time female chaplain, and a further eighteen sessional female chaplains.
Chaplaincy has thereby become a significant way for British Muslim
women to serve the community in professional religious roles. The Prison
Service Chaplaincy undertook a major recruitment drive in late 2008, and

---

[13] This is evident in the growth of academic 'in-service' training courses for chaplains, such as the
MTh in Chaplaincy studies offered by St Michael's College, Llandaff, in association with Cardiff
University.
[14] I am grateful to Ahtsham Ali, the Muslim Advisor to the Prison Service Chaplaincy, for this
information, correct in July 2009.

so the total number of Muslim prison chaplains has been rising steadily in recent years. This makes the Prison Service one of the largest employers of Muslim religious professionals in Britain. In the health service in 2009, there were four full-time Muslim chaplains (of whom one was female) and forty-six part-time chaplains (of whom fourteen were female). They were supported by an additional fifty-seven volunteers (of whom ten were female).[15] The armed forces recruited a full-time civilian Muslim chaplain in 2005, and there are now an increasing number of Muslim chaplains associated with educational institutions.

Chaplaincy is a significant growth area in terms of employment opportunities for qualified Muslim religious professionals. As a result of the early formation of *Deobandī* seminaries in Britain (see chapter 4), many of these chaplaincy posts have been taken up by graduates of these institutions, especially from the seminary at Bury.

Owing to this growth in employment, Muslim chaplains are developing distinctive professional (and sector-specific) identities, as is evident in the formation of associations to represent their interests.[16] There are now a sufficient number of Muslim chaplains, especially in the Prison Service, to enable specific in-service training that provides opportunities for Muslim scholars to discuss legal, social and political questions from the perspective of their differing schools of thought. Chaplaincy is not only stimulating 'professionalization', therefore, but also offers significant opportunities for internal (intra-faith) religious debate.[17]

The longer-term consequences of Muslim involvement in chaplaincy are yet to be seen, but one possible outcome is that Muslim chaplains might have a professionalizing effect on community-based religious leadership, both within and outside mosques.[18] This is already happening in

---

[15] I am grateful to Chowdhury Mueen-Uddin, Director of Muslim Spiritual Care in the NHS, from the Muslim Council of Britain for this information, correct in February 2009.

[16] For example: the Muslim Chaplains Association (for prison chaplains), established 2007; the Islam Resource Group at the College of Health Care Chaplains (NHS), established in 2002; and the Association of Muslim Chaplains in Education (mainly further and higher education), established in 2008.

[17] The process of professionalization is being stimulated further still by the opportunity to undertake educational programmes devoted to the study of Muslim chaplaincy, especially the Certificate in Training of Muslim Chaplaincy provided by Markfield Institute of Higher Education in Leicester. Over 100 students have taken their course in recent years.

[18] This prospect has recently been explored by Imam Asim Hafiz as part of a Master's dissertation, Faculty of Continuing Education, Birkbeck College, University of London, 2008, 'Muslim Chaplaincy: An examination of what it offers mosque-based imams in contemporary Britain'. The harmonization of British and EU employment law in December 2003 meant that all ministers of religion have full employment rights in terms of pay, conditions and legal redress, but this does not prevent poor employment practice.

a small number of cases, where former chaplains have used the skills and 'professionalism gained from experiences in chaplaincy' (Birt 2005b) to develop independent community work characterized by a new style of professionalism. Mosque-based imams have little or no access to continuing professional development. They often suffer poor terms and conditions and may therefore be increasingly influenced by the better employment prospects that clearly accompany chaplaincy work. This awareness may in due course encourage mosque committees to offer equivalent employment conditions, thereby potentially raising standards of professional leadership in mosques.

The overall number of Muslim chaplains in Britain is relatively small, but their significance and potential is clearly understood within government. As publicly funded employees, Muslim chaplains are vulnerable to strategies of government power and control, and especially efforts to reinforce what a 'good imam' or a 'bad imam' is like, and the qualities he or she should embody (Birt, J. 2006). This is evident in a Communities and Local Government project begun in 2009, intended to formulate a set of standards and recruitment processes for institutions employing Muslim faith leaders. These standards very appropriately seek to ensure that Muslim chaplains have good communication skills, some aptitude for pastoral care delivery, and a sound understanding of policies and procedures that govern public institutions. However, it is also made clear that with these competencies there are assumed attitudes and behaviours that would undermine one of the traditional roles of the *'ulamā'*, namely the expectation that, when necessary, they reserve the right to act as critical independent voices in relation to those in power. An analysis of the proposed new standards for Muslim chaplains reveals the dominance of secular principles in British public institutions, and an assumed willingness to be open to working with people from a variety of religious and non-religious backgrounds. Warnings about the implications of this have already been sounded in relation to Christian healthcare chaplaincy:

There is much to be commended in this open-minded, concerned attitude for people of all faiths and none. It is a great advance on tribalism, exclusivism, and xenophobia. However ... chaplains may be tempted to downplay the importance of their own tradition and identity within that tradition in the interests of being universally accepting and acceptable. In the long term, this can only weaken their value as speakers of a particular language and representatives of a particular religious community and tradition. (Pattison 2001: 41)

If this was not enough to give pause for thought, Birt has already noted that 'contemporary public policy works from an "Anglican template" with respect to the formation of Muslim religious leaderships' (Birt, J. 2006: 689). Muslim chaplains are therefore unwittingly caught up in a process that they may not fully appreciate. The proposed new standards for Muslim chaplains in public institutions are revealing of a particular kind of religious engineering that is not being undertaken in relation to other religious traditions in Britain. Quite simply, Muslim chaplains are implicated in a larger government concern with British Muslim religious leadership, at a time when 'the British imam has become a central figure in tackling extremism' (Birt, J. 2006: 687).

It is questionable whether Muslim communities and institutions in Britain have a sufficiently developed infrastructure to engage in this debate, let alone deliver its intended outcomes, as equal partners. For example, it is proposed that an 'eligible' Muslim chaplain will have formal endorsement from national, regional or local organizations, or from a professional chaplaincy association. However, the relatively recent formation of professional Muslim bodies, some of which have yet to establish their own identity, means that they are not sufficiently developed to be in a position to formally judge the qualifications or suitability of those aspiring to become chaplains. In a context where the role of 'Muslim chaplain' is itself so new, attempts to evaluate the degree to which a person measures up to externally imposed criteria for a competent public religious 'professional' are complicated. They will involve difficult decision-making about the legitimacy of different forms of Islamic religious knowledge and training, and personal qualities and characteristics (such as 'empathy' or 'sensitivity') that are tricky, if not impossible, to assess. Given the decentralized and highly diverse character of Muslim communities in Britain, this is potentially divisive, premature, and counterproductive to an otherwise gradual transformation of Muslim religious leadership.

## GOVERNMENT INFLUENCES

The subject of imams in Britain, their origins, their competence, their role, their employment status and their training, has now become a matter of open debate and public policy. The government is playing an increasingly active role in shaping the future religious leadership of Muslims in Britain in a number of distinctive ways and, as a consequence, the distance between the religious sphere of the *'ulamā'* and the political sphere of the government has gradually begun to close. Some British Muslim organizations are concerned and sceptical about the 'intentions of the Government which [is] perceived to have an agenda of control for the training and accreditation of imams' (Rahman *et al.* 2006, authors of the Muslim Council of Britain report, *Voices from the Minaret: MCB Study of UK Imams and Mosques*, May 2006). 'It is within the policy context of interfaith, community cohesion and counter-terrorism … that policy on British imams is now being formed' (Birt, J. 2006: 694). Britain is not alone in this effort. Across Europe, considerable resources have been devoted to 'deporting, monitoring, coercing and training imams' (Haddad and Balz 2008: 228). While some European countries have been more actively engaged in the effort to influence Muslim religious training and to 'reprogram imams' (Haddad and Balz 2008: 229) (especially in the Netherlands), this is gradually beginning to change in Britain, especially through two initiatives announced in the Home Office document, *Preventing Violent Extremism: A strategy for delivery* (May 2008). One of these initiatives involves 'the establishment of a board of leading Muslim scholars to help articulate an understanding of Islam in Britain' (Home Office 2008: 4). The second key project is the Muslim Faith Leaders Review, funded by the UK Department for Communities and Local Government. The funding and structural support for this project as part of the PVE/ Prevent agenda immediately makes the Review a highly politicized undertaking, especially where it aims to map the variety of training institutions and, perhaps more controversially, where it aims to evaluate their suitability for the professional training of Muslim religious specialists in Britain.

The Review has so far established the existence of up to fifty facilities for acquiring Islamic religious knowledge in Britain, some of these being 'virtual', such as www.sunnipath.com. There is a considerable overlap between the institutions identified in the Review and those that were the subject of previous surveys of training institutions (Birt 2005b; Gilliat-Ray 2006). Among the challenging issues that the Review seeks to address are ways to enable collaboration between mainstream institutions of higher and further education in Britain, and centres of Islamic religious training such as *dāru'l-'ulūm*. This is because many young men and women graduating from these institutions, perhaps aged twenty-one or twenty-two, have no recognizable qualifications beyond GCSE level, and certainly none that have currency in the world of mainstream education. This can frustrate their employment opportunities or onward educational development. Thus the Review is, among other things, exploring potential ways in which some formal academic recognition can be brought to the traditional South Asian *dars-i niẓāmī* curriculum.

Many of the objectives of the Review are commendable, especially where they are concerned with the formation of imams who are perhaps better able to meet the needs of younger people, and who are better prepared for the challenges they may face in the world of employment, especially as (prison) chaplains. However, the timing and methods of the Review may be inimical to the successful achievement of these aims, and they may frustrate the process of organic, internally driven developments that were already underway:[19]

> Government efforts may in fact be stifling debate within European communities. Government intervention is probably impeding the construction of an organic European-Muslim (or French-Muslim, British-Muslim, etc.) identity that would otherwise develop over time. (Savage, 2004: 42)

As governments continue to demonize radical Islam and to intimidate Muslim communities into cooperating with state security services, they force immigrant communities into defensive postures, making them into suspects, or even enemies rather than partners. Consequently, Muslim communities are focused on their struggle against government intimidation rather than on their internal struggle to marginalize radicalism. (Haddad and Balz 2008: 229)[20]

The way in which these controversial debates unfold in the coming few years will also be partly shaped by the outcomes of the Higher Education Funding Council for England (HEFCE) investment of £1 million into the field of Islamic studies, now designated as 'strategically important' (Robinson 2007), following the publication of the Siddiqui Report in 2007 (Siddiqui 2007).

Pressure is therefore simultaneously being placed upon the higher education sector and upon traditional centres of Islamic religious training in Britain. The values that underpin 'academic freedom' are now being pitted against the values of 'religious freedom' held by Islamic colleges and seminaries, against a distinctive government agenda background. The issues involved in this process are complex:

> Guided as it is by international and domestic politics, the most striking feature of these contributions to the national debate about Islam is the ontological (and faintly theological) assumption that there is a 'true' (read: moderate) Islam, that, once 'properly' appreciated and disseminated, will expose the views of the 'extremists' for what they really are: perversions, fantasies, distortions and lies. The debate is presented as one about truth and falsehood, but what it is actually about is social authority. Who controls the discourse of what is 'authentic' or

---

[19] For instance, the adapted *dars-i niẓāmī* curriculum, taught in the medium of English (rather than Urdu) at Ebrahim Community College, London.
[20] See Savage (2004).

'real'? Who speaks on behalf of Islam and what fields of knowledge constitute expertise? (Robinson 2007)

Traditionally trained Muslim religious professionals who are able to span the worlds of the seminary and the higher education academy are perhaps an especially important group of people to support and empower within this complex debate. As yet, the number of individuals who have the competence and qualifications to carry this task forward is small, but their numbers are set to grow.

### A MUSLIM 'PARISH PRIEST'?

The role of imams in Britain is broadening to include pastoral care, youth work and counselling, as well as traditional ritual, scholarly and spiritual leadership. British Muslims are arguably seeking a form of local religious leadership that can to some extent approximate to the role of the Christian priest or minister, or the Jewish rabbi. However, there is a divergence of opinion among imams themselves about the wisdom or suitability of this development. The following comments recorded during interviews with two imams in Britain in 2004 (one British-trained) amplify one side of the debate:[21]

The imam should be really a replica of what the Priest does ... or for that matter the Rabbi. They cannot be less.

Sometimes I look at the priest in the Christian tradition and what they do. They do so much pastoral work and other work within the community, within society, that I think imams also should be sharing that burden. I have many many Christian priests who are friends and some of them have actually been approached by Muslims with their problems. And you can see that it is an indicator of the fact that the imams are not accessible or are not reaching out to these people. (British-trained imam)

In contrast, British-born imams who took part in a focus group discussion as part of Geaves's research in 2007 (Geaves 2008) had very different perspectives. Geaves noted that

generally there was little opposition to the need to 'professionalize' the *ulema*, although there was an awareness of *the risk that imams could be turned into parish priests and would no longer be fitting the Islamic model of the ulema*. (Geaves 2008: 109, emphasis mine)

These diametrically opposing views arising from British-born, British-trained Muslim religious professionals are indicative of a lack (perhaps a

---

[21]  See note 6 above for the details of this project.

very healthy lack) of consensus about their present and future role. This kind of divergence of opinion is also seen in relation to other issues. For example, some are committed to perceptions of the essentially sacred and inviolate nature of the traditional *dars-i niẓāmī* curriculum of religious training typical in the Indian subcontinent, while others are open to the possibilities for review and revision of this curriculum for the British context. Regardless of whether, or even how, such different perspectives are resolved, it is perhaps becoming unrealistic for a single person, the imam, to try to fulfil growing expectations and newly developing roles. An interviewee for research in 2003–4[22] noted:

> Somebody in a mosque may expect their mosque imam to be, you know, a super duper *mufti*, a huge intellectual figure, engaged in interfaith dialogue, engaged in politics, engaged with the council, fundraising for the community, giving them pastoral care, as well as leading the prayer and running the mosque. I think that is a very unrealistic expectation. So I think one of the things we need to do is break down all of those different roles and somehow distribute that authority and that power throughout the community. (British Muslim scholar, Leicester, 12 December 2003)

If this re-division of religious work is to be achieved, it will depend upon the capacity of mosque communities and religious organizations to fund it, and the ability of imams themselves to exert more influence in the shaping of their role.

### CONCLUSION

Muslim religious leaders in Britain are under pressure from a variety of quarters, and changes are underway. One of the most significant catalysts for change is the recent emergence of a number of dynamic and young imams, mostly British-trained. They can move between several cultural and linguistic worlds with confidence, and they are likely to have a significant influence in reshaping perceptions and roles of imams in Britain in the future, particularly away from 'the rather forbidding image many young people have about religious teachers – the *maulvis* and *maulanas*' (Mondal 2008: 39).

However, 'whenever charisma emerges among the ulema, it tends to decrease their historic attachment to established traditions' (Ghozzi 2002: 318), and already there is some evidence of a diminishing of specific sectarian identities. A British imam recently reflected: 'I don't see myself

---

[22] See note 6 above for the details of this project.

as *Deobandī* anymore. I see myself as serving British Muslims.'[23] It would appear that sectarian alliances and identities derived from 'back home' are perhaps slowly becoming less meaningful to some British-trained imams, as they appear to be among British Muslims as a whole. In some ways this bodes well for the future role of imams in Britain. Like their Christian counterparts, they are increasingly likely to have to find ways of working co-operatively across those boundaries of interpretation and tradition which have historically separated them, achieving at least a 'working level of ideological harmony that can be activated either to counteract internal divisive or disruptive forces, or to defeat external hostilities and pursue collective goals' (Ghozzi 2002: 318). The context of contemporary Britain is providing opportunities for new arrangements of co-operation.

The role of an imam is to some extent shaped by circumstances, history and tradition. Many mosque communities in Britain remain constituted from a particular linguistic or ethnic group, and the performance of the imam's role has therefore been shaped by distinctive local expectations about the remit of his post, the message he will preach and so on. Yet already it is possible to discern tension between past traditions and new social realities. There are now two countervailing forces at work. Conservative forces are seeking to preserve the definitive character of the scholarly role and traditions of the *'ulamā'* (most evident in the continued delivery of the traditional *dars-i niẓāmī* curriculum in the *dāru'l-'ulūm*). At the same time charisma, entrepreneurialism and government agendas are producing diversity in knowledge and expertise relevant to, and shaped by, the realities of life for Muslims in Britain. The syllabus of religious learning is being adapted to support this process. The long-term challenge of counterbalancing the demands of tradition and change lies largely with the new generation of British-born, British-trained imams.

---

[23] Quotation from research interview conducted by Fiaz Ahmed in December 2003. See note 6 above for details of this project.

# CHAPTER 8

# Mosques

## INTRODUCTION

British Muslims have devoted more energy and resources to the creation of mosques than perhaps to any other institution. There are between approximately 850 and 1,500 mosques in Britain today. They vary considerably in size, architecture, function and history. It is difficult to determine the precise number of mosques because not all premises are registered as places of worship with local authorities, and much depends upon the criteria used to define a mosque. The producers of the 'Model Mosque' competition run by the UK-based Islam Channel in 2008 estimated that 1,500 mosques existed in Britain, whereas the *Muslim Directory UK 08/09* lists 849 mosques. One academic authority notes the existence of approximately 1,000 mosques, including unregistered premises (McLoughlin 2005b).

It may at first seem rather pointless to try to ascertain precise numbers, but the significance becomes more apparent when the process of establishing a mosque is seen instead as the 'Islamization of space' in Britain (Eade 1993). The number of mosques and their location are indicators of broader issues, such as the changing religious landscape of Britain, the degree to which British Muslims are investing in a long-term future in this country, and the scope of Muslims to prevail in their plans with respect to local planning authorities (Gale 2004). This chapter traces the establishment of mosques in Britain from small converted terraced houses to large, purpose-built, multi-functional community centres. Consideration is also given to the internal and external politics that surround mosques. This will involve some discussion of the internal tensions among local Muslim communities on issues such as mosque governance and access for women, as well as wider community debates about the physical and symbolic place of mosques in local neighbourhoods, urban politics and the recent securitization agenda (Brown 2008).

Mosques crystallize many issues that pertain to Muslims in Britain more generally. For example, the complex politics concerning the management of particular mosques reflect broader issues about the leadership of British Muslims in general. Where some mosques have started to assume a role in the delivery of local authority-funded social welfare provision, or 'Preventing Violent Extremism' initiatives, this illustrates, in microcosm, changing local and national government policy responses to religious minorities, and especially to Muslims. Behind the physical existence of a mosque there are social and political interests that reflect many of the issues relating to Islam in Britain more generally. Mosques are not just bricks and mortar, but places for the production of Islamic discourse and for the sustaining of Muslim identity in the context of wider British society.

The establishment of mosques needs to be understood within broader Islamic traditions, and some explanation of terminology is therefore a helpful starting point. The word 'mosque' or *masjid* derives from the Arabic root word *sajada*, which means 'to prostrate'. It is a universal term referring to any place or building used for prayer:

> The social house of worship is called a *masjid* because prostration is understood as the *salat's* highpoint ... It symbolizes the utter submission and surrender (*islam*) of the human being to God. (Murata and Chittick 2000: 14)

A mosque is respected as a place of worship requiring certain etiquettes, but it is not set apart as a sacred or holy place through consecration or some other religious ritual (Gale 2007; Turner 1981).[1] This is partly a reflection of Islamic tradition. A saying of the Prophet Muhammad recounts that 'the whole earth is made as a place of worship'.[2] The word 'mosque' can have a meaning that is so general and universal that it has not only been applied to the places of worship established by Muslims, but also to

> pre-Islamic sanctuaries in Arabia, the churches and temples of other religions, and places where worship occurred without benefit of buildings at all. Even if the mosque should have to be closed for repairs, or cannot accommodate all on a great occasion the adjacent courtyard [or street] remains adequate as an authentic *masjid,* for the building is not essential. (Turner 1981: 138–9, 146)

Throughout the history of Islam, mosques have usually served as much more than premises for the performance of prayers. They exist at the heart

---

[1] For a fuller discussion of 'sacred places' in relation to the law in England, see Edge (2002).

[2] I. Al Bukhari (2007). 'Prayers (Salat)', in Muhammad Muhsin Khan (trans.), *The Translation of the Meanings of Sahih Al-Bukhari: Arabic–English*. Riyadh: Darussalam. Vol. 1, Book 8, No. 429.

of the community and all the obligations associated with the five 'pillars' of Islam involve mosques in one way or another. For example, pilgrims going to Makkah to perform their lifetime obligation (*hajj*) are usually supported by the prayers, and sometimes by the finances, of their local worshipping community. This makes their journey in some senses a vicarious experience for their co-worshippers. Mosques are spaces for discussion and debate, for the settlement of disputes, for the performance of rites of passage, for education and for social welfare. These multiple functions reflect the importance in Islam of integrating prayer with other activities, and the spiritual merits of simply being in the mosque. Numerous *Ḥadīth* relate the rewards of actions associated with mosques, such as building them, travelling to them and sitting in them (Alavi 2004).

The furnishing and internal decoration of mosques varies, but there are some common features. For example, there are no seats in a mosque. The congregation sits on the floor, which is usually carpeted in such a way as to indicate the rows that worshippers should form for prayer. There will usually be a *minbar*, which is a pulpit or a set of steps from which the Friday sermon is delivered, and which is placed to one side of the *miḥrāb* (niche, indicating the direction for prayer). There are usually no pictures or images depicting living beings, but there may be images of geometric patterns or calligraphy on the walls or in the windows. Clocks on the wall indicate times for each of the five daily prayers. Apart from the requirement of a place for ritual ablutions (*wudū'*), some means of separating men and women (such as a curtain) and the necessity to face Makkah, there are no other essential architectural or functional components:

The ease with which a mosque may be created is attributable to the portable nature of Islam and the simple functional requirements of the mosque (cleanliness and orientation to Mecca) which means that Muslim ritual requires no 'sacred space' and can be practiced anywhere. The architectural requirements for a mosque are few ... (Nasser 2005: 73)

However, some of the typical architectural features of mosques in Muslim majority countries, such as minarets (useful for the projection of the *muezzin's* voice), have become symbolically charged in Britain, particularly when major new mosque-building projects have sought to include these features in the design.

## BRITAIN'S FIRST MOSQUES: 1860–1945

There appear to have been three distinctive kinds of people behind the establishment of early British mosques. These were Muslim traders (often associated with the shipping industry), Orientalists (some of whom converted to Islam), and Islamic scholars and missionaries.[3] Scholars with an interest in the Orient and its religions were inspired to travel to Muslim countries and in some cases this led to their conversion to Islam. As we saw in chapter 2, one such scholar was Henry Quilliam, an English solicitor who journeyed to Morocco and became a Muslim in 1884. He returned to Britain in 1887 and established the first officially designated mosque in Liverpool. However, Quilliam was evicted by his landlord because of his new-found Islamic faith, and was forced to find new premises. This nonetheless provided an opportunity to develop the mosque's activities, and in 1891 the Liverpool Mosque and Institute was founded. This encompassed not only facilities for prayer, but also a home for orphans, a publishing outlet and a school. Although the Liverpool Mosque and Institute was not purpose built, when the Institute moved to Brougham Terrace in 1889 the interior was adapted to reflect typical North African mosque architecture.[4] The use of the site was fraught with many of the same difficulties that Muslims face in Britain today regarding premises for worship. There were local concerns regarding the 'public advertisement' of Islam, especially via the *adhān,* the call to prayer (Beckerlegge 1997).

The first purpose-built mosque, established in 1889 in Woking, Surrey, owes its existence to the efforts of a Hungarian Orientalist scholar, Dr Gottlieb Leitner. Leitner had for many years served as the Registrar of the University of Punjab, but in his retirement he settled in Woking, and established an Oriental Institute in 1884. However, he knew that a mosque would be a necessary facility to attract students. Leitner's friend and patron in Lahore, Her Highness Shah Jahan, the Begum of Bhopal, sponsored the mosque-building project. It was designed by English architect W. I. Chambers, who drew inspiration from the architectural styles that he had studied in the India Office Library (Brown 2004). While it attracted less controversy than the Liverpool mosque, there were still concerns about its architectural features, in this case regarding the dome (Ryan and Naylor 2002). The Woking mosque depended heavily upon the personal connections and influence of Leitner himself, but its existence survived his death in 1899, and it went on to become a symbol and centre of South Asian Muslim activity in Britain for many years afterwards: 'Its recognition as the centre of Islam in Britain was reflected, as ever, in its regular stream of visits by dignitaries from all over the Muslim

[3] See Gailani (2000) for a more detailed history of Britain's early mosques.
[4] See www.abdullahquilliamsociety.org.uk

Figure 6. Shah Jahan Mosque, Woking, Surrey (author's own image)

world' (Ansari 2004: 134). It remains open today, and continues to be a landmark in British Muslim history.

The East London Mosque is often regarded as the first mosque in London and, like many other mosques, took a long time to become established (Ansari 2004). In 1910, a group of notable Muslim figures started the London Mosque Fund. Initially, they rented a small room for Friday prayers, but by 1926, funds had grown sufficiently to draft a Deed of Declaration of Trust. In 1940, three houses were purchased on Commercial Road in London's East End, and the mosque opened for Friday prayers on 1 August 1941.[5] Like the Liverpool Mosque and Institute, it served as much more than simply a place for worship. For example, it provided a base for the *Jamiatul Ittahadul Muslimim* (Society for Muslim Unity), which gave charitable help to local Muslims (Ansari 2004). As with its Liverpool counterpart, the East London Mosque also had to find new premises during its history. Following a compulsory purchase order in 1975, the mosque had to be re-sited and a replacement mosque was not

[5] A longer and more detailed account of the mosque's history can be found at www.eastlondon-mosque.org.uk/about_2.htm

built until 1985, on Whitechapel Road. In 2004, the mosque undertook a new building project to meet the needs of the growing Muslim population in the area.

Outside London, the first half of the twentieth century saw the development of Islamic centres in towns and cities that had attracted Muslim settlement owing to their heavy industry and shipping trades, such as Cardiff, Glasgow and South Shields. Reflecting the predominance of Arabs, often of Sufi orientation, some of these centres were *zāwiyahs* (literally, 'nook' or 'corner'), although they functioned in much the same way as mosques in providing a focus for religious and social activity. These centres were distinctive for being run in most cases by individual religious teachers, and the *zāwiyahs* in Britain owe their existence in particular to Shaykh Abdullah Ali al-Hakimi, of the *'Alawī* Sufi order (Ansari 2004). For example, the entrance to what is known locally as 'the Somali mosque' in Butetown, Cardiff, has a plaque by the entrance commemorating its establishment by al-Hakimi in 1936. Again, the mosque has changed its site and architecture several times since its establishment.

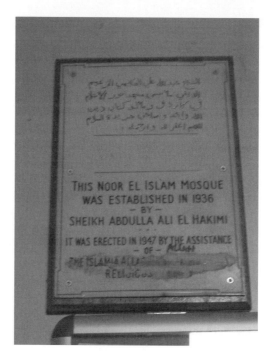

Figure 7. Plaque inside Nur al-Islam Mosque, Cardiff

## MOSQUE CONSTRUCTION: 1945 TO THE PRESENT

If Britain's colonial history accounts for the establishment of mosques in the nineteenth century, the same can be said for the second half of the twentieth century when mosques were established by the new wave of Muslim migrants to Britain after the Second World War. Many of the same patterns of mosque construction from the nineteenth century were repeated once again, but this time on a larger scale. These various stages of mosque construction reflect the growth, evolution, fortunes and aspirations of Muslims in Britain. Most mosques founded in the 1950s and 1960s were 'house mosques', mainly established by South Asian Muslim immigrants. These were often very modest since there was no certainty that these Muslims would remain in Britain, and resources were limited. The relatively recent emergence of custom-built mosques reflects a new confidence about the long-term and established place for Muslims in British society. Contrary to popular perception, the construction of many of Britain's mosques has been funded by British Muslims themselves, giving an important sense of 'ownership' of the structure and of 'belonging' to the locality in which it is based (Werbner 2006: 132). With the exception of some of the larger mosques, such as the London Central Mosque in Regent's Park, or the Jame Masjid in Birmingham (once officially known as the President Saddam Hussein Mosque), most of Britain's mosques have evolved from limited community resources (Gailani 2000). The establishment of mosques and supplementary schools indicated a shift within the migrants' self-perception from being sojourners to being settlers. The investment needed for a mosque, and for an imam to lead prayers and teach children, both reflected and in some cases even precipitated community formation (Lewis 1994).

'House mosques' were domestic residences that were internally modified to accommodate religious gatherings. Internal walls would be removed to make sufficient room for congregational prayers. Typical features of mosque design, such as a pulpit or niche to indicate the direction for prayer, sometimes had to be symbolic. Worshippers in these makeshift premises noted their unsatisfactory character, especially when they could not stand shoulder to shoulder as one congregation during prayers but were spatially separated on different floors or landings (Insoll 2001; Marranci 2004). Given the size of Muslim communities in Britain at this time, such premises often accommodated Muslims from a variety of religious and ethnic backgrounds. Speaking about this era, Sher Azam, former President of the Bradford Council of Mosques, recalls:

What happened is that when we came to Britain … there were no *Deobandīs,* no *Barelwīs,* no *Ahl-i Hadith,* nobody. We were glad to have a mosque and to be able to pray. Whoever established it usually was going to do it his own way, in his own tradition, but we were glad to see him whether *Deobandī* or *Barelwī.* We didn't mind what it was as long as Islam was practiced. (Geaves 1996b: 159)

The establishment of the first mosque in Bradford occurred in 1960, in a terraced house on Howard Street (Barton 1986). It was used by both Pakistanis and Bengalis, and by both *Deobandīs* and *Barelwīs.* By 1969, however, a separate Bengali mosque had been established. This was also a 'house mosque', located within a predominately Bengali area of settlement, on Cornwall Road. This example of early mosque construction in Bradford illustrates well the natural point of fission that usually leads to the creation of new mosques. Premises either become too small or, as is more often the case, worshippers begin to exert their own distinctive ethnic and linguistic identity or ideological preferences. This process is often contentious, as particular factions break away to establish a new congregation which conforms to their particular interpretation of Islamic practice. In the 1980s, the 80,000 Muslims in Birmingham were already served by no fewer than fifty-five mosques, sometimes with several on the same street (Wolffe 1993: 148).

'House mosques' remain the most common kind of mosque in Britain today. However, they have sometimes undergone considerable changes in status, from temporary centres not registered with local authorities, to permanent and formally registered mosques. This is particularly true where neighbouring properties have been acquired to expand facilities and to accommodate growing numbers of worshippers. Sometimes the original residential property, or properties, have been demolished, to make way for a new purpose-built facility on the same site.

The proximity of these facilities to residential communities reflects the importance of having a place of worship that is within easy walking distance. Children can, for example, walk from their home or school to the nearby *maktab* or *madrasah* safely without having to cross busy main roads. Moreover, Muslim elders with restricted mobility find the mosque a convenient place to gather, not only for daily prayers but also for social support and 'pious repose' (Kahera 2002: 376). Some mosques have become important resources for women, accommodating a crèche, a counselling and advisory service, a library or a study circle. However, the physical expansion and evolution of 'house mosques' into larger, more active community centres, particularly where this has involved the incorporation of traditional external mosque design, has often been subject to restrictive application of the planning laws and contested understandings about what counts as 'authentic' local architecture.

As Muslim communities have grown in size and wealth, some congregations have deliberately acquired much larger premises for their worship and social functions, these often being former churches, synagogues, cinemas, factories or warehouses. The number of redundant churches and chapels coming onto the property market in the 1970s and 1980s reflected the changing fortunes of some Christian churches in Britain. This meant that many former Christian places of worship were converted into mosques. Furthermore, factories and other premises on 'brownfield' sites offered new opportunities. The 'rehabilitation of redundant buildings was often an important means of tackling the functional and physical obsolescence of the industrial built heritage, imbuing these buildings with new cultural and functional meaning' (Nasser 2006: 380).

With relatively little structural alteration, these buildings could be converted into mosques, often with associated social facilities such as wedding halls and kitchens. To achieve this, various decorative devices have been employed to strip away the former 'identity' and to create a new, distinctive visual appearance. Commonly this has featured Arabic lettering, a star and crescent motif, green paintwork or decorative arches. Exactly this kind of process of adaptation and re-imagining has taken place at the Shah Jalal mosque on Crwys Road in Cardiff.[6] Formerly a Welsh Calvinistic Methodist Chapel, it is now one of the Bangladeshi community's principal mosques. The transformation of the building has been achieved by adjustments to its typical chapel architecture, by the addition of lettering on the vestibule arch and through the addition of stars and crescents on the turrets.

When mosques are converted in this way, especially from former chapels or churches, 'the presence of the Other' (Nasser 2006: 384) is made manifest. So too, however, is the dynamic nature of culture and the scope for 'architectural hybridity' (Nasser 2006: 386). As ongoing cultural productions, buildings do not have a consistent or timeless identity but are manipulated and transformed according to changing needs and interests.

Many architecturally impressive purpose-built mosques have been built in Britain in recent years, and the three different types of mosques – 'house', 'converted' and 'purpose-built' – now co-exist in the religious landscape. As Muslim communities from different schools of thought

---

[6] For more details about this building, including architectural plans, see www.glamro.gov.uk/ check/Building%20of%20a%20Capital%202/A_Worship.html

Figure 8. Welsh Calvinistic Methodist Chapel, Cardiff, 1899 (see Figure 9).
Reproduced by kind permission of Tempus Publishing Ltd

and different ethnic groups have become more established, sometimes 'the building of highly elaborate mosques represents an intense (and expensive) form of status competition between Muslim groups and personalities' (McLoughlin 2005b: 1053). Moreover, 'architecture can embody the interactions between individuals and groups in a given society, particularly when these interactions occur under sustained relations of power and resistance' (Gale 2004: 28). In this way, although there is no functional

Figure 9. The Shah Jalal Mosque, Cardiff (the lettering on the vestibule arch
reads in English: 'NONE BUT ALLAH IS WORTHY OF WORSHIP.
MUHAMMAD IS HIS MESSENGER' (author's own image)

necessity for either a dome or minaret, some Muslim communities have
insisted upon their construction because they recognize that 'the dome
in the British context is perceived by non-Muslims as the form by which
Islam is recognizable' (Nasser 2005: 74). The inclusion of a dome and/or
minaret is therefore seen as symbolically and politically important as a
means of both signalling and legitimizing the community's presence. It
serves another important purpose by linking Muslims to 'an imagined
tradition' (Nasser 2005: 74) of their own.

Many of Britain's purpose-built mosques, particularly those in major
British cities, are often called 'central' mosques. The distinction between
a local mosque and a central mosque is similar in some respects to the
distinction between a local 'parish' church and a cathedral. A number of major British cities, such as Birmingham, Edinburgh, Glasgow,
London and Manchester, have a central mosque. They often act as a focal
point for Islamic activities, for example hosting major conferences, providing legal services such as *Shari'ah* Councils or offering facilities for
funerals. Werbner noted the 'symbolic primacy' (Werbner 2002a: 29) of
Manchester Central Mosque relative to other mosques in the city, and the
controversies that have often surrounded it as a result.

Because purpose-built central mosques have this 'symbolic primacy' (Werbner 2002a: 2), they have often also taken on a strategic role at the interface between Muslim communities and the wider society. Their distinctive architecture and staffing capacity has meant that they have played an important educational role for non-Muslims, for example hosting visits by school religious education classes, or the training of public sector professionals. Central mosques are better able to welcome such visitors, and they provide for many non-Muslims their only direct exposure to Islamic communities in Britain. Similarly, when Muslim or non-Muslim dignitaries visit particular towns or cities, the central mosque makes an ideal platform for mutual recognition and affirmation. Other purpose-built mosques can take on the same role, a good example being the Jamia Masjid Gamkol Sharif in Birmingham, built in the 1990s.[7] This building performs an important function for the City Council when visiting diplomats visit the City (Gale 2004), since it can be promoted as a good example of effective multiculturalism and the successful integration of religious buildings into urban cityscapes.

The architectural design of purpose-built mosques reflects two main styles. The first is a traditional and historic Islamic architectural style, typical of mosques in the Middle East, which comprises a large central dome with a minaret to one side. An example of this is London Central Mosque. Alternatively, some British custom-built mosques embody a contemporary 'localized' interpretation of traditional Islamic styles. A good example is the central mosque in Edinburgh, which successfully fuses Scottish and Islamic architectural styles, and is a fitting reflection of the emergence of a distinctive Scottish Muslim identity. The exterior decoration of the mosque merges vernacular art with Kufic calligraphy employing vivid patterns that run along the circumference of the entire building. The check-like patterns correspond to Scottish tartans, a design feature that was intended to strengthen ties of solidarity with the people in the city. The architect has also used octagonal towers to reflect the folk image of a Scottish castle:

Superficially, the mosque can be considered a hybrid of architectural styles just as British born Muslims can be considered hybrids of identity. But the final design of the Central Mosque is the architect's interpretation of his perceived hybridity, just as each Muslim life is their own interpretation of their hybridic experience. The individual interpretation of this ... means that there is no consensus on how

----

[7] See also Werbner (2002b).

Table 4. *Mosques and Muslim populations in five British cities*

|  | Muslims in 2001 | Total mosques | Purpose-built | Percentage purpose-built |
|---|---|---|---|---|
| Birmingham | 140,033 | 116 | 10 | 9 |
| Bradford | 75,188 | 44 | 6 | 13 |
| Cardiff | 11,261 | 10 | 2 | 20 |
| Leicester | 30,885 | 25 | 5 | 20 |
| Manchester | 125,219 | 31 | 5 | 16 |

to live a British Muslim way of life just as there is no consensus and no rules on how mosques in non-Muslim countries can be built. (Li 2003)

It is difficult to assess precisely how many of Britain's mosques are purpose built. The best general estimate can be derived from looking at the number of such mosques relative to the total number of mosques in particular cities. From the table above, we can estimate that in towns and cities with sizeable Muslim populations, purpose-built mosques are likely to constitute between 9 per cent and 20 per cent of all mosques.[8]

Today, the institutionalization of Islam through formally established mosques is evident right across Britain, but also in the workplace and other public settings such as universities and prisons. At least three major London prisons have a mosque: HMP Pentonville, Feltham YOI and HMP Wandsworth, two of which were funded through the offices of the Islamic Cultural Centre (Regent's Park Mosque).[9] There was a mosque at the Millennium Dome in Greenwich (Gailani 2000; Gilliat-Ray 2005a; Gilliat-Ray 2005b), the first to be sited in a public leisure attraction. A sound-proofed prayer room has been established at Ewood Park football stadium, for supporters of Blackburn Rovers, and some other football clubs have followed this example. Prayer rooms set aside primarily for Muslim use are now becoming commonplace in many 'non-places' (Auge 1995) such as airports, shopping centres and motorway service stations (such as the M6 Hilton Park Services). But as mosques have become more numerous and often more visible in the urban landscape, they have also become more vulnerable to vandalism and attack, particularly in the wake

---

[8] I am grateful to Chris Hewer, Dilwar Hussain, Atif Imtiaz and Fiaz Ahmed for figures regarding mosque construction in Birmingham, Leicester, Bradford and Manchester, respectively.
[9] I am grateful to Maqsood Ahmed and Ahtsham Ali for this information.

of international events (Werbner 2002a). Recent additions to the premises of many mosques have been security fences and CCTV cameras.

## THE ROLE AND FUNCTION OF MOSQUES

The role of mosques in Britain has subtly altered over time, according to the changing needs of Muslim communities. Most mosques established in the early 1960s and 1970s were almost solely places for the performance of the five daily prayers, for the *Jum'a* prayer on Fridays and for the celebration of religious festivals. With the gradual enlargement in the size and number of mosque premises, there has also been an expansion in their role and function. As well as providing spaces for prayer and other religious gatherings, they also often nowadays accommodate facilities for learning, social functions (for example, weddings), training, missionary work and advisory or *Sharī'ah* Council services, particularly in the larger central mosques. They are also centres of transnational networks, hosting visits by international scholars and preachers, and thereby fostering for many British Muslims a sense of connection to the wider Muslim world.[10] Mosques have also 'played a large part in Muslims' social and political organisation' (McLoughlin 2005b: 1046), and many have served as bases for mounting local and national campaigns.

A driving force behind the establishment of mosques has been the perceived need to create an institution for the maintenance and nurture of religious identity, especially among British-born Muslim youth. Most mosques today therefore operate a *maktab* or *madrasah*, an after-school class for the teaching of classical Qur'ānic Arabic and *Islamiyyat* (Islamic studies). Mosques are the institution through which many young Muslims are socialized into Muslim communities, where they internalize traditions and beliefs, and find a pathway into the adult membership of the mosque. In this way, mosques in general and *makātib* in particular have an important role for young Muslims in regulating social behaviour and fostering collective sentiments of belonging to a shared religious community. As Wardak's research on Muslims in Edinburgh demonstrates:

the internalisation of communal norms and the expression of the feelings of communality and unity, which are clearly present in the language of the collective prayer ('we', 'us', versus 'you alone') have important implications for controlling individual and social undertakings. Of equal importance, from a social control point of view, is the public expression of shared sentiments and the

---

[10]  For a British Muslim perspective on the role and function of mosques see Maqsood (2005).

feelings of unity by the faithful during the *Jom'a* [*sic*] prayer; it is a renewal of the worshippers' commitment to their shared sets of moral and religious values. (Wardak 2002: 217)

As noted at the start of this chapter, mosques reflect many of the issues pertaining to Muslims in Britain more generally. Therefore from the early 1990s, mosques took on particular significance as sites for resisting the perceived discrimination against Islam and Muslims, especially following the Rushdie Affair. Raza writes:

The potential of the mosque can be seen in the case of the Rushdie affair. That was the only cause for which mosques have shown some defiance. (Raza 1991: 54)

Since then, mosques have further evolved as sites for building a sense of community, 'belonging' and identity in the face of discrimination: 'Oppressed groups can, through a politics of identity *and a politics of place*, reclaim rights, resist and subvert' (Jacobs and Fincher 1998: 2, cited in Ryan and Naylor 2002: 41, emphasis added). For Ziauddin Sardar:

a mosque was the essential accoutrement for strangers desperate to build a home in a new land. In such places the air itself was a history of struggle and aspiration in inauspicious circumstances. Wherever there is a mosque there will usually be someone camping out for the night [sleeping in the mosque]. It is the norm that when all else fails, the mosque offers a place of refuge: material and spiritual, real or metaphysical. (Sardar 2004: 1)

## THE GOVERNANCE OF MOSQUES

The day-to-day life and operation of most mosques is governed by committee. The mosque committee constitutes the political and financial leadership of the mosque, while the imam provides religious leadership (though sometimes the imam will also be a committee member). Becoming a mosque committee member, or Chair, is not necessarily a democratic process, since it is often likely to rest upon kinship and other social ties. As noted above, in the early post-Second World War period, Muslims from a variety of schools of thought and ethnic backgrounds often shared the same mosque premises. From time to time, there were tensions within mosque committees as rival factions struggled to assert their own particular interpretations of Islamic norms and practice. Sometimes, internal mosque rivalries had (and continue to have) the unintended but inevitable consequence of alienating many young British-born Muslims from mosques: 'young men simply avoid the mosque altogether, finding the

sectarian arguments and factional fights incomprehensible and unpleasant'
(Werbner 2002a: 249). Today, the tensions surrounding the governance
of mosques are increasingly inter-generational, as younger British-born
Muslims pressurize committees, not only for greater representation but
also for increased recognition of their needs and interests. The pressure
group MPAC has routinely campaigned for more youthful representation
on mosque committees.[11]

Mosques rely on income generated from a variety of sources in order
to maintain their upkeep and to support their personnel. Some operate a
fixed subscription system for members, while others rely on ad hoc informal donations, especially on Fridays. Income might also be generated
through the teaching of children, the hosting of an event or conference, or
the rental of property. Laws which regulate charitable organizations commonly provide the structure through which most (but not all) mosques
manage their staffing and finances. This is because 'Britain has no generally applicable legal framework for religious communities' (Nielsen
2004: 45). While there is no legal requirement to register mosques with
the Charity Commissioners, many communities choose to do so since it
provides advantages in the form of certain tax exemptions. Registration
with the Registrar General also makes it possible to conduct a legally
valid marriage ceremony within a mosque, provided that it is conducted
by either a civil official or a 'recognized' mosque employee.

The most recent comprehensive quantitative study of mosques in
Britain has been undertaken by the UK Charity Commission (Coleman
2009). This study worked with initial information for 1,102 mosques and
Islamic centres, but ultimately reduced the sample size to 716, resulting
in the probable omission from the survey of many unregistered and less
formally established Islamic centres in Britain. The resulting survey data
provides valuable basic information on 255 British mosques, in terms of
their size and structure, their activities and service provision, and their
funding and governance.

## MOSQUES AND THE POLITICS OF THE BUILT ENVIRONMENT

The development of mosques has altered the social, religious, political and
physical landscape of many British towns and cities, and this has sometimes been accompanied by some degree of controversy (Birt and Gilliat-

---

[11]  For example 'MPAC Back Young Muslim Challenge in Mosque Election', www.mpacuk.org

Ray 2009). The establishment of a mosque indicates that the symbolic and political dynamics of a community or locality are somewhat altered. This is especially evident when, for example, a disused chapel or synagogue is converted into a mosque. Such a transformation is an indicator of new local identities and politics. It marks the start of a new phase of history. Regardless of architecture, a mosque is a 'very concrete and material sign of domination and power' (Allievi 2003: 344), the more so when it is purpose built. The bricks and mortar make a 'visual claim on public space' (Eade 1996b: 223), and where mosques are permitted to broadcast the call to prayer, often only for the midday and afternoon prayer, this makes for a further 'acoustic' claim on the non-material spaces of a locality. Mosque-building has been vital in order to enable British Muslims to exercise a sense of belonging:

the conquest of space, its inscription with a new moral and cultural surface ... is an act of human empowerment ... in sacralising spaces, Muslims also root their identities qua Muslims in a new locality and embody the moral right of their communities to be 'in' this new environment. (Werbner 1996b: 309)

Ownership of land does not bring with it the automatic right either to continue with or to change its usage. Many variations in use are subject to approval via national planning law, administered by local planning authorities under the terms of the Town and Country Planning Act 1990 and relevant guidance. Where local planning committees use their authority to grant or refuse planning permission for the establishment of mosques, they inadvertently exercise the power to 'condense and mediate the relations between social groups' (Gale 2004: 18).

At present there are no national guidelines for planning decisions concerning places of worship. There have therefore been considerable local variations in the outcomes of planning applications to build mosques (Gale and Naylor 2003).[12] Planning decisions are further complicated by currents in national and transnational politics (Nye 2000; Ryan and Naylor 2002). Historically, the non-Muslim and local authority response to the emergence of mosques has been mixed. In some cases they have been seen as exotic and picturesque, and in others as aesthetically and socially disruptive (Ryan and Naylor 2002). Closely related to a perceived visual incongruity of mosques is the characterization of their users as 'bad neighbours'. Such prejudicial views seek to normalize the social customs of the local majority population, while locating the members of the

---

[12] The same kind of regional variation in responses to mosque construction is also evident in other parts of Europe. See, for example, Landman (1991).

minority concerned as beyond the boundary between 'us' and 'not us' (Gale and Naylor 2003: 394).

Local debates about the construction of mosques usually centre either upon historical precedent or aesthetic considerations such as architectural heritage and urban conservation, or upon more mundane or practical matters such as parking facilities and traffic congestion in the surrounding streets. These are legitimate concerns, but behind the overt objections to the new, visible and audible presence of Muslims, there are often deeper, unconscious, assumptions about the future trajectory of individual places based upon their past history, and the perceived 'symbolic appropriation of territory' (Allievi 2003: 344). This inevitably results in 'hegemonic representations of what does, and does not, constitute "Britishness"' (McLoughlin 1998a: 214), and highly selective understandings about who 'belongs' and who does not. Such discriminatory constructions of belonging are particularly visible in local newspapers (Fekete 2008), and it is clear that many of the most public contests concerning mosque construction are fought not only in planning committees but also via the local press. For example, during debates about the East London Mosque (Eade 1996b) and the London Fazl Mosque (Ryan and Naylor 2002), local newspapers had a significant role in recording, dramatizing and politicizing these debates, further highlighting the visibility of Muslims in each area.

In East London, letters pages in local newspapers became a significant 'site' for heated debates about the relative noise of church bells and the Muslim call to prayer. The tolling of church bells was considered to be 'acceptable' noise pollution, while a proposal for the call to prayer was regarded as 'alien' (Ryan and Naylor 2002).[13] Negative opposition here betrayed notions of cultural exclusivism which failed to recognize the changing character of the locality. Selective constructions of 'us' and 'them' amount to a 'double ethnicization ... of "Englishness" on the one side and "Islam" on the other' (Eade 1996b: 231) which over-simplifies and homogenizes complex multi-faceted identities. Some members of the ethnic majority tend to read the re-inscription of 'old' spaces with 'new' cultural meanings in terms of an ever-expanding (Islamic) 'threat' to 'the English way of life' (McLoughlin 2005b: 1048). Negative planning

---

[13] The call to prayer has always been controversial in Britain. *The Islamic World* in July 1896 noted that the *muezzin* (one who makes the call to prayer) was stoned having called the *adhān*. In Liverpool, the local newspaper regarded the public 'advertisement' of Muslim practice to be 'most incongruous, unusual, silly, and unwelcome', reminding local residents of the 'Eastern humbug detested by Western folk' (*Liverpool Review,* 28 November 1891, p. 14, cited in Beckerlegge 1997: 253)

decisions, although 'couched in the neutral language of planning and notions of "amenity", are often underpinned by notions of prejudice and difference' (Ryan and Naylor 2002: 56), leading Gale and Naylor to conclude that the 'overriding experience of religious expression in British cities is one dogged by exclusionary practices, whether by recalcitrant planning authorities or unwelcoming residents' (Gale and Naylor 2003).

However, there are examples of good practice and more sympathetic engagement with local Muslim communities seeking to establish places of worship. Often this sympathy has emerged in tandem with the growing stature and recognition of the Muslim community in general. Sympathy for mosque-building projects has sometimes been engendered through the successful brokerage undertaken by Muslims who have achieved public recognition and prestige in the wider business and civic community (Gale and Naylor 2003). They have been able to play an important mediating role between mosque communities and local authorities, persuading the latter of the social or economic value of mosque construction.

Some mosque communities have themselves become more astute at the articulation of the same kind of inclusive, multicultural narratives that some Councils want to stress in their discourse on urban development. This is usually achieved when planning applications stress that the new religious premises will be a resource for the 'whole community', and will provide social capital through the delivery of employment-related skills or language training courses open to all (Edge 2002; McLoughlin 2005b). An example of this co-incidence of Council and mosque interests was evident in 1992 when Leicester City Council sold some of its land to enable the construction of a new mosque, at a quarter of its market value. As well as benefiting local Muslims, the Council could use the mosque-building project to demonstrate its commitment to the development of an inclusive, multicultural city. Some mosque buildings can therefore be seen to have emerged out of a common language of inclusion and multiculturalism expressed by both politicians and Muslim activists alike.

The interests underpinning the mutual public discourse on mosque construction are nonetheless likely to be quite different, leading to a discrepancy in the way that the state or local authorities envisage mosques, as against local mosque communities themselves (McLoughlin 1998a). It is also quite possible for local authorities to change their stance in relation to the same buildings. A good example of this has occurred in Birmingham where the central mosque has seen a transition 'from an initial ambivalence – and even hostility – to more recent endorsements, as [it has] been increasingly celebrated as [a] signifier of Birmingham's cultural diversity'

(Gale 2004: 31). Moreover, mosques are now bound up in a new 'security framework', and seen as important sites for 'counter-radicalization' initiatives (Brown 2008).

Mosque communities can play an active and often very creative role in shaping their local environment. New building projects are increasingly sensitive to their wider community setting, and where possible try to incorporate features that will make them attractive for Muslims and non-Muslims alike, such as the provision of a cafeteria open for all. The new mosque in Cambridge, currently under construction, will include an Islamic garden providing 'a haven of peace for all comers'.[14] Mosque communities are able to mount sustained and politically astute campaigns, not only to secure their own buildings but also to challenge other, unwelcome, local planning applications. They are increasingly becoming concerned to preserve or rectify the decency and sobriety of the immediate vicinity of mosques, so extending their sphere of influence beyond the boundaries of the building and into the local community. The headline 'Muslims to fight bar bid near mosque' (*Edinburgh Evening News*, 12 November 2004) was indicative of such efforts. So too was the successful campaign against the lingerie company Sloggi, which sited immodest advertising posters near mosques in the north of England. The Advertising Standards Agency passed a ruling banning the advertisement near mosques. Local Muslims had regarded the poster as 'insulting', and as constituting 'environmental pollution' ('Not near the mosque', *Asian News,* 28 June 2004). The pollution in this case was clearly of a moral nature. So far from being simply passive 'victims' of failed planning applications in relation to the building of mosques, there is now increasing evidence that Muslims are becoming successful participants in urban life, with mosques themselves being one of the primary settings for engagement with local politics and decision-making.

MOSQUES AND MUSLIM BURIAL

Just as mosques and Islamic centres are clear and identifiable markers of Muslim presence in Britain, Muslim cemeteries and burial spaces are significant sites for establishing and affirming Islamic inclusion. Provision for cemeteries is largely determined by local authorities, under the terms of the Local Government Act 1972. During the nineteenth century, Muslims who died in Britain were usually buried in unconsecrated

---

[14] See www.cambridgemosqueismoving.org.uk/faq/faq.html

ground, or ground allocated to non-conformist traditions (Ansari 2007). Over the past century, it has become commonplace for Muslims to be buried in separate sections at public cemeteries, and most large towns and cities now have a distinctive 'Muslim' section. Associated with this, many local authorities have in place arrangements to facilitate 'same day' burials at weekends and on public holidays, in keeping with Islamic tradition.

There are now a number of famous historical Muslim burial sites in Britain, such as Brookwood Cemetery near Woking in Surrey, which contains the graves of well-known figures in the history of Islam in Britain, such as Syed Ameer Ali (1846–1928), Abdullah Quilliam (1856–1932) and Lord Headley (1855–1935). Distinctive sections of this burial ground have become associated with Muslims from different 'schools of thought'. One of the first private cemeteries for the sole use of British Muslims was established in 2002. The Gardens of Peace near London claims to be the largest Muslim burial ground in Europe, containing space for 10,000 graves.[15]

## WOMEN AND MOSQUES

The predominant experience of Muslim women in relation to British mosques has been one of exclusion and marginalization. Both within and outside Muslim communities there are some who, incorrectly, assume that women are 'not allowed' in mosques: 'Male elders tend to claim the mosque, the most "serious" and "prestigious" Islamic space, as their own' (McLoughlin 2005b: 1049). So while mosques are theoretically open to all, 'they can in practice operate all sorts of closures most especially in terms of gender and generation' (McLoughlin 1998a: 215). It is nonetheless important to understand at the outset that 'the restrictions on women are not original, for they stood behind the men in Muhammad's time [for prayer] and are more socio-cultural than derivative from views on spatial sanctity' (Turner 1981: 145). Louay Safi, Executive Director of the Leadership Development Centre for the Islamic Society of North America (ISNA), states clearly that

the Prophet was concerned about the possible exclusion of women by overzealous men and so unequivocally instructed the community to make sure that women are not prevented from attending the mosque ... the arguments against women's participation in the mosque boil down to the principle of *dar'al mafāsid*

---

[15] www.gardens-of-peace.org.uk

(prevention of corruption). Such a principle cannot be invoked to invalidate an established right sanctioned by Islamic law. (Safi 2005: 149)

In the early days of mosque construction in Britain, particularly in the 1960s and 1970s, the ratio of women to men was heavily imbalanced since communities were still largely characterized by temporary, male, single residents. The resources available for prayer facilities at this time were limited; this chapter has charted the emergence of the early 'house mosques', which were often overcrowded and unsuitable. They did, however, at least provide a venue for Friday prayer which was obligatory for the predominantly male Muslim community. The exclusion of women from mosques was often therefore a matter of practicality: there was simply no space. In the warmer climes of the Middle East, mosque congregations often spill out onto surrounding streets in order to accommodate worshippers, but this is less feasible (although it still occurs) in the often cold and damp conditions of Western Europe.

As more 'converted' and 'purpose-built' mosques began to emerge in the 1970s and 1980s, some of them incorporated a women's gallery, or a female section. A number of central mosques in Britain now have facilities for women, and among the mosques in Cardiff, several have a women's prayer space. However, even when women are able to access these mosques, they remain bastions of male dominance. They are often inhospitable places for women, and there are numerous indications that women's presence is regarded as less significant than that of men.

The physical separation of male and female worshippers is usually to the disadvantage of women. Often they can neither satisfactorily hear nor see what is happening in the main prayer hall. The size of their facilities is often much smaller than for men, and generally inferior. For example, one of the mosques in Cardiff has a female section, but the community 'ran out of money' for the specially designed carpeting indicating the rows worshippers should form for prayer suggesting that 'the forms of women's prayers are not considered as important as those of men' (Marshall 1994: 64–5, cited in Mazumdar and Mazumdar 2002). Sometimes, the space reserved for female worshippers becomes a multi-purpose space, perhaps for storage, or it is appropriated by men at Eid or for other functions: 'Many mosques relegate women to small, dingy, secluded, airless, and segregated quarters with their children' (Safi 2005: 151). Women's spaces are in this way uniquely subject to the kind of transformations and adaptations that confirm their 'back stage' participation in mosque life, in contrast to the 'front stage' role of men (Goffman 1959). The behaviour that takes place in these 'back stage' regions is often more informal (frequently compounded by the presence of young children at play), making it more difficult for women to engage in serious religious practice in mosques.

Despite this evidence of women's marginalization, there has been a growth of religious gatherings among women, and 'an autonomous movement among Muslim women outside the mosques' (Modood *et al.* 1997: 303). Muslim women are actively reshaping, reinterpreting, and reconstructing their religious lives outside the home (Mazumdar and Mazumdar 2002), creating alternative opportunities for religious gathering and participation. They have countered their 'exclusion' from mosques by finding alternative ways of engaging in community action and decision-making, such as establishing their own independent religious study circles as well as women-only organizations offering access to sporting facilities, educational initiatives or employment. In the 1960s and 1970s, mosques constituted the dominant British Muslim institution, but as Muslim communities have grown and developed, there are now a plethora of organizations in which women take a full and active part. To some extent, their exclusion or marginalization from mosques now matters far less for their overall participation in British Muslim life.

It is therefore somewhat ironic that the effort to make mosques more 'woman-friendly' has been actively promoted in government circles since 2005 as part of the 'Prevent' strategy. Women are seen as 'witnesses to a moderate and liberal Islam ... support for women's access to mosques is seen as a way of shoring up the "radical middle" of liberal Islam' (Brown 2008: 481).[16] This construction of British Muslim women has the effect of reinforcing a homogenizing gendered stereotype that is also bound up with erroneous and paternalistic assumptions that Muslim women need 'saving' in order that their rights might be fulfilled.

Supporting women's access to mosques is not simply about counter-radicalization, however, but has wider implications, where it becomes

a means for assessing how integrated and cohesive British Muslim communities are because it is assumed that equality (for women) is an inherent value of the 'British way of life'. This strategy of linking narratives of multicultural cohesive communities to counter-terrorism via mosque reform appears as a repetition of orientalist imagery, where women's roles in society and religions become the benchmark by which societies are judged as 'civilised'. (Brown 2008: 483)

---

[16] Here 'radical middle' is an allusion to the 'Radical Middle Way' project, www.radicalmiddleway. co.uk/ – a 'revolutionary grassroots initiative aimed at articulating a relevant mainstream understanding of Islam that is dynamic, proactive and relevant to young British Muslims'.

The battle for 'hearts and minds' being undertaken as part of 'Prevent', and an emphasis upon the role that women might play in this process via their access to mosques, has the effect of distracting attention from the more significant socio-economic factors which affect Muslim community life and well-being. The evidence for educational underachievement, poor housing and ill-health uncovered through the 2001 Census appears to have become increasingly obscured amid post-7/7 politics and the emphasis on counter-radicalization, especially where this focuses upon British Muslim institutions such as mosques and their personnel.

## CONCLUSION

It was recently remarked that the East London Mosque has throughout its long history provided an example for other British mosques to follow (Alfaradhi 2004). Muslims in Britain could in fact look back further in their history, to the Liverpool Mosque and Institute in the nineteenth century, for another example of 'good practice'. The opening of the London Muslim Centre in June 2004, an initiative of the East London Mosque, has provided not only an important local resource, but also a template for the kind of religious facility that many British Muslims around the country yearn for. The new London Muslim Centre, built by the local Muslim community for £4 million (with an overall budget of £9 million), has been praised as a 'triumph of community spirit' (*Muslim Weekly*, 18–24 June 2004). It has not only religious facilities, but also dedicated areas for education and social activity (Hussain 2006). There is a library, a gym, state-of-the-art technology and a crèche to enable women's full participation. The new Centre, the largest of its kind in Western Europe, aims to serve the diverse needs of the community, spiritually, socially, economically and culturally, and to reach out to the local non-Muslim population. It is this combining of 'mosque' with multi-purpose 'community centre' (premises which in many other towns and cities are spatially separate) that potentially enables the full participation of all members of the community. It is the kind of resource that will make a difference not only to the Muslims in East London, but also beyond London, as the success of this new initiative resonates further afield and sets a new standard for the kind of religious facility that British Muslims aspire to.[17]

---

[17] Another recent initiative, reflecting a collaboration between the Guide Dogs for the Blind Association and the Muslim Council of Britain, has led to a religious ruling allowing a Muslim worshipper in Leicester to take his guide dog to the mosque. The saliva of dogs is regarded as

Indeed, there is growing competition among British mosques to become beacons for their communities, in part fostered by the 'Model Mosque' contest on the UK-based *'Islam Channel'*. This contest, established in 2007, aims to 'improve standards within UK mosques ... to promote and share best practice ... to recognise and reward the best mosques ... and to combat negative media portrayal of mosques'.[18] Entrants are advised that the criteria for the competition do not rest upon the size or architecture of the mosque, but upon the services it provides to local Muslims and the relations it has with the wider community. What is particularly striking about this competition is the fact that it has the distinctive feel of a 'reality TV' show.[19] This is as suggestive of the 'embeddedness' of Muslims in British life and culture as the physical establishment of mosques themselves.

'unclean' in Islam, but special facilities have been created at the mosque for Vargo to wait while his owner is at prayer (BBC News Online, 24 September 2008, http://news.bbc.co.uk/1/hi/england/leicestershire/7633623.stm, accessed 6/1/09).

[18] www.islamchannel.tv

[19] This is not the first example of mosques and Muslim communities becoming the subject of entertainment. Another example is the TV series *Little Mosque on the Prairie*, an award-winning Canadian TV sitcom: www.cbc.ca/littlemosque

# CHAPTER 9

# *Gender, religious identity and youth*

## INTRODUCTION

Much research on gender in relation to British Muslims so far has focused on women, and especially the emerging generation of young British-born Muslim girls.[1] The hopes and expectations of young women in relation to marriage and education, for example, have been studied in some depth (Afshar 1998; Basit 1995; Dwyer 1999c; Jawad and Benn 2003; Khanum 1992a; Knott and Khokher 1993; Mirza 1989). The problems facing women in terms of social control by religious authorities (Sahgal and Yuval-Davis 1992) and issues such as forced marriages, domestic violence and female circumcision have emerged as major concerns. However, ethnographic research on gender in the past decade has shifted its focus towards Muslim men, and especially young men (Alexander 2000; Archer 2009; Hopkins 2006).[2] Likewise, there have been some important recent studies involving British Muslim women that centralize their emerging economic and civic roles, rather than highlighting stereotypical concerns with marriage and the family. New topics, including youth work with Muslim girls (Cressey 2007) and participation in the labour market and civil society (see for example Ahmad *et al.* 2003; Benn 2003; Bowlby and Lloyd Evans 2009), are now being tackled seriously and with new insights.

This chapter surveys the literature concerning British Muslim masculinity and femininity, and critically evaluates gender and gender relations among Muslims in Britain more broadly. In the past decade, academic attention has shifted markedly from a preoccupation with the private world and concerns of women and girls, towards an exploration of the masculinity of young Muslim men, especially as located in the visible and

---

[1] At least one reason for this imbalance may be the straightforward availability of women as participants in research projects, in contrast to men who are more likely to be at work.

[2] One of the earliest studies of Muslim adolescent boys in Britain was undertaken as an MPhil thesis (Reed 1974), but the significance of gender is not prominent in this study.

public realm of the street (Alexander 1998; Archer 2001). The discussion then extends to an examination of how female and male styles of dress are manifested in the public sphere. These dress codes have been used and understood in various ways, by both Muslims and non-Muslims, as indicators of identity, community and belonging. The aim of this discussion is not to reinforce an unhelpful concentration upon what Muslim women and men look like, particularly in a context where dress, and particularly the hijab, is already 'semiotically over-charged' (Tarlo 2007a: 135). The aim is instead to consider what changing styles of dress and self-presentation signify about British Muslim expressions of femininity, masculinity and identity, and indeed, about Islam in Britain more broadly.

Much of this chapter is necessarily concerned with exploding myths and stereotypes which have revolved around the supposedly passive or oppressed Muslim woman (Ahmad 2006; Benn and Jawad 2003; Brah 1996; Dwyer 2000) and the allegedly deviant, criminal Muslim male (Alexander 2000). The chapter therefore begins with a very brief examination of gender relations in Islam.[3] This is because Islamic texts and the popularly promoted exemplars of 'femininity' and 'masculinity' attributed to early Islamic history are often used as benchmarks in contemporary evaluations of gender and gender relations.

## GENDER RELATIONS IN ISLAM: A BRIEF OVERVIEW

The *Qur'ān* makes no distinction between men and women in terms of their equality as human beings (Ahmed 1992; Jawad 1998). In terms of their religious obligations and moral duties, they are equally accountable.[4] Islamic sources describe the rights and responsibilities that men and women have towards one another. These are founded upon mutual respect and complementarity. A Muslim woman therefore has in principle every right to develop herself as an individual and to contribute to her society. This is expressed in particular through her right to education, her right to choose her own spouse, her right to own and dispose of property as she sees fit, and her right to participate in public life. From the outset, 'Islam bestowed a separate personal and economic identity on women: they did not become the chattel of their husband, but retained their name and property and had inalienable rights of inheritance from both their parents and their husband' (Afshar 1998: 109). A series of rights and responsibilities

---

[3] For a fuller discussion of gender relations in Islam see for example (Jawad 1998; Roald 2001).
[4] See for example *Sūrah* 3: 194; *Sūrah* 33: 32: *Sūrah* 16: 95.

are conferred on women in their various roles as daughters, sisters, wives and mothers, and a parallel series of rights and responsibilities are conferred on men, as sons, brothers, husbands and fathers.

Motherhood is one of the most valued roles for a Muslim woman, because she is seen as the most suitable parent to take on primary responsibility for the nurture and education of the next generation. A saying of the Prophet recalls that 'paradise is under the feet of mothers', and there are Qur'ānic verses that explicitly call for kindness and respect to be shown towards mothers (for instance, *Sūrah* 46: 15). Motherhood is by no means the only role for women, however, and they are free to contribute their skills and talents to society as they see fit. There are many Muslim women in Britain who combine professional roles such as teaching, social work or medicine alongside their roles as mothers, while some women may for various reasons be unable to (or prefer not to) marry or to become mothers.

If the nature of femininity is exemplified in the lives and conduct of the Prophet Muhammad's wives and daughters, the nature of masculinity in Islam is exemplified through the personal example of the Prophet Himself, and in the writings and example of notable Islamic scholars subsequently. For example, Imam al-Qushayri wrote in his famous *Risāla*:

The root of chivalry is that the servant strive constantly for the sake of others. Chivalry is that you do not see yourself as superior to others. The one who has chivalry is the one who has no enemies. Chivalry is that you be an enemy of your own soul for the sake of your Lord. Chivalry is that you act justly without demanding justice for yourself. Chivalry is [having] ... beautiful character.[5]

An exemplar of this wisdom is the figure of 'Alī, the last of the 'Rightly Guided' caliphs, and son-in-law of the Prophet Muhammad. He came to represent the archetype of youthful manly perfection on account of his selflessness, courage, generosity, honour and nobility (Birt 2000).

At the time of the Prophet Muhammad, women attended mosques and took part in public religious debates with men. They were 'not passive, docile followers but were active interlocutors in the domain of faith as they were in other matters ... thus the *Hadīth* narratives show women acting and speaking out of a sense that they were entitled to participate in the life of religious thought and practice' (Ahmed 1992: 72). Following the Prophet's death, his widows assumed positions of authority, esteem and influence in the early Muslim community. However, discrepancies

[5] Abu'l –Qasim al-Qushayri, *al-Risāla*, cited in Murata (1992: 267).

have arisen between ideals enshrined in Islamic thought and teaching, and the realities facing Muslim women in everyday life. It was not long after the death of the Prophet Muhammad that Muslim women found their newly defined God-given rights being denied to them (Afshar 2008). They have in various ways been struggling for recognition of these rights ever since.

Women of all faiths and races have often carried a particular burden as bearers of family honour, and this is certainly true in Muslim societies (Afshar 1998). Women are moreover seen as guardians of collective identity by virtue of their role as mothers and educators of the next generation. As a result, their physical bodies have often become subject to a particular kind of ordering and regulation which reflects a distinction between the domestic, private, female realm of the home, and the public, masculine space beyond it (Mohammad 2005b). The sexual purity of women is regarded as essential for marriage and the formation of successful Muslim families and societies. This requires strict control of their sexuality and the monitoring of their interaction with men to whom they are not related, especially in the public realm. Modesty in women's dress and demeanour is required if the good reputation of the family is to be maintained (Wilson 2006). The process of migration has often resulted in the intensification and reinforcing of gender roles and ideals bound up with honour and reputation, as new communities seek to maintain their values, sometimes in the face of hostility and discrimination (Dwyer 2000). However, there also exists an awareness of how the honour of men and women is interdependent. In her study of Pakistani Muslims in Manchester in the 1970s and 1980s, Pnina Werbner noted that both husband and wife derived status and reputation from vicarious participation in their respective networks (Werbner 1990: 130).

FEMININITY AND MUSLIM WOMEN IN BRITAIN

There is now an extensive research literature which looks at issues such as marriage (Ahmad 2006; Basit 1996; Basit 1997a; Charsley 2007; Mirza 1989) or education (Abbas 2003; Basit 1995; Haw 1998) or identity and ethnicity (Butler 1999; Dwyer 1999b; Knott and Khokher 1993) among young Muslim girls in Britain (especially those born and raised in Britain, and particularly those from South Asian backgrounds). Compared with this, the voices and experiences of women who are from other ethnic origins, or who are in their middle or later years, are harder to find, although there are some studies that provide important exceptions (Afshar *et al.* 2001;

Berns McGowan 1999; Gardner 2002; Phillipson *et al.* 2003; Werbner 1990). The extent of literature does, however, enable evaluation of the changing experiences of Muslim women in Britain over the past four decades. This section explores these experiences, with particular emphasis on the participation of women in the labour market, and in civil society.

There are at least 800,000 Muslim women in Britain today (Communities and Local Government, *Empowering Muslim Women: Case Studies* 2008). These are women whose families are located in Britain owing to the migration at some point of a person (normally a man) on whom they (or their mother or grandmother) are, or have been, economically dependent (Lloyd Evans and Bowlby 2000: 473). This relationship of 'dependence' may, however, have changed, even becoming reversed in some circumstances. Especially following the Second World War, many (but not all) Muslims came to Britain from relatively poor, uneducated, rural or semi-rural South Asian backgrounds. Neither men nor their womenfolk (who often arrived later) were likely to be fluent English speakers. Many found the urban culture of large British cities hostile, unfamiliar and disorientating, especially compared to the close-knit rural communities they had often left behind.[6] Suddenly, 'their language, their faith, their traditions and rituals all [ceased] to be the norm … [while] many moved from warm open spaces into small cold surroundings where they had almost no skill and know-how in dealing with the most basic requirements of everyday life' (Afshar *et al.* 2005: 267). It would be easy to assume, as many popular stereotypes suggest, that South Asian Muslim women in Britain in the 1970s or 1980s were therefore confined to the home, and were denied agency or power both within and outside the domestic sphere. Explanations for the lower employment rate of British Muslim women have, for example, often involved simplistic and uninformed assumptions about gender roles in Islam. These have presumed that Muslim women are 'not allowed' to work outside the home (Brah 1993; Brah 1996: 70).[7] However, research evidence indicates a different and more complex story. How women spend their time (whether in paid or unpaid work), and their overall relationship to the labour market,

---

[6] The transition and upheaval involved in migration from rural South Asian villages to urban British cities is vividly captured Monica Ali's novel *Brick Lane* (Ali 2003).

[7] This stereotype is unfortunately sometimes reinforced by ignorance of women's rights in Islam *within* Muslim communities, as this quotation indicates: 'But in our Islam, working outside the home for women is not allowed; as much as they can stay in the home, it's better for them' (Pakistani woman, age thirty-five, with five children) (Dale 2002: 7).

provides an initial lens through which some of the changing experiences of Muslim women in Britain may come into focus.[8]

## WOMEN, WORK AND THE LABOUR MARKET

'Paid employment is only one form of work' (Brah 1993: 449), and in most societies women have been largely responsible for housework and the care of dependents. Women have nonetheless often been engaged in various forms of 'home' working which supports the family income, such as craftwork, agricultural work, or the processing and storage of food. Many South Asian Muslim women coming to Britain in the 1970s and 1980s were engaged in informal economic activity prior to migration (especially, given their mostly rural origins, related to agriculture) alongside their domestic 'work' in the home (Ahmad 2006: 274; Khanum 1994: 108, cited in Phillipson *et al.* 2003: 9). The take-up of auxiliary work in Britain as opportunities arose was therefore part of an existing practice.

As a consequence of changes in the wider labour market and economy (especially the decline in the manufacturing industry, the rise of global multinationals, and the growth of the clerical and service sector), South Asian Muslim women found themselves steadily drawn into the workplace, not least to support the income of low-paid or unemployed men (Brah 1996; Dwyer 2000). This work was often undertaken alongside responsibility for above-average-sized or extended-family households, and limited funds to purchase labour-saving devices such as washing-machines. The opportunities available to women varied, according to their capacity in English, their qualifications and external constraints, such as the structure of the local economy. Various forms of 'home' working, and especially machining at home for the textile and clothing industry, provided a way for women to contribute to family income while maintaining family responsibilities (Brah 1993).[9] Many women were aware that, while convenient for them, such work was often exploitative, isolating and costly in terms of their health and well-being. Those women who entered the labour market more formally often did so strategically, perhaps to support a particular family occurrence, such as a wedding or a visit to Pakistan. These were events that confirmed their roles at the centre of domestic life and management of family affairs (Werbner 1990). Subsequent research

---

[8] The availability of empirical evidence unfortunately limits this discussion almost entirely to women of South Asian background, though there are possibilities for extending general insights to Muslim women from other ethnic groups.

[9] This kind of work is often invisible in employment statistics (Brah 1996: 70).

has confirmed that this kind of strategic employment continued through-out the 1990s (Lloyd Evans and Bowlby 2000).

Pakistani Muslim women in Manchester in the 1970s and 1980s were proactive in creating sociable and supportive networks which empowered them, individually and collectively, both within and outside the labour market:

Incoming South Asian women demanded, and regained, power in the family by reasserting their traditional role in the management of extensive gendered and familial networks in Britain. In order to achieve their status as active makers and sustainers of this interdomestic domain of sociality, women often had to enter the wider labour market. In some sense, then, they become 'modern' but their power and agency resided in their reassertion of a traditional role. (Werbner 1990: xvii)

However, in the British context this traditional role was often being undertaken free from the gaze of older female relatives, such as a mother-in-law, and some of the women in Werbner's research valued the independence that this kind of occupation afforded. Migration freed them from a number of constraints and restrictions that would have been imposed had they not migrated (Werbner 1990: 129). In parallel, and for women of all generations, having children could be an important means for ending isolation and for limiting restricting influences coming from menfolk. The requirement to take children to school and collect them, for instance, allows for conversation at the school gates that in turn provides an opportunity for extending friendship networks. Once children are at school, women simply have more time for their own enterprises.

Like their Pakistani counterparts, Bangladeshi Muslim women who arrived in Britain some thirty years ago quickly established strong social networks which enabled them to cope with multiple caring roles, poor-quality overcrowded housing, poverty and ill health (Phillipson *et al.* 2003). For some women, arrival in Britain meant taking up new opportunities that would have been impossible in Bangladesh, including education, and, for some, careers and employment:

I have done ESOL classes and am doing a childcare course. I wanted to join the childcare course two years ago but they said my English wasn't good enough so I took the ESOL classes and now they have accepted me (Halima [Bangladeshi]). (Phillipson *et al.* 2003: 46)

Some Bangladeshi women have faced insurmountable barriers to their own educational or employment ambitions, but they are nevertheless optimistic about the prospects for their daughters:

They can study as much as they want to. They can work. Their life has more meaning and use here. In our country they see women as useless, not here. They have more worth here. It is better for them in every way here (Zaima [Bangladeshi]). (Phillipson *et al.* 2003: 47)

Patriarchal attitudes have nonetheless shaped British Muslim women's experience of the labour market across the generations, and their participation has been, and continues to be, 'structured by a multiplicity of ideological, cultural and structural factors' (Brah 1993: 456). For example, the income of Muslim wives in paid employment would be regarded by some husbands (and, indeed, some wives) as undermining the primary male role as breadwinner (Ahmad *et al.* 2003: 29; Brah 1993: 452; Howe 2007: 14), or as a shaming indication of either greed or poverty (Lloyd Evans and Bowlby 2000: 467). For others, family honour could be irrevocably damaged in a context where a Muslim woman was working alongside unrelated males.

Some women take pride in the fact that they do not, or need not, undertake paid employment, whereas others positively value the independence, choice and freedom that paid work or a career can offer (Dale 2002; Dale *et al.* 2002). Employment can confer a range of non-financial rewards for British Muslim women, such as an identity 'not circumscribed solely by domestic roles ... and an opportunity to forge a set of relationships distinct from family networks' (Ahmad *et al.* 2003: 16). Undertaking voluntary work has been a useful intermediate route for some British Muslim women in their transition into the labour market. Community or voluntary work and its connotations of selfless service can be used to negotiate potential family or community reservations, while giving women the opportunity to gain independence or to develop skills (Lloyd Evans and Bowlby 2000).

A consistent finding from studies that have taken place across several decades is the importance that British Muslim women attach to choice about whether or not to work (Ahmad *et al.* 2003; Brah 1993: 450; Brown 2006). Even among those whose family and caring responsibilities or competence in English are keeping them out of the labour market, many would like the opportunity to exercise choice in the decision about whether to engage in paid employment (47 per cent in a sample of eighty-one Bangladeshi women in 2001/2) (Phillipson *et al.* 2003: 39). For Brah, this represents 'a critical commentary on those views that hold women's participation in the labour market to be undesirable ... and the hegemonic claims of such perspectives' (Brah 1993: 450).

Despite this picture of strategic employment and multiple unpaid working roles on the part of many British Muslim women, figures from the 2001 Census indicate that the formal economic inactivity rate of British Muslim women is almost double that of other faith groups. Statistics show that 68 per cent of Muslim women are economically inactive (Bunglawala 2004). Recent Labour Force Survey and Department for Work and Pensions data collected in 2006/7 places the figure even lower at 66 per cent (compared to 26 per cent for all women) (Communities and Local Government, 'Empowering Muslim Women: Case Studies', 2008: 9). However, these statistics hide considerable disparities within and between communities (Ahmad *et al.* 2003; Brah 1996; Dale *et al.* 2002). For example, Indian Muslim women are much more likely to be in paid employment than women from Pakistani and Bangladeshi Muslim backgrounds. Nearly half of Pakistani and Bangladeshi women over the age of twenty-five are looking after the home and family full time, compared to just over 30 per cent for all Muslim women aged twenty-five and over (Beckford *et al.* 2006: 18, 35, figure 1.8). So although religious considerations and expectations surrounding motherhood are clearly significant factors in determining overall rates of female Muslim employment, they are by no means the only ones. The lack of formal qualifications is significant. Amongst Pakistanis and Bangladeshis (who make up 70 per cent of Muslims in the UK), 40 per cent of women of working age have no formal qualifications at all. This compares especially unfavourably with white women among whom only 17 per cent have such a lack of qualifications (Communities and Local Government, 'Empowering Muslim Women: Case Studies', 2008).

For those British Muslim women who are in the labour market, there is a strong preference for particular kinds of employment that are consistent with expectations of honour and reputation. This means that careers that positively enhance family honour, such as medicine, dentistry, pharmacy, accountancy, teaching or law (Ahmad *et al.* 2003; Benn 2003; Mohammad 2005b), are especially preferred.

Medicine [is a] prestige career. People like to say 'My daughter is a doctor'. (Mohammad 2005b: 193)

Such is the degree of honour attached to these 'prestige' occupations that more Pakistani women now enter 'the professions' than Pakistani men (11 per cent and 9 per cent, respectively). Indeed, their overall rate of entry is higher than that of white British women (Mohammad 2005b: 185). This high level of achievement reflects the differential outcomes of education between Muslim girls and boys at school.

For those women who do not enter the professions, there is often a parental preference for employment that might be regarded as 'transparent' in terms of its setting. Recent research with Pakistani women in Britain by the geographer Robina Mohammad illustrates some of the factors that affect and regulate women's engagement in the labour market, and considers the corresponding gendering of public space and occupations (Mohammad 2005b). She notes that some kinds of work are regarded as distinctively masculine, while others are distinctively feminine (an observation also confirmed by earlier research (Brah 1993; Howe 2007)). One of the criteria used to determine this distinction is the space–time setting in which the job is performed. For example, the mobility and flexibility inherent in taxi driving, combined with its enclosed and individualized character, makes it less spatially or temporally fixed than shop or factory work. It is thus decidedly masculine, and therefore unsuitable for an 'honourable' Muslim woman. In fact, any kind of work involving extensive travel, even of a professional kind, may be frowned upon where it takes young women/daughters away from the regulatory gaze of parents (Ahmad *et al.* 2003). Ironically, therefore, although a Muslim woman working in a shop may be subject to a greater number of encounters with unrelated men, 'these encounters are regulated by the disciplinary gaze of the store and the public as a whole, including parents, who can make an inspection of their daughter's performance anytime' (Mohammad 2005b: 195).

Muslim women continue to face and overcome various obstacles to their engagement in the labour market that emanate both from within and outside their own communities. It is an environment of potential prejudice and Islamophobic hostility for Muslim women, bound up with stereotypical and gendered assumptions about them and their ability to 'fit in':

Muslim women are having to confront not only the sexist assumptions from within their own communities ... but also from British society as a whole. Thus, although their parents' culture may place restrictions on their lifestyles, the sexist and racist stereotypes that exist in British society restrict them even further. Standing up for their rights as women means challenging traditional gender relations within Pakistani and Bangladeshi culture, but it also means fighting against their image as exploited and oppressed 'victims' which pervades British 'common sense' notions of Muslim women in general. (Butler 1999: 149)

I have been to interviews and you can tell as soon as you walk in that they don't really want you. There was this one interview I went to and it was mostly a white firm, in the interview they were really targeting some funny questions at me, like would you be able to work evenings being a Muslim, or do you know there are a lot of men working here so would your family mind and do you wear a scarf at all … (Pakistani woman, 19, full-time sales assistant). (Dale 2002: 12)

In the light of comments such as these, the effort of some employers to accommodate the needs of Muslim women is to be applauded, such as the adaptation of the Metropolitan Police uniform for female Muslim officers who wear hijab.

Although the Employment Equality (Religion or Belief) Regulations 2003 aim to eliminate the scope for religious prejudice in the workplace, it persists in more subtle or indirect forms, and women are likely to remain engaged in the struggle to resist other people's uninformed assumptions about them well into the future (Anwar and Shah 2000). Yet the labour market is not the only site of resistance. British Muslim women have been pro-actively engaged in civil society and self-help projects for at least the past three decades, championing their rights and placing themselves at the forefront of social action.

## WOMEN'S EMPOWERMENT AND PARTICIPATION IN CIVIL SOCIETY

Long before the creation of national and local Muslim women's organizations, Muslim women in Britain habitually supported one another in informal networks. Werbner's research with Pakistani Muslim women in Manchester in the 1970s described the various pro-active measures that women took to sustain themselves socially, spiritually and emotionally, following their arrival in Britain. A good example was the organization of *Qur'ān* readings, a relatively simple ritual which involves reading the entire *Qur'ān* in one sitting, each person taking turns to read one or more of the thirty portions of the text. These gatherings were convened by women in their homes, and were described as 'important locuses of inter-household women-centred sociability' (Werbner 1990: 156).[10] It was from gatherings such as these that Qur'ānic 'study circles' *(ḥalaqāt)* emerged. These provided regular and more formalized opportunities for groups of women to learn about their faith together, usually led by a woman with in-depth knowledge of Islamic sources, and were held in homes

---

[10] This ritual is still important for British Muslim women, especially in the context of illness or other domestic crises (Rozario and Gilliat-Ray 2007).

or community centres or in mosques. Today there are well-established Islamic 'study circles' for women – young and old – throughout Britain.[11]

In parallel with this kind of spiritual empowerment, Muslim women also formed self-help organizations, particularly associated with the development of literacy and language skills in order that they could speak publicly on their own behalf and further their prospects in the labour market (Burlet and Reid 1998). Alongside such self-development programmes, other forms of activism were pursued. Kundnani notes that 'myriad women's groups in Asian communities have been dealing with issues like forced marriage for decades' (Kundnani 2007a: 139), rarely receiving any funding or support from mainstream organizations (Wilson 2006). Looking back, these initiatives undoubtedly enhanced the confidence of many women and their potential to engage in the labour market and civil society. Ultimately, however, they did relatively little to increase direct political representation. This is because the women's organizations engaged in social action often faced dual resistance, both from conservative male community leaders, and from a state apparatus that often endorsed these community leaders and therefore resisted the funding of women's activism (Burlet and Reid 1998).[12] Muslim women nonetheless found innovative and effective ways of overcoming this resistance.

Being excluded from decision-making, Muslim women, who tend to be in the frontline of meeting social needs, have been forced to make themselves relevant. While you may not necessarily see them at photo calls and high powered delegations you will see them getting training in education, media, social work, health care and counselling. Muslim women are now a quiet but potent presence in statutory bodies and other public arenas increasingly becoming team managers, directors of departments and chairs of committees. Women's organisations have led the way in setting agendas and developing much needed social welfare projects that support families and heal communities. (Khan 2004b: 25)

A good example of such an agenda-setting organization is the well-established high-profile An-Nisa Society in London,[13] founded in 1985. It works to improve the provision of Muslim-sensitive social services, and to influence government policy on issues that affect women and families.

---

[11] This point was confirmed by Humera Khan, An-Nisa Society, London, during an interview on 15 January 2004, but as yet there has been little or no systematic research of these 'study circles' for British Muslim women.

[12] Brown (2006: 422) notes that local state agencies, in an effort to embrace multiculturalism and anti-racism, were also reluctant to intervene where 'Asian women [were] concerned … guided by the belief that the Asian community [has its] own internal mechanisms to resolve problems … [the result being] the denial to Asian women of advice and help offered to other women'.

[13] www.an-nisa.org

Figure 10. 'Women with the right attitude' – Khalida and Humera Khan of the
An-Nisa Society. Reproduced by kind permission of Peter Sanders

An-Nisa aims to bridge the gap between local service providers in the statutory sector on the one hand, and often poorly funded community-based voluntary initiatives on the other. Over the course of the past two decades, its members have worked on a wide range of projects, relating to health (mental and physical), parenting (including fatherhood), arts and culture. Its staff have made pioneering contributions to national networks and media.

Individual British Muslim women have become increasingly prominent in all spheres of national public life, from politics (for example, Salma Yaqoob and Baroness Uddin), to entertainment (with comics such as Shazia Mirza), the academy (for example, Professors Mona Siddiqui and Halah Afshar OBE), business (with entrepreneurs such as Perween Warsi) and journalism (such as Anila Baig, *The Sun*).[14] In recent years, they have also had roles in national bodies representing Muslims in the public sphere, such as the Muslim Council of Britain (Unaiza Malik, former Treasurer) and the British Muslim Forum (Zareen Roohi Ahmed, former Chief Executive). Such women offer a powerful challenge to stereotypical images of Muslim women as either 'passive' or 'oppressed', as well as highlighting individuality and diversity among Muslim women. As role models who clearly demonstrate that they have been empowered by their faith rather than constrained by it, they challenge media and secularist discourses which assume that Muslim women's 'liberation' will arise from assimilation into 'Western' and (European) Enlightenment

---

[14] See the website www.salaam.co.uk for the profiles of *numerous* prominent British Muslim women. The names I have cited are simply indicative.

values (Kundnani 2007a: 139).[15] Such figures also have the potential to free other Muslim women from the burden of essentialist assumptions that, innately, women cannot perform such roles. For too long, Muslim women have been 'judged by others – by peers, teachers, colleagues at work – as being representative of a group rather than as diverse individuals … young women found themselves constantly judged or essentialized as *"a typical Muslim girl"'* (Dwyer 2000: 480, emphasis original).

This challenge to the assumption that Muslim women will be 'liberated' by Western secularist ideologies is a struggle that has taken place not only with non-Muslim liberals, but also with a strand of radical feminist thinking within Islam itself. So, for instance, 'Women against Fundamentalism' was an organization that emerged in the wake of the Rushdie affair in 1989 (Sahgal and Yuval-Davis 1992), and was active until 1997. This group was distinctive for rejecting the idea that Muslim women might find liberation from within Islam, favouring the view that Western secularism could provide the sole route for the achievement of women's rights (Glavanis 1998: 403). Prominent activists within this movement, such as Nira Yuval-Davis and Gita Saghal, were particularly critical of 'fundamentalism' as it affected British Muslim women, placing the blame squarely on an assumed synergy between Islamist ideology on the one hand, and the 'Orientalist' assumptions of the British state on the other. Government backing or sponsorship of Muslim community organizations that reflect some of the religious movements examined in chapters 3 and 4 were regarded as directly and indirectly oppressive for women.

A significant weakness in this line of secularist feminist thinking however is its uncritical reproduction of an either/or dichotomy between progressive, secular modernity on the one hand and reformist/revivalist Islamic thought, with its sometimes conservative ideas regarding the regulation of women's bodies and sexuality, on the other (Glavanis 1998; McKerl 2007). By juxtaposing Islam and secularism in this way, the kind of innovation, resistance, reinterpretation and self-empowerment that British Muslim women have been engaged in from within Islam (as the An-Nisa Society demonstrates in practical terms) is effectively devalued. So too is the capacity of women to take up multiple strategic positionings in relation to their faith, to their families, to their communities and to

---

[15] Muslim women have long struggled with external perceptions: 'Whether she is exoticised, represented as ruthlessly oppressed in need of liberation, or read as a victim/enigmatic emblem of religious fundamentalism, she is often perceived as the bearer of "race" and cultures that are constructed as inherently threatening to the presumed superiority of western civilisations' (Brah 1993: 447).

the state, as the need has arisen (Brown 2006; Hall 1992). The assumption that Muslim women need to renounce their Islamic identity as a prerequisite for emancipation results in 'a new kind of superiority entrenched in the name of feminism' (Kundnani 2007a: 139). Furthermore, a discourse of secularism and feminism which assumes that Muslim women require liberation into the supposedly 'progressive' ideologies of the West develops from a viewpoint that seems to take it for granted that 'Western women are secular, liberated and in total control of their lives when this is not the case' (McKerl 2007: 207). It is also noticeable that the issues that are widely assumed by politicians, or the media, to be most problematic for Muslim women seem to reflect a particular preoccupation with questions of freedom (dress, movement, body, sexuality) (McKerl 2007), with little or no regard for the issues that probably affect them far more, such as poor-quality, overcrowded accommodation, poverty or access to equitable health care (Rozario and Gilliat-Ray 2007).

As we have seen in relation to the position of Muslim women in the labour market, the exclusion or oppression of women often results from a complex interplay of social, economic, political and patriarchal processes. For some women, Islamic religious movements have been an important means for resisting exclusion and for finding a feminist discourse for the expression of their Islamic rights from within their tradition (Afshar 1998; Butler 1999; Samad 1998). Their ability to differentiate between cultural attitudes and more normative Islamic tradition and teaching has enabled them to 'lever open spaces that were foreclosed by the older generation' (Samad 1998: 436). The Qur'ānic and Islamic study circles established by Muslim women back in the 1970s have provided an avenue for women to become conversant with Islamic sources, and this has enabled them to articulate their Islamic rights (Afshar 1998: 119).

In the wake of the London bombings of July 2005, Muslim women have increasingly been recruited into the government's anti-radicalization and anti-terrorism strategy. Several government-backed initiatives involving Muslim women have been launched in recent years, including the 'Muslim Women Talk' campaign (2005–7),[16] and the National Muslim Women's Advisory Group (2008 –).[17] It is of course desirable that Muslim women are given a voice at local and national level and an opportunity to speak directly to government. However, speaking primarily to already

[16]  www.muslimwomentalk.com
[17]  For a YouTube clip of the launch see www.number-10.gov.uk/output/Page14454.asp; and for a list of participants, www.gnn.gov.uk/Content/Detail.asp?ReleaseID=349213&NewsAreaID=2

prominent and articulate Muslim women has the potential to inadvertently exclude those from older generations, or those who have limited
capacity in English.[18] Indeed, there is relatively little information or transparency about the process of selection to these forums. Other critical
questions need to be asked. For example, will there be a redistribution
of power and resources as a result of these initiatives, or will they remain
merely 'talking shops'? In a report published by Communities and Local
Government in January 2008 (*Empowering Muslim Women: Case Studies*),
the phrase 'preventing violent extremism', and the role that women
might play in this process, occurs no fewer than four times in a one-page
Introduction. Empowering Muslim women for their own sake seems to
be secondary to the anti-radicalization agenda ('Dealing with the real
issues', *Labour Review,* April 2008). Critical evaluation of the way that
government works with Muslim communities now seems overdue.

## WORK, MASCULINITY AND MUSLIM MEN IN BRITAIN

Compared to the abundant literature on British Muslim women, there
are relatively few studies of British Muslim men and masculinity, reflecting in part the relatively recent emergence of masculinity as a subject for
academic research (Archer 2001: 80). There have nonetheless been some
important studies of labour and migration, and education and identity,
which place an emphasis on the world of Muslim men from a variety of
(mainly South Asian) backgrounds (Alam and Husband 2006; Alexander
2000; Archer 2001; Gardner 1998b; Hopkins 2006; Kalra 2000). An
emerging consensus is that the meaning of manhood is framed in relation
to power relations and negotiations with other men and women, in particular localities, and in reference to other social divisions such as class,
race and religion. Most research on Muslim men undertaken so far has
focused on the younger generation. For this reason, Virinder Kalra's study
of employment and labour relations in Oldham is especially valuable,
since it compares and contrasts the economic activity and inactivity of
men across several generations (Kalra 2000).

Muslim men (notably those of South Asian background) have
been especially vulnerable to socio-economic changes, and particularly the decline of the manufacturing industry in Britain. The negative

---

[18] See Raz (2006) for a collection of quotations and voices from Muslim women on a range of
topics, collected as part of the Muslim Women's Network report *She Who Disputes: Muslim
Women Shape the Debate* (2006) at the Women's National Commission.

consequences for men arising from the closure of large textile mills in the north of England in the 1970s and 1980s, and the need to find alternative forms of income, is vividly captured in Kalra's study of employment in Oldham, *From Textile Mills to Taxi Ranks* (Kalra 2000). A particularly valuable aspect of Kalra's study is his analysis of the consequences of these labour changes in terms of the organization of space, time and relationships between men, their community and their families, and – of special significance here – their sons. For example, for the older generation of men, unemployment from the mills (and little prospect of re-employment) provided a new opportunity to engage in 'work' associated with the extended family, such as attending funerals or collecting grandchildren from school. This strengthened their relationships with immediate kin and members of their wider kinship group (*birādarī*). While some men certainly resorted to spending long hours at home watching television following their redundancy, others found new ways of organizing their time. This usually revolved around mosques and extended family life cycles. Their new circumstances enabled a renewed commitment to Islam, which offered them an alternative way of organizing their day, week or year, as well as a moral framework for understanding their situation (Kalra 2000: 147). This was especially so in a context where affirmation of masculinity through the role of breadwinner had been compromised (Brah 1996: 57).[19] The mosque also provided a natural and convenient place to pass their time in a situation where many of them were living in overcrowded or poor-quality accommodation.

Kalra shows how wider transformations in the British economy also affected the work patterns of younger men in Oldham. By virtue of their age and responsibilities, these younger men were forced to enter the service economy, developing businesses that relied on their own self-employment. Catering, market-trading and taxi-driving were particular areas of growth, as was the garment trade – this of course providing a particularly good opportunity for women to support the domestic enterprise through machining at home (Werbner 1990: 133). For those men who developed new self-employed businesses, the flexibility afforded to them by organizing their own time also allowed a renewed engagement with Islam.[20] However, these changes in employment had (and continue to have) major

[19] This increasing engagement with Islam is also noted in Gardner (1998b: 170–1) in her research with Bengali male elders. However, she also records a sense of regret and loss as a result of unemployment and declining health among the male elders she interviewed (p. 162).
[20] Research that records the revival of interest in religion among Muslims in Britain (unfortunately and unhelpfully this is often framed as extremism) usually attributes this to a defensive

consequences for family life and the fulfilment of fatherhood roles. The catering trade invariably means regular late-night shift work, which clearly has implications for support of a spouse and contact time with young children (Birt 2008b).

## MUSLIM MALE YOUTH: REBELLION, RESISTANCE AND REALITY

Growing up through adolescence often involves experimentations with identity and some degree of youthful rebellion. The fact that Islam is sometimes used as a resource as part of this process should not come as a surprise. Thus in his research with young Muslim men in Bradford, Samad noted that a 'hard' macho masculinity is sometimes deliberately constructed using Islamic discourse, often with little awareness of the meanings and nuances:

> membership of Hamas or Hizb-ut-Tahrir was noted ... yet these same individuals were unaware who Shias were, and how they differed from Sunnis, and did not know what Hamas or Hizb-ut-Tahrir represents. Neither were they observant in their religious rituals, except in superficial terms, and also they were often in trouble with the police for petty crimes, drugs, etc. Thus the daubing of walls in Manningham with the slogan 'Hamas Rules OK' or supporting anti-Semitic, homophobic and misogynist organisations such as Hizb-ut-Tahrir, was more an act of rebellion and defiance rather than the rise of 'fundamentalism'. It is all about being 'hard'. (Samad 1998: 434)

'Hanging out' on local streets, or in motor cars, provides an alternative space for otherwise unoccupied males. Overcrowding is a key factor, but not necessarily the only factor that propels young men out of the house, since many will have been raised with the assumption that the domestic space of the home is predominantly feminine space, while space outside the home is masculine (Mohammad 1999: 130). An interviewee for Marta Bolognani's research on crime and deviance among Pakistani Muslims in Bradford illustrates this social construction of space:

> When I first came over to Bradford I asked my sister in law's brother, where do your guys ... where is the most popular hang out place for Muslims? I think you know anyway for white communities there is your pub, your club, etc. etc., so there's lots to do, but for Muslim communities ... well, the answer I got when I went around and they showed me around, it's cars! You see a car there, and you

and passive reaction against Islamophobia, racism, exclusion or cultural alienation (Kibria 2008) among a number of factors, but rarely takes account of the multitude of factors much closer to home which might also be driving this process, especially among men.

see 5 guys sitting in a car, and some of them even have the portable televisions. Because for them that is their space, this is the space, this is the private space, they don't get that at home. They live at home, maybe someone is married, his wife lives at home, you know ... maybe a brother, married, the other brother lives at home, the sister lives at home and you have got a two-bedrooms house. And that's what they do, drive around, sitting in cars (Imran, teacher in his early thirties). (Bolognani 2009: 143)

In the wake of the New York/World Trade Center and 7/7 attacks, the young British Muslim male has become increasingly vulnerable to labelling as 'radical' or 'terrorist' (Dwyer *et al.* 2008), so amplifying another stereotype formed after the Rushdie Affair and the 'Northern Riots' of 2001, that young Muslim men are out of control, deviant, problematic, criminal, violent, and failing educationally and socially (Alexander 2004; Archer 2009; Burlet and Reid 1996; Macey 1999a; Webster 1997; Wilson 2006: 50).[21] Young Muslim men have been 'increasingly constructed as intrinsically fanatical "ultimate Others"' (Phoenix 1997, cited in Wilson 2006: 51). It is not difficult to find media reporting and academic research (Goodey 1999; Macey 1999b) that supports such a pathologized conception of Muslim male youth.

Such stereotyping ultimately positions young Muslim men in a marginal space, not only beyond inclusion in wider British society but also outside Islamic conceptions of ideal masculinity. Fortunately, there are examples of research which expose and challenge the assumptions that underpin the studies that have promulgated such stereotypes, restoring a degree of agency, individuality and subjectivity to young Muslim men (Alam and Husband 2006; Alexander 2000; Hopkins 2006). These offer a more nuanced, and balanced, assessment of the situation of Muslim male youth, because they record the 'structural' barriers that many young Muslim men face, such as economic inactivity or educational disadvantage. At the same time, such studies also portray Muslim male dynamism, positive resistance and creativity, and this profiling in itself challenges simplistic assumptions of supposed failure and marginality. As a consequence, the fluid and contextual nature of Muslim masculinity is evident. Hopkins demonstrates, for instance, the 'diverse, heterogeneous

---

[21] Writing about young male identity in general, Jonathan Rutherford notes that male redundancy in the 1980s created 'cultures of prolonged adolescence in which young male identities remain locked into the locality of estate, shops and school' with the consequence that deviant behaviour become a 'means to gaining prestige for a masculine identity bereft of any social value or function' (Rutherford 1998: 22). Thus the problems and issues facing young Muslim males should not be isolated from the problems facing non-Muslim males of the same generation.

and multifaceted nature of youthful Muslim masculinities that are simultaneously gendered, sexualised and classed, and influenced by generation
and location' (Hopkins 2006: 349).

## 'BROTHERS' AND 'SISTERS': YOUNG MUSLIM MALE ATTITUDES TO WOMEN

Some researchers have suggested that there is a link between the construction of ethnic minority Muslim male identity and resistance to racism
(Wetherell 1993, cited in Archer 2001: 83). Feelings of powerlessness
engendered by experiences of racism (and other forms of marginalization,
discrimination or exclusion) can be assuaged through the construction of
a masculine identity that is empowered by deliberate control, 'ownership'
and subordination of women (Dwyer 1999a; Dwyer 2000). Evidence to
support such a claim in relation to British Muslim men can be located
from comments made by interviewees in Claire Dwyer's research with
young British Muslim women near London, of which the following was
typical:

They [i.e. the boys] always bring their religion into it as well. In Islam it is like
all Muslims are supposed to be brothers and sisters, but not really, not literally.
But you know, they say that they're our brothers so they've got to protect us
(Ghazala, 18). (Dwyer 2000: 479)

Marie Macey conducted research following the Bradford disturbances in
1995[22] in which she noted how Islam was used by young Muslim men as
a key resource to control women, both Muslim and non-Muslim, though
in ways that showed a contradictory relationship to Islam. For example,
successfully ridding particular inner city streets from the nuisance of
prostitution became an Islamic cause for some young men, despite their
simultaneous involvement in other 'un-Islamic' behaviour, such as drug-
dealing (Macey 1999a: 854). Macey reports the various ways in which the
activities of young Muslim women were 'policed' by young men, through
direct intimidation as well as through more subtle forms of surveillance
such as reporting the 'shameful' behaviour of daughters to their parents.
Macey's conclusions about the role of Islam in the process of controlling
women are disrupted, however, by the findings of other work that suggests
that Muslim men in fact have many different ways of relating to women,
especially where they are literally or figuratively regarded as 'sisters'.

---

[22] See Burlet and Reid (1998) for an account of the Bradford disturbances.

In her study *The Asian Gang* (Alexander 2000), it was apparent that where relations between male friends were characterized by mutual respect, care and protection these same attitudes were often extended to include the female relatives or sisters of these friends:

As with 'brothers', the category of 'sister' extended beyond the bounds of imme-diate family to encompass the sisters of friends and other young women in the local community, along with its incumbent rights and responsibilities. Jamal commented, 'your friend's sister is like your sister'. (Alexander 2000: 207)

The term 'sister' is widely used in Islam and in other religious traditions as a convenient linguistic device to convey a non-sexualized form of rela-tionship, meaning that these women can be placed within an orbit of care and respect which reflects the fact that they are the sisters of their friends, or the daughters of their mother's friends. South Asian languages have an extensive vocabulary to denote different family relationships, which amp-lify and support non-sexualized relations between men and women. The young men in Alexander's study recognized that, as 'sisters', these young women were in principle 'off-limits' in terms of illicit relationships, and that a duty of care should be extended towards them.

The young men nonetheless also recognized the fact that relation-ships did sometimes occur between 'sisters' and men from other areas. However, the same attitudes of protection (not harassment) still prevailed, by their acting as confidants, and not telling the young women's brothers/ male relatives, in order to protect all parties. It is too simplistic, therefore, to imagine that gender relations are wholly characterized by oppressive Muslim male surveillance and control of women, justified in the name of Islam. At least one reason why such a conceptualization is inadequate is that it ignores the strategies that Muslim women use, often very effect-ively, to resist, renegotiate and reject community control (Mohammad 2005a). Macey's portrayal of male violence as a means of controlling women, while reflecting a reality for some women, has the unfortunate effect of reinforcing a stereotype of British Muslim women as helpless victims of brutish men, a stance that unwittingly denies them their actual agency and autonomy.

The young Muslim men in Bradford who took part in a recent research project were aware that they had become the focus of a moral panic cen-tred on their supposed 'outdated patriarchal dominance of women' (Alam and Husband 2006: 51), among other stereotypes. They were concerned to find ways of addressing and responding to these negative, dominant, majority ethnic constructions of their identity, and were to some extent successful through the outcomes of the research project itself. By demonstrating the manifest ways in which they were positively connected in Bradford and in their own social networks, they were able to resist stereotypical pathologizing images of themselves as victims of oppression, or as culturally schizophrenic (Alam and Husband 2006: 54). Through their testimonies, it becomes clear that there is no such thing as a single 'Bradford-Pakistani' community, and they themselves provided evidence of the capacity of young Muslim men for positive agency and dynamic resistance. Even with the odds stacked so heavily against them by externally imposed constructions coming from policy-makers, think-tank reports and academics (Cantle 2002; Ouseley 2001), their knowledgeable engagement with their environment was clear. 'The auto-critique of their communities by the young men in this study mocks the certainties and monolithic rhetoric of many of the majority commentaries' (Alam and Husband 2006: 57).

Between Macey's portrayal of male violence towards women, and Alexander's accounts of duty and care towards 'sisters', there lie some important realities about the way in which Muslim men express worries in relation to women. These concerns appear to be framed, in part, in terms of opposition towards white, non-Muslim males. This locates Muslim gender relationships within wider power and gender relations in British society:

Young men's resistance to the 'westernisation' of Muslim women could be seen as resistance to the internal psychological 'colonizing' of Asian/Muslim women by the dominant (white male) culture ... in other words, I suggest that the young men's discursive attempts to assert control over their Muslim female peers through 'tradition' (opposing the influence of 'British' [white/western] values among Asian women) should be read in conjunction with the boys' positioning of themselves in relation, and opposition, to white men. (Archer 2001: 97)

Narratives of ownership and control of women, expressed through an assertive Muslim masculinity, can also be seen as unconscious attempts by men to distance themselves from some of the abiding Orientalist stereotypes of Asian/Muslim men, as effeminate, victims of racism, or studious (Archer 2001; Hopkins 2006). Interestingly, and more consciously, however, these same men are also aware of the contradictions and 'double standards' inherent in their attitudes (Jacobson 1998: 62). Many of them know that Islam accords equal status to men and women, and yet at the same time they collude in an assumption that gendered inequalities are somehow the inevitable outcome of (South Asian) culture, or the preferences of women themselves. These 'contradictory masculine subject positions ... promote a form of sexist equality' that young men do not seem inclined to challenge (Hopkins 2006: 341). Not only are they aware of the contradictions inherent in their attitudes, but they also recognize the sheer hypocrisy that often accompanies it. Most of the empirical research on young Muslim men in Britain reveals that some of them had, or have had, girlfriends (usually white, non-Muslim), and they know that these relationships fall outside the boundaries of acceptable behaviour in Islam. The relative freedom of these young men to travel is often denied to their 'sisters', and they are well aware of the choice and freedom that comes with their social and geographic mobility.

All this points to the reality that Muslim masculine identities are not innate, but are constructed in relation to particular social and historical contexts, and in reference to a variety of social structures (Ouzgane 2003: 232; Samad 1998). Avtar Brah's concern that we should distinguish between 'young Pakistani women' as an object of social discourse and young Pakistani women as concrete historical subjects (Brah 1993: 449) can equally be applied to young men in order that we better appreciate that, like their female counterparts, young Muslim men 'are a diverse and heterogeneous category of people who occupy a multiplicity of subject positions ... their everyday lives [being] constituted in and through matrices of power embedded in intersecting discourses and material practices' (Brah 1993: 449).

One of the ways in which men might construct their subject positions is through dress and physical appearance. Again, compared to the (over)abundant literature on Muslim women and their appearance/dress (especially), there is apparently no research as yet which evaluates British Muslim masculinity in relation to clothing and personal 'style'.[23] This is surprising given the increasing interest in the creation of Islamic lifestyles among Muslims in Britain supported by various media, such as *'emel'*, a Muslim lifestyle magazine launched in 2003 which carries a regular 'fashion' page, including styles for men.

British Muslim men are becoming increasingly visible in their adoption of 'Islamic' styles of clothing, such as the wearing of prayer caps (*kufi*), Arab headdresses (*keffiyeh*) or Arab-style robes (for example, the *thobe*).[24] Whether this reflects changing sartorial practice, or simply greater media exposure, is difficult to assess. Regardless of the answer, explicit links

---

[23] This point was confirmed in a personal communication with Dr Peter Hopkins (2008), author of numerous papers and articles relating to Muslim masculinity.

[24] These items of clothing are known by different names in various parts of the Muslim world.

have been made in recent years between Muslim male radicalization and the adoption of 'Islamic' dress in the popular press (Lewis and Laville 2006; Taseer 2005). The appearance of British Muslim men (and women) has also been debated and commented upon in relation to the supposed separateness and perceived lack of integration of Muslims in the public sphere (Birt, Y. 2006b; Sardar 2006; Wynne-Jones 2008). If the media want evidence that British Muslims are supposedly insufficiently committed to the values and politics of British society (Afshar *et al.* 2005), the expression of Muslim identity through visibly different religious dress is one means of backing such an assertion. The way in which British Muslim masculinity and femininity is articulated through dress is perhaps more helpfully situated, however, within wider academic debates about British Muslim identity, community and the regulation and performance of the body in religious communities.

## MASCULINITY, FEMININITY, ISLAM AND DRESS

Islam offers believers comprehensive guidance on a range of issues, including dress.[25] There is no such thing as 'Islamic' dress, but simply a set of basic standards and requirements for both men and women; Qur'ānic verses regarding dress are often as applicable to men as they are to women. Men must minimally (that is, at least) cover from the navel to the knee, while the Prophet Muhammad instructed women to cover their bodies except for their face and hands. The majority of Muslims interpret this to include covering of the hair. Both men and women are required to wear clothes that are loose, opaque, dignified, modest and clean. Clothing should reflect gender, and thus both men and women are encouraged to express their masculinity and femininity through dress. Apart from these basic expectations, Muslims are free to wear whatever they choose although the style of dress believed to have been worn by the Prophet

---

[25] There are many Arabic words used to refer to women's 'Islamic' dress which reflect the part of the body being covered, local dialect and historical eras. 'Hijab' is a generic word to signify the general practice of veiling, and it can be most accurately translated as 'to cover, wrap, curtain, veil, screen or partition'. The word 'hijab' is often mentioned almost interchangeably with the word *purdah*, but the word *purdah* refers more accurately to the general seclusion of women, and the wearing of a veil or hijab will be part of this. Various words such as 'hijab', and *jilbab* have entered popular and media discourse in the past decade. Very briefly, the hijab usually refers to a covering of the head and hair; a *burqa* is a single garment covering the entire body with a 'shuttlecock' style masking of the face; a *chador* is again a single garment worn to cover the body and head; a *niqab* refers to a face veil, and a *jilbab* signifies a long loose robe or gown, usually worn over other clothing.

Muhammad, His Companions and His Wives is sometimes regarded as an example to emulate, and thus an indicator of piety.

The subject of Muslim women's dress has often figured significantly in academic studies of gender (Ahmad 1998; Dwyer 1999c; Franks 2000; Mirza 1989). Various themes are prominent, such as the assumption that women's propriety (and thus the honour of the community) could be assumed through their dress (Dwyer 2000), despite the fact that women themselves sometimes confess to the maintenance of outward conformity while simultaneously engaging in inner rebellion. This might be manifest in the practice of going out wearing one style of dress, only to change into another having arrived at the intended destination (Mohammad 2005a). The role of women's bodies and their dress in 'performing the boundary that marks the imagined, psychic and physical space of the "community"' (Mohammad 2005a: 385) is also evident. However, a predominant theme contained within the research literature is the increasing take-up of the hijab by British-born Muslim girls, and the numerous meanings that this has for them. For example, some have adopted the hijab as an indicator of increased piety and commitment to Islam, while others have used it as a strategy for negotiating parental approval for participation in higher education or the workforce (Mohammad 1999; Nagel and Staeheli 2009). In many accounts, it becomes clear that the adoption of the hijab is often a self-conscious statement signifying resistance, agency and empowerment, bound up with the articulation of a distinctive British Muslim identity vis-à-vis wider society and traditional parental culture (Mondal 2008).

It is impossible to dislocate this process from the wider political and social context, shaped in the past three decades by such events as the Rushdie Affair, the Gulf Wars, 9/11, 7/7 and the 'cartoon' crisis in 2006.[26] Cumulatively, these events have served to intensify the visibility of Islam in the public sphere, and it is possible to make links between these events and the amplification of Muslim identity through dress:[27]

[26] The 'cartoon' crisis refers to the publication of twelve cartoons of the Prophet Muhammad in the Danish newspaper *Jyllands-Posten* on 30 September 2005. Many Muslims around the world regarded them as blasphemous and Islamophobic.

[27] The potential for dress to be used as a form of collective resistance and defence – without necessarily involving increased piety or observance of Islam – is evident in the character of 'Karim' in Monica Ali's novel *Brick Lane*, released as a film in 2008. Despite becoming increasingly involved in an adulterous relationship, Karim simultaneously becomes more visibly 'Muslim' by adopting a style of dress that distinguishes him as religious, such as a prayer cap and a beard that becomes longer and thicker as the film progresses. This seems to be set against the backlash of 9/11, and increasing levels of Islamophobia in Tower Hamlets, London.

An 18 year old Muslim woman from Luton told me: 'Afghanistan was attacked, Iraq is being bombed, Muslims are dying – that's why I am wearing the hijab these days. I want people to know I am a Muslim. I am proud of my culture.' (Wilson 2006:24)

... the 'war on terror' has succeeded in making a large number of people feel alienated, and, as a result defensive about their cultural heritage. A few people react to demonisation by becoming invisible. The natural impulse of many is instead to do the opposite, to become fully paid-up members of the tribe which is being denigrated, in order to show their defiance ... for men it might be growing long beards, wearing the kind of get up their grandparents once walked around in. (Shariatmadari 2006)

The effort to shape public space through dress can thus be read as an active 'performance of difference' (Göle 2002: 187) by British Muslims whereby symbols and codes embedded in Islam are adopted to signify resistance to the subjugation of Muslim identity in the Western world. They simultaneously convey empowerment through belonging to, and identification with, an imagined global community, the *ummah* (Mohammad 2005a: 381), while also suggesting a 'material' rejection of Western/British liberal modernity, secularism and its associated politics. Such discourse is actively articulated in some Islamic reform movements in Britain today, such as *Ḥizb al-Taḥrīr*, which regards Islamic dress codes as a means of 'rejecting and resisting "the West" from within the West' (Tarlo 2005: 14) while also actively proselytizing. Hijab is a 'flag for Islam' for them (Tarlo 2007a: 144). Such statements actively reverse the popular media stereotype of the oppression or passivity of Muslim woman who wear the headscarf:

it is the 'Western woman' who is the real victim of patriarchal oppression and whose imprisonment is visibly apparent in her revealing clothes and bodily exposure, which make her endlessly vulnerable to the oppressive penetration of the male gaze ... By contrast, the 'the Muslim woman' is held up as an icon of modesty and contentment, capable of thinking for herself, of being judged for who she is rather than what she looks like. (Tarlo 2005: 15)

Embedded within such a discourse is evidence of the way in which the body can become a site onto which 'different power relations are mapped in particular times, places and contexts' (Mohammad 2005a: 379). Muslim men and women in Britain today who identify themselves as visibly Muslim through their dress are rarely doing so passively, especially where they have come from families which placed an emphasis on traditional modest dress (e.g. *shalwar kameez*), rather than more explicit markers of Islamic identity (Afshar *et al.* 2005). By wearing a headscarf, or a long beard and Arab-style robe, they are deliberately amplifying their religious identity and upsetting the status quo: 'They are playing with ambivalence, being both Muslim and modern without wanting to give up one for the other ... they are outside a regime of imitation, critical of both subservient traditions and assimilative modernity' (Göle 2002: 181).

The resources available for the expression of British Muslim masculinity and femininity, especially through dress and clothing, have grown in recent years because of the increased availability of Islamic consumer goods sold in a variety of retail outlets, and via the internet. Scarves, prayer caps, robes and other 'Islamic' dress form part of a growing international industry of Muslim consumerism, from halal chocolate and hoodies with Islamic motifs to Barbie doll look-alikes (Tarlo 2005; Yaqin 2007). The sartorial style of British Muslim musicians, such as Aki Nawaz,[28] provides a template for possible expressions of Muslim masculinity through dress (Saini 2004), while high-profile British Muslim women, such as Humera Khan, reflect a cosmopolitan style that is individual yet identifiably Muslim (Tarlo 2007b).

### CONCLUSION

Femininities and masculinities are embodied, negotiated and performed in and through different spaces of home, work, school, street, shopping centre, and within particular social, cultural and economic situations, to produce different social relations and discursive practices (Dwyer 1999b: 136). Though there are some common themes and patterns in terms of gender and gender relationships among Muslims in Britain,

the lived cultures that young Muslim[s] ... inhabit are highly differentiated varying according to such factors as country of origin, rural/urban background of households prior to migration, regional and linguistic background in the subcontinent, class position in the subcontinent as well as in Britain, and regional location in Britain. British Asian [Muslim] cultures are not simply a carry over from the subcontinent, but rather, they are organically rooted in regional and local specificities in Britain. Hence, Asian [Muslim] cultures of London may be distinguished from their counterparts in Birmingham. (Brah 1993: 448)

The expression of masculinity and femininity is therefore continually changing in the light of new social, political and economic circumstances, and there are important regional variations. Expressions of identity are also highly variable within and between different ethnic groups. For

---

[28] www.fun-da-mental.co.uk

example, some Muslims of Arab origin insist that their religious identity is an entirely private matter, and they reject the idea of a 'British Muslim' identity, where this has come to be associated with the politicization of Islam (Nagel and Staeheli 2009: 105).

Some key themes emerge from this overview of gender and gender relations among Muslims in Britain. Throughout the discussion, ideas of power, agency and empowerment have been predominant, suggesting that both individually and corporately Muslim men and women have found ways of resisting impositions, assumptions and pathologies that have come from both within and outside the Muslim 'community'. Muslim men and women have found myriad ways of disrupting power relations and 'Orientalist' stereotypes, with the implicit 'gaze reversal' (Franks 2000: 920) that comes with the adoption of hijab or *niqab* being just one example.

CHAPTER 10

# *Engagement and enterprise*

### INTRODUCTION

Particular themes have dominated research and writing about Muslims in Britain in the past three decades. These themes include youth, migration, education, gender, mosques and religious leadership. This book has discussed these important aspects of Muslim life in Britain, and has examined some of the results of inquiry into them. However, it is evident that the way in which these topics have been considered, both in academic writing and more particularly in public and media discourse, has occasionally created a somewhat pathologized, two-dimensional impression of British Muslims. There is a sense in which Muslims have, in some studies and reports, been reduced to a function of their religion, and other dimensions of identity and experience have been ignored. Since 9/11 and 7/7 in particular, there has been relatively little interest in the everday experience of 'ordinary' British Muslims. A new stigmatizing discourse fuelled by an 'anti-Muslim political culture' (Kundnani 2007a: 126) and the politics of the 'Preventing Violent Extremism' agenda has come to focus upon the apparent otherness of Muslims in Britain, which is assumed to be closely connected to the nature of Islam itself. As a consequence of such a distracting and distorting characterization, other important narratives have become obscured.[1]

This chapter therefore aims to reveal some of the significant but rarely examined ways in which British Muslims are integral to British civil society today. These spheres have received less academic attention and, by their very nature, they have been subject to less media speculation or political commentary. While often relatively uncontroversial in public debate, and beyond the radar of much mainstream media interest, they are nonetheless fundamental to the lives of many Muslims in Britain. The focus of

---

[1] See also Hesse and Sayyid (2006).

this chapter is therefore particularly upon the involvement of Muslims in various domains, such as entertainment and the arts, media, sport, politics, and trade and commerce.

Day-to-day life for many British Muslims features not only moral and religious issues, but also much more mundane questions about living in Britain. These often involve active choices about lifestyle, such as which television channels or films to view, which newspapers and magazines to read, which financial products to purchase, how to decorate the home, which charities and voluntary sector organizations to engage with, and which sports to play or teams to support, as well as end-of-life decisions about where to be buried after death. Over the past three decades, British Muslims have slowly been developing institutions, organizations, personalities and products that arguably suggest the subtle development of a distinctive British Muslim 'culture' that is becoming deeply rooted in British society, and which adds to the variety, complexity and flourishing of life in Britain today. The scholarship, trade and entrepreneurialism of Muslims, so vital to British institutions during the course of history (see chapter 1), is finding new forms of contemporary expression, and is emerging especially out of the experiences of Muslims who have been born and raised in Britain.

## THE BROADCAST, PRINT AND ELECTRONIC MEDIA

The media have a significant influence in British society, as elsewhere, in determining how the public view certain groups of people, or particular issues. This is especially the case in relation to Islam and Muslims in Britain (Moore *et al.* 2008; Poole 2002; Poole and Richardson 2006; Said 1997). The extent and nature of mainstream media coverage is simultaneously suggestive of the embedded nature of Muslim communities in Britain, and also of their assumed marginalization, threat and difference. Tarlo notes in particular the 'media hunger in the West for images of covered women whose concealment seems to serve as a visual shorthand for lack of integration, oppression and threat' (Tarlo 2007a: 144).

While it is of course important to document the shape and consequences of negative media portrayals of Islam and Muslims, as a number of scholars have successfully done (Meer 2006; Poole 2002; Poole and Richardson 2006), this chapter is more particularly concerned with charting the development and significance of new media in Britain produced by Muslims themselves. The emergence of newspapers, magazines, television channels and websites deserves attention, not only because it counters the largely negative images conveyed in the mainstream press, but also because these media are bought, read, consumed or watched by thousands of British Muslims across the country, often on a daily basis. The opinions that Muslims have about a range of contemporary issues are likely to be shaped in part by media such as the *Muslim News*,[2] the *Muslim Weekly*[3] and the Islam Channel,[4] or visits to websites such as www.IslamOnline.net or www.mpacuk.org, or indeed a range of other websites and blogs originating from British domains (Siapera 2006). It is therefore worth noting the role these media might have in shaping views and attitudes, especially of younger, English-speaking British Muslim professionals who comprise their particular consumer base.

Unfortunately, there has been very little research to establish precise patterns of consumption across the range of publications and media, although the British Muslim magazine *Q News* (now lapsed) established that its 60,000 readers were second- and third-generation British Muslims and non-Muslim educators, policy-makers and parliamentarians (Moll 2007). This profile is likely to be similar for other English-language, British Muslim media. As to reasons for consumption, recent research has established that Muslims primarily want to learn about national and international current affairs from a distinctive Islamic perspective (Ahmed 2005: 118), although the opportunity to gain religious knowledge and to support British Muslim enterprise also motivates consumers.

A number of factors have stimulated the development of British Muslim media over the past three decades. The emergence of particular publications reflects wider socio-political developments and changes, both within and beyond Muslim communities. So, for example, the Rushdie Affair in the late 1980s and early 1990s generated hostile mainstream media coverage of Islam in Britain, and indicated the absence of media for the articulation of distinctively British Muslim opinions and responses.[5] Simultaneously, during the 1980s and 1990s, a new generation of British-born, English-speaking Muslims were looking for media with English as the *lingua franca*. While they might have been proficient speakers of community languages, this was not necessarily indicative of an ability to read and write them as well. So new British Muslim media emerged in parallel with a new generation of British-born Muslims whose first language for the purposes of written media consumption was English, and who were looking for media which reflected their concerns

---

[2] www..muslimnews.co.uk    [3] www.themuslimweekly.com
[4] www.islamchannel.tv    [5] See preface, note 2, for resources about the 'Rushdie Affair'.

and interests (Ahmed 2005). International world events, especially as they were affecting Muslim countries and peoples (such as the Gulf War and Bosnia) also created a thirst for news which reinforced an emerging sense of shared belonging to the *ummah*. The comments of a participant in a research project about British Muslim media were typical: 'I certainly feel part of an active community. I feel less isolated, better informed about Islamic issues' (Ahmed 2005: 121).

The *Muslim News,* one of the most enduring English-language British Muslim publications, was first produced in February 1989, shortly after *The Satanic Verses* was published. It was founded with the explicit object-ive of offering British Muslims a newspaper reflecting their concerns and interests. At a time when mainstream media were failing to articulate Muslim opinions and perspectives, the *Muslim News* had an important role to play in offering a platform for Muslims to lobby and campaign on a range of issues. Published monthly, and with a current circulation of around 140,000 (many copies being distributed free in mosques and Islamic centres in Britain), it has become one of the most significant channels for the dissemination of news reflecting British Muslim inter-ests, via both its print and on-line versions. The *Muslim News* has in many ways become more than just a newspaper. Its 'Awards for Excellence' were launched in 2000 as a means to recognize and reward achievements by, or for the benefit of, Muslims. The Awards gala dinner, usually hosted in a top London hotel, has become one of the premier social events in the British Muslim calendar, and usually features celebrities from the world of politics or royalty. The Awards provide an opportunity to be proud of successes and talents, and to showcase particular skills and role mod-els. The *Muslim News* has in these ways become a key British Muslim institution.

It was only a matter of time before publications reflecting Muslim interests entered the mainstream media market (Ahmed 2005: 112). In 2005, this became a reality when the glossy monthly Muslim life-style magazine *emel*, established in 2003, took shelf space not only in Muslim-owned bookstores but also in major British supermarkets (such as Tesco), newsagents (WH Smiths) and high-street bookshops (Waterstones). In the title, 'em' (M) stands for Muslim and 'el' (L) for Life, while *emel* is the Arabic word for 'hope' or 'aspiration'. With a readership of 20,000 and with 3,000 subscribers,[6] this magazine aims to promote 'everyday Muslims and the ordinary life of ordinary people' (Byrne 2005) through

---

[6] www.emel.com

its features on parenting, family relationships, health, finance, interior decoration, food, fashion and travel, as well as comment and opinion pieces. Like other lifestyle publications, however, the glamorous standards of living and consumer spending choices that are sometimes featured in *emel* are unlikely to resonate with the experiences of many 'ordinary' British Muslims, whose material and economic circumstances place such a lifestyle well out of reach. Nonetheless, what the magazine does indicate is both a new self-confidence and an impatience with the traditional confines of Muslim identity on the part of economically upwardly mobile young Muslim professionals.

Over the course of the past twenty years, British Muslim media have had an important role in

simultaneously deconstructing mainstream media discourse through a construction of their own discursive alternative … These media show us how some British Muslims see themselves and would like others to see them, thus moving beyond the subjugation of what Werbner calls 'external definition'. (Moll 2007, citing Werbner 1991)

British Muslim media have been at the forefront of the effort to articulate what it means to be a Muslim living in Britain. The newspaper and then magazine *Q News* was perhaps the most energetic publication to engage in this project, and its demise represents a significant loss in the debate about the position of Muslims in Britain. The new Muslim media have been important in the emerging discourse on British Muslim life, and they have played a significant role in framing particular debates and agendas. Perhaps equally significant, however, is the degree to which British Muslim intellectuals are contributing to debates about society, identity, economy and politics. This is evident from the number of British Muslims contributing to magazines such as *Prospect*, and the willingness of such magazines to explore Islamic themes beyond the usual stereotypes.

British Muslims are involved in a wide range of creative arts and niche industries, and their faith is often a source of inspiration and motivation for their work as photographers, calligraphers, interior designers, artists, musicians, playwrights, fashion designers, novelists, film-makers, organic farmers, jewellers and poets, to name just a few of their diverse creative professions. The humanity, talent and individuality portrayed through their profiles in British Muslim media outlets are a powerful counter to stereotypical images of Muslims in the mainstream media, and they reinforce the range and complexity of identities. An artistic representation of this creativity is provided in a series of photographic images conveying Muslims' contributions to British society. The Muslim photographer Peter Sanders has created an exhibition to demonstrate how British Muslims have successfully managed 'The Art of Integration'.[7]

## ARTS AND ENTERTAINMENT

An entire social and cultural infrastructure is emerging among young Muslims that provides 'Islamic' alternatives in areas of entertainment and social life (Ahmed 2005: 122; Nieuwkerk 2008). Given the demographics of the British Muslim population, we should not be surprised by the rapid growth in artistic cultural forms in recent years which reflect the experiences of young British Muslims, despite the resistance that many Muslim parents of the 1970s and 1980s had to their children's involvement in drama, poetry or art at school:

Up until a decade ago, the British Muslim scene was (on balance) a comedy, art and culture-free zone. Pick up the listings section from any Muslim magazine from the 1980s and 1990s and there would be plenty of religious conferences, talks and discussions to attend all over the UK. But few sources to amuse or entertain. (Masood 2006a: 62)

Given the relatively recent emergence of British Muslim arts and entertainments, by which I mean artistic productions that have Islamic themes at their core, it is unsurprisingly a subject area that has received little academic attention. It is nevertheless possible to contextualize the development of British Muslim engagements with the arts. Several emergent artistic forms are useful barometers for examining the changing ways in which British Muslims have viewed themselves, their history, their politics and their place in British society. For example, an analysis of song lyrics or the lines from a stand-up comic are a readily available means for examining perspectives on a wide range of issues. This is because musicians, artists and comedians have to be sensitive to audience reception and must make their work resonate with the experiences of their listeners or viewers.

Compared to some other arts or forms of entertainment, 'music is more popular, more democratic and more far-reaching in both production and consumption' (Baily and Collyer 2006: 167), and this makes it a valuable starting point for discussion. If one were to conduct a survey to identify

---

[7] See www.petersanders.co.uk and www.artofintegration.co.uk

the most famous British Muslim today, the results would be likely to reveal the global popularity of British Muslim musicians and singers such as Yusuf Islam (formerly known as Cat Stevens) or Sami Yusuf, rather than British Muslim politicians, journalists or religious scholars. Both musicians have produced recordings that sell by the million around the world and their concerts attract audiences numbering in the hundreds of thousands. Sami Yusuf can easily fill London's Wembley Arena, for instance.

There has been a continuing lack of consensus among Muslim scholars about the degree to which music is permitted or forbidden in Islam (Baily 2006; Kabeer 2007). Some regard the human voice, accompanied by certain percussive instruments, as acceptable; others do not. Regardless of the different opinions that exist or the religious justifications behind them, for young British Muslims 'these remain at best academic debates ... the majority won't think twice before downloading music to an iPod' (Masood 2006a: 62). Some of these downloads reflect a nascent British Muslim musical scene.

Muslim migrants to Britain in the 1960s and 1970s brought their various traditional musical and artistic forms with them. For example, *qawwālī*, a type of Sufi religious music unique to South Asia (Baily 1990), could be heard among many Muslims in Britain who had originated from rural backgrounds in the Indian subcontinent, usually via imported cassette tapes or through occasional performances by renowned touring practitioners such as the late Nusrat Fateh Ali Khan (Lewis 1994: 81). This devotional music contributed to a sense of cultural solidarity, but made little or no impact on the wider mainstream music scene. Rooted in a specific cultural past, it provided 'a source of comfort, a partial antidote to the hostility experienced in the new society, reinforcing and responding to feelings of nostalgia' (Baily and Collyer 2006: 171).

During the late 1980s and early 1990s, and motivated in part by the Rushdie Affair and experiences of racism, British-born musicians began to use music as a form of activism and as a means to express political resistance and anti-imperialist sentiments. In this climate, inspired by the audacity and energy of the punk movement, musicians such as Aki Nawaz in Bradford, 'seamlessly punk rocker-Muslim and frontman of Islamic funk-rap band Fun Da Mental' (*emel*, February 2007, p. 22) led the way in the creation of a new, vibrant grassroots British Muslim musical aesthetic.

If the energy behind Aki Nawaz's anger and politics was too forceful for some, Sami Yusuf has become a palatable and very popular alternative for many British Muslims in the past five years. His polished and very personable self-presentation, expressed through Islamic devotional songs (*nasheeds*) conveying messages of love, mercy, peace and tolerance, makes him a decidedly 'good' Muslim. In an interview for *emel* in 2004, he asserted his mission to promote the message of Islam, to provide a 'halal' alternative to the profanity, drugs and sexualized messages of mainstream popular music, and to give young Muslims a chance to take pride in their faith (Ahmad 2004). His young, fashionable, attractive image has made him accessible to an international audience, who in turn use mainstream distribution techniques to access his work, from downloadable Apple iTunes to mobile phone ringtones.

Music is a powerful medium for dealing with new realities, and second- and third-generation migrants often therefore use innovative forms of artistic expression to assert and negotiate their identities in contrast to their parental or grandparental heritage. These new forms are often a synthetic fusion of inherited traditions with popular local styles, thereby borrowing from several sources to articulate something new. Hip hop and rap have become especially popular musical styles in the past decade, and their reliance upon vocals and a strong beat alone means that contentious debates about the permissibility of 'music' within Islam can to some extent be circumnavigated. So it was that in 1996 the first British rap group, Mecca2Medina (M2M), was created, inspired by the American Muslim hip hop scene popularized by artists such as Mos Def and Native Deen. Four albums later, and as partici- pants in a British Council tour of Nigeria to promote their 'distinctly British form of Islam',[8] this group has served as a catalyst for the emer- gence of many other British Muslim hip hop groups. Pearls of Islam, established in 2005, is the first British Muslim women-only group to engage in musical performance using voice, poetry and drumming.[9] A new magazine to support the lifestyle and worldview of those attracted to Islamic hip hop, *Platform Magazine,* was first published in November 2006.

An interesting dimension of the new transglobal Islamic hip hop scene is the stylistic connections that it has with the *Qur'ān*:

The very means by which the Quran was revealed to the Prophet – that is, orally and in large part, through rhymed prose – exhibits parallels to the linguistic and literary mode of delivery found in hip hop lyrical production. (Alim 2005: 266)

---

[8] www.globallocal.co.uk/Mecca2Medina.html
[9] www.freewebs.com/pearlsofislam/index.htm

It can be used to convey information about Islam, as well as providing a means for social protest. It is also an attempt by young Muslims to claim Islam for themselves, and is arguably a reaction to

> other people telling young Muslims what to think about their religion ... they felt they had a different opinion to express and they just decided to use their talents to express it. It's not just in hip hop, it's in other forms of culture and art, and in business, film and broadcasting too ... (Birt 2007a)

Although it is perhaps exaggerated to state that 'these are the new role models for British Muslims – artists, singers, activists' (Moll 2007), they are nevertheless becoming a dynamic force in the emergence of British Muslim cultural life. Islamic rappers in Britain have something in common with their American counterparts, where 'Islamic hip hop is embedded in the larger project of developing an authentic American Muslim culture' (Kabeer 2007: 125).

Meanwhile, as the past decade has seen the rapid growth in youth-based musical production, there has been a similar flourishing of skill among British Muslim creative artists, some of whom have international reputations. Younger British-born Muslims often express gratitude to their parents for giving them the opportunity to explore their creative talents, since this has frequently involved the negotiation of cultural perceptions that artistic professions are less respectable than the established careers of law, business or medicine (al-'Alam 2003). A stimulus for the growth of artistic work has been the establishment of VITA, Visual Islamic and Traditional Arts, an educational institution in London whose patron, HRH the Prince of Wales, takes a close personal interest in the educational work of students taking professional degrees in the arts. A direct consequence of recent burgeoning talent is the opportunity it has presented for British Muslim artists to display their work in major national exhibitions, both in Britain and abroad.

One of the most cherished art forms among Muslims is calligraphy, a form of art that is both seen and read. A saying of the Prophet claims that a person who writes beautifully the *Bismillah* ('In the name of God') will enter paradise (Schimmel 1995). By now, there are a number of well-known British Muslim calligraphers, such as Ali Omar Ermes, and the work of these artists is becoming accessible and popular through major exhibitions, such as the Young British Muslim Artists gallery at IslamExpo, London, 2008.[10] Many artists use their work as a means of

---

[10] http://islamexpo.info/index.php?option=com_content&task=view&id=72&Itemid=121

remembrance of God (*dhikr*), hence the name that one artist has given to his brand, 'Visual Dhikr'.[11] Birmingham-based Mohammed Ali is acquiring an international reputation for his distinctive form of 'urban spiritual art', which he has named 'Aerosol Arabic'.[12] His inspiration comes from the modern urban art of graffiti, woven together with the grace and eloquence of Islamic Arabic calligraphy. Part of the rationale for his method is the opportunity to make Islam accessible, especially to young British Muslims. He notes that as a youth himself:

if I'd have seen graffiti in Arabic I would have followed my faith more – it would have inspired me. It seemed like religion was for old folks, and I want to give it back to the kids. I wanted to take an art form that belonged on the street and connect with ordinary people through the divine meaning contained in the book of Allah. Be proud of your identity as a Muslim. Do it with confidence. (Mohammed, A. 2004)

Meanwhile, the involvement of Muslims in the performing arts has disrupted stereotypical public perceptions of Islam as 'a sombre, austere if not angry faith in which the act of having fun needs divine license' (Masood 2006a: 62). For example, Khayaal is a professional theatre company that was founded in 1997 in order to specialize in performances of classical Islamic plays and literature. It aims to present innovative 'wisdom-orientated performing arts entertainment that explores the literature, heritage, culture and arts of the Muslim world'.[13] Its productions are popular with both Muslim and non-Muslim audiences.

However, Shappi Khorsandi and Shazia Mirza, two British women of Muslim background, have struggled to win acceptance for their work as stand-up comics from within their own communities, despite their international success in mainstream comedy circuits. Shazia Mirza's fluctuating self-presentation as a Muslim has been evident in her changing persona and material in recent years, and she no longer promotes herself as a distinctively 'Muslim' comedienne. From her early days in comedy, when she became distinctive for wearing a hijab on stage (but not off stage), and for her famous post-9/11 line, 'My name is Shazia Mirza ... at least that's what it says on my pilot's license', she now promotes a form of entertainment that relies less upon material derived from her upbringing in a devout Pakistani home in Birmingham. In a belief that 'the greatest comedy transcends all religions and colours' (Akbar 2006),

---

[11] www.visualdhikr.com    [12] www.aerosolarabic.com
[13] www.khayaal.co.uk

her jokes are today less about ethnicity or religion, and more about everyday matters such as shopping and budget airlines. For example, Ryanair is described by Shazia Mirza as 'just a council estate in the air' (Review from Edinburgh Fringe Festival, 2008), but the degree to which her jokes about low-cost retail chains, cheap airlines or excess body hair will successfully travel to international audiences remains to be seen.

Mirza's comedy has been controversial among Muslims in Britain, but US comics have won more wholehearted support from British Muslim audiences, and they may help to stimulate more British Muslim comics. Comedians such as Ahmed Ahmed and the comic trio Allah Made Me Funny seek to 'normalize' Muslims through their work, and they deliberately 'poke fun at themselves, their communities, government and human nature and the tricky predicament of living in post 9/11 America'.[14] Their popularity among British Muslim audiences reflects a growing confidence and willingness to see the humorous side of being a Muslim in the modern world, with jokes about poor time-keeping among Muslims and faulty sound systems in mosques (Jalil 2004):

Despite the potential pitfalls, British television executives are on the hunt for classy, funny comedy from Muslims who can laugh at themselves, while at the same time generating humour that crosses cultural boundaries. Jokes about the Qur'an may well be banned, but gags about men in polygamous marriages might just slip through the veil. (Masood 2006a: 63)

This section has surveyed just a very small sample of creative work produced by British Muslims. There are many other talented British Muslim artists and performers who are taking the message of Islam, and the inspiration they derive from their faith, into exhibitions, concert halls and theatres around the world. The best among them have secured appreciation from both Muslims and non-Muslims, and have thereby contributed to the opening of new discourses on identity and individuality, and on religion in society. This is clearly an area for future research.

Continuing with the theme of leisure and entertainment, boxing, cricket and rugby are among the sports in which British Muslim men have had a particular involvement.[15] Readers of the British Muslim and mainstream press will have noted the triumphs of Nasser Hussain (first

[14] www.allahmademefunny.com
[15] A research project was undertaken in 2003/4 to examine, among other things, the circumstances which enable British Muslim women to engage in sporting activity (Kay 2006). The project's findings established that the participation of practising British Muslim women is often conditional upon family approval which itself rests upon absolute certainty that Islamic norms in relation to gender relations are observed. The *Muslim News* has been a key sponsoring force behind

British Muslim captain of the England cricket team), or boxing champions 'Prince' Naseem Hamid, Danny Williams and 2004 Olympic medalist Amir Khan (Khan, A. 2006). In the world of rugby, Ikram Butt became the first British Muslim to play for England (Butt 2009). While not wishing to diminish the significance of these achievements, it is the way in which they have been represented in the media, by politicians and by British Muslims themselves, that is perhaps most worthy of reflection. The idea that these individuals are 'role models' for the successful integration of British and Muslim identities – as they are so often promoted – must be critically evaluated on account of the way in which these discourses are situated within the politics of 9/11, 7/7 and the subsequent 'war on terror', as well as the politics of particular areas of Britain following the disturbances of 2001 (Burdsey 2007). While considering issues of representation, this section also considers why boxing and cricket are two sports that have enabled British Muslim successes while, paradoxically, many British Muslims are happy to support the England football team (Bagguley and Hussain 2005) despite their relative lack of actual representation or participation in the national team (Burdsey 2006a).

British Muslim involvement in, exclusion from or support for particular sports or national teams provides a lens through which we can critically evaluate issues of identity, belonging, nationalism, cultural capital and racism: 'From Orwell to Tebbit, cricket has been used as a metaphor for English nationalism. It has been a test for belonging and unbelonging' (Alibhai-Brown 2005). In April 1990, just before the cricket Test series between England and India, Conservative politician Norman Tebbit made a speech in Parliament which asserted that if British Asians and Afro-Caribbeans chose to live in Britain, they should be willing to support the national team on account of the fact that

[i]f you come to live in a country and take up the passport of that country, and you see your future and your family's future in that country, it seems to me that is your country. You can't just keep harking back. (Norman Tebbit, cited in Werbner 1996a: 104)

Similar sentiments were expressed eleven years later, when England cricket captain Nasser Hussain expressed disappointment at the degree to which British Pakistanis supported Pakistan rather than England in the Test series at Edgbaston in May 2001: 'I cannot really understand why those

the participation of British Muslim women in the International Islamic Women's Games, held every four years in Iran.

born here, or who came here at an early age like me, cannot support or follow England' (Burdsey 2006, citing Campbell 2001). In Tebbit's case, it was particularly unfortunate that he chose cricket as the sport against which national loyalty might be tested, since he failed to recognize the historical and political significance of cricket in relation to colonialism. This is perceptively explored by Daniel Burdsey, a sociologist of sport and leisure:

Cricket is one of the few arenas in which the Indian subcontinent and its diaspora can assert an ephemeral challenge to western hegemony. India and Pakistan regularly play against England and, in recent decades, have been frequently victorious. Despite, or because of, the role of cricket in British imperialism in India, the game now enables a temporary disruption of this historical connection, whereby former colonial peoples are able to compete with, and even defeat, England. Within the context of colonial subordination and contemporary racisms, international cricket can operate as a means of cultural resistance for British Asians. Supporting a South Asian nation … forges a symbolic link with the subcontinent, enabling the celebration of tradition and feelings of belonging with the nation from which they or their forebears migrated. (Burdsey 2006a: 21, 17)

Burdsey goes on to note that spectatorship and performative support of Indian or Pakistani cricket teams at international matches, expressed through chanting, flags and musical instruments, is a way of engaging with cricket at a level that offers the chance of participation, in contrast to the likelihood of excluding structures and institutions that exist in local, amateur clubs: 'British Asians can be alienated by the class-specific connotations … together with a hegemonic "traditional (white) Englishness" which means that the game is often equated with village greens, church spires and the quaffing of real ale' (Burdsey 2006a: 21). Not surprisingly, therefore, many 'Asian/Muslim' cricket teams and leagues have emerged in parallel with predominantly 'white' local teams and leagues, particularly in the north of England (Ansari 2004; Burdsey 2006b).

Similar parallel teams and leagues now exist for football, a sport in which, at the time of writing, British Muslims have been unable to make any significant impact at national level. It becomes easier to understand their relative lack of participation by considering the cultural capital necessary to enter the 'field':

Traditionally, the scouting procedures by which young players are recruited by professional clubs have revolved around an established network of relations between parents, school teachers, amateur club managers and county selectors, and their inside knowledge of, and contacts within, local professional clubs. Therefore, for those players seeking to enter the local professional sphere from amateur youth football, having an existing contact within the professional game is a significant advantage. In most cases, however, this is something that British Asians do not possess. (Burdsey 2004: 766)

A direct consequence of this indirect exclusion at the entry level is the inability of British Muslims to enter the senior levels of football management, which would make change and greater inclusion more likely. Further exclusionary practice is the 'laddish' culture that often accompanies both amateur and professional football, especially the drinking of alcohol, gambling and the watching of pornographic movies after the game is over (Burdsey 2004). This obviously makes the involvement of observant Muslims in the social life of footballing culture difficult. Finally, there is a considerable academic literature charting the deeply embedded culture of racism that goes with the world of football and compounds other forms of exclusion (Carrington 1998).

In contrast to football, British Muslims have achieved considerable success in the boxing ring, despite the fact that a well-known British Muslim scholar, the late Dr Zaki Badawi, thought that 'fighting in a ring with spectators cheering you on is clearly not acceptable in Islam' (*Q News*, August 1998, p. 31). Despite this view, the achievements of Amir Khan, Danny Williams and Prince Naseem Hamid in particular have provided an opportunity for their promotion as 'role models' of integration for young British Muslims by politicians, 'community leaders' and social activists in both the Muslim and non-Muslim press.

For example, British Muslim journalist Fareena Alam wrote in *The Observer* of her anticipation of Amir Khan's victory at the Athens Olympics in 2004, and the fact that, should he win, it would mean the defiance of 'the stereotype of the Muslim as an indigestible minority or cultural parasite ... British Muslims are rarely celebrated as heroes' (Alam 2004). In a similar vein, and following Khan's victory, former Secretary General of the Muslim Council of Britain, Sir Iqbal Sacranie, claimed that 'the heart-lifting sight of Amir's family at the ringside proudly dressed in the red, white and blue of the Union Flag was far more powerful than any number of worthy speeches from politicians'.[16] Khan's victory was described as 'an answer to our prayers' (Alam 2004), while the *Muslim News* saw Khan as 'Britain's emerging star, [and] the face of British multiculturalism' (Azim 2004).

However, critical evaluation and deconstruction of the discourses that emerged around Khan's victory illustrate that he was appropriated

---

[16] 'Amir Khan – British, Muslim and Proud!', www.mcb.org/features

by, and subjected to, a complex politics bound up with New Labour's 'multiculturalist nationalism' (Fortier 2005, cited in Burdsey 2007). By being positioned as a role model through selective media reproduction of particular quotations or images which emphasized his 'Britishness' over his religious identity, Khan was inadvertently contributing to a distinctive New Labour project which sought to promote Britain as an inclusive and tolerant society in which it is possible, through 'traditional' British values of hard work and discipline, to be successful. This positioning carried with it an implicit assumption about the lack of positive role models in the (Muslim) community that he is perceived to represent (Burdsey 2007: 621). His success is framed as the outcome of being a 'good' British Muslim, as against the deviance of 'bad' British Muslims who fail to affirm their 'Britishness'.

## POLITICAL REPRESENTATION AND PARTICIPATION

There are various ways and means by which British Muslims have engaged in political action, each of which reflects a different understanding of how they should strategically construct their identities and subsequently mobilize in order to achieve particular outcomes. A typology for various forms of participation has been set out by Dilwar Hussain from the Islamic Foundation in Leicester (Hussain, D. 2004: 183). He has characterized Muslim political participation involving working outside the system; working for an alternative system; joining existing parties; setting up a Muslim party; lobbying; and local action.

The representation of Muslims in mainstream local and national politics has been of interest to academics for several decades, not least because political incorporation is a significant measure of the wider recognition and involvement (Anwar 1979: 136). Furthermore, 'growing numbers of Muslims have come to regard formal political mechanisms as an effective way of getting their problems addressed, if not solved' (Ansari 2004: 234). The evidence to support this assertion can be found in research which has documented the growing involvement of British Muslims in local politics (Anwar 1979; Purdam 2000; Purdam 2001). Additionally, more recent work documents and evaluates Muslim participation in new post-9/11 political parties and movements, such as the Stop the War Coalition and the Respect Party (Phillips 2008). Muslim involvement in local and national politics has taken different forms over time, and has been influenced by events and factors within and outside British Muslim communities.

High concentrations of Muslims in particular towns and cities in Britain have direct implications for local politics, political mobilization and voting patterns. In the 1970s, when Muslim communities were becoming more established as a result of the reunification of families, their political concerns were particularly related to immediate needs, especially in terms of housing, social welfare, immigration and education. Organizations were established to lobby and campaign on these issues, and Muslims began to influence local political decision-making by serving as local councillors. Purdam's research outlined the growing trajectory of this involvement, the demographic profile of Muslim councillors (Purdam 2000) and their sometimes controversial relationship with the Labour Party (Purdam 2001).

In May 1996, there were 160 Muslim local councillors in Britain, and their distribution among the main political parties is indicative of historical Muslim community support for different parties with 153 Labour, six Liberal, and one Conservative (Purdam 2001). Their presence reflected areas of Muslim concentration, and so there were twelve Muslim councillors on Birmingham City Council, and eleven in Bradford. Purdam predicted future growth in the number of British Muslim councillors, and indeed by 2005 there were 230 Muslim local government councillors in Britain (Anwar 2008).

One of the most high-profile British Muslim councillors in Britain today is Salma Yaqoob, co-founder of the Respect Party, current vice-chair of the Party, and councillor for the Sparkbrook ward in Birmingham since 2006. From this platform, she has increasingly acquired a reputation for public comment on a range of issues, and has contributed to recent academic publications (Yaqoob 2007). She has successfully galvanized both Muslim and non-Muslim anti-war protesters, while focusing on common concerns for *R*espect, *E*quality, *S*ocialism, *P*eace, *E*nvironment, *C*ommunity and *T*rade Unions as part of a broader anti-imperialist, anti neo-liberalist stance. Respect was formed in 2004, and was built upon the

energy of the anti-war movement ... [It] aimed to occupy the political space opened up by the Labour Party's shift to the right. Respect contested the 2005 general election, winning a parliamentary seat in Tower Hamlets and coming a close second in Birmingham Sparkbrook. (Phillips 2008: 109)

A legacy of the partnership between Muslims and non-Muslims in the anti-war movement means that 'political capital remains to be channeled and political and human relationships remain, in some latent form, for when they are wanted and needed' (Phillips 2008: 110).

At the time of writing, there are four Muslim members of parliament (MPs) in the House of Commons out of a total of 646 MPs:[17] 'However, to reflect the numbers of Muslims in Britain there should be more than 20 MPs of Muslim origin' (Anwar 2008: 132). Similarly, while there are presently nine Muslims in the House of Lords, to reflect the Muslim population in Britain there should be at least another eighteen (Anwar 2008: 132). The vice-chair of the Conservative Party, Saeeda Warsi, is a Muslim, as is the deputy president of the Liberal Democrat party, Fiyaz Mugal. Young British Muslims have been increasingly joining Whitehall departments, and the Prime Minister and other senior politicians now regularly attend and host events that reflect British Muslim festivals and interests. It is commonplace for the leaders of all three main political parties to publish '*Eid* Greetings' in the British Muslim press.

Among the nine Muslim peers in the House of Lords, of whom Baroness Pola Uddin is the first British Muslim woman to be made a peer, several have become especially prominent in national and international life, often playing key ambassadorial roles. For example, Lord Nazir Ahmed of Rotherham became a headline figure in 2007 for his part in the successful effort to secure the release of a British schoolteacher from custody in Sudan. However, Lord Ahmed has not shied away from condemnation of his government, particularly on issues affecting British Muslims. For example, he openly criticized Tony Blair's foreign policy in 2006, and likewise registered his disgust at the decision to offer British novelist Salman Rushdie a knighthood in 2007.

In terms of British Muslim voting patters, there has been a long tradition of support for the Labour Party, based on a widespread assumption that their policies were more sympathetic to Muslim interests, especially on issues such as employment and public service. Given the fact that many British Muslims arriving in the UK in the post-Second World War years were employed in manual occupations with strong trade union representation, the link to the Labour Party was natural. This was reinforced in 1997, when New Labour gave Muslims a voice in Westminster via support for the establishment of the Muslim Council of Britain (Masood 2006a) and likewise responded to Muslim campaigns for voluntary aided schools. However, over the years British Muslim political affiliation has diversified, and perceptions of the Labour Party have been severely damaged on account of foreign policy and the recent 'war on terror'.

---

[17] They are Shahid Malik – Dewsbury; Sadiq Khan – Tooting; Khalid Mahmood – Birmingham; Mohammad Sarwar – Glasgow.

The indications of increasing British Muslim participation in the political life of the UK suggest growing political capital and a recognition that change in their local or national situation can only come about through engagement and action.[18] However, some British Muslims have sought to establish distinctively 'Muslim' political parties, and this found clearest expression in the formation of the Islamic Party of Great Britain, established in 1989. However, its political success has been virtually non-existent, and even in towns and cities with large Muslim populations, such as Bradford, the IPGB failed to make an impact. Dilwar Hussain speculates that some of the reasons for this lay in the IPGB's failure to win the trust of Muslim voters, the narrowness of its agenda, and a failure to engage sufficient community participation (Hussain, D. 2004).

So far, there has been just one significant example of a British Muslim attempt to create an alternative, parallel political system, this being the establishment of the 'Muslim Parliament' in 1992 under the leadership of the late Dr Kalim Siddiqui (Khanum 1992b). He argued that Muslims would be unlikely to ever secure real power in Westminster, and should therefore create their own political structure as a forum for debate on issues of concern. The idea was that British Muslims should become self-sufficient in terms of their social and political needs. In the immediate years following the publication of *The Satanic Verses*, when it seemed that British Muslim voices were unheard in what were perceived to be indifferent or discriminatory mainstream political circles, it was not surprising that an Islamic institution calling for political separateness should emerge. However, the energy of the Muslim Parliament derived almost entirely from the charismatic personality of Siddiqui himself, and so when he died, in 1996, many of his ambitions were unrealized. But this created an opportunity for an appraisal of strategy, and his successor, Dr Ghayasuddin Siddiqui, changed the emphasis away from high-profile ideologically driven thinking, and towards a more 'consensual, pragmatic modus operandi'.[19] Today, the Muslim Parliament is perhaps best understood as a 'lobbying' group, and campaigns on a range of issues affecting British Muslims, such as forced marriages, civil liberties and education.

Chapter 4 outlined the emergence of various local and national lobbying and 'representative' organizations established by British Muslims, while the range of civil society and local action groups aiming to support

---

[18] For insight into self-perceptions and attitudes of young British Muslims as political actors see Appleton (2005a; 2005b).
[19] www.muslimparliament.org.uk

British Muslim needs is now well documented in publications such as the *Muslim Directory* (MDUK Media). This 'Yellow Pages' of Muslim organizations captures the extent to which British Muslims have success-fully established local and national organizations to meet their needs, such as telephone helplines, bookshops, publishing houses, educational bodies, nurseries, sporting organizations, women's groups, environmen-tal projects, professional networks (e.g. dentists, doctors, teachers, law-yers, youth groups, chaplains, educationalists, researchers), charities,[20] media and human rights groups. Some of these organizations are reg-istered charities, or well-established voluntary sector organizations, and they have often been at the front line of delivering local services. But they have also played an important role in providing people with the skills and networks which have enabled them to go on to become effective local and national lobbyists. The Muslim voluntary sector is still relatively young, and, while being blessed with individuals of energy and commitment, there is a vicious circle of deficits that frustrates further development.

Over the past two decades, and with the Rushdie Affair a key turning point, there has been a major shift in British Muslim political consciousness and engagement. The Rushdie Affair highlighted a relative lack of mobil-izing power, and was a catalyst in the formation of the Muslim Council of Britain. The election of New Labour accelerated growing Muslim involvement in political structures, while the events of, and the attacks on, London on 7 July 2005 have generated further political consciousness and willingness to mobilize, often in collaboration with non-Muslims. In 2008, increasing numbers of British Muslims found themselves impli-cated as 'advisors' or participants in the 'Preventing Violent Extremism' agenda, and its associated programmes.[21] Whether these programmes will have the government's intended and desired outcome, or will generate British Muslim alienation on the basis of the assumptions that underpin the 'Prevent' or 'PVE' agenda, remains to be seen and will no doubt be documented by academics in the coming years.

## TRADE AND COMMERCE

Where chapter 5 briefly examined British Muslims and employment, this section focuses less on participation in the labour force, and more on the

---

[20] Given that 'charity' is one of the five pillars of Islam, it is not surprising that, by now, there are some very well-established and successful British Muslim charities, such as Islamic Relief and Muslim Aid, to name just two.

[21] www.communities.gov.uk/communities/preventingextremism

multicultural marketplace, British Muslim entrepreneurialism, consumer culture and the role of traders as cultural intermediaries (Jamal 2003). Just as the introduction of 'coffee houses' into London in the seventeenth century created an arena for inter-cultural exchange of ideas and products, so the introduction of foods, fashions, music and other 'ethnic' products into Britain as a result of British Muslim migration and settlement has provided an opportunity for experimentation in tastes, themes and sounds that can be marketed among consumers from a variety of backgrounds. Much of this multicultural production and consumption rests upon the enterprise of South Asian Muslim retailers. The process of cultural exchange through food and consumption has not, however, been one-way. Among the Muslim and non-Muslim interviewees in Ahmad Jamal's research in Bradford, some Muslim households had developed their own Friday-night takeaway traditions, consisting of fish and chips or pizza (Jamal 2003).

British Muslims are also consumers and producers in an emerging global market characterized by increasing 'halalization' (Fischer 2008b: 829), whereby a range of products – not just food but also cosmetics and pharmaceuticals – are becoming officially certified as Islamically permitted. For example, at the most mundane level every box of Kellogg's cornflakes sold in corner shops or supermarkets around Britain now carries certification by the Halal Food Authority (HFA) as 'halal', while at the other end of the spectrum the global Islamic banking and finance industry is concerned with 'halal' financial products. This section therefore also briefly considers some of the social and economic implications of the process of 'halalization' that is increasingly shaping British Muslim consumers' choices, and ultimately, perhaps their identity itself.

The first halal butcher's shop in Britain is said to have been opened by Haji Taslim Ali in East London in the 1940s (Adams 1987: 40). Before the widespread emergence of such halal meat-trading outlets, early Muslim migrants to Britain were faced with a number of choices about food consumption, particularly in relation to meat. Some felt that their circumstances, often characterized by crowded, shared accommodation and long working hours, warranted a relaxation of normal Islamic dietary laws. In such cases, some felt it was permissible to eat meat slaughtered by 'the people of the book' (Jews and Christians), as long as it was not pork, and thus when meat was affordable it was purchased from ordinary butchers. For those who felt this was an unacceptable compromise, there were two possibilities. One was to become vegetarian, while another was to resort to do-it-yourself halal slaughter, as one interviewee from Bradford explained:

Initially for meat there wasn't any. Then one individual discovered a process whereby he could go and buy a sheep, have it killed at the farm, and bring over to the house and we would share it – and this sheep was obviously slaughtered in the halal fashion so everybody was eligible (Bradford Heritage Recording Unit, 1994, 50). (Hamlett *et al.* 2008: 100)

In the early days of Muslim settlement after the Second World War, food shops selling spices and flavourings to cater for other ethnic groups, such as Poles and Jews (Hamlett *et al.* 2008), were also frequented by Muslims. However, particularly during the 1960s and 1970s there was a growth in small businesses established to provide products and services to enable the material retention of South Asian and Muslim lifestyles, especially in terms of food and dress. Goods (particularly fruit and vegetables) were (and still are) often displayed on the pavement outside the shop frontage, reflecting the use of public space in South Asian towns and villages:

the mainly rural origin of many post-colonial migrants has had some influence on the way that the public spaces of Birmingham have been appropriated and adapted. It has certainly had an impact on the ambience of streets both visually and audibly. The displaying of goods on the pavement by its nature generates high concentrations of people and slows down movement along the street. This contributes to the sense of 'busy-ness' and liveliness of many of these streets. (Nasser 2005: 69)

Small retail stores were therefore important sites for social interaction and the exchange of news (Hamlett *et al.* 2008), as well as being an important dimension of the institutionalization of British Muslim settlement. As one researcher put it, 'names and scripts on shop fascias mimic its communities; "Desh Sangeet", "Sylhet Food Store", "Rahman Butchers", "Malik Travel", "Lahore Restaurant"' (Nasser 2005: 72):

One interviewee reflected on this process in distinctly religious terms.

During our initial days we could not find all these things [ethnic commodities] … I mean these vegetables and spices … like palak [spinach], dhania [coriander], bhindi [okra] … and halal meat … and even shalwar kameez [ethnic dress]. There were only limited things available … and now I think it is Allah's fazal [grace] that you find all these things. (Jamal 2003: 6)

The growth and development of the ethnic minority population in Britain over time has created the market conditions for small- and large-scale entrepreneurial activity, from local grocery stores and curry houses, to 'Asian' supermarkets, and wholesale and retail electrical enterprises.

Where many of these businesses once tended to serve a limited ethnic minority market, some have successfully expanded to serve a wider mainstream consumer base from a variety of backgrounds, often on account of their competitive pricing strategies.

The self-employment industry that is perhaps particularly associated with South Asian Muslims is the restaurant trade. In 1997, the overall ethnic restaurant market in the UK was worth £3 billion, with over half of this market dominated by Indians, Pakistanis and Bangladeshis (Ram *et al.* 2000). Within what is known as the 'Balti Quarter' in Birmingham (a deliberate designation by the City Council to attract tourism), some sixty restaurants have a combined annual turnover of approximately £8.5 million (Ram *et al.* 2002): 'In Britain, the consumption of food and drink in restaurants, from takeaway outlets and other sources outside the home, is undergoing a rapid expansion ... with a 46% leap in ethnic food consumption' (Ram *et al.* 2002: 28). 'Curry' is now one of the nation's favourite foods (Kalra 2004). Behind the production of the 'Balti Quarter' in Birmingham, local Muslim and South Asian communities have

willingly engaged in this strategic mobilization of a commercially viable and adequately consumable notion of their culture as a means of opening up economic opportunities within Birmingham's culturally hegemonic context. This phenomenon emphasises the powerful aspect of capital accumulation: the production and consumption of culture as a marketing tool in the process of place-making not just for authorities, but also for settlers mediating and engaging with powerfully organized commercialism. (Nasser 2005: 72)

The representation of these areas as 'exotic landscapes', whether the 'Curry Mile' in Manchester or the 'Balti Quarter' in Birmingham, involves reframing them, from places 'of production (serving the needs of the BrAsian community) to [places] of consumption (by the larger society)' (Nasser 2006: 391).

Alongside deliberate council promotion of difference for commercial gain, some of the reasons for the growth in the 'curry' market can be accounted for by wider social changes, such as the increase in one-person households, higher disposable incomes and greater personal spatial mobility. Furthermore, there is an increasing association of leisure with food, as indicated by the celebrity status of TV chefs and the increased publication of magazines and books associated with the food industry. All this has influenced mainstream supermarket retailers, such as Marks & Spencer, Tesco and Asda, which now carry 'ethnic' and halal merchandise in selected stores to satisfy the new demands of the marketplace

(Fischer 2008b; Jamal 2003). In this way, 'halal is being lifted out of its traditional base in halal butchers to become part of "world food" ranges in major supermarkets' (Fischer 2008a: 17).

'Indian' takeaways and restaurants, predominantly owned and staffed by Bangladeshis and Pakistanis in Britain, are sites for significant cultural exchange, according to Jamal (Jamal 2003). For him, consumption and retailing carry the potential for 'tolerance of different ways of being and living' (Jamal 2003: 9), and material products provide the raw material for construction and maintenance of multiple and co-existing identities. Where the Muslim-owned corner shop sells 'ethnic' produce alongside mainstream commodities, the consumer becomes familiar with, and engages with, these products, sometimes changing their consumption patterns. Jamal's optimistic views are supported by Narayan, who notes that

relish for the food of 'Others' may help to contribute to an appreciation of their presence in the national community, despite ignorance about the cultural contexts of their foods – these pleasures of the palate providing more powerful bonds than knowledge. We risk privileging the mind too much if we ignore the ways in which a more carnal relish may sometimes make for stronger appreciation than intellectual 'understanding'. (Narayan 1995: 80, cited in Kalra 2004: 33)

But such a picture of the integrative potential of food and consumption is challenged by Kalra, in his analysis of the 'political economy' of the ubiquitous samosa (Kalra 2004). The cultural commentator Jatinder Verma, quoted by Kalra notes:

I do not think that imaginatively we have become multicultural. I think in diet we have, absolutely, but I don't think that has translated from our stomachs to our brains yet. (Jatinder Verma, cited in Kalra 2004: 24)

The growth of small Asian- and Muslim-owned retail businesses, including restaurants, has resulted in the emergence of economic infrastructures to support them, such as Asian banks, insurance and tax services, import and export businesses, and accountancy firms. The recent growth of Islamic banking and finance in Britain is another dimension of this development, and there are now five stand-alone Islamic banks and twenty conventional banks with *Sharī'ah*-compliant products. It is a growth industry, and very much associated with the global 'halalization' (Fischer 2008b) of Muslim lifestyles, which is itself partly driven by an apparent religious revivalism.

The British Muslim lifestyle magazine *emel* is now sold and marketed internationally, and its success is a reflection of a new concern with 'halal' lifestyles. The global trade in halal products is now estimated at US$150 billion, among the roughly 1.3 billion Muslims worldwide (Fischer 2008b). With their command of English, and often strong multicultural ties as a result of migration, British Muslims are in a particularly effective position to capitalize upon this global trade. At present, however, the approach to the certification of halal products in Britain is fragmented and disunited (Fischer 2008a). The existence of a number of rival certification bodies (e.g. the Halal Food Authority and the Halal Monitoring Committee) is to some extent a microcosm of wider debates and tensions among British Muslims on issues of unity and identity, and about 'what Islam is, or ought to be' (Fischer 2008a: 7). Until these are resolved, it may be difficult for British Muslims to develop and market British halal brands internationally.

Where British Muslims have been able to make a significant impact in terms of international activity, and in an entirely businesslike way, is in the charitable sector. There are now numerous British Islamic charities operating internationally, such as Muslim Aid (established in 1985), Muslim Hands (established in 1993) and, perhaps the largest and most well-known, Islamic Relief, founded in Birmingham in 1984 with an initial donation of twenty pence. Today, it has field offices around the globe, and in the face of international disasters (such as the Kashmir earthquake in October 2005) it works alongside other global charitable organizations, such as Oxfam and UNICEF (Masood 2005). Masood notes that 'the charity's recipients do not have to be Muslim, or religious at all, to be eligible for assistance', and he credits Islamic Relief as being 'the world's first international NGO with origins in Islam' (Masood 2005). It is significant and noteworthy that this development emerged in Britain, not in the Middle East or the Indian subcontinent.

THE INDUSTRY OF HERITAGE

In recent years, there have been concerted efforts to document, celebrate and revive an appreciation of the history of Islam and Muslims in Britain. A number of key British Muslim websites[22] have extensive documentation about British Muslim history, and a book published by the Muslim Council of Britain (MCB) in the aftermath of 11 September 2001 also documented the history of Islam in Britain (Sherif 2002). Work undertaken by academics, public institutions, and by British Muslims themselves to

[22] Such as www.salaam.co.uk

illuminate British Muslim history is of course valuable in its own right. However, it is the degree to which this is happening that is perhaps most interesting.

There are well-established 'Islamic' collections in a number of British museums and galleries such as the British Museum, the Oriental Museum, the Royal Museum of Scotland, the Ashmolean Museum and the St Mungo Museum of Religious Life and Art. There is also a dedicated exhibition '1001 Inventions: Muslim Heritage in our World' associated with www.muslimheritage.com which seeks to revive knowledge and understanding of Muslim contributions to science, medicine and technology (Hassani *et al.* 2006). Museums around Britain were involved in the nationwide Festival of Muslim Culture in 2006–7, sometimes engaging in projects in collaboration with local Muslim communities (as in Cardiff). However, research evidence points to a degree of ambivalence on the part of some British Muslims about the display of 'Islam' in museum settings (Heath 2007). While they appreciate the opportunity for more positive public representations of Muslims through Islamic art and heritage, certainly in comparison to negative media framing, at the same time, some are critical of displays of 'Islamic bits and pieces' which, for them, fail to reflect the all-encompassing way of life that is so valued by many observant Muslims, and is arguably impossible to portray through 'things'. Where museum displays of Islamic arts or textiles were once predominantly bound up with an Orientalist, colonial/post-colonial enterprise concerned with acquiring aesthetically pleasing decorative arts from the Empire, today the basis for pro-active connection to an Islamic past is perhaps suggestive of something else entirely. It could be seen as an effort to embrace an Islamic present, and an attempt to take the past history and contemporary presence of Muslims in Britain rather more seriously, on its own terms. If there is any merit in this evaluation, it signals something positive for the future.

Alongside academic and institutional efforts to revive and re-evaluate the display of Islamic material culture (Petersen 2008), British Muslims have simultaneously been involved in perhaps a more grounded, grassroots but equally physical, material and political effort to claim their history and presence in Britain, not through 'bits and pieces' but more through space and place. For example, the Abdullah Quilliam Society, established in Liverpool in 1998, is working to restore the Brougham Terrace premises bought by Quilliam in 1889. This is in order to highlight the Muslim roots in Britain … it is a heritage site for us … important especially for the younger generation who are searching for roots in this area … we can say your roots are here … this truly is the birthplace of Islam in Britain. (IslamOnline.net 2009)

Not surprisingly, a government adviser from English Heritage was equally affirming: 'it is an immensely important monument to Islam in Britain' (IslamOnline.net 2009). The conservation efforts that surround the Woking Mosque are equally historic and significant.

Amid the politics of counter-terrorism and the assumed 'separation' and 'segregation' of British Muslims in the media, conservation projects of this kind, especially in Liverpool, are indicative of quite the opposite. They reflect a deep sense of belonging (and a wish to belong). As a forward-looking investment in the future and an effort at self-empowerment and pride, the Liverpool project is arguably a very 'British' thing to do. Through the effort to revive a connection to an historic British Muslim institution, the efforts of Liverpool Muslims are a beacon for the potential of Islam and Muslims in Britain in the future. At a time when British Muslims have often felt that their 'identity is made by others' (Omaar 2006: 9), the Liverpool project is a form of positive enculturation, and history has provided a resource for asserting a deep-seated and very real sense of belonging and identity.

How surprising and perhaps unfortunate it is, then, that a government-funded 'PVE' anti-radicalization think-tank founded in London in 2008 has equally claimed the power of history, by calling itself The Quilliam Foundation. Supported by £1 million of taxpayers' money, and having earned the scepticism of a number of major British Muslim organizations on account of its leadership by two former members of *Ḥizb al-Taḥrīr*, this new project in fact suffers from a manifest failure to understand the real significance of Liverpool, and more especially the person of Quilliam himself. Living at the height of colonial rule, Abdullah Quilliam was seen as an

anti-imperial agitator and was unashamedly pro-Ottoman … He questioned the virtue of Muslim imperial subjects fighting on behalf of the Empire against their fellow brethren in the Sudan. Quilliam wrote his subversive pan-Islamist tracts in favour of defensive jihad, ummatic solidarity and the support and defence of the beleaguered caliphate. At least in the mid-1890s, he seemed to be a staunch Islamist, to use the current terminology, and thus seems an unlikely candidate for the latest fashion in Britislam-makeovers. (Birt 2008a)

The name 'Quilliam' therefore has begun to mean different things to different people, at least for now. This example is indicative of how religious 'resources' (including historic figures) can be appropriated in different times and places, and in order to serve different interests.

## CONCLUSION

In his speech to the Islamic Finance and Trade Conference in London in October 2008, Jack Straw MP claimed that the overall contribution of British Muslims to the UK economy was over £31 billion.[23] This statement, although almost certainly an underestimate, is a reflection not only of British Muslim trading and enterprise but also of the increased spending power and choices bound up with the growing production and consumption of a British Muslim cultural aesthetic. This chapter has surveyed some of the various manifestations of this aesthetic, and the other non-commercial ways in which Muslims are embedded within some of the social, political and cultural institutions of our society. From eighteenth-century coffee to twenty-first-century 'halal' cornflakes, it is apparent that British Muslims have been successful at establishing tastes and consumption trends that have appeal and significance beyond limited Muslim-only enclaves. Thus, it is likely that the burgeoning Islamic banking and finance sector will, in time, be increasingly able to advertise financial products to the mainstream on account of the ethical principles that underpin this market. When this becomes a reality, it will be a significant indicator of the place of religion in society, and the role that Muslims have played in reversing everyday assumptions about the secular character of British society.

This chapter has glimpsed the work and significance of British Muslim comics, artists, actors, sporting personalities, writers and traders. These cultural producers disrupt established notions of what Muslims in Britain are like, and although they may be relatively few in number, their significance is disproportionate in terms of their capacity to act as key cultural and social interlocutors. They stand alongside many other 'ordinary' British Muslims who display a commitment to living and working in a particular locality, who take an interest in local politics, vote in elections, play sport at the weekends, and enjoy the work of entertainers, artists and novelists. Whereas Muslim 'extremists' seek to re-create the political or military domination of Islam during particular historical periods, those British Muslims who offer their talents and entrepreneurialism to the flourishing of British society may be more effectively 'revolutionary' but

---

[23] From the text of Jack Straw's speech; see www.justice.gov.uk/news/sp301008a.htm.

in subtle rather than overt ways. They demonstrate that being a British Muslim is not just about 'being religious', but is also about being a good human being, and contributing to the flourishing of society. One of the interviewees in Mondal's study of young British Muslims reflected that

for her, Islam emphasises an ethics of everyday life that is not specifically about observing particular rituals and practices or about holding certain beliefs but rather it is a means of regulating one's relationships with others, a way of living based around being good to others. (Mondal 2008: 33)

# Epilogue

The religious identity of Muslims in Britain has come to the fore over the past two decades. The presence of Muslims in Britain has not only changed the character of religion in Britain as a whole, but has 'given it an importance which is out of step with native trends' (Modood 1998: 384). A distinctively Muslim presence in British society in a fully involved, if not fully evolved, way is an established fact. What is less well appreciated is just how pervasive – and increasingly influential – this is. At various points throughout this book, it has been necessary to note the manifest contradictions between popular images of British Muslims and their lived reality.

In many ways, this volume has comprised a journey, tracing where Muslims in Britain have come from, geographically and ideologically, to a consideration of their present situation. But what about the future? What can Islam, as a major world religion, offer to British society today at a time of international economic decline, but also a time, if momentarily, of hope and expectation with the election of President Barack Obama whose own journey has been both remarkable and unprecedented? In this closing 'last word', I want to explore briefly some of the opportunities.

British Muslims have, unwillingly, seen themselves become the subject of public debate and focus for social and security policy in British society as a result of global events and trends. They are 'increasingly subject to a forced telling of the self in UK public life' (Archer 2009: 88). However uncomfortable this may be, the 'spotlight' does also provide opportunities to inhabit a wider canvas and influence an emerging social agenda in Britain more positively, and there are signs of a dawning appreciation that this is so:

Muslims living in the non-Islamic West face an unparalleled opportunity. Theirs is a promising exile: a freedom of thought, action, and inquiry unknown in the contemporary Muslim world ... those who can break free from the inertial ties of national and ethnic personas will be the ones who will forge an Islamicity hitherto unexperienced. (Haider 1996: 77)

Many commentators suggest that, in future, the most important strains of Islam will emerge in the peripheries of the Muslim world, in Europe, in South-East Asia and even in America. (Mondal 2008: 46)

There is also some tangible evidence that this process is already underway. During research in 2003/4, one respondent observed that

there's a kind of revival of religious affiliation amongst young Muslims that's overwhelmingly traditional in nature. It's more conservative even than their parents in many instances, you know. Although it is liberal in surprising ways at the same time … it doesn't quite add up. They are redrawing the boundaries of what piety is. And I think it is more political. I think it is more activist. I think it is more scriptural.[1]

The conscious identification of paradox here is crucial. The paradox sits also within a much wider one. There is clearly an opportunity for the renewal, revival (*tajdīd*) and reinvigoration of Islamic traditions among Muslims to emerge specifically as a result of their situation in contemporary Britain. However, in a number of less obvious ways, the presence of an outward-looking, questioning Islamic community in Britain is equally significant for the potential flourishing and reinvigoration of British society as a whole. British Muslims can contribute to the exploration, debate and resolution of deeper moral and philosophical issues, common in principle to everyone.

Take, for example, the issue of the environment. The *Qur'ān* asserts that human beings are 'guardians' of the earth (*khalīfah*), and that through striving and struggle they should seek to establish a society and way of living that reflects justice, equality, balance and thoughtful stewardship of the earth's resources. Such a worldview centralizes the idea that the earth and its abundance are not 'ours' to possess, but are on loan, entrusted to us for current and future generations (Amery 2001). This 'long view' of the future, shaped by the idea of personal responsibility and generational succession, is arguably significant and valuable in a society that is almost exclusively focused upon the shorter-term priorities of politicians and industrialists (Benthall 2003). British Muslims accordingly have a philosophical and practical contribution to make to debates concerning a sustainable balance between individual responsibility and the common good of society as a whole. Inspired by such Islamic principles, British Muslims

---

[1] See chapter 7, note 6.

are already forging alliances with environmental networks, and contributing to international debates about conservation (Khalid 2002).

The Islamic view of the environment is nonetheless also a holistic one, encompassing not only the material and biological, but also the cultural, the social and the economic. The principles of order, balance and proportion, implict in Islamic law, are in place to enable justice and peace in relationships between humans and their world. The act of charitable giving, one of the 'pillars' of Islam, is for example intended to create economic balance, and the equitable redistribution of resources. The wealthy have an obligation to give, in the same way that the less wealthy have an obligation to receive. It is a mechanism that ensures economic and material balance for the good of society, as well as for the salvation of individuals. By now, British Muslims have established a number of major charities which support projects both in Britian and further afield. They have been actively engaged in the voluntary sector, and in projects which rest upon the giving of self and the giving of time. These initiatives challenge normative assumptions about the necessarily 'private' place of religion in society, and they arguably reflect, and contribute to, a wider effort for more satisfying and meaningful relationships, local engagement and sustainable living.

The international Muslim intellectual Tariq Ramadan has argued that European Muslims should not limit themselves to integration 'on the margins' (Ramadan 2004: 5), but should fully engage in and contribute to the building of their societies, bringing forth the universal principles of Islam, such as justice, balance and a 'search for the common good' (*istiṣlāḥ*). He has written at length on the way that Islamic sources can be interpreted by Muslims afresh, to make this process possible. It will not be easy. If this is the challenge facing British or 'European' Muslims in relation to their religious tradition, what does this demand from those who are inevitably engaged in the process too, implicity or explicitly, by virtue of the fact that they are living alongside Muslims and sharing the same schools, streets and neighbourhoods? What can Muslims expect, or hope for?

Integration is not a one-way process in which *they* come closer, culturally, to *us*. Instead, integration is surely a two-way process involving dialogue, give and take, and mutual accommodation. (Mondal 2008)

The idea of effort or 'struggle' (*jihād*) contains an imperative and exhortative challenge to everyone to strive for the 'common good'. *Jihād* is often interpreted by Muslims as a matter of individual personal striving, away from the negative human tendencies of jealousy, envy or greed, and towards greater God-consciousness (*taqwā*), piety and obedience. It is a term that should, however, have resonances beyond Islam, potentially providing inspiration to anyone concerned with the effort to live by standards and ideals that demand personal endeavour and personal sacrifices for their achievement. The idea of struggle can be mutually interpreted and adopted as a common, shared, collective process to try to address intransigent and difficult social, economic and environmental challenges, bringing the resources of many different traditions and interpretations to the table.

Ramadan poses a challenge to European Muslims by suggesting that

Muslims will get what they deserve: if, as watchful and participating citizens, they study the machinery of their society, demand their rights to equality with others, struggle against all kinds of discrimination and injustice, establish real partnerships beyond their own community and what concerns themselves alone, it will be an achievement that will make political security measures, discrimination, Islamophobic behaviour, and so on drift away downstream. (Ramadan 2004: 7)

Arguably, European societies will also 'get what they deserve' according to the terms upon which they meet and engage with Muslims. If Muslims are respected as equal partners in society, rather that relegated to an 'imagined borderland' (Ramadan 2004: 53), then a real process of integration will extend far beyond tolerance to a more positive mutual enrichment. The current political climate makes this a challenging possibility, but one that is surely worth striving for, given the benefits that it might bring for future generations.

# *Appendix: Source notes for researchers*

The quality and type of quantitative and qualitative data about Muslims in Britain over the past four decades has varied, as have the methodological and disciplinary approaches used to gather new data. This appendix outlines some of the diversity of literature and sources, thereby helping readers with an interest in doing further research and reading to identify the various genres of literature, and other sources of information.

Data derives from a variety of disciplinary perspectives, especially from religious studies, sociology, Islamic studies, ethnic and racial studies, anthropology, geography, politics and history. A broad palette of academic research methods has been deployed to gather data. Qualitative research methods, especially interviews, case studies, documentary and archival research, have added considerable depth and texture to our current knowledge. Unfortunately, hardly any survey research with any time-depth has so far been carried out with Muslims in Britain. In part, this reflects the relatively recent development of what can be termed 'British Muslim studies'.

**Muslim communities in particular locations in the UK**. One source for reaching an understanding of Muslims in Britain today is anthropological and sociological publications over the past forty years which have involved research with Muslims in particular locations in Britain, such as Manchester, Rochdale, Bradford, Oxford, London and Birmingham (Jacobson 1998; Joly 1995; Lewis 1994; Scantlebury 1995; Shaw 2000; Werbner 2002a). Some of these studies have been undertaken solely in relation to Muslims as Muslims, but in other cases in relation to ethnic groups which are predominantly Muslim and have settled in significant numbers in particular locations in Britain, such as Bangladeshis in East London (Gardner 2002) or Yemenis in South Shields (Lawless 1995). The value of these studies has been the publication of usually very detailed, ethnographic, empirical data, and they have contributed to an overall picture of Islam in Britain. However, given that the internal composition and dynamics of Muslim communities in particular towns and cities of Britain can sometimes differ considerably, insights derived from one location cannot always be generalized to another.

**Census data on ethnicity and other large-scale quantitative studies**. Over the past four decades (and particularly since 1991), a greater understanding of Muslims in Britain has come about through extrapolation from data relating to race and ethnicity in the decennial Census, and in other large-scale quantitative studies (see for example Anwar 1993b). By examining the size, demographic characteristics and socio-economic fortunes of, for example, Pakistanis or Bangladeshis, some insights about the situation of Muslims in Britain could be ascertained. Besides the Census, other important studies include the Labour Force Survey and Home Office Citizenship Surveys.

**National studies of ethnic minorities**. Another important source of data about Muslims in Britain has been national surveys of ethnic minorities, where religion is one element of investigation. Studies of this kind have been regularly conducted by the Policy Studies Institute since 1966.[1] These projects have focused upon race and ethnicity, but in the last survey in 1994 the religious identity of participants was recorded. However, these projects have so far only ever been able to partially capture the experience of Muslims in Britain as a whole, because some Muslims in Britain are not regarded as being part of an ethnic 'minority' group. White British converts to Islam, for example, have been invisible in such studies, as have Muslims from other much smaller and diverse ethnic groups, such as Arabs, Bosnians or Turks.

**Studies on Muslims 'in the West' or 'in Europe', which include Muslims in Britain**. The mass migration of Muslims into Western Europe has spawned numerous publications about the migration histories, settlement patterns and relative socio-economic 'fates' of Muslims in France, Germany, Belgium, Italy, Denmark and so on. Muslims in Britain have usually been included as part of these academic works, and so this genre of scholarship has contributed to our understanding of the situation of British Muslims relative to Muslims living in other minority contexts in Europe (Abedin and Sardar 1995; Cesari and McLoughlin 2005; Fetzer and Soper 2004; Nielsen 2004; Peach and Vertovec 1997; Werbner and Modood 1997).

---

[1] These surveys were: Brown (1984); Daniel (1968); Modood *et al.* (1997); Smith, B. P. (1977). The 1997 'Fourth Survey' took into account the religious identity of participants.

**Research about particular ethnic groups in Britain which are predominantly Muslim**. Included within this genre of literature are works that have not only illustrated the experiences of Muslims of South Asian background (such as Pakistanis or Bangladeshis in Britain), but also those Muslims who originate from other ethnic backgrounds, such as Iranians (Spellman 2004), diverse Arab groups including Saudis, Egyptians and Yemenis (Al-Rasheed 2005; Halliday 1992a; Karmi 1997; Nagel 2001), Turks (Enneli *et al.* 2005; Kucukcan 1999; Yilmaz 2004), Kurds (Griffiths 2002) and Somalis (Berns McGowan 1999; El-Solh 1993; Griffiths 2002). The religious life and experiences of such groups form a greater or lesser part of these studies, but most of them make some reference to the lived experience of being Muslims in British society.[2]

**Studies about 'religion in Britain'**. The increasing religious diversity of British society over the past fifty years has led to the emergence of new sociological literature about religion in modern British society. Given that Muslims constitute the largest religious minority group in the UK, their situation has sometimes figured significantly in this literature, and we have been able to evaluate their presence in the UK relative to other religious communities and against the background of Britain's religious history (Brierley 1999; Bruce 1995; Davie 1994).

**British Muslim community publications**. Over the past thirty years, the emergence of British Muslim publishing houses and media and research organizations and the evolution of a new generation of British Muslim scholars have helped to create and sustain the production of information that reflects 'insider', community-based perspectives. As a result, it is arguable that the inevitable power relations that shape a field of study and its production are being contested and rebalanced in favour of Muslim interests and viewpoints.

**Topic-specific studies**. In recent decades, there have been a number of publications that narrate the story of Muslims in Britain as whole. Good examples of this genre include historical accounts of the settlement of Muslims in Britain (Ansari 2004; Matar 1998), or commentaries which attempt to evaluate the overall situation of Muslims in Britain (Raza 1991). But in the past two decades, there has been extensive research and writing which considers Muslims in Britain in relation to particular issues. The following are indicative of the range of topics that have now been studied in some depth: education (both within and outside the state system);

---

[2] See also the Change Institute reports, April 2009 (London: Communities and Local Government).

internal diversity; migration and employment; identity; youth; health; family; politics and social policy; media; 'Islamophobia'; law and discrimination; gender; conversion; mosques and other Islamic institutions; religious and political leadership; and interfaith dialogue.

**Crisis-driven publications**. Numerous publications and studies about Islam and Muslims in Britain have emerged in the wake of major incidents and crises. Significant events have often thrown into sharp relief the overall situation of Muslims in Britain, and have brought into the open key issues and debates that might have otherwise remained hidden or latent if not for a particular event or crisis. So following the Rushdie Affair, the Gulf War, 9/11, the 'Northern riots' in 2001, and then the London bombings of July 2005, a range of books, reports and articles have been written in response. These works might be considered as mirrors which reflect the immediate concerns and issues surrounding Muslims in Britain as a result of the particular incident. A predominant concern of these kinds of publications has been issues such as cohesion (Cantle 2002), multiculturalism and equality, and the place of Muslims in British society (Modood 1990b), and, more recently, radicalization and religious extremism, and the pressures placed upon British Muslims in the wake of the 'war on terror' (Brown 2008; Hussain and Bagguley 2005; Modood 2005b). Within this category of literature we also need to include the new and growing phenomenon of opinion polls and semi-academic 'think-tank' reports and studies, often compiled in some haste by researchers without an established track record of researching Islam in Britain.[3] These have done little to improve understanding of Muslims in Britain, because they are rarely underpinned by the normal protocols of scholarly peer review, ethical scrutiny or in-depth social scientific methodological awareness.

**Journalistic reports about Muslims in Britain**. Crises and major international occurrences involving Muslims create particular news agendas. In the wake of 9/11, for example, British Muslims increasingly came under the journalistic spotlight, leading simultaneously to both derogatory articles and stories, and also more informed and balanced portrayals. Sometimes, the topics that constitute the substance of media articles are revealing for the assumptions they betray about what readers are likely to regard as most interesting, newsworthy or significant about Muslims in Britain. Feature articles might therefore appear about the

---

[3] A good example of this kind of literature is the reports published by the Policy Exchange (MacEoin 2007; Mirza *et al.* 2007). Few of the authors of these often controversial and high-profile studies have any academic track record as published scholarly researchers of Islam in Britain, and they usually rely heavily on desk-based and internet resources.

'richest' or 'most influential' Muslims in Britain, Muslim support for the Labour Party, or the antics of Muslim youth enjoying the freedom of the university campus, for example. This of course says little about the daily lived realities that comprise British Muslim experiences. Some of the better-quality media contributions include the BBC 'Islam Season' in 2002, with many of the programmes being made by, or featuring, British Muslims who were able to articulate their own narratives and experiences. In the same year, *The Guardian* printed a series of in-depth articles about Muslims in Britain, many of which involved the collection or compilation of new data. In 2005, *The Guardian* hosted a series of conferences with young British Muslims, resulting in a published collection of informative essays (Bunting 2005).

**Novels, films, and autobiographical works authored by, or about, British Muslims**. As the experience of Muslims in Britain has developed over time, the possibility for new kinds of literature and information has emerged, such as autobiographical works which offer personal reflections on life as a Muslim in the UK. A good example of such a work is Rageh Omaar's *Only Half of Me: Being a Muslim in Britain* (Omaar 2006), which tells the story of his childhood upbringing in Britain as a young Somali Muslim. Ziauddin Sardar's *Desperately Seeking Paradise: Journeys of a Sceptical Muslim* (Sardar 2004) recounts his first-hand experiences of encounters with particular Muslim groups in Britain in the 1970s, and life as an 'Asian' in Britain in *Balti Britain: Journeys through the British Asian Experience* (Sardar 2008). Other recent memoirs include Imran Ahmad's *Unimagined* (Ahmad, I. 2007), Sarfraz Manzoor's *Greetings from Bury Park* (Manzoor 2007), Na'ima B Robert's *From my Sister's Lips* (Robert 2005), Moazzam Begg's *Enemy Combatant: A British Muslim's Journey to Guantanamo and Back* (Begg 2006), Ed Husain's *The Islamist* (Husain 2007) and recently Shelina Zahra Janmohamad's *Love in a Headscarf* (Janmohamed 2009). Fictional works which reflect aspects of British Muslim life and experience include the novels of well-known authors such as Hanif Kureishi (*My Beautiful Laundrette*; *The Black Album*) and Monica Ali (*Brick Lane*), as well as lesser-known Muslim novelists such as Farhana Sheikh (*The Red Box*), Tariq Mehmood (*Hand on the Sun*; *While There is Light*), Zahid Hussain (*The Curry Mile*), Nadeem Aslam (*Maps for Lost Lovers*) and Leila Aboulela (*Coloured Light*; *Minaret*; *The Translator*).

Over the past few years, a number of films have been made which depict aspects of British Muslim experience, such as *Britz* (2007), *The Road to Guantanamo* (2006), *Love + Hate* (2005), *Yasmin* (2004), *Ae Fond Kiss* (2004), *East is East* (1999) and *My Son the Fanatic* (1997). These cinematographic works, despite their almost inevitable exaggerations and caricaturing of Muslims (and predominant concern with 'culture clash'), must be regarded as part of the overall production of knowledge about Islam and Muslims in Britain, especially since outside academic or educated circles they perhaps constitute a significance source of impressions or information about the lives and experiences of British Muslims.

**Blogs and websites**. Recent years have seen the exponential growth of 'blogs' and websites[4] which provide a forum for individuals to reflect, criticize, activate and muse upon the situation of Muslims in Britain. These new sites are deserving of further academic attention, providing as they do a unique insight into a range of personal and political perspectives about the situation of Muslims in Britain today.[5]

**Other resources**. There is now a thriving British Muslim information industry, mainly directed towards Muslim needs and interests. A good example is the *Muslim Directory* (MDUK Media) which produces a comprehensive 'Yellow Pages' of Muslim businesses and services, mosques and Islamic organizations around the UK, sports and activities, and charities as well as general religious guidance on birth rites, funerals and wills. MDUK Media has a database of over 300,000 Muslim households in the UK, which means that marketing of Islamic products and services can become better targeted. It is notable that major British organizations are increasingly using such resources to target communities that they otherwise might not reach. These include bodies such as the Food Standards Agency (raising awareness about food labelling and healthy eating) and the British Heart Foundation (campaigning on heart disease and life-saving skills).

The information resources now available to researchers are extensive, and the growing availability of on-line searchable databases helps scholars to locate key material. Researchers based in academic institutions can now benefit from the ability to locate existing and new publications through such things as:

- ZETOC Alert – Electronic 'Table of Contents' (www.mimas.ac.uk). Researchers can create personalized search criteria and indicate 'keywords' to ensure that they are 'alerted' to new publications in their field.

---

[4] See for example: www.salaam.co.uk
[5] See Yahya Birt's 'blog' and especially an evaluation of some of the most vibrant British Muslim blogs: 'Roll up, Roll up! Vote for the best of the British Muslim blogosphere' (Birt 2007b), www.yahyabirt.com/?p=116

- Electronic databases, such as the British Humanities Index, Social Sciences Index and Abstracts (ASSIA), ATLA Religion Database, Web of Knowledge, are all important abstracting and indexing tools.
- *Index Islamicus* describes itself as 'the leading bibliography on Islam and the Muslim world since 1906' (www.brill.nl/indexislamicus) and is arguably an essential resource for researchers on Islam and Muslims today.

# Glossary

| | |
|---|---|
| *Adab* | etiquette or manners |
| *adhān* | call to prayer |
| *'ālim* (plural, *'ulamā'*, feminine, *'ālima*) | religious scholar |
| *Allāh* | God |
| *Amīr* | leader |
| *Ayatollah* | senior *Shī'a* scholar/cleric |
| *barakah* | blessing |
| *bid'ah* | religious innovation |
| *birādarī* | kinship network (South Asian term) |
| *dars-i niẓāmī* | classical South Asian religious syllabus |
| *dāru'l-'ulūm* | religious seminary |
| *da'wah* | invitation |
| *dhikr* | remembrance of God |
| *dīn al-fitra* | natural religion of humankind |
| *Eid* (also transliterated as *'Īd al-Aḍhā* and *'Īd al-Fiṭr*) | religious festivals in Islam |
| *fatāwā* (sing. *fatwā*) | legal opinion |
| *fiqh* | jurisprudence |
| *Ḥadīth* | sayings of the Prophet Muhammad |
| *ḥāfiz* (plural, *ḥuffāẓ*) | one who has memorized the *Qur'ān* |
| *ḥajj* | pilgrimage to Makkah |
| *ḥalaqāt* | study circle |
| *Ḥanafī* | school of *Sunni* Islamic law |
| *Ḥaẓrat* | honorific title of respect for a religious teacher or 'master' |
| *'ibādāt* | worship |
| *Ijmā* | consensus |
| *ijtihād* | interpretative effort |

| | |
|---|---|
| *'ilm* | knowledge |
| *iṣlāḥ* | reform |
| *isnād* | chain of transmission |
| *istiṣlāḥ* | taking account of the public good |
| *izzat* | honour |
| *jihād* | to strive |
| *jinn* | spirits |
| *Jum'a* | Friday prayers |
| *kāfir* | those deemed to be non-Muslims |
| *Khalīfah* | ruler, or steward/guardian |
| *khaṭīb* | one who gives the Friday sermon |
| *khuṭbah* | Friday sermon |
| *Khilāfah* | Islamic state |
| *lascar* | seafarer |
| *madhhab* (plural, *madhāhib*) | one of the schools of Sunni Islamic law |
| *madrasah* (plural, *madāris*) | institution for advanced religious learning |
| *maktab* (plural, *makātib*) | institution for elementary religious learning |
| *masjid* (plural, *masājid*) | mosque |
| *Maslak* | school of thought |
| *Maulānā* | respected religious scholar |
| *Maulvī* | a learned man |
| *miḥrāb* | niche indicating the direction for prayer |
| *minbar* | steps from which the Friday sermon is delivered |
| *muezzin* | one who makes the call to prayer |
| *muftī* | scholar who can issue legal opinions |
| *mullah* | religious teacher |
| *murīd* | disciple of a Sufi religious teacher |
| *nasheed* | devotional song |
| *nikāḥ* | marriage contract or ceremony |
| *ribā* | usury/interest |
| *qāḍī* | a judge |
| *qāri'* (plural, *qurrā'*) | one who has learned correct technique for recitation of the *Qur'ān* |
| *qawwālī* | Sufi devotional song |

| | |
|---|---|
| *qirā'āt* | the correct technique for recitation of the *Qur'ān* |
| *qiyās* | analogy |
| *qurbāni* | sacrifice of an animal to mark a festival or celebration, with meat distributed to the poor |
| *ṣadaqah* | voluntary charitable giving |
| *ṣalāt* | compulsory daily prayer, performed five times a day |
| *ṣalāt al-janāzah* | funeral prayer |
| *Shahādah* | to witness that 'There is no God but God, and Muhammad is His Messenger' |
| *Shāfi'ī* | one of the schools of *Sunni* Islamic law |
| *Sharī'ah* | principles and practices for Islamic belief, behaviour and worship |
| *shaykh* (plural, *shuyūkh*) | spiritual teacher |
| *shirk* | idolatry |
| *silsilah* | chain of Sufi teachers |
| *Sunnah* | example of the Prophet Muhammad |
| *sūrah* | chapter of the *Qur'ān* |
| *tajdīd* | renewal or revival of Islam |
| *tajwīd* | principles for correct recitation of the *Qur'ān* |
| *taqlīd* | imitation |
| *taqwā* | God-consciousness |
| *tarbiyat* | religious nurture, especially of children |
| *ṭarīqah* | Sufi order |
| *tawḥīd* | the indivisible oneness of God |
| *'ulamā'* (singular, *'ālim*) | religious scholars |
| *ummah* | worldwide Muslim community |
| *unani tibb* | system of medicine derived from Islam |
| *wuḍū'* | ritual cleansing prior to worship |
| *zāwiyah* | religious centre |

# References

Abbas, T. 2002a. 'The home and the school in the educational achievements of South Asians', *Race, Ethnicity and Education* **5** (3): 291–316.

2002b. 'Teacher perceptions of South Asians in Birmingham schools and colleges', *Oxford Review of Education* **28** (4): 447–71.

2003. 'The impact of religio-cultural norms and values on the education of young South Asian women', *British Journal of Sociology of Education* **24** (4): 411–28.

(ed.) 2005. *Muslims in Britain: Communities under Pressure*, London: Zed Books.

Abedin, S. and Sardar, Z. (eds.) 1995. *Muslim Minorities in the West*, London: Grey Seal.

Adams, C. 1987. *Across Seven Seas and Thirteen Rivers: Life Stories of the Pioneer Sylheti Settlers in Britain*, London: Eastside Books.

Afshar, H. 1989. 'Gender roles and the moral economy of kin among Pakistani women in West Yorkshire', *New Community* **15** (2): 211–35.

1993. 'Schools and Muslim girls: gateway to a prosperous future or quagmire of racism? Some experiences from West Yorkshire', in Barot, R. (ed.), *Religion and Ethnicity: Minorities and Social Change in the Metropolis*, Netherlands: Kok Pharos, pp. 56–67.

1998. 'Strategies of resistance among the Muslim minority in West Yorkshire: impact on women', in Charles, N. and Hintjens, H. (eds.), *Gender, Ethnicity and Political Ideology*, London: Routledge, pp. 107–26.

2008. 'Can I see your hair? Choice, agency and attitudes: the dilemma of faith and feminism for Muslim women who cover', *Ethnic and Racial Studies* **31** (2): 411–37.

Afshar, H., Aitken, R. and Franks, M. 2005. 'Feminisms, Islamophobia and identities', *Political Studies* **53**: 262–83.

Afshar, H., Franks, M., Maynard, M. and Wray, S. 2001. 'Empowerment, disempowerment and quality of life for older women', *Generations Review* **11** (4): 1153–61.

Ahmad, F. 2006. 'The scandal of "arranged marriages" and the pathologization of BrAsian Families', in Ali, N., Kalra, V. and Sayyid, S. (eds.), *A Postcolonial People: South Asians in Britain*, London: Hurst, pp. 272–88.

2007. 'Muslim women's experiences of higher education in Britain', *American Journal of Islamic Social Sciences* **24** (3): 46–69.

Ahmad, F., Modood, T. and Lissenburgh, S. 2003. *South Asian Women and Employment in Britain*. London: Policy Studies Institute, Report No. 891.

Ahmad, I. 2007. *Unimagined*. London: Aurum.

Ahmad, N. 1998. 'Hijabs in our midst', in Rutherford, J. (ed.), *Young Britain: Politics, Pleasures and Predicaments*, London: Lawrence and Wishart, pp. 74–82.

Ahmad, Q. 1966. *The Wahabi Movement in India*, Calcutta: Firma K. L. Mukhopadhayay.

Ahmad, S. 2004. 'Play it again, Sami', *emel*, March/April, pp. 80.

Ahmed, A. 1993. *Living Islam: From Samarkand to Stornoway*, London: BBC Books.

Ahmed, L. 1992. *Women and Gender in Islam*, New Haven and London: Yale University Press.

Ahmed, T. S. 2005. 'Reading between the lines: Muslims and the media', in Abbas, T. (ed.), *Muslim Britain: Communities under Pressure*, London: Zed Books, pp. 109–26.

Aithie, P. 2005. *The Burning Ashes of Times: From Steamer Point to Tiger Bay*, Bridgend, Wales: Seren.

Akbar, A. 2006. 'Why Shazia Mirza wants to shake off her "Muslim comic" label', *The Independent*, 28 October.

Akhtar, S. 1989. *Be Careful with Muhammad*, London: Bellew.

Akram, M. 1975. 'Pakistani migrants in Britain: a note', *New Community* **4** (1): 116–18.

al-'Alam, R. 2003. '*Exclusive interview with Visual Dhikr artist*', www.mcb.org.uk/features/features.php?ann_id=154 (accessed 19/9/08).

Al-Khoei, Y. 2000. 'Obituary of Mulla Asghar Ali Jaffer', *The Independent*, 5 April.

Al-Rasheed, M. 2005. 'Saudi religious transnationalism in London', in Al-Rasheed, M. (ed.), *Transnational Connections and the Arab Gulf*, London: Routledge, pp. 149–67.

Alam, F. 2004. 'Muslim boxing hero who unites us all', *Observer*, 29 August.

Alam, M. Y. and Husband, C. 2006. '*British-Pakistani men from Bradford: linking narratives to policy*', London: Joseph Rowntree Foundation.

Alavi, K. 2004. *The Mosque within a Muslim Community*, Birmingham: UK Islamic Mission.

Alexander, C. 1998. 'Re-imagining the Muslim community', *Innovation: The European Journal of Social Sciences* **11** (4): 439–50.

2000. *The Asian Gang: Ethnicity, Identity, Masculinity*, Oxford: Berg.

2004. 'Imagining the Asian gang: ethnicity, masculinity and youth after "the riots"', *Critical Social Policy* **24** (4): 526–49.

Alfaradhi, R. 2004. 'A New Dawn in East London', *Q News*, **357**: 9.

Ali, M. 2003. *Brick Lane*, London: Doubleday.

Alibhai-Brown, Y. 2005. 'England oh England', *The Independent*, 21 September.

Alim, S. Y. 2005. 'A new research agenda: exploring the transglobal hop hop umma', in Cooke, M. and Lawrence, B. (eds.), *Muslim Networks: From Hajj to Hip Hop*, Chapel Hill, NC: University of North Carolina Press, pp. 264–74.

Allan, G. and Crow, G. 2001. *Families, Households and Society*, London: Palgrave Macmillan.

Allan, J. 1914. 'Offa's imitation of an Arab dinar', *The Numismatic Chronicle and Journal of the Royal Numismatic Society* **XIV** (Fourth Series): 77–89.

Allievi, S. 2003. 'Relations and negotiations: issues and debates on Islam', in Marechal, B., Allievi, S., Dassetto, F. and Nielsen J. (eds.), *Muslims in the Enlarged Europe: Religion and Society*, Leiden: Brill, pp. 331–68.

Ally, M. 1979. *The Growth and Organisation of the Muslim Community in Britain*, Birmingham: Selly Oak Colleges, CSIC.

Amer, F. 1997. *Islamic supplementary education in Britain – a critique. PhD thesis*, University of Birmingham.

Amery, H. 2001. 'Islam and the environment', in Faruqui, N., Biswas, A. and Bino, M. (eds.), *Water Management in Islam*, Tokyo, New York, Paris: United Nations University Press, pp. 39–48.

Ansari, H. 2002. 'The Woking Mosque: a case study of Muslim engagement with British society since 1889', *Immigrants and Minorities* **21** (3): 1–24.

  2003. 'The Muslim presence in Britain: making a positive contribution', www.rhul.ac.uk/EthnicMinority-Studies/MuslimPresenceInBritain1.pdf (accessed 10/10/05).

  2004. *The 'Infidel' within: Muslims in Britain, 1800 to the Present*, London: Hurst.

  2007. '"Burying the Dead": making Muslim space in Britain', *Historical Research* **80** (210): 545–66

Anwar, M. 1979. *The Myth of Return*, London: Heinemann Educational Books.

  1983. 'Education and the Muslim community in Britain', *Muslim Education Quarterly* **1** (3): 9–23.

  1993a. 'Muslims in Britain', in Abedin, S. and Sardar, Z. (eds.), *Muslim Minorities in the West*, London: Grey Seal, pp. 37–50.

  1993b. *Muslims in Britain: 1991 Census and Other Statistical Sources*, Birmingham: CSIC.

  2008. 'Muslims in Western states: the British experience and the way forward', *Journal of Muslim Minority Affairs* **28** (1): 125–37.

Anwar, M. and Bakhsh, Q. 2003. *British Muslims and State Policies*, Coventry: CRER, University of Warwick.

Anwar, M. and Shah, F. 2000. 'Muslim women and experiences of discrimination in Britain', in Blaschke, J. (ed.), *Multi-Level Discrimination of Muslim Women in Europe*, Berlin: Edition Parabolis, pp. 203–48.

Appleton, M. 2005a. 'The political attitudes of Muslims studying at British universities in the post-9/11 world (part 1)', *Journal of Muslim Minority Affairs* **25** (2): 171–92.

2005b. 'The political attitudes of Muslims studying at British universities in the post-9/11 world (part II)', *Journal of Muslim Minority Affairs* **25** (3): 299–316.

Archer, L. 2001. '"Muslim brothers, black lads, traditional Asians": British Muslim young men's constructions of race, religion and masculinity', *Feminism and Psychology* **11** (1): 79–105.

2003. *Race, Masculinity and Schooling: Muslim Boys and Education*, Maidenhead: Open University Press.

2009. 'Race, "face" and masculinity: the identities and local geographies of Muslim boys', in Hopkins, P. and Gale, R. (eds.), *Muslims in Britain: Race, Place and Identities*, Edinburgh University Press, pp. 74–91.

Asad, T. 1993. *Genealogies of Religion: Discipline and Reasons of Power in Islam and Christianity*, London: John Hopkins University Press.

Asif, I. 2006. *Hijaz College: students of Islamic religious sciences in contemporary British society*, MA dissertation, Lund University.

Aspinall, P. 2000. 'Should a question on "religion" be asked in the 2001 British census? A public policy case in favour', *Social Policy and Administration* **34** (5): 584–600.

Auge, M. 1995. *Non-Places: Introduction to an Anthropology of Supermodernity*, London: Verso Books.

Azami, R. A. 2000. *Ahl-e-Hadith in Britain: History, Establishment, Organisation, Activities and Objectives*, London: TaHa Publishers.

Azim, I. 2004. 'Amir Khan, Britain's emerging star', *Muslim News*, 24 September.

Aziz, S. 2006. 'Creating the Bakri Monster', *Islamica*, **17**: 59–62.

Badawi, Z. 2004. 'Fatwa shopping', www.channel4.com/culture/microsites/S/shariahtv/rules.html (accessed 19/08/04).

Bagguley, P. and Hussain, Y. 2005. 'Flying the flag for England: citizenship, religion and cultural identity among British Pakistani Muslims', in Abbas, T. (ed.), *Muslim Britain: Communities under Pressure*, London: Zed Books, pp. 208–21.

Baily, J. 1990. 'Qawwali in Bradford: traditional music in the Muslim communities', in Oliver, P. (ed.), *Black Music in Britain*, Buckingham: Open University Press, pp. 153–62.

2006. '"Music is in our blood": Gujarati Muslim musicians in the UK', *Journal of Ethnic and Migration Studies* **32** (257–70).

Baily, J. and Collyer, M. 2006. 'Introduction: music and migration', *Journal of Ethnic and Migration Studies* **32** (2): 167–82.

Bak, G. 1999. 'Different differences: locating Moorishness in early modern English culture', *Dalhousie Review* **76**: 197–216.

Baksh, N., Cantle, T., Lempriere, J. and Kaur, D. 2008. *Understanding and Appreciating Muslim Diversity: Towards Better Engagement and Participation*, Coventry: Institute of Community Cohesion.

Balchin, C. 2007. 'God's waiting room', www.channel4.com/culture/microsites/C/can_you_believe_it/debates/allahsdoor.html (accessed 5/7/09).

Bano, S. 1999. 'Muslim and South Asian women: customary law and citizenship in Britain', in Werbner, P. and Yuval-Davis, N. (eds.), *Women, Citizenship and Difference*, London: Zed Books, pp. 162–77.

2007. 'Muslim family justice and human rights: the experience of British Muslim women', *Journal of Comparative Law* **2** (2): 38–66.

Barton, S. 1986. *The Bengali Muslims of Bradford: A Study of their Observance of Islam with Special Reference to the Function of the Mosque and the Work of the Imam*. Leeds: Community Religions Project, University of Leeds.

Basit, T. 1995. 'I want to go to college: British Muslim girls and the academic dimension of schooling', *Muslim Education Quarterly* **12** (3): 36–54.

1996. '"Obviously I'll have an arranged marriage": Muslim marriage in the British context', *Muslim Education Quarterly* **13** (2): 4–19.

1997a. *Eastern Values, Western Milieu: Identities and Aspirations of Adolescent Muslim Girls*, Aldershot: Ashgate.

1997b. '"I want more freedom, but not too much": British Muslim girls and the dynamism of family values', *Gender and Education* **9** (4): 425–39.

Bearman, P., Bianquis, T., Bosworth, C. E., Donzel, E. v. and Heinrichs, W. P. (eds.) 2007. *Encyclopaedia of Islam*, Leiden: Brill.

Beckerlegge, G. 1997. 'Followers of "Mohammed, Kalee and Dada Nanuk": the presence of Islam and South Asian religions in Victorian Britain', in Wolffe, J. (ed.), *Religion in Victorian Britain*. Manchester University Press, pp. 221–70.

Beckford, J., Gale, R., Owen, D., Peach, C. and Weller, P. 2006. *Review of the Evidence Base on Faith Communities'*, London: Office of the Deputy Prime Minister.

Beckford, J. and Gilliat, S. 1998. *Religion in Prison: Equal Rites in a Multi-Faith Society*, Cambridge University Press.

Begg, M. 2006. *Enemy Combatant: A British Muslim's Journey to Guantanamo and Back,* London: Free Press.

Benn, T. 2003. 'Muslim women talking: experiences of their early teaching careers', in Benn, T. and Jawad, H. (eds.), *Muslim Women in the United Kingdom and Beyond*, Leiden: Brill, pp. 131–50.

Benn, T. and Jawad, H. 2003. 'Preface', in Benn, T. and Jawad, H. (eds.), *Muslim Women in the United Kingdom and Beyond*, Leiden: Brill, pp. xiii–xxv.

Benthall, J. 2003. 'The greening of Islam?', *Anthropology Today* **19** (6): 10–12.

Berns McGowan, R. 1999. *Muslims in the Diaspora: The Somali Communities of London and Toronto*, Toronto: University of Toronto Press.

Bijlefeld, W. A. 1984. 'On being Muslim: the faith dimension of Muslim identity', in Haddad, Y., Haines, B. and Findly, E. (eds.), *The Islamic Impact*, New York: Syracuse University Press, p. 220.

Birt, J. 2005a. 'Lobbying and marching: British Muslims and the state', in Abbas, T. (ed.), *Muslim Britain: Communities under Pressure*, London: Zed Books, pp. 92–106.

2005b. 'Locating the British Imam: the Deobandi "Ulama" between contested authority and public policy post-9/11', in Cesari, J. and McLoughlin, S. (eds.), *European Muslims and the Secular State*, Aldershot: Ashgate, pp. 183–96.

2005. 'Wahhabism in the United Kingdom: Manifestations and Reactions', in al-Rasheed, M. (ed.), *Transnational Connections in the Arab Gulf and Beyond*, London: Routledge, pp. 168–84.

2006. 'Good Imam, Bad Imam: civic religion and national integration in Britain post 9/11', *The Muslim World* **96** (October): 687–705.

Birt, J. and Gilliat-Ray, S. 2009. 'Mosque conflicts in Europe: the case of Great Britain', in Allievi, S. (ed.), *Mosque Controversies in Europe*, Rome: Ethnobarometer.

Birt, Y. 2000. 'True and false masculinity', *Q News*, **325**: 19–21.

2003. 'Lies! Damn lies! Statistics and conversion'. *Q News*, **350**: 20.

2006a. 'Between nation and umma: Muslim loyalty in a globalizing world', http://islam21.net/docs/uploads/Islam21Mar06.pdf (accessed 24/10/07).

2006b. 'The veil and the limits of English tolerance', www.yahyabirt. com/?p=36 (accessed 14/1/08).

2006c. 'What the Moroccan ambassador knew', www.yahyabirt.com/?p=29 (accessed 5/6/2009).

2007a. 'Muslim hip hop UK: an interview with Tony Ishola', www.yahyabirt. com/?p=117 (accessed 18/9/08).

2007b. 'Roll up, roll up! Vote for the best of the British Muslim blogosphere', www.yahyabirt.com/?p=116 (accessed 29/12/08).

2008a. 'Abdullah Quilliam: Britain's first Islamist?' www.yahyabirt. com/?p=136 (accessed 22/12/08).

2008b. 'Takeaway lives', *emel*, February, p. 18.

Bodi, F. 2006. 'Let us speak for ourselves', *The Guardian*, 18 July.

Bolognani, M. 2009. *Crime and Muslim Britain: Race, Culture and the Politics of Criminology among British Pakistanis*, London: I B Tauris.

Bowlby, S. and Lloyd Evans, S. 2009. '"You seem very westernised to me": place, identity and othering of Muslim workers in the UK labour market', in Hopkins, P. and Gale, R. (eds.), *Muslims in Britain: Race, Place and Identities*, Edinburgh University Press, pp. 37–54.

Boyle, H. 2004. *Contemporary Quranic Schools: Agents of Preservation and Change*, London: Routledge.

Brah, A. 1993. '"Race" and "culture" in the gendering of labour markets: South Asian young Muslim women and the labour market', *New Community* **19** (3): 441–58.

1996. *Cartographies of Diaspora: Contesting Identities*, London: Routledge.

Brah, A. and Phoenix, A. 2004. 'Ain't I a woman? Revisiting intersectionality', *Journal of International Women's Studies* **5** (3): 75–86.

Brierley, P. 1999. *Religious Trends 2000/2001*, London: Christian Research.

Brown, C. 1984. *Black and White Britain*, London: Heinemann.

Brown, D. 1996. *Rethinking Tradition in Modern Islamic Thought*, Cambridge University Press.

Brown, K. 2006. 'Realising Muslim women's rights: the role of Islamic identity among British Muslim women', *Women's Studies International Forum* **29** (4): 417–30.

2008. 'The promise and peril of women's participation in UK mosques: the impact of securitisation agendas on identity, gender and community', *British Journal of Politics and International Relations* **10** (3): 472–91.

Brown, M. 2000. 'Religion and economic activity in the South Asian population', *Ethnic and Racial Studies* **23** (6): 1035–61.

Brown, P. 1971. *The World of Late Antiquity: From Marcus Aurelius to Muhammad*, London: Thames and Hudson.

Brown, R. (ed.) 1890. *The Adventures of Thomas Pellow of Penryn, Mariner, Three and Twenty Years in Captivity among the Moors*, London: T. F Unwin.

Brown, S. 2004. 'The Shah Jahan Mosque, Woking: an unexpected gem', *Conservation Bulletin* **46** (Autumn): 32–4.

Bruce, S. 1995. *Religion in Modern Britain*, Oxford: OUP.

Bugby, J. E. 1938. 'Moslems in London', *The Muslim World* **28**: 76–9.

Bunglawala, Z. 2004. *Aspirations and Reality: British Muslims and the Labour Market*, Budapest: Open Society Institute.

Bunt, G. 1998. 'Decision-making concerns in British Islamic environments', *Islam and Christian-Muslim Relations* **9** (1): 103–13.

Bunting, M. (ed.) 2005. *Islam, Race and Being British*, London: The Guardian & Barrow Cadbury Trust.

Burdsey, D. 2004. '"One of the lads?" Dual ethnicity and assimilated ethnicities in the careers of British Asian professional footballers', *Ethnic and Racial Studies* **27** (5): 757–79.

2006a. '"If I ever play football, Dad, can I play for England or India?" British Asians, sport and diasporic national identities', *Sociology* **40** (1): 11–28.

2006b. 'No ball games allowed? A socio-historical examination of the development and social significance of British Asian football clubs', *Journal of Ethnic and Migration Studies* **32** (3): 477–96.

2007. 'Role with the punches: the construction and representation of Amir Khan as a role model for multiethnic Britain', *The Sociological Review* **55** (3): 611–31.

Burlet, S. and Reid, H. 1996. 'Riots, representation and responsibilities: the role of young men in Pakistani-heritage Muslim communities', in Shadid, W. A. R. and Koningsveld, P. S. v. (eds.), *Political Participation and Identities of Muslims in non-Muslim States*, Kampen, Netherlands: Kok Pharos, pp. 144–57.

1998. 'A gendered uprising: political representation and minority ethnic communities', *Ethnic and Racial Studies* **21** (2): 270–87.

Burnett, C. 1997. *The Introduction of Arabic Learning into England (Panizzi Lectures)*, London: British Library Publishing Division.

Butler, C. 1999. 'Cultural diversity and religious conformity: dimensions of social change among second-generation Muslim women', in Barot, R., Fenton, S. and Bradley, H. (eds.), *Ethnicity, Gender and Social Change*, London: Macmillan, pp. 135–51.

Butt, I. 2009. *Tries and Prejudice: The Autobiography of England's First Muslim Rugby International*, Leeds: Scratching Shed Publishing Ltd.

Byrne, C. 2005. 'Muslim magazine goes mainstream', *The Independent*, 29 September.

Cabinet Office. 2003. 'Ethnic Minorities and the Labour Market', London: Cabinet Office.

Campbell, D. 2001. 'Hussain Lashes British Asians as Unpatriotic', *Observer*, 27 May.

Cantle, T. 2002. *Community Cohesion: A Report of the Independent Review Team*, London: Home Office.

Cantwell Smith, W. 1961. *Islam in Modern History*, New York: Mentor Books.

Carr, B. 1992. 'Black Geordies', in Colls, R. and Lancaster, B. (eds.), *Geordies: Roots of Regionalism*, Edinburgh University Press.

Carrington, B. 1998. '"Football's coming home". But whose home? And do we want it? Nation, football and the politics of exclusion', in Brown, A. (ed.), *Fanatics, Power, Identity and Fandom in Football,* London: Routledge, pp. 101–23.

Carroll, L. 1997. 'Muslim women and "Islamic divorce" in England', in Helie-Lucas, M.-A. and Kapoor, H. (eds.), *Dossier 19,* London: Women Living Under Muslim Laws (WLUML), pp. 51–74.

Castles, S. and Kosack, G. 1973. *Immigrant Workers and Class Structure in Western Europe*, London: Oxford University Press.

Cesari, J. and McLoughlin, S. (eds.) 2005. *European Muslims and the Secular State*, Aldershot: Ashgate.

Change Institute/Communities and Local Government. 2009a. 'The Iraqi Muslim Community in England', London: Change Institute/Communities and Local Government.

2009b. 'The Somali Muslim Community in England: Understanding Muslim Ethnic Communities', London: Change Institute/Communities and Local Government.

Charsley, K. 2007. 'Risk, trust, gender and transnational cousin marriage among British Pakistanis', *Ethnic and Racial Studies* **30** (6): 1117–31.

Cheal, D. 2002. *Sociology of Family Life*, London: Palgrave Macmillan.

Chew, S. 1937. *The Crescent and the Rose: Islam and England during the Renaissance*, New York: Octagon 1974.

Clark, P. 1986. *Marmaduke Pickthall: British Muslim*, London: Quartet Books.

Cobbold, E. 2008. *Pilgrimage to Mecca*, London: Arabian Publishing Ltd.

Cochrane, L. 1994. *Adelard of Bath: The First English Scientist*, London: British Museum Press.

Cohn-Sherbok, D. (ed.) 1990. *The Salman Rushdie Controversy in Interreligious Perspective*, Lampeter: Edwin Mellen Press.

Coleman, L. 2009. *Survey of Mosques in England and Wales*, London: Charity Commission.

Colley, L. 2000. 'Going native, telling tales: captivity, collaborations and Empire', *Past and Present* **168** (Aug): 170–93.

2002. *Captives*, New York: Pantheon Books.

Collins, S. 1957. *Coloured Minorities in Britain: Studies in Race Relations Based on African, West Indian and Asiatic Immigrants*, London: The Lutterworth Press.

Commins, D. 1991. 'Taqi al-Din Al-Nabhani and the Islamic Liberation Party', *The Muslim World* **LXXXI** (3–4): 194–211.

Communities and Local Government. 2008. 'Empowering Muslim Women: Case Studies', www.communities.gov.uk/publications/communities/empoweringmuslimwomen (accessed 29/1/08).

Connor, K. 2005. '"Islamism"in the West? The life-span of the Al-Muhajiroun in the United Kingdom', *Journal of Muslim Minority Affairs* **25** (1): 117–33.

Cressey, G. 2007. 'Muslim Girlswork: the ultimate separatist cage?' *Youth and Policy* **92** (1): 33–46.

Dahya, B. 1973. 'Pakistanis in Britain: transients or settlers?', *Race* **14** (3): 241–77.

  1974. 'The nature of Pakistani ethnicity in industrial cities in Britain', in Cohen, A. (ed.), *Urban Ethnicity*, London: Tavistock, pp. 77–118.

Dale, A. 2002. 'Social exclusion of Pakistani and Bangladeshi women', *Sociological Research Online* **7** (3).

Dale, A. Shahaeen, N. Kalra, V. and Fieldhouse, E. 2002. 'Routes into education and employment for young Pakistanis and Bangladeshi women in the UK', *Ethnic and Racial Studies* **25** (6): 942–68.

Dalrymple, W. 2002. 'Your country badly needs you. And your beard', *The Guardian*, 9 November.

Daniel, N. 1979. 'The impact of Islam on the laity in Europe from Charlemagne to Charles the Bold', in Weltch, A. T. and Chachia, T. (eds.), *Islam: Past Influence and Present Challenge*, Edinburgh University Press, pp. 105–25.

Daniel, W. 1968. *Racial Discrimination in England*, London: Penguin.

Davie, G. 1994. *Religion in Britain since 1945: Believing Without Belonging*, Oxford: Blackwell.

  2000. *Religion in Modern Europe: A Memory Mutates*, Oxford University Press.

Donohue, J. and Esposito, J. (eds.) 2007. *Islam in Transition: Muslim Perspectives*, Oxford University Press.

Draper, I. 1985. *A Case Study of a Sufi Order in Britain*, MA dissertation, University of Birmingham.

Draper, M. 2004. 'Sufism in Glastonbury: alternative spiritualities, alternative adaptations', in Westerlund, D. (ed.), *Sufism in Europe and North America*, London: Curzon RKP, pp. 144–56.

Dunlop, A. 1990. 'Lascars and labourers: reactions to the Indian presence in the West of Scotland during the 1920s and 1930s', *Scottish Labour History Society Journal* **25**: 40–57.

Dwyer, C. 1999a. 'Contradictions of community: questions of identity for young British Muslim women', *Environment and Planning A* **31**: 53–68.

  1999b. 'Negotiations of femininity and identity for young British Muslim women', in Laurie, N., Dwyer, C., Holloway, S. and Smith, F. (eds.), *Geographies of New Femininities*, Harlow: Pearson Education Ltd, pp. 135–202.

1999c. 'Veiled meanings: young British Muslim women and the negotiations of differences', *Gender, Place and Culture* **6** (1): 5–26.

2000. 'Negotiating diasporic identities: young British South Asian Muslim women', *Women's Studies International Forum* **23** (4): 457–86.

Dwyer, C. and Meyer, A. 1995. 'The institutionalisation of Islam in the Netherlands and in the UK: the case of Islamic Schools', *New Community* **21** (1): 37–54.

Dwyer, C. Shah, B. and Sanghera, G. 2008. '"From cricket lover to terror suspect" – challenging representations of young British Muslim men', *Gender, Place and Culture* **15** (2): 117–36.

Eade, J. 1993. 'The political articulation of community and the Islamisation of space in London', in Barot, R. (ed.), *Religion and Ethnicity*, Netherlands: Kok Pharos, pp. 29–42.

1996a. 'Ethnicity and the politics of cultural difference: an agenda for the 1990s', in Ranger, T., Samad, Y. and Stuart, O. (eds.), *Culture, Identity and Politics*, Aldershot: Avebury, pp. 57–66.

1996b. 'Nationalism, community, and the Islamization of space in London', in Metcalf, B. (ed.), *Making Muslim Space in North America and Europe*, Berkeley: University of California Press, pp. 217–33.

Edge, P. 2002. 'The construction of sacred places in English law', *Journal of Environmental Law* **14** (2): 161–83.

Eickelman, D. and Piscatori, J. (eds.) 2004. *'Muslim Politics'*, Oxford: Princeton University Press.

El-Fadl, K.A. 2001. 'Islam and the theology of power', www.merip.org/mer/mer221/221_abu_el_fadl.html (accessed 10/1/08).

El-Solh, C.F. 1993. '"Be True to Your Culture": gender tensions among Somali Muslims in Britain', *Immigrants and Minorities* **12** (1): 21–46.

Ellis, M. 2004. *The Coffee-House: A Cultural History*, London: Orion Books.

Enneli, P., Modood, T. and Bradley, H. 2005. *Young Turks and Kurds: A Set of 'Invisible' Disadvantaged Groups*, London: Joseph Rowntree Foundation.

Esposito, J. 1992. *The Islamic Threat: Myth or Reality?*, Oxford: OUP.

Esposito, J. and Voll, J. 2001. *Makers of Contemporary Islam*, Oxford University Press.

Evans, N. 1980. 'The South Wales Race Riots of 1919', *LLafur: Journal of the Society for the Study of Welsh Labour History* **3** (1): 5–29.

1985. 'Regulating the reserve army: Arabs, blacks and the local state in Cardiff, 1919–1945', *Immigrants and Minorities* **4** (2): 68–115.

Ewing, K. P. 1980. *The Pir or Sufi Saint in Pakistani Islam*, University of Chicago Press.

FAIR. 2002. *Employment Status in Relation to Statutory Employment Rights*, London: FAIR, The Muslim College, Al-Khoei Foundation.

Farazi, I. 2004. 'Sacred Culture of the Bean', *Q News*, **354**: 16–17.

Faruqi, Z.-u.-H. 1963. *The Deoband School and the Demand for Pakistan*, Bombay.

Faust, E. 2000. 'Close ties and new boundaries: Tablighi Jamaat in Britain and Germany', in Masud, M. (ed.), *Travellers in Faith: Studies of the Tablighi Jamaat as a Transnational Islamic Movement for Faith Renewal*, Leiden: Brill, pp. 139–60.

Fekete, L. 2008. 'Cultural Cleansing?', *European Race Bulletin* Winter (62).

Fernea, E. W. 1995. 'Family', in Esposito, J. (ed.), *The Oxford Encyclopaedia of the Modern Islamic World*, Oxford University Press, pp. 458–61.

Fetzer, J. and Soper, J. C. 2004. *Muslims and the State in Britain, France and Germany*, Cambridge University Press.

Fischer, J. 2008a. 'Feeding secularism: the halal market in London', www.ku.dk/Satsning/religion/sekularism_and_beyond/pdf/Fischer_Paper.pdf (accessed 9/12/08).

  2008b. 'Religion, science and markets', *European Molecular Biology Organisation* **9** (9): 828–31.

Fortier, A.-M. 2005. 'Pride politics and multiculturalist citizenship', *Ethnic and Racial Studies* **28** (3): 559–78.

Franks, M. 2000. 'Crossing the borders of whiteness? White Muslim women who wear the hijab in Britain today', *Ethnic and Racial Studies* **23**: 917–29.

Fryer, P. 1984. *Staying power: the history of black people in Britain*, London: Pluto Press.

Fuchs, B. 2000. 'Faithless empires: pirates, renegados, and the English nation', *English Literary History* **67** (Spring): 45–69.

Gailani, F. 2000. *The Mosques of London*, Henstridge, Somerset: Elm Grove Books.

Gale, R. 2004. 'The multicultural city and the politics of religious architecture: urban planning, mosques and meaning-making in Birmingham, UK', *Built Environment* **30** (1): 18–32.

  2007. 'The place of Islam in the geography of religion: trends and intersections', *Geography Compass* **1** (5): 1015–36.

Gale, R. and Naylor, S. 2003. 'Religion, planning and the city: the spatial politics of ethnic minority expression in British cities and towns', *Ethnicities* **2** (3): 387–409.

Gardner, K. 1998a, 'Death, burial and bereavement amongst Bengali Muslims in Tower Hamlets, East London', *Journal of Ethnic and Migration Studies* **24** (3): 507–23.

  1998b, 'Identity, age and masculinity amongst Bengali elders in East London', in Kershen, A. (ed.), *A Question of Identity*, Aldershot: Avebury, pp. 160–78.

  2002. *Age, Narrative and Migration: The Life Course and Life Histories of Bengali Elders in London*, Oxford: Berg.

Gatrad, A. R. 1994a. 'Medical implications of Islam for women and children', *Maternal and Child Health* July 1994: 225–7.

  1994b. 'Muslim customs surrounding death, bereavement, postmortem examinations, and organ transplants', *BMJ* **309** (20–27 August): 521–3.

Geaves, R. 1995. 'The reproduction of Jamaat-i-Islami in Britain', *Islam and Christian-Muslim Relations* **6** (2): 187–210.

1996a. 'Cult, charisma, community: the arrival of Sufi pirs and their impact on Muslims in Britain', *Journal – Institute of Muslim Minority Affairs* **16** (2): 169–92.

1996b. *Sectarian Influences Within Islam in Britain with reference to the concepts of 'ummah' and 'community'*, Leeds: Community Religions Project.

2000. *The Sufis of Britain*, Cardiff: Cardiff Academic Press.

2005. 'The dangers of essentialism: South Asian communities in Britain and the 'world religions' approach to the study of religions', *Contemporary South Asia* **14** (1): 75–90.

2008. 'Drawing on the past to transform the present: contemporary challenges for training and preparing British Imams', *Journal of Muslim Minority Affairs* **28** (1): 99–112.

2010. *Islam in Victorian Britain: The Life and Times of Abdullah Quilliam*, Leicester: Kube Publishing Ltd.

Gelsthorpe, V. and Herlitz, L. 2003. *Listening to the Evidence: The Future of UK Resettlement*, London: Home Office.

Gent, B. 2005. 'Intercultural learning: education and Islam – a case study', in Jackson, R. and McKenna, U. (eds.), *Intercultural Education and Religious Plurality*, Oslo Coalition on Freedom of Religion or Belief, pp. 43–53.

2006. *Muslim Supplementary Classes and the Wider Learning Community*, Ed.D thesis, Coventry, University of Warwick.

Gent, B. and Redbridge SACRE. 2003. *Muslim Madrasahs in Redbridge*. Briefing Paper no. 4.

Ghozzi, K. 2002. 'The study of resilience and decay in ulema groups: Tunisia and Iran as an example', *Sociology of Religion* **63** (3): 317–34.

Gilliat, S. 1997. 'A descriptive account of Islamic youth organisations in the UK', *American Journal of Islamic Social Sciences* **14** (1): 99–111.

Gilliat-Ray, S. 2000. *Religion in Higher Education: The Politics of the Multi-faith Campus*, Aldershot: Ashgate.

2005a. 'From "chapel" to "prayer room": the production, use, and politics of sacred space in public institutions', *Culture and Religion* **6** (2): 287–308.

2005b. '"Sacralising" sacred space: a case study of "prayer space" at the Millennium Dome', *Journal of Contemporary Religion* **20** (3): 357–72.

2005c. 'Sheikh Saeed', *Agenda: Journal of the Institute of Welsh Affairs*, Winter 2005/06: 5.

2006. 'Educating the 'ulema: centres of Islamic religious training in Britain', *Islam and Christian-Muslim Relations* **17** (1): 55–76.

2008. 'From "visiting minister" to "Muslim chaplain": the growth of Muslim chaplaincy in Britain, 1970–2007', in Barker, E. (ed.), *The Centrality of Religion in Social Life: Essays in Honour of James A. Beckford*, Aldershot: Ashgate, pp. 145–60.

2010. 'The first registered mosque in the UK, Cardiff, 1860: the evolution of a myth'. *Contemporary Islam*, 10.1007/s11562-010-0116-9.

Glavanis, P. 1998. 'Political Islam within Europe: a contribution to the analytical framework', *Innovation: The European Journal of Social Sciences* **11** (4): 391–410.

Goffman, E. 1959. *The Presentation of Self in Everyday Life*, London: Penguin.

Goldziher, I. 2007. 'Djamal al-Din al-Afghani, al-Sayyid Muhammad b. Safdar', in Bearman, P., Bianquis, T., Bosworth, C. E., Donzel, E. v. and Heinrichs, W. P. (eds.), *Encyclopaedia of Islam*, Leiden: Brill,.

Göle, N. 2002. 'Islam in Public: New Visibilities and New Imaginaries', *Public Culture* **14** (1): 173–90.

Goodey, J. 1999. 'Victims of racism and racial violence: experiences among boys and young men', *International Review of Victimology* **5** (3).

Gouldner, A. 1973. *For Sociology: Renewal and Critique in Sociology Today*, London: Allen Lane.

Grierson, P. 1974. 'Muslim coins in thirteenth-century England', in Kouymjian, D. (ed.), *Near Eastern Numismatics, Iconography, Epigraphy and History: studies in honour of George C. Miles*, Beirut: American University of Beirut, pp. 387–91.

Griffiths, D. 2002. *Somali and Kurdish Refugees in London*, Aldershot: Ashgate.

Haddad, Y. and Balz, M. 2008. 'Taming the Imams: European governments and Islamic preachers since 9/11', *Islam and Christian-Muslim Relations* **19** (2): 215–35.

Hafez, S. 2003. *Safe Children, Sound Learning: Guidance for Madressahs*, Huddersfield: Kirklees Metropolitan Council.

Haider, G. 1996. 'Muslim space and the practice of architecture', in Metcalf, B. D. (ed.), *Making Muslim Space in North America and Europe*, Berkeley: University of California Press, pp. 31–45.

Haim, S. 1982. 'Sayyid Qutb', *Asian and African Studies* **16** (1): 147–56.

Hall, S. 1992. 'New ethnicities', in Donald, J. and Rattansi, A. (eds.), *'Race', Culture and Difference*, London: Sage/Open University, pp. 252–9.

Halliday, F. 1992a, *Arabs in Exile: Yemeni Migrants in Urban Britain*, London: I B Tauris.

  1992b, 'The millet of Manchester: Arab merchants and the cotton trade', *British Journal of Middle Eastern Studies* **19** (2): 159–76.

Halstead, M. 1986. 'To what extent is the call for separate Muslim voluntary aided schools in the UK justifiable?', *Muslim Educational Quarterly* **3** (2): 5–26.

  2004. 'An Islamic concept of education', *Comparative Education* **40** (4): 517–29.

  2005. 'Muslims in the UK and Education', in Choudhury, T. (ed.), *Muslims in the UK: Policies for Engaged Citizens*, Budapest: Open Society Institute, pp. 101–92.

Hamid, S. 2007. 'Islamic political radicalism in Britain: the case of Hizb-ut-Tahrir', in Abbas, T. (ed.), *Islamic Political Radicalism: A European perspective*, Edinburgh University Press, pp. 145–59.

  2008a. 'The attraction of "authentic" Islam: Salafism and British Muslim youth', in Meijer, R. (ed.), *Salafism as a Transnational Movement*, London: Hurst,.

2008b. 'The development of British Salafism', *ISIM Review* **21** (Spring): 10–11.

Hamlett, J., Bailey, A., Alexander, A. and Shaw, G. 2008. 'Ethnicity and consumption: South Asian food shopping patterns in Britain, 1947–1975', *Journal of Consumer Culture* **8** (1): 91–116.

Haneef, S. 1979. *What Everyone Should Know about Islam and Muslims*, Lahore: Kazi Publications.

Haque, Z. 2000. 'The ethnic minority "underachieving" group? Investigating the claims of "underachievement" amongst Bangladeshi pupils in British secondary schools', *Race, Ethnicity and Education* **3** (2): 146–68.

Harrison, G. B. 1931. *A Second Elizabethan Journal: Being a Record of Those Things Most Talked of During the Years 1595–1598*, London: Routledge and Kegan Paul.

Hashem, M. 2006. 'Contemporary Islamic activism: the shades of praxis', *Sociology of Religion* **67** (1): 23–42.

Hashmi, N. 2003. *A Muslim School in Bristol? An Overview of the Current Debate and Muslim School Children's Views*, Centre for the Study of Ethnicity and Citizenship, Bristol University.

Hassani, S. Woodcock, E. and Saoud, R. (eds.) 2006. *1001 Inventions: Muslim Heritage in Our World*, Manchester: Foundation for Science Technology and Civilisation.

Haw, K. 1998. *Educating Muslim Girls: Shifting Discourses*, Milton Keynes: Open University Press.

Haynes, J. (ed.) 1986. *The Humanist as Traveler: George Sandys's Relation of a Journey begun An. Dom. 1610*, London/Toronto: Fairleigh Dickinson University Press.

Heath, I. 2007. *The Representation of Islam in British Museums. BAR International Series 1643*, Oxford: Archeopress.

Herrin, J. 1989. *The Formation of Christendom*, Princeton University Press.

Hesse, B. and Sayyid, S. 2006. 'Narrating the postcolonial political and the immigrant imaginary', in Ali, N., Kalra, V. and Sayyid, S. (eds.), *A Postcolonial People: South Asians in Britain*, London: Hurst, pp. 13–31.

Hewer, C. 2001. 'Schools for Muslims', *Oxford Review of Education* **27** (4): 515–27.

Hill, C. 1969. *Immigration and Integration*, Oxford: Pergamon Press.

Hinsliff, G. 2002. 'Speak English at home, Blunkett tells British Asians', www.guardian.co.uk/politics/2002/sep/15/race.immigrationpolicy (accessed19/4/08).

Holt, P. 1972. *17th Century Defender of Islam: Henry Stubbe (1632–76) and His Book*, London: Dr Williams's Trust.

Hopkins, P. 2006. 'Youthful Muslim masculinities: gender and generational relations', *Trans Inst Br Geogr NS* **31**: 337–52.

Hourani, A. 1991. *Islam in European Thought*, Cambridge University Press.

Howe, M. 2007. 'Shifting Muslim Gender and Family Norms in East London', New York, Paper presented at the American Sociological Association, 11 August.

Huq, M. 1975. 'How many Muslims in Britain?' *The Muslim*, August–September: 142.

Husain, E. 2007. *The Islamist*, London: Penguin.

Hussain, D. 2004, 'Councillors and Caliphs: Muslim political participation in Britain', in Seddon, M. S., Hussain, D. and Malik, N. (eds.), *British Muslims between Assimilation and Segregation: Historical, Legal and Social Realities*, Leicester: The Islamic Foundation, pp. 173–200.

  2006. 'Bangladeshis in East London: from secular politics to Islam', www.opendemocracy.net (accessed 21/11/08).

  2007. 'Identity formation and change in British Muslim communities', in Wetherell, M., Lafleche, M. and Berkeley, R. (eds.), *Identity, Ethnic Diversity and Community Cohesion*, London: Sage, pp. 34–9.

  2008. 'Islam', in Lodge, G. and Cooper, Z. (eds.), *Faith in the Nation: Religion, Identity and the Public Realm in Britain*, London: IPPR, pp. 39–46.

Hussain, S. 2004, 'An introduction to Muslims in the 2001 census', www.bristol.ac.uk/sociology/ethnicitycitizenship/intromuslims_census.pdf (accessed 10/11/04).

  2005. 'An annotated bibliography of recent literature on "invisible" Muslim communities and new Muslim migrant communities in Britain', www.compas.ox.ac.uk/publications/papers/Muslim%20Communities%20Annotate%20Bibliography%20090306.pdf (accessed 17/4/08).

  2008. *Muslims on the Map: A National Survey of Social Trends in Britain*, London: I B Tauris.

Hussain, Y. and Bagguley, P. 2005. 'Citizenship, ethnicity and identity: British Pakistanis after the 2001 "Riots"', *Sociology* **39** (3): 407–25.

Insoll, T. 2001. 'The archaeology of Islam', in Insoll, T. (ed.), *Archaeology and World Religion*, London: Routledge, pp. 123–47.

Iqbal, M. 1977. 'Education and Islam in Britain: a Muslim view', *New Community* **5** (4): 397–404.

IslamOnline.net. 2009. '*Restoring Britain's oldest mosque*', www.islamonline.net/servlet/Satellite?c=Article_C&cid=1230650228217&pagename=Zone-English-News%2FNWELayout (accessed Islam Online, 5/1/09).

Jacob, J. 1983. *Henry Stubbe, Radical Protestantism and the Early Enlightenment*, Cambridge University Press.

Jacobs, J. and Fincher, R. 1998. *Cities of Difference*, London: Guildford Press.

Jacobson, J. 1998. *Islam in Transition: Religion and Identity among British Pakistani Youth*, London: LSE/Routledge.

Jalil, J. 2004. 'Muslim comedians laugh at racism', http://news.bbc.co.uk/1/hi/world/americas/3796109.stm (accessed 19/9/08).

Jamal, A. 2003. 'Retailing in a multicultural world: the interplay of retailing, ethnic identity and consumption', *Journal of Retailing and Consumer Services* **10** (1): 1–11.

Jawad, H. 1998. *The Rights of Women in Islam*, Basingstoke: Macmillan.

Jawad, H. and Benn, T. 2003. *Muslim Women in the United Kingdom and Beyond*, Leiden: Brill.

Jeffery, P. 1976. *Migrants and Refugees*, Cambridge University Press.

Johnston, P. 2006. 'Reid meets the furious face of Islam', *The Telegraph*, 21 September.

Joly, D. 1984. *The Opinions of Mirpuri Parents in Saltley, Birmingham, about their Children's Schooling*, Birmingham: CSIC.

 1995. *Britannia's Crescent: Making a Place for Muslims in British Society*, Aldershot: Avebury.

Jones, N. 1978. 'The adaptation of tradition: the image of the Turk in Protestant England', *Eastern European Quarterly* **12** (2): 161–75.

Kabeer, S.A. 2007. 'Rep that Islam: the rhyme and reason of American Islamic hip hop', *The Muslim World* **97** (January): 125–41.

Kahera, A.I. 2002. 'Urban enclaves, Muslim identity and the urban mosque in America', *Journal of Muslim Minority Affairs* **22** (2): 369–80.

Kalin, I. 2004. 'Roots of misconception: Euro-American perceptions of Islam before and after September 11', in Lumbard, J. (ed.), *Islam, Fundamentalism, and the Betrayal of Tradition: Essays by Western Muslim Scholars*, Bloomington, Indiana: World Wisdom, pp. 143–90.

Kalra, V. 2000. *From Textile Mills to Taxi Ranks: Experiences of Migration, Labour and Social Change*, Aldershot: Ashgate.

 2004. 'The political economy of the samosa', *South Asia Research* **24** (1): 21–36.

Karmi, G. 1997. *The Egyptians of Britain: A Migrant Community in Transition*, Centre for Middle Eastern and Islamic Studies, University of Durham.

Kay, T. 2006. 'Daughters of Islam: family influences on Muslim young women's participation in sport', *International Review for the Sociology of Sport* **41** (3–4): 357–73.

Kechichian, J. 1986. 'The role of the 'ulama' in the politics of an Islamic state: the case of Saudi Arabia', *International Journal of Middle East Studies* **18** (1): 53–71.

Kelly, P. 1999. 'Integration and identity in Muslim schools: Britain, United States and Montreal', *Islam and Christian-Muslim Relations* **10** (2): 197–217.

Kerbaj, R. 2009. 'Muslim population "rising 10 times faster than rest of society"', *Times Online*, 30 January.

Khalid, F. 2002. 'Islam and the environment', in Timmerman, P. (ed.), *Encyclopaedia of Global Environmental Change*, Chichester: John Wiley, pp. 332–9.

Khan, A. 2006, *A Boy from Bolton: My Story*, London: Bloomsbury.

Khan, A.T. 1810. *Travels of Mirza Abu Taleb Khan in Asia, Africa and Europe during the years 1799–1083. Written in Persian and translated by Charles Stewart*, London: Longman, Hurst, Rees and Orme.

Khan, H. 2004a. 'Fatherless ummah', *Q News*, **355**: 32–3.

 2004b. 'Who speaks for British Muslims?', *Q News*, **354**: 24–5.

 2007. *In conversation with Muslim dads*, London: Fathers Direct/An-Nisa Society.

Khan, S. 2006, 'New Sufis for New Labour', *Muslim News*, 25 August.

Khanum, S. 1992a. 'Education and the Muslim girl', in Yuval-Davis, N. and Sahgal, G. (eds.), *Refusing Holy Orders: Women and Fundamentalism in Britain*, London: Virago Press, pp. 124–40.

1992b. 'The search for power', *New Statesman and Society* **5** (184): 14–15.

1994. *We just buy illness in exchange for hunger: experiences of health care, health and illness among Bangladeshi women in Britain*, PhD thesis, Keele University.

Khattak, S. K. K. 2008. *Islam and the Victorians: Nineteenth Century Perceptions of Muslim Practices and Beliefs*, London: I B Tauris.

'Khwaja Kamal-ud-Din – the torch-bearer of Islam', 1922. *Islamic Review* **10**: 8–11.

Kibria, N. 2008. 'The "new Islam" and Bangladeshi youth in Britain and the US', *Ethnic and Racial Studies* **31** (2): 243–66.

Kidwai, A. 1987. 'Translating the untranslatable: a survey of English translations of the Quran', *Muslim World Book Review* **7** (4): 66–71.

King, J. 1997. 'Tablighi Jamaat and the Deobandi mosques in Britain', in Vertovec, S. and Peach, C. (eds.), *Islam in Europe: the politics of religion and community*, Basingstoke: Macmillan Press, pp. 129–46.

King, O. 2006. 'Criticism for new Muslim organisation', www.guardian.co.uk/religion/Story/0.,1824131.00.html (accessed 28/9/06).

Knott, K. and Khokher, S. 1993. 'Religious and ethnic identity among young Muslim women in Bradford', *New Community* **19** (4): 593–610.

Kose, A. 1996. *Conversion to Islam: A Study of Native British Converts*, London: Kegan Paul.

Kramer, M. 2003. 'Coming to terms: fundamentalists or islamists?' *Middle East Quarterly* **10** (2): 65–78.

Kucukcan, T. 1999. *Politics of Ethnicity, Identity and Religion: Turkish Muslims in Britain*, Aldershot: Ashgate.

Kundnani, A. 2007a. *The End of Tolerance: Racism in 21st Century Britain*, London: Pluto Press.

2007b. 'Integrationism: the politics of anti-Muslim racism', *Race and Class* **48** (4): 24–44.

Landman, N. 1991. 'Muslims and Islamic Institutions in the Netherlands', *Journal Institute of Muslim Minority Affairs* **12** (2): 410–32.

Lapidus, I. 2002. *A History of Islamic Societies*, Cambridge University Press.

Lawless, R. 1994. 'Religion and politics among Arab seafarers in Britain in the early twentieth century', *Islam and Christian-Muslim Relations* **5** (1): 35–56.

1995. *From Ta'izz to Tyneside: An Arab Community in the North East of England in the Early 20th Century*, University of Exeter Press.

1997. 'Muslim migration to the north east of England during the early twentieth century', *Local Historian* **27** (4): 225–44.

Leiken, R. and Brooke, S. 2007. 'The moderate Muslim Brotherhood', http://find.galegroup.com/itx/start.do?prodID=EAIM (accessed 29/10/07).

Lewis, B. 1993. *Islam and the West*, Oxford University Press.

Lewis, P. 1994. *Islamic Britain: Religion, Politics and Identity among British Muslims*, London: I.B. Tauris.

2006a. 'Mosques, 'ulama' and Sufis: providers of bridging social capital for British Pakistanis?' *Contemporary South Asia* **15** (3): 273–87.

2006b. 'Only connect: can the ulema address the crisis in the transmission of Islam to a new generation of South Asians in Britain?', *Contemporary South Asia* **15** (2): 165–80.

2007. *Young, British, and Muslim*, London: Continuum.

Lewis, P. and Laville, S. 2006. 'Ordinary friends who grew devout together', *The Guardian*, 12 August.

Li, K. 2003. 'Scotland's Tartan Mosque', *Dialogue: Newsletter of the Public Affairs Committee for Shi'a Muslims*, June: 4.

Lloyd Evans, S. and Bowlby, S. 2000. 'Crossing Boundaries: racialised gendering and the labour market experiences of Pakistani migrant women in Britain', *Women's Studies International Forum* **23** (4): 461–74.

Maan, B. 2008. *The Thistle and the Crescent*, Argyll: Argyll Publishing.

MacEoin, D. 2007. *The Hijacking of British Islam: How Extremist Literature is Subverting Mosques in the UK*, London: Policy Exchange.

Macey, M. 1999a. 'Class, gender and religious influences on changing patterns of Pakistani Muslim male violence in Bradford', *Ethnic and Racial Studies* **22** (5): 845–66.

1999b. 'Religion, male violence, and the control of women: Pakistani Muslim men in Bradford, UK', *Gender and Development* **7** (1): 48–55.

MacLean, G. 2007. *Looking East: English Writing and the Ottoman Empire before 1800*. London: Palgrave Macmillan.

Makdisi, G. 1974. 'The Scholastic method in Medieval education: an inquiry into its origins in law and theology', *Speculum* **49** (4): 640–61.

1976. 'Interaction between Islam and the West', *Revue des Etudes Islamiques* **54**: 273–312.

Malieckal, B. 1999. '"Hell's Perfect Character": the black woman as the Islamic Other in Fletcher's The Knight of Malta', *Essays in Arts and Sciences* **28** (October): 53–68.

Mandaville, P. 2001. *Transnational Muslim Politics: Reimagining the Ummah*, London: Routledge.

2005a. 'The Salafi movement: violence and the fragmentation of commu- nity', in Cooke, M. and Lawrence, B. (eds.), *Muslim Networks: From Hajj to Hip Hop*, Chapel Hill, NC: University of North Carolina Press, pp. 208–34.

2005b. 'Sufis and Salafis: the political discourse of transnational Islam', in Heffner, R. (ed.), *Muslim Politics: Pluralism, Contestation, Democratisation*, Princeton University Press, pp. 302–25.

Manzoor, S. 2007. *Greetings from Bury Park: Race. Religion. Rock 'n' Roll*, London: Bloomsbury.

Maqsood, R. W. 2005. *The Role of the Mosque in Britain*, London: Muslim Parliament of Great Britain.

Marechal, B. 2008. *The Muslim Brothers in Europe: Roots and Discourse*, Leiden: Brill.

Marranci, G. 2004. 'Constructing an Islamic environment in Northern Ireland', *Built Environment* **30** (1): 17–29.

Marshall, J. 1994. 'The mosque on Erb Street', *Environments* **22** (2): 55–66.

Martin, P. Creese, A. Bhatt, A. and Bhojani, N. 2004. *A Final Report on Complementary Schools and their Communities in Leicester*, University of Leicester School of Education.

Masood, E. 2005. 'The globalisation of Islamic relief', www.opendemocracy.net/ globalization/relief_3072.jsp (accessed 22/6/09).

    2006a. *British Muslims: Media Guide*, London: British Council.

    2006b. 'Islam's reformers', *Prospect*, **124**: 20–3.

Mastnak, T. 2002. *Crusading Peace: Christendom, the Muslim World, and the Western Political Order*, London: University of California Press.

Masud, M. K. (ed.) 2000. *Travellers in Faith: Studies of the Tablighi Jamaat as a Transnational Islamic Movement for Faith Renewal*, Leiden: Brill.

Matar, N. 1993. 'The renegade in English seventeenth-century imagination', *Studies in English Literature* **33** (3): 489–506.

    1997. 'Muslims in seventeenth-century England', *Journal of Islamic Studies* **8** (1): 63–82.

    1998. *Islam in Britain: 1558–1685*, Cambridge University Press.

    2001. 'English accounts of captivity in North Africa and the Middle East: 1577–1625', *Renaissance Quarterly* **54** (2): 553–72.

Mayer, J.-F. 2004. 'Hizb ut-Tahrir – the next al-Qaida, really?' http://hei.unige. ch/psio/fichiers/Meyer%20Al%20Qaida.pdf (accessed 7/11/07).

Mazumdar, S. and Mazumdar, S. 2002. 'In mosques and shrines: women's agency in public sacred space', *Journal of Ritual Studies* **16** (2): 165–79.

'MCB comeback?' 2007. *Prospect*, **138**: 6.

McDermott, M. and Ahsan, M. 1980. *The Muslim Guide: for Teachers, Employers, Community Workers and Social Administrators in Britain*, Leicester: Islamic Foundation.

McKerl, M. 2007. 'Multiculturalism, gender and violence: multiculturalism – is it bad for women?' *Culture and Religion* **8** (2): 187–217.

McLoughlin, S. 1998a. 'The mosque-centre, community-mosque: multi-functions, funding and the reconstruction of Islam in Bradford', *Scottish Journal of Religious Studies*. **19** (2): 211–27.

    1998b. 'A-part of the Community? The politics of representation and a Muslim school's application for state funding', *Innovation: The European Journal of Social Sciences* **11** (4): 451–70.

    2005a. 'Migration, diaspora and transnationalism: transformations of religion and culture in a globalising age', in Hinnells, J. (ed.), *Routledge Companion to the Study of Religion*, London: Routledge, pp. 526–49.

    2005b. 'Mosques and the public space: conflict and cooperation in Bradford', *Journal of Ethnic and Migration Studies* **31** (6): 1045–1066.

2005c. 'The state, new Muslim leaderships and Islam as a resource for public engagement in Britain', in Cesari, J. and McLoughlin, S. (eds.), *European Muslims and the Secular State*, Aldershot: Ashgate, pp. 55–70.

Meer, N. 2006. '"Get off your knees": print media public intellectuals and Muslims in Britain', *Journalism Studies* 7 (1): 35–59.

2007. 'Muslim schools in Britain: challenging mobilisations or logical developments?', *Asia Pacific Journal of Education* 27 (1): 55–71.

Metcalf, B. 1982, *Islamic Revival in British India: Deoband 1860–1900*, Princeton University Press.

1993. 'Living Hadith in the Tablighi Jama'at', *Journal of Asian Studies* 52 (3): 584–608.

2002. *'Traditionalist' Islamic Activism: Deoband, Tablighis, and Talibs*, Leiden: ISIM.

2008. *Husain Ahmad Madani: The Jihad for Islam and India's Freedom*, Oxford: Oneworld.

Metcalf, D. M. 1982, 'Anglo-Saxon coins I: seventh to ninth centuries', in Campbell, J. (ed.), *The Anglo-Saxons*, London: Phaidon Press, pp. 62–3.

Miah, S. 2005. 'How the East London Mosque's imam encouraged Sajid Miah to work with young people', *Voluntary Voice (London Voluntary Service Council)* (**188**): 19.

Milton, G. 2004. *White Gold: The Extraordinary Story of Thomas Pellow and North Africa's One Million European Slaves*, London: Hodder and Stoughton.

Mirza, H. S. 2002. 'Women and society', http://news.bbc.co.uk/hi/english/static/in_depth/uk/2002/race/women_and_society.stm (accessed 19/05/06).

Mirza, K. 1989. *The Silent Cry: Second Generation Bradford Women Speak*, Birmingham: CSIC.

Mirza, M., Senthilkumaran, A., and Zein, J. 2007. *Living Apart Together: British Muslims and the Paradox of Multiculturalism*, London: Policy Exchange.

Mitchell, R. 1969. *The Society of the Muslim Brothers*, London: Oxford University Press.

Modood, T. 1989. 'Religious anger and minority rights', *Political Quarterly* (July): 280–4.

1990a. 'British Asian Muslims and the Rushdie affair', *Political Quarterly* 61 (2): 143–60.

1990b. 'Muslims, race and equality in Britain: post-Rushdie reflections', *Third Text* 11 (Summer): 127–34.

1998. 'Anti-essentialism, multiculturalism and the "recognition" of religious groups', *Journal of Political Philosophy* 6 (4): 378–99.

2005a. *Multicultural Politics: Racism, Ethnicity and Muslims in Britain*, Edinburgh University Press.

2005b. 'Remaking multiculturalism after 7/7 Tariq Modood – openDemocracy', www.opendemocracy.net/conflict-terrorism/multiculturalism_2879.jsp (accessed 30/9/05).

2006. 'Ethnicity, Muslims and higher education entry in Britain', *Teaching in Higher Education* **11** (2): 247–50.

Modood, T., Berthoud, R., Lakey, J., Nazroo, J., Smith, P., Virdee, S. and Beishon, S. (eds.) 1997. *Ethnic Minorities in Britain: Diversity and Disadvantage*, London: Policy Studies Institute.

Mogra, I. 2004. 'Makatib Education in Britain: a review of trends and some suggestions for policy', *Muslim Education Quarterly* **21** (4): 19–27.

2005. 'Moving forward with Makatib: the role of reformative sanctions', *Muslim Education Quarterly* **22** (3&4): 52–64.

Mohammed, Ali. 2004. '*Aerosol Arabic: graffiti for God*', www.bbc.co.uk/birmingham/faith/2004/05/aerosol_arabic.shtml (accessed 19/9/08).

Mohammad, R. 1999. 'Marginalisation, Islamism and the Production of the "Other's" "Other"', *Gender, Place and Culture* **6** (3): 221–40.

2005a. 'British Pakistani Muslim women: marking the body, marking the nation', in Nelson, L. and Seager, J. (eds.), *A Companion to Feminist Geography*, Oxford: Blackwell, pp. 379–97.

2005b. 'Negotiating spaces of the home, the education system, and the labour market: the case of young, working-class, British Pakistani Muslim women', in Falah, G.-W. and Nagel, C. (eds.), *Geographies of Muslim Women: Gender, Religion and Space*, New York: Guildford Press, pp. 178–200.

Mohammed, K. 2005. 'Assessing English translations of the Qur'an', *Middle East Quarterly* **12** (2): 59–72.

Moll, Y. 2007. 'Beyond beards, scarves and halal meat: mediated constructions of British Muslim identity', *Journal of Religion and Popular Culture* **15** (Spring): 1–32.

Mondal, A. 2008. *Young British Muslim Voices*, Oxford: Greenwood World Publishing Ltd.

Moore, K. Mason, P. and Lewis, J. 2008. *Images of Islam in the UK: The Representation of British Muslims in the National Print News Media 2000–2008*, Cardiff School of Journalism, Media and Cultural Studies.

Mukadam, A. and Mawani, S. 2009. 'Excess baggage or precious gems? The migration of cultural commodities', in Hopkins, P. and Gale, R. (eds.), *Muslims in Britain: Race, Place and Identities*, Edinburgh University Press, pp. 150–68.

Munson, Z. 2001. 'Islamic mobilization: social movement theory and the Egyptian Muslim Brotherhood', *The Sociological Quarterly* **42** (4): 487–510.

Murad, A. H. 1997. 'British and Muslim?' www.islamfortoday.com/murad05.htm (accessed 7/10/2005).

2003. 'Ward the Pirate', *Seasons*, Spring/Summer: 61–4.

2005. *Muslim Songs of The British Isles*, London: The Quilliam Press Ltd.

Murata, S. 1992. *The Tao of Islam: A Sourcebook on Gender Relationships in Islamic Thought*, New York: State University of New York Press.

Murata, S. and Chittick, W. 2000. *The Vision of Islam*, London: IB Tauris.

Mustafa, B. 1999. 'Education for integration: case study of a British Muslim high school for girls', *Journal of Muslim Minority Affairs* **19** (2): 291–8.

Nafi, B. 2004. 'The rise of Islamic reformist thought and its challenge to traditional Islam', in Taji-Farouki, S. and Nafi, B. (eds.), *Islamic Thought in the Twentieth Century*, London: I B Tauris, pp. 28–60.

Nagel, C. 2001. 'Hidden Minorities and the politics of "race": the case of British Arab activists in London', *Journal of Ethnic and Migration Studies* **27** (3): 381–400.

Nagel, C. and Staeheli, L. 2009. 'British Arab perspectives on religion, politics and "the public"', in Hopkins, P. and Gale, R. (eds.), *Muslims in Britian: Race, Place and Identities*, Edinburgh University Press, pp. 95–112.

Narayan, U. 1995. 'Eating cultures: incorporation, identity and Indian food', *Social Identities* **1** (1): 63–86.

Nasser, N. 2005. 'Expressions of Muslim identity in architecture and urbanism in Birmingham, UK', *Islam and Christian–Muslim Relations* **16** (1): 61–78.
    2006. 'Metropolitan borderlands: the formation of BrAsian Landscapes', in Ali, N., Kalra, V. and Sayyid, S. (eds.), *A Postcolonial People: South Asians in Britain*, London: Hurst & Company, pp. 374–91.

Nazroo, J. 1997. 'Health and health services', in Modood, T., Berthoud, R., Lakey, J., Nazroo, J., Smith, P., Virdee, S. and Beishon, S. (eds.), *Ethnic Minorities in Britain: Diversity and Disadvantage*, London: Policy Studies Institute, pp. 224–58.

Neal, F. 1988. *Sectarian Violence: The Liverpool Experience, 1819–1914: An Aspect of Anglo-Irish History*, Manchester University Press.

Nielsen, J. 1981. 'Muslim education at home and abroad', *British Journal of Religious Education* **3** (3): 94–9.
    1989. 'Muslims in English schools', *Journal Institute of Muslim Minority Affairs* **10** (1): 223–45.
    2004. *Muslims in Western Europe*, Edinburgh University Press.

Nieuwkerk, K. v. 2008. 'Creating an Islamic cultural sphere: contested notions of art, leisure and entertainment. An introduction', *Contemporary Islam* **2** (2): 169–76.

Norfolk, A. 2007. 'Muslim group behind "mega-mosque" seeks to convert all Britain', *The Times*, 10 September.

North, C. 1986. *Islam in Schools and Madrasahs*, MA dissertation, Birmingham, University of Birmingham.

Nye, M. 2000. *Multiculturalism and Minority Religions in Britain*, London: Curzon.

O' Neill, S. and McGrory, D. 2006. *The Suicide Factory: Abu Hamza and the Finsbury Park Mosque*, London: Harper Collins.

O' Sullivan, J. 2003. 'Defender of his faith', *The Guardian*, 15 January.

Odone, C. 2008a. *In Bad Faith: The Betrayal of Faith Schools*, London: Centre for Policy Studies.

2008b. 'Learning to be British and Muslim', www.timesonline.co.uk/tol/news/uk/education/article4231194.ece (accessed 15/8/08).

Omaar, R. 2006. *Only Half of Me: Being a Muslim in Britain*, London: Viking.
  2005. *Muslims in the UK: Policies for Engaged Citizens*, 2005. Hungary, Budapest: Open Society Institute.

Open Society Institute. 2002. *Monitoring Minority Protection in the EU: The Situation of Muslims in the UK*, Budapest: Open Society Institute, EU Accession Monitoring Program.

Osler, A. and Hussain, Z. 2005. 'Educating Muslim girls: do mothers have faith in the state sector?', in Abbas, T. (ed.), *Muslim Britain: Communities under Pressure*, London: Zed Books, pp. 127–43.

Ouseley, S. H. 2001. *Community Pride – Not Prejudice: Making Diversity Work in Bradford*, Bradford: Bradford Vision.

Ouzgane, L. 2003. 'Islamic masculinities: an introduction', *Men and Masculinities* **5** (3): 231–5.

*The Oxford Dictionary of Islam*. 2003. Oxford University Press.

Parker-Jenkins, M. 1995. *Children of Islam: A Teacher's Guide to meeting the needs of Muslim pupils*, Stoke on Trent: Trentham Books.
  2002. 'Equal access to state funding: the case of Muslim schools in Britain', *Race, Ethnicity and Education* **5** (3): 273–89.

Parr, A. (ed.) 1996. *Three Renaissance Travel Plays: The Travels of the Three English Brothers, the Sea Voyage, the Antipodes*, Manchester University Press.

Pattison, S. 2001. 'Dumbing down the spirit', in Orchard, H. (ed.), *Spirituality in Health Care Contexts*, London: Jessica Kingsley Publishers, pp. 33–46.

Peach, C. 2006. 'Muslims in the 2001 Census of England and Wales: gender and economic disadvantage', *Ethnic and Racial Studies* **29** (4): 629–55.

Peach, C. and Vertovec, S. (eds.) 1997. *Islam in Europe: The Politics of Religion and Community*, Basingstoke: Macmillan.

Pearl, D. and Menski, W. 1998. *Muslim Family Law*, London: Sweet & Maxwell.

Pedziwiatr, K. 2007. 'Creating new discursive arenas and influencing the policies of the state: the case of the Muslim Council of Britain', *Social Compass* **54** (2): 267–80.

Penn, R. and Lambert, P. 2002. 'Attitudes towards ideal family size of different ethnic/nationality groups in Great Britain, France and Germany', *Population Trends* **108** (Summer): 49–58.

Peskes, E. and Ende, W. 2007. 'Wahhabiyya', www.brillonline.nl/subscriber/entry?entry=islam_COM-1329 (accessed 23/10/2007).

Peter, F. 2003. 'Islamic activism, interfaith dialogue and identity politics: the Islamic Foundation in Leicester, 1972–2003', in Koningsveld, P. S. v. (ed.), *Proceedings of Leiden Institute for the Study of Religions*, University of Leiden.

Petersen, A. 2008. 'The archaeology of Islam in Britain: recognition and potential', *Antiquities* **82** (318): 1080–92.

Phillips, D. 2006. 'Parallel lives? Challenging discourses of British Muslim self-segregation', *Environment and Planning D: Society and Space* **24**: 25–40.

2009. 'Creating home spaces: young British Muslim women's identity and conceptualisations of home', in Hopkins, P. and Gale, R. (eds.), *Muslims in Britain: Race, Place and Identities*, Edinburgh University Press, pp. 23–36.

Phillips, R. 2008. 'Standing Together: the Muslim Association of Britain and the anti-war movement', *Race and Class* **50** (2): 101–13.

Phillipson, C., Ahmed, N. and Latimer, J. 2003. *Women in Transition: A Study of the Experiences of Bangladeshi Women Living in Tower Hamlets*, Bristol: The Policy Press.

Phoenix, A. 1997. 'The place of "race" and ethnicity in the lives of children and young people', *Educational and Child Psychology* **14** (3): 5–24.

Phoenix, A. and Pattynama, P. 2006. 'Intersectionality', *European Journal of Women's Studies* **13** (3): 187–92.

Pool, J. J. 1892. *Studies in Mohammedanism*, London: Archibald Constable & Co.

Poole, E. 2002. *Reporting Islam*, London: I B Tauris.

Poole, E. and Richardson, J. (eds.) 2006. *Muslims and the News Media*, London: I B Tauris.

Porter, V. and Ager, B. 1999. 'Islamic amuletic seals: the case of the Ballycottin cross brooch', in Gyselen, R. (ed.), *La science des crieux: sages, mages, astrologues (Res Orientales 12)*, Bures-sur-Yvette: Groupe pour l'étude de la civilisation du Moyen-Orient, pp. 211–18.

Purdam, K. 2000. 'The political identities of Muslim local councillors in Britain', *Local Government Studies* **26** (1): 47–64.

2001. 'Democracy in practice: Muslims and the Labour Party at the local level', *Politics* **21** (3): 147–57.

Radcliffe, L. 2004. 'A Muslim lobby at Whitehall? Examining the role of the Muslim minority in British foreign policy making', *Islam and Christian–Muslim Relations* **15** (3): 365–86.

Rahman, S., Ahmed, S. T. and Khan, S. 2006. *Voices from the Minaret: MCB study of UK Imams and Mosques*, London: Muslim Council of Britain.

Ram, M., Jones, T., Abbas, T. and Sanghera, B. 2002. 'Ethnic minority enterprise in its urban context: South Asian restaurants in Birmingham', *International Journal of Urban and Regional Research* **26** (1): 24–40.

Ram, M., Sanghera, B., Abbas, T., Barlow, G. and Jones, T. 2000. 'Ethnic minority business in comparative perspective: the case of the independent restaurant sector', *Journal of Ethnic and Migration Studies* **26** (3): 495–510.

Ramadan, T. 2004. *Western Muslims and the Future of Islam*, Oxford University Press.

2007. *The Messenger: The Meanings of the Life of Muhammad*, London: Penguin/Allen Lane.

Raz, A. 2006. *She Who Disputes: Muslim Women Shape the Debate*, London: Women's National Commission.

Raza, M. S. 1991. *Islam in Britain*, Leicester: Volcano Press.

Reddie, R. 2009. *Black Muslims in Britain*, Oxford: Lion.

Reeber, M. 1990. *Islam, Islamism and Secularity*, Birmingham: CSIC.

Reed, P. 1974. *Moslem adolescent boys in Batley*, M.Phil. thesis, University of York.

Riley-Smith, J. 1987. *The Crusades: A Short History*, London: The Athlone Press.
2002. *What Were the Crusades?*, Basingstoke: Macmillan.
2008. *The Crusades, Christianity and Islam*, New York: Columbia University Press.

Rippin, A. 2005. *Muslims: Their Religious Beliefs and Practices*, London: Routledge.

Roald, A. S. 2001. *Women in Islam: The Western Experience*, London: Routledge.

Robert, N. B. 2005. *From My Sister's Lips*, London: Bantam Press.

Robinson-Dunne, D. 2003. 'Lascar sailors and English converts: the imperial port and Islam in late 19th-century england', Washington DC, 12–15 February, Seascapes, Littoral Cultures and Trans-Oceanic Exchanges, www.historycooperative.org/proceedings/seascapes/dunn.html, (accessed 31/1/06).
2006. *The Harem, Slavery and British Imperial Culture: Anglo-Muslim Relations in the Late Nineteenth Century*, Manchester University Press.

Robinson, C. 2007. 'Today's lecture: the good Muslim', *Times Higher Education Supplement*, 13 July.

Roff, W. 1983. 'Whence cometh the law? Dog saliva in Kelantan, 1937', *Comparative Studies in Society and History* **25** (2): 323–38.

Rozario, S. 2009. 'Allah is the scientist of scientists: modern medicine and religious healing among British Bangladeshis', *Culture and Religion* **10** (2): 177–99.

Rozario, S. and Gilliat-Ray, S. 2007. *Genetics, Religion and Identity: A Study of British Bangladeshis*, Cardiff University School of Social Sciences Working Paper Series no. 93.

Rutherford, J. 1998. 'Introduction', in Rutherford, J. (ed.), *Young Britain: Politics, Pleasures and Predicaments*, London: Lawrence & Wishart, pp. 7–30.

Ruthven, M. 1997. *Islam: A Very Short Introduction*, Oxford University Press.

Ryan, J. and Naylor, S. 2002. 'The mosque in the suburbs: negotiating religion and ethnicity in South London', *Social and Cultural Geography* **3** (1): 39–59.

Safi, L. 2005. 'Towards women-friendly mosques', *American Journal of Islamic Social Sciences* **22** (3): 148–57.

Sahgal, G. and Yuval-Davis, N. (eds.) 1992. *Refusing Holy Orders: Women and Fundamentalism in Britain*, London: Virago Press.

Said, E. 1997. *Covering Islam: How the Media and the Experts Determine How We See the Rest of the World*, London: Vintage.

Saifullah-Khan, V. 1975. *Pakistani Villagers in a British City*, PhD thesis, University of Bradford.
1976. 'Pakistanis in Britain: perceptions of a population', *New Community* **5** (3): 222–9.

Saini, A. 2004. '"Islam for me was more punk than punk": Aki Nawaz interviewed', www.opendemocracy.net/globalization-world/article_2138.jsp (accessed 6/2/08).

Salter, J. 1873. *The Asiatic in England: Sketches of Sixteen Years' Work among the Orientals*, London: Seeley, Jackson & Halliday.

1895. *The East in the West*, London: Partridge.

Samad, Y. 1998. 'Media and Muslim identity: intersections of generation and gender', *Innovation: The European Journal of Social Sciences* 11 (4): 425–38.

Sanyal, U. 1996. *Devotional Islam and Politics in British India*, Delhi: Oxford University Press.

Sardar, Z. 1996. 'At last we can stand up and be counted', *New Statesman* 129 (4492): 24.

2004. *Desperately Seeking Paradise: Journeys of a Sceptical Muslim*, London: Granta Books.

2006. 'Jack Straw's thinly veiled abuse of power', *New Statesman* 135 (4814): 23–4.

2008. *Balti Britain: A Journey through the British Asian Experience*, London: Granta Books.

Savage, T. 2004. 'Europe and Islam: crescent waxing, culture clashing', *Washington Quarterly* 27 (3): 25–50.

Scantlebury, E. 1995. 'Muslims in Manchester: the depiction of a religious community', *New Community* 21 (3).

Scarfe Beckett, K. 2003. *Anglo-Saxon Perceptions of the Islamic World*, Cambridge University Press.

Schacht, J. 2007. 'Muhammad "Abduh"', in Bearman, P., Bianquis, T., Bosworth, C.E., Donzel, E.v. and Heinrichs, W.P. (eds.), *Encyclopaedia of Islam*, Leiden: Brill.

Schimmel, A. 1995. 'Calligraphy', in Esposito, J. (ed.), *Oxford Encyclopaedia of the Modern Islamic World*, Oxford University Press, pp. 243–7.

Schoenherr, R. 1987. 'Power and authority in organised religion: disaggregating the phenomenological core', *Sociological Analysis* 47 (Summer): 52–71.

Scott, J. 1997. 'Changing households in Britain: do families still matter?' *Sociological Review* 45 (4): 591–620.

Scott, J., Treas, J. and Richard, M. (eds.) 2007. *The Blackwell Companion to the Sociology of Families*, Oxford: Wiley Blackwell.

The Search for Common Ground: Muslims, non-Muslims and the UK Media. A report commissioned by the Mayor of London, 2007. London: Greater London Authority.

Seddon, M.S. 2003. 'Muslim Travellers in Eighteenth-Century Britain', www. islamic-foundation.org.uk/articles/muslimTravellers.htm (accessed 24/1/06).

Serjeant, R.B. 1944. 'Yemeni Arabs in Britain', *The Geographical Magazine* 17 (4): 143–7.

Sha'ban, F. 1991. *Islam and Arabs in Early American Thought: The Roots of Orientalism in America*, North Carolina: Acorn Press.

Shah-Kazemi, S.N. 2001. *Untying the Knot: Muslim women, divorce and the Shariah – a study of the Muslim Law Shariah Council, UK*, London: Nuffield Foundation.

Shahin, E. E. 1995. 'Salafiyah', in Esposito, J. (ed.), *Oxford Encyclopaedia of the Modern Islamic World*, Oxford University Press, pp. 463–9.

Sharafuddin, M. 1994. *Islam and Romantic Orientalism: Literary Encounters with the Orient,* London: I B Tauris.

Shariatmadari, D. 2006. 'Two Types of Veiling', www.opendemocracy.net/faith-europe_islam/two_veils_3989.jsp (accessed 21/1/08).

Shaw, A. 1988. *A Pakistani Community in Britain*, Oxford: Blackwell.

2000. *Kinship and Continuity: Pakistani Families in Britain*, The Netherlands: Harwood Academic Publishers.

2001. 'Kinship, cultural preference and immigration: consanguineous marriage among British Pakistanis', *Journal of the Royal Anthropological Institute* **7**: 315–34.

Sheikh, A. and Gatrad, A. R. (eds.) 2000. *Caring for Muslim Patients*, Abingdon: Radcliffe Medical Press.

Sherif, J. 2002. *Historical Roots of Islam in Britain', in The Quest for Sanity: Reflections on September 11 and the Aftermath*, London: Muslim Council of Britain, pp. 163–74.

Sherwood, M. 1988. 'Racism and Resistance: Cardiff in the 1930s and 1940s', *LLafur: Journal of the Society for the Study of Welsh Labour History* **5** (4): 51–71.

Shirwani, H. 1999. 'Conference bug strikes Imams', *Q News*, **312**: 20–1.

Siapera, E. 2006. 'Multiculturalism, progressive politics and British Islam online', *International Journal of Media and Cultural Politics* **2** (3): 331–46.

Siddiq, S. M. 1934. 'Islam in England', *Islamic Review* **22** (1–2): 14–25.

Siddiqui, A. 2007. *Islam at Universities in England: meeting the needs and investing in the future*, London: Department for Innovation, Universities and Skills.

Sikand, Y. 1998. 'The origins and growth of the Tablighi Jamaat in Britain', *Islam and Christian–Muslim Relations* **9** (2): 171–92.

1999. 'Women and the Tablighi Jama'at', *Islam-and-Christian-Muslim–Relations* **10** (1): 41–53.

2006. 'The Tablighi Jama'at and politics: a critical re-appraisal', *Muslim World* **96** (Jan): 175–95.

Simms, R. 2002. '"Islam is our Politics": a Gramscian Analysis of the Muslim Brotherhood (1928–1953)', *Social Compass* **49** (4): 563–82.

Simpson, L. 2004. 'Statistics and Racial Segregation: measures, evidence and policy', *Urban Studies* **41** (3): 661–81.

Sinclair, K. 2008. 'Islam in Britain and Denmark: deterritorialized identity and reterritorialized agendas', *Journal of Muslim Minority Affairs* **28** (1): 45–52.

Sivan, E. 1989. 'Sunni Radicalism in the Middle East and the Iranian Revolution', *International Journal of Middle Eastern Studies* **21** (1): 1–30.

Skovgaard-Petersen, J. and Graf, B. (eds.) 2009. *Global Mufti: The Phenomenon of Yusuf al-Qaradawi*, London: Hurst.

Smith, B. P. 1977, *Islam in English Literature*, New York: Caravan Books.

Smith, D. 1977, *Racial Disadvantage in Britain*, London: Penguin.

Sonn, T. 2004. *A Brief History of Islam*, Oxford: Blackwell.

Southern, R. W. 1962. *Western Views of Islam in the Middle Ages*, Massachusetts: Harvard University Press.

Southworth, J. 2005. '"Religion" in the 2001 Census for England and Wales', *Population, Space and Place* **11**: 75–88.

Spalek, B. and Wilson, D. 2001. 'Not just "visitors" to prisons: the experiences of Imams who work inside the penal system', *Howard Journal* **40** (1): 3–13.

Spellman, K. 2004. *Religion and Nation: Iranian Local and Transnational Networks in Britain*, Oxford: Berghahn Books.

Sporton, D., Valentine, G. and Nielsen, K. 2005. 'Post-conflict identities: practices and affiliations of Somali refugee children', www.identities.group. shef.ac.uk/pdfs/Briefing%20Somali%20Migration%20to%20the%20UK. pdf (accessed 10/1/08).

Stopes-Roe, M. and Cochrane, R. 1990. *Citizens of this Country: The Asian British*, Clevedon: Multilingual Matters.

Syed, A. 1984. *Pakistan, Islam, Politics and National Solidarity*, Lahore.

Taji-Farouki, S. 1996. *A Fundamental Quest: Hizb al-Tahrir and the Search for the Islamic Caliphate*, London: Grey Seal.

   2000. 'Islamists and the threat of Jihad: Hizb al-Tahrir and al-Muhajiroun on Israel and the Jews', *Middle Eastern Studies* **36** (4): 21–46.

Tarlo, E. 2005. 'Reconsidering stereotypes: anthropological reflections on the jilbab controversy', *Anthropology Today* **21** (6): 13–17.

   2007a. 'Hijab in London: metamorphosis, resonance and effects', *Journal of Material Culture* **12** (2): 131–56.

   2007b. 'Islamic cosmopolitanism: the sartorial biographies of three Muslim women in London', *Fashion Theory* **11** (2/3): 143–72.

Taseer, A. 2005. 'A British Jihadist', www.prospect-magazine.co.uk/article_details.php?id=6992 (accessed 5/2/08).

Tayob, A. 1999. *Islam in South Africa: Mosques, Imams, and Sermons*, Gainesville: University Press of Florida.

Tibi, B. 2007. 'The totalitarianism of Jihadist Islamism and its challenge to Europe and to Islam', *Totalitarian Movements and Political Religions* **8** (1): 35–54.

Tinker, C. 2006. 'Islamophobia, social cohesion and autonomy: challenging the arguments against state funded Muslim schools in Britain', *Muslim Education Quarterly* **23** (1&2): 4–19.

Turner, H. 1981. 'The history of Islam's Mosques: a critical analysis', *Scottish Journal of Religious Studies*. **2** (2): 135–50.

Tyerman, C. 2004. *Fighting for Christendom: Holy War and the Crusades*, Oxford University Press.

Vertigans, S. 2007. 'Militant Islam and Weber's social closure: interrelated secular and religious codes of exclusion', *Contemporary Islam* **1** (3): 303–21.

Visram, R. 2002. *Asians in Britain: 400 Years of History*, London: Pluto.

Vitkus, D. 2001. 'Trafficking with the Turk: English travelers in the Ottoman Empire during the early seventeenth century', in Kamps, I. and Singh, J. (eds.), *Travel Knowledge: European 'Discoveries' in the Early Modern Period*, pp. 35–52.

Voll, J. 1983. 'Renewal and reform in Islamic history: tajdid and islah', in Esposito, J. (ed.), *Voices of Resurgent Islam*, Oxford University Press, pp. 32–47.

Waddy, C. 1990. *The Muslim Mind*, London: Grosvenor Books.

Walvin, J. 2005. 'Black people in Britain', in Tibbles, A. (ed.), *Transatlantic Slavery: Against Human Dignity*, Liverpool University Press, pp. 79–83.

Wardak, A. 2002. 'The mosque and social control in Edinburgh's Muslim community', *Culture and Religion* 3 (201–19).

Ware, J. 2006. 'MCB in the dock', www.prospect-magazine.co.uk/article_details.php?id=7980 (accessed 26/11/2007).

Warraich, S. and Balchin, C. 2006. *Recognising the Un-Recognised: inter-country cases and Muslim marriages and divorces in Britain*, London: Women Living under Muslim Laws (WLUML).

Watt, W.M. 1972. *The Influence of Islam on Medieval Europe*, Edinburgh University Press.

Webster, C. 1997. 'The construction of British "Asian" Criminality', *International Journal of the Sociology of Law* 25 (1): 65–86.

Weller, P. 2004. 'Identity, politics and the future(s) of religion in the UK: the case of the religion questions in the 2001 decennial census', *Journal of Contemporary Religion* 19 (1): 3–22.

2009. *A Mirror for Our Times: The Rushdie Affair and the Future of Multiculturalism*, London: Continuum.

Werbner, P. 1990. *The Migration Process*, Oxford: Berg.

1996a. '"Our blood is green": cricket, identity and social empowerment among British Pakistanis', in MacClancey, J. (ed.), *Sport, Identity and Ethnicity*, Oxford: Berg, pp. 87–111.

1996b. 'Stamping the earth with the name of Allah : Zikr and the sacralizing of space among British Muslims', *Cultural Anthropology* 11 (3): 309–38.

2002a. *Imagined Diasporas among Manchester Muslims*, Oxford: James Currey Publishers.

2002b. *Pilgrims of Love: The Anthropology of a Global Sufi Cult*, London: Hurst.

2006. 'Seekers on the Path: different ways of being a Sufi in Britain', in Malik, J. and Hinnells, J. (eds.), *Sufism in the West*, London: Routledge, pp. 127–41.

Werbner, P. and Modood, T. (eds.) 1997. *The Politics of Multiculturalism in the New Europe: Racism, Identity and Community*, London: Zed Books.

Wetherell, M. 1993. *Masculinity as Constructed Reality*, Norway, Constructed Realities: Therapy, Theory and Research.

Wiktorowicz, Q. 2005. *Racial Islam Rising: Muslim Extremism in the West*, Oxford: Rowman & Littlefield Publishers, Inc.

Williams, R. 2008. 'Civil and religious law in England: a religious perspective', www.archbishopofcanterbury.org/1575 (accessed 17/4/08).

Wilson, A. 2006. *Dreams, Questions, Struggles: South Asian Women in Britain*, London: Pluto Press.

Winchester, D. 2008. 'Embodying the faith: religious practice and the making of a Muslim moral habitus', *Social Forces* **86** (4): 1753–80.

Winter, T. J. 2004. 'The poverty of fanaticism', in Lumbard, J. (ed.), *Islam, Fundamentalism, and the Betrayal of Tradition: Essays by Western Muslim Scholars*, Indiana: World Wisdom pp. 283–94.

Wolff, P. 1968. *The Awakening of Europe*, London: Penguin.

Wolffe, J. 1993. 'Fragmented universality: Islam and Muslims', in Parsons, G. (ed.), *The Growth of Religious Diversity: Britain from 1945. Volume 1 – Traditions*, London: Routledge, pp. 133–72.

Wormald, P. 1982. 'The age of Offa and Alcuin', in Campbell, J. (ed.), *The Anglo-Saxons*, London: Phaidon, pp. 101–28.

Wynne-Jones, J. 2008. 'Bishop warns of no-go zones for non-Muslims', www.telegraph.co.uk/news/main.jhtml;jsessionid=DU51SAEZ4MGRZQFIQMGSFF4AVCBQWIV0?xml=/news/2008/01/06/nislam106.xml (accessed 14/1/08).

Yaqin, A. 2007. 'Islamic Barbie: the politics of gender and performativity', *Fashion Theory* **11** (2–3): 173–85.

Yaqoob, S. 2007. 'British Islamic political radicalism', in Abbas, T. (ed.), *Islamic Political Radicalism: A European perspective*, Edinburgh University Press, pp. 279–94.

Yilmaz, I. 2004. 'Marriage Solemnization among Turks in Britain: the emergence of a hybrid Anglo-Muslim Turkish Law', *Journal of Muslim Minority Affairs* **24** (1).

Zaman, M. Q. 2007. *Ashraf Ali Thanawi: Islam in Modern South Asia*, Oxford: Oneworld.

Zebiri, K. 2008. *British Muslim Converts: Choosing Alternative Lives*, Oxford: Oneworld.

# Index

# Index